The Dream of Reason

American Consciousness and Cultural Achievement
from Independence to the Civil War

for Eric Mottram

The Dream of Reason

American Consciousness and Cultural Achievement
from Independence to the Civil War

Clive Bush

St. Martin's Press   New York

All rights reserved. For information, write:
St. Martin's Press, Inc., 175 Fifth Avenue, New York, N.Y. 10010
Printed in Great Britain
Library of Congress Catalog Card Number 77-93574
ISBN 0-312-21960-1
First published in the United States of America in 1978

Table of Contents

Acknowledgements

I am indebted to the following persons and institutions whose generous help in time and money made the following book possible. First the Newberry Library of Chicago for a grant-in-aid for two months in the summer of 1968. I should especially like to thank Lawrence Towner and James Wells for their hospitality, and David Stam and Don Krummel for their interest and advice. Second I would like to thank the Cassel Foundation and the University of Warwick for a travel grant which enabled me to visit important galleries and libraries in the mid-West and on the East Coast of the United States. The University of Warwick also advanced a small loan towards the cost of the plates. I have benefited from the advice of Mrs E. A. Stadler at the Missouri Historical Society, Milton Kaplan in the print room of the Library of Congress, Garnet McCoy of the Archives of American Art and Edward Countryman of the University of Warwick. I am grateful to John Reed of the English Department of Wayne State University for both his academic interest and hospitality while visiting the Detroit Institute of Arts. I am enormously indebted for help of many kinds from the extended concourse of the Hadas family in St Louis and New York. From 1972–3 I was in receipt of a fellowship from the American Council of Learned Societies held at Yale University which enabled me to complete the manuscript. I hope this book discharges some of the immense personal debts to Mr and Mrs Matt Coyle of West Haven, the Drs Laura and Elias Manueledes, Guyla and Ika Kodolanyi and William Westney.

My chief intellectual debt is to Eric Mottram, poet and critic, whose pioneering work in American culture in this country is unequalled for its generosity of sympathy and uncompromising critical intelligence. My chief general debt is to Rachel Thatcher with whom I shared many ideas of the work in its formative stages. Not only did her expert advice in matters relating to the history and philosophy of science frequently find its way into the following pages, but her consistent scrutiny of the manuscript, her enthusiasm, scepticism and intellectual commitment made the writing of this book a near unmitigated pleasure.

Preface

This book is an experiment. It is addressed to readers with some knowledge of early nineteenth-century American culture, though it is not confined to them. More particularly it is addressed to anyone with an interest in crossing cultural boundaries, and who also looks to find in literature, art and the history of science and technology ways of focusing and rehearsing the large questions of society and the nature of human achievement. Complex and unfamiliar though some of the material is, it should not be beyond anyone interested enough in American culture to have given, say, Melville's *Moby Dick* a serious and thoughtful reading. This book is a late twentieth-century attempt to look in fresh ways at the early years of what is arguably the most powerful and dominant culture of our time: American, capitalist, representative democracy. Some of the material will be familiar, much will not be. The scheme of the book itself I believe enables us to look in clear and important ways at interactions in the field of artistic experience which have been neglected owing to current specialization dogmas: dogmas which in recent years have shown encouraging signs of breaking down. So instead of looking separately at the well-established themes of American culture of this period—the 'American Adam', 'the frontier', gothic sexual sensibility in fiction, the machine and pastoralism, the Puritan inheritance or the idea of virgin land—this book asks the reader to look at them together. The structure I hope facilitates this process. The organizing pattern of the book is deeply influenced by the central chapters of Norman O. Brown's famous work, *Love's Body*: 'Person', 'Representative', 'Head', and 'Boundary'. The details of the private and public drama of political representation under the conditions of repression which he describes are as much part of the American experience as reflections on it. I draw on the patterns of Brown's analysis to describe the conventional realities of American consciousness of this period. By conventional I mean what seeks to confirm not recreate the existing reality. Unlike Brown, however, I do not go from 'Liberty' to 'Nothing'. My argument is that the successful American art of this period does resist both the European artistic legacy and the acquisitive, anti-intellectual, business-oriented, expansionist and materialist cultural bias of the new republic's own making. This book then intends to seek out the pockets of creative resistence, finitely and concretely achieved, in a still generally undervalued period of America's cultural past. The disastrous consequences of early American capitalism are not ignored.

The structure of the book is designed to articulate and clarify some significant moments of this 'drama of consciousness'. It attempts to show how Americans made their own selections from the European cultural legacy and adapted them to their own purposes. What is presented is a kind of 'drama of consciousness'. It is a drama because I have tried to trace creatively a set of cultural events and artistic performances tending toward the catastrophe of the Civil War. The set of events I have selected does not illustrate a plot of conventional linear kind, rather it briefly illumines a series of moments between man and man, and between man and landscape. The resultant 'actions' or activities, whether in literature, painting, technology, or exploration, are seen as achieved realities capable of analysis from multi-disciplinary critical positions. The aim is to rescue a live tradition, to recognize, as I shall argue, at what is an apparent moment of total failure (the Civil War), a number of finite achievements in this period of American culture in order to encourage communities dedicated to change on both sides of the Atlantic.

This book then seeks ways of interpreting, through multiple levels of data, the relation of the self to a new sociogeographic space during the first 80 or so years of an independent American culture. The plot of this fiction, though presented nonlinearly, is a simple one. It begins with a figure and ends with a landscape. First we look at some aspects of the European legacy in the models America inherited to express its own consciousness. Then comes the figure in the landscape, the hero rapidly turning into the American representative man. The landscape he inhabits is the new continent of America, the mode of vision, a European one of conflict. The land is something either to be feared or symbolized as prospective utopia. The pattern of conflict, war and peace, gives the hero, a representative, it is argued, his *raison d'etre*. The following two chapters illustrate some models of peaceful and warlike consciousness across a wide range of arts and technology. The second half of the book deals with the landscape. Inherited attitudes confront the reality of a new space. So we look at the land itself, the indigenous peoples and its fauna and flora.

The concluding chapter, 'Landscape', attempts to unite all the major themes and indicate a direction of development. In some ways the arrangement of the book is almost artificially formal in order to allow as much play of response as possible between the materials. The *general* features of the inheritance are built into the book's structure in order to emphasize the particular and local achievement.

In a period of change, such as that which characterized the years following the American Revolution, the inherited European theories of culture and society underwent much modification, even to the point of rejection. That might sound tentative, especially since the effort of most formal university departments of American studies is towards discovering the 'Americanness' of any particular manifestation of their own civilization. Such an aim is, however, taken for granted in this study, but it is felt that it can only be properly realized in juxtaposition with European cultural phenomena. The structure of the book represents a kind of drama, a drama whose origins, as the first chapter will show, stretches back into classical antiquity and early Christian civilization. It is a drama of consciousness beginning with the Revolution, extending to the Civil War, and read in the cultural events of the turbulent years in between.

First and foremost the American Revolution was a political event, an historical power struggle with an accompanying ideology. The view of reality encompassed by that ideology is suggested by the title of the book, *The Dream of Reason*. This title is meant to be understood poetically, not in any philosophical or logical way. Rather it is an image which indicates a movement of understanding, now engaging connotations of the immediate cultural threshold of the American Revolution, 'the Age of Reason', now indicating a more 'Romantic' definition of active imaginative consciousness, now becoming a satiric comment on the failure of idealism before a more pragmatic reality. It is an image intended to hold within itself the effort of creative consciousness. The structure or field of that effort is formal and is derived immediately (its ultimate sources can only be indicated in antiquity) from the eighteenth-century philosophers. The idea of dividing the book into two complementary halves comes therefore from the great French natural philosopher Buffon with his division of knowledge into the large categories of civil and natural history. It seemed particularly appropriate, given the materials used, to transfer this central statement to indicate the European inheritance structurally in the book. The aim is to keep the generalities continually present without being bound to them.

So in the first half, 'Civil History', the nature of culture and
civilization is examined under the large and fundamental categories
of the hero, war and peace. It contains crucial questions about the
nature of America's response to its inheritance. What is the role of
the hero in democracy? What is the nature of individual and social
sovereignty? What is meant by *representation* in art and in the
drama of state? Are they connected? What is the relation of the
spectator to the drama of representative democracy? How are the
conceptions of war and peace related to the need for heroes? It is
suggested that the best of American culture answers these questions
in new ways.

These problems take us into American portraiture, political
biography, quasi-philosophical works by Carlyle and Emerson, and
into *Moby Dick*. In the chapter, 'The Arts of Peace', we look at the
conceptions of peace and civilized order over a range of cultural
phenomena, from American scientific work to the visual arts and
to poetry. The scope is not intended to be perverse in its catholicity,
but itself indicates that daring, if at times overly nationalistic,
American attempt to dissolve the European categories in new
definitions of cultural possibility. In the chapter, 'The Arts of War',
there is a similar pattern. The claim that American achievement
lay in its industrial and technological progress is taken seriously.
For example Colt's famous arms factory at Hartford is examined
as a complex cultural occasion. The concluding chapter of part one
shows how a new medium of scientific representation, the photograph, challenged directly all the inherited assumptions about the
hero, war and peace.

In the second part we look at some aspects of the general interest
in natural history current at this time. It will be seen how a general
metaphysic of categorization and classification provided a set of
a priori ideas which had profound social as well as scientific implications. In the first chapter, the writings of Jefferson, Crèvecoeur
and Bartram are discussed to show how men, deeply aware of European culture, come to terms with the American continent politically
and scientifically. The next chapter, on government expeditions
demonstrates scientific consciousness operating in the context
of exploration and discovery. The remaining four chapters on
Indians, animals, birds and landscape reflect the divisions of the
typical eighteenth-century work on natural history, and discuss the
implications of these categories as well as looking closely at particular examples. The final chapter on landscape draws together all
the themes of the book: representation, political theatre, the social
implications of scientific and technological development, of new

modes of literature and vision and the relation of the American individual to a newly emerging sociogeographical space.

Most importantly the book's structure provides new and flexible ways of explicitly criticizing its subject. While the main intention of the following pages is to create and discover vital lines of American cultural tradition in all their uniqueness and particularity, the disastrous effects of the European legacy are not neglected. Anger and critical objectivity are not mutually exclusive qualities, and the critical discussion contains both as the more socially disruptive results of this first period of American culture are examined.

A book of this nature depends heavily on other scholars and writers in the field. Without the specialized monograph, the academic critical works on the large themes of American culture, this book would not have been possible, either in terms of information and ideas, or in a potential audience. The line of distinguished American cultural historians who have written on the American Adam, or on the frontier, or on manifest destiny, or on the themes of pastoral versus technological consciousness, or on the idea of virgin land, or on the Puritan inheritance, or on American literature, inform this study in crucial ways. Wherever possible I have indicated my debt to them, while I apologize for much that has been almost unconsciously absorbed in the following pages. As well as the scholars, however, there is an important range of writers outside the university which has influenced this work: Thorsten Veblen, Louis Mumford, Buckminster Fuller to name but a few. These writers' originality of synthesis and, in some, humanity of social concern is in a vital American tradition, and gives the more un-orthodox scholar greater confidence. But my largest debt is to the classic American writers themselves. If this book helps to revalue and encourage the reading of Melville, Thoreau and Whitman out-side the boundaries of conventional critical response, then the effort will have been worthwhile. Finally the book seeks to provide ways of seeing this period of American culture in ways relevant to our own time. It does not seek to found a methodology, neither does it provide definitive judgements about other men's achievements. The selection of material is personal in the hope that individual directness of preference communicates more interestingly and ultimately more socially than conventional academic modes. The book attempts to break down our stiflingly specialized categories of cultural response, its direction is to open up debate and *suggest* the still unrealized richness of those pockets of creative resistance which even in this early period of American culture have proved to be of enduring value.

PART I Civil History

I

Origins of the Dream of Reason

In the summer of 1968 a number of Columbia University students were arrested for wilfully distributing copies of *The Declaration of Independence* to passers-by in New York. Their gesture and its consequences demonstrated an acute sense of political irony and historical consciousness. The eighteenth-century *Declaration,* in all its sweet reasonableness, was seen to be confronted by the naked facts of power in twentieth-century urban society and soundly defeated. With it went that dream of a commonsense reality founded on the laws of nature and nature's God. It was placed under arrest in the name of a law more interested in power than reason. And yet the seeds of its defeat were there in the original premises. For, as will become clear in the course of this study, one of the consequences of this rational vision was a separation of magnanimous moral intent and pragmatic power-seeking. The connections between the two were left unstated and undetermined. By what authority might a self-evident truth be established and who could measure the limits of prudence? Nonetheless, however precarious their premises, the consciousness of wrong gave force and relevance to the *Declaration of Independence.* In contemporary America, those disenfranchized by colour, poverty or political conviction may still find in these phrases an authority for their protest—focused not on a crazy and tyrannical king, but on a reasonable administration pathologically incapable of admitting error. Inside the boundaries of state a small minority of students and the black poor may object to 'the quartering [of] large bodies of armed troops among us,' and to those responsible for the suffering abroad, the initial rage of the *Declaration* against the king has an uncomfortable ring:

> He is at this time transporting large armies of foreign mercenaries to compleat the works of death, desolation, and tyranny, already begun with circumstances of cruelty and perfidy scarcely paralleled in the most barbarous ages, and totally unworthy the head of a civilized nation.

The American Revolution itself was fought, won and then lost
in the name of reason. In 1776 we have the curious spectacle of a
society contemplating radical change in the name of law and order.
In theory and practice, however, its dream of natural harmony was
charged with ambiguity. Liberty itself had been called for in the
name of representation, the drama of kingship was being taken over
by the drama of compact, representation and confederation, and
the sons were already quarrelling over the father's inheritance. The
law of nature had replaced the law of divine right, and in return for
direct political involvement, the individual was replaced by an
'individualism' which secured the personal, not political, rights of
speech, religion and property. Throughout the following century,
the great American myths are in conflict with the actualities of
American society. The myth of 'Virgin Land' accompanied the
necessities of individual property and boundary-creating agriculture,
the 'American Adam' traded his God-given individuality for more
Mammon-oriented associations, and the 'Frontier' became the
dream of the mushrooming urban centres. Even that strange Americanization of European gothic fictional types, the dream of black-
white male love in the wilderness most famously expounded by
Leslie Fiedler, which haunted the American literary imagination,
might be seen to counterbalance the loss of sexual respect to both
man and woman involved in the monogamous pieties of the nineteenth-century family, built according to the needs of economic
efficiency and torn by the guilt involved in a vast exploitation of
natural resources and indigenous populations.[1]

The period between the *Declaration of Independence* and the
Civil War is one of the most fascinating of all cultural epochs.
Politically it witnessed the change from a small-town, pastoral
'Jeffersonian' democracy to a more urban and industrial oligarchy,
with, from at least 1845 onwards, practical imperial ambitions based
on military power. The dream of reason failed, however, because of
the inherent contradictions of its vision of reality and it is to the
writers, artists and artisans of this first independent period of
American culture that we must turn in order to chart the causes
of its failure.[2]

[1] The major books on these individual topics are as follows:
Henry Nash Smith, *Virgin Land, the American West as Symbol and Myth* (Cam., Mass.,
1950); R. W. B. Lewis, *The American Adam: Innocence, Tragedy and Tradition in the
Nineteenth Century* (Chicago and Cambridge, 1955); E. S. Fussell, *Frontier: American
Literature and the American West* (Princeton, 1965); Leslie Fiedler, *Love and Death in
the American Novel* (New York, 1960).

[2] The best book so far which attempts to generalize about the relations of literature
and technology is Leo Marx's *Machine in the Garden: Technology and the Pastoral Ideal
in America* (New York, 1964).

To determine the origins of the American Revolution, bourgeois in character, with its powerful myths eternally receding from practice, we must go back to Renaissance Europe and to that union of Puritanism and scientific discovery which gave the American mind its peculiar cast and sense of reality. We can conveniently point to two important writers and thinkers who helped to articulate the properties of the frame of mind that encountered and experienced the New World for the first time. The first is Peter Ramus (1515–86) a Puritan philosopher and logician whose English successors brought neo-Platonism to New England and the second is Francis Bacon (1561–1626), the publicist of the scientific revolution.[3] The effect of the issues which these writers created and codified have a relevance to the American consciousness which goes far beyond philosophy.

Out of the matrix of Ramus's thought we can distinguish three important areas: education, science and method. All three were characterized by a general change from an oral and manuscript culture to one which placed increasing emphasis on printing and on visual demonstration. In education, (before Ramus's time), for example, the qualities which were stressed were essentially dramatic. In oral dialogue, gesture and aphorism as means of gaining a point were determined by the strict rules of rhetorical discourse. Speaker and audience were involved in a debate where the consequences were immediate and social. The change from oral pedagogy to book learning was promoted largely through the invention of movable types in printing. Commentators like Walter Ong and Marshall McLuhan have brought new light to bear on the effects these inventions have had on the whole scope and direction of learning.[4] Ramus advocated a 'method' which insisted on clarity, sequential order and prudence by arranging hierarchies of significance in the stages relating the particular to the general. The method found an ally in the formal relationships brought about by the lay-out of type and diagram possible in the new printed book. With Ramus's own emphasis on book learning and the formal institutionalization of syllabus (itself a result of specialization and diagrammatic attitudes to knowledge) the acquisition of knowledge became a private, individualistic activity separating thought from action and debate.

[3] The best book on Ramus is Walter Ong's *Ramus, Method and the Decay of Dialogue* (Cam., Mass., 1958) and there are long discussions also in Perry Miller's pioneering work, *The New England Mind* (New York, 1938). The best recent book on Bacon is Paolo Rossi's *Francis Bacon: from magic to science: translated from the Italian by Sacha Robinovich* (London, 1968).

[4] See Marshall McLuhan, *The Gutenberg Galaxy* (London, 1962).

Ong and McLuhan, however, have distorted some of the results of
their useful and necessary investigations. The contemporary analogies
are sometimes too simplistic and ahistoric to stand up to close inspection. Ong, for example, laments the depersonalization of the
learning process consequent upon the Ramian method. 'Millions
of schoolboys were inducted into an understanding of language and
of the world around them by making their way conjointly through
individual texts arranged in identical spatial patterns.'[5] None the
less the printing press was the single biggest factor in democratizing
the educational system and it simultaneously did away with the
educationally dubious value of painful memorization. However
visually diagrammatic and didactic Ramus appears to be to his
distinguished contemporaries, the new privately-considered judgement gave the shy, the oppressed, the hitherto subservient and
mystified a means of understanding. In stressing the impersonality
of method and syllabus, with its own irrational claim to authority,
Ong has assumed that the result visually reflects the method. Does
he suppose that a million schoolboys all make similar responses?
To identify means and ends so closely and to assume that a mass
homogeneity of response is the inevitable result, is a social and
ultimately a political mistake.

   Ong directly links 'Ramism' with the revolution in the concept
of space which characterized both the scientific revolution and the
painter's art. 'The development of Copernican space, so much more
truly spatial than Aristotle's less abstract space, climaxed in the
work of Jan van Eyck, which Erwin Panofsky has so masterfully
analysed in his *Early Netherlandish Painting* and elsewhere; . . .'[6]
Ramian analysis is based on this new conception of space. It is also
based on the concept of 'anatomy', itself a result of the increased
prestige of the medical sciences with their emphasis on quantification and classifaction spatially presented. We shall see later how
perspective, the new concepts of space and the classification system
in medical science and natural history become major issues in the
visual, literary and technological work of the first independent
period of American culture.

   The most important effect of Ramus's work was in its onslaught
on the status quo. To understand the ambiguous nature of this
onslaught it is necessary to understand the precise meaning of his
conception of reason. Generally it is assumed that in place of the
'Aristotelian' method of logic (simple terms, proposition and
discourse) he substituted the 'Platonic' concept of dialectic. We

   [5] Walter Ong, p. 314.
   [6] Ibid., p. 314.

shall see how, as in Bacon's work, the difference is more apparent than real. The terms Aristotelian and Platonic are merely convenient handles (even to sixteenth- and seventeenth-century thinkers) to distinguish between specifically Renaissance issues of newness and tradition. All that is Platonic in Ramus's thought is his vague sense of dualism. His real contribution was to found a visual method of classification on the nonvisual assumption of dualism or dialectic. This dialectic was composed of what he called *invention* and *judgement.* It was a means of explaining rather than an explanation in itself. Invention is the imaginative part of the process. It divides things into visible parts by making distinctions. Judgement is the reshuffling of the distinctions into the whole. By applying the same method, all branches of knowledge could be shown to have the same coherent and highly abstract order. In practice the process of invention assumed that a man was possessed of an inner sense which could perceive which of two propositions was a true one. Followers of Ramus in New England asserted that his method, applied intuitively, articulated the law of nature itself. The method then mystically determines the law. Ramus himself had already begun to illustrate his method with analogies drawn from physics. What really appealed, however, to Ramus's followers was the simplicity and orderliness of the system and the easy means of visualizing the relations of the parts of knowledge to the whole. The visual and diagrammatic patterns of Ramus's method emphasized the how rather than the why of things. The separation of argument from the means of effecting argument tends to make analysis the justification not the cause of action. The political consequences of such reasoning are disturbing, and we can trace the peculiar influence of this way of thinking in American philosophy right through to the philosophers of pragmatism at the end of the nineteenth century.

It is well known that Ramus was denounced by the synod of Nîmes in 1572 for proposing that congregations should have the power to elect their own pastors. The fact is often proudly cited by scholars working on the origins of democratic thought in modern history. It is not democracy, however, but *representative* democracy which comes at the end of this particular process. The connection between the Ramian method and so-called democratic thought is the new power to visualize a representative system. The sense of communication between the part and the whole and between the ideal and the particular is guaranteed by the mystical mechanical reality of the visual model.

Ong and McLuhan are somewhat nostalgic for premechanical

models of education and civil polity. There seems little point in
justifying either oral or visual methods as better models for contemporary concerns. The mechanical philosophy, the system of
classification according to dialectic, and the conception of space as
homogenous and uniform are just as potentially dehumanizing
for the purposes of propaganda, as the less linearly organized information of a medieval cathedral or the rhetorical laws of scholastic
discourse.

It is commonly thought that when we turn to Francis Bacon the
period of direct Ramian influence is over. But there remained a
direction of intellectual purpose and an attitude of mind which
informs Bacon's own thought. His *Advancement of Learning* (1605),
for example, is permeated with Ramian preoccupations which show
how a specific intellectual and historical attitude has become a condition of learning. Like Ramus, Bacon is at pains to debunk the
prestige of Aristotelian scholasticism, to advertise the importance of
method, clarity and logic, to separate the vast complex of medieval
learning into more manageable classes and then to claim for those
classes an authenticity located in nature itself. There is the same
shift of emphasis towards the visually demonstrable fact and a sense
of order. Bacon himself is a man standing with his feet firmly planted
in medieval culture, an Aristotelian using Ramian methods to prove
that he was not narrow-mindedly scholastic. McLuhan is right to
stress that Bacon is in fact *modern* in only a limited sense and in a
way which would not have been thought very important by most
of his contemporaries. It is his advocacy of the new in a backward-
looking manner and his enthusiastic plea for the importance of
technology that makes him significant as a precursor of the early
American world picture. In *The Advancement of Learning* he said:

> . . . we see commonly the levity and inconstancy of men's judgements,
> which till a matter be done, wonder that it can be done; and as soon as
> it is done, wonder again that it was no sooner done: as we see in the
> expedition of Alexander into Asia, which at first was prejudged as a vast
> and impossible enterprise; and yet afterwards it pleaseth Livy to make
> no more of it than this: *Nil aliud quam bene ausus vana contemnere*; and
> the same happened to Columbus in the western navigation. But in in-
> tellectual matters it is much more common; as may be seen in most of
> the propositions of Euclid; which till they be demonstrate, they seem
> strange to our assent; but being demonstrate, our mind accepteth of
> them by a kind of relation (as the lawyers speak), as if we had known
> them before.[7]

[7] Francis Bacon, *The Advancement of Learning* (London, 1962 for 1605) p. 32.

Bacon is pleading for a suspension of disbelief in relation to hypothesis and possibility. The chief figure in both his extremely significant examples is the practical man conducting expeditions for the purposes of exploration and the extension of power. The man who acts disproves the theorist. Analogous to this is the proof which governs mathematical proposition. The demonstration justifies the act of faith. The last phrase of the quotation shows the latent Aristotelianism of Bacon's thought, with its suggestion that 'art' discovers better what is already known in nature. The asssociation, however, of the practical active hero, particularly in the area of conquest and exploration, with the psychology of mathematical proof and a revised attitude to the new, works against his medievalism. The passage is typical of Bacon's life-long attempt to fuse the practical and mechanical arts with a more contemplative scientific philosophy. As Rossi, an Italian historian of science, points out, the division between useful and theoretical knowledge goes back to the pre-Socratics and is a division inherent in a slaveocracy.[8] It was the new artisan class of the Elizabethan period who helped to put together mathematics and technology, to facilitate the exploration of the New World and to start a process which was to invade philosophy itself with the pervasive metaphor of the machine. In geography, navigation, astronomy, medicine and military invention the methods of technology were beginning to give the law to scientific investigation. The theoretical basis or justification was found not in dialectic but in Euclidian geometry. Visual demonstrable proof replaced pure speculation; use, not contemplation, justified action. The mathematicians of the Elizabethan period were consultants to the exploring expeditions both national and 'commercial'. During the nineteenth century, the Americans, exploring their own continent as their Elizabethan ancestors had explored the Atlantic and the Eastern seaboard of America, recapitulated both the psychological and physical nature of the Renaissance discovery experience. Gresham College was to the explorers of the early seventeenth century what the Philadelphia Philosophical Society was to the expeditions of Lewis and Clarke.

One of the common and unstated aims of all these methods was domination, control and the exploitation of man and nature. A lively and genuine curiosity was mingled with greed. For the emerging American scientific and technological explorer there existed many conflicts between the ideal they had of themselves as impersonal, internationally cooperative labourers for the common good

---

[8] See Paolo Rossi, *Philosophy, Technology and the Arts in the Early Modern Era* (New York, 1970, orig. *I Filosofi e le Macchine*, Milan, 1962).

and actual scholarly competition and pettiness, between the pursuit of theoretical and practical knowledge, between their claims that the scientific mind was the prerequisite of democracy and those stubborn facts of the human condition which lay outside their analyses, between the actual conditions of discovery and the popular adulation of scientific and technological advancement as a tool of undifferentiated human progress.

Both the neo-Platonism of Ramus and the new prestige of technology which Bacon helped to link with a new conception of scientific method are important factors in the discovery of America. The neo-Platonic school in America pushed Ramus's characterization of nature as an *art* of God to new conclusions. If the visible manifestation was linear, orderly, classifiable, clear and logical, the source of ideal ought to have exhibited the same characteristics. It is easy to see why neo-Platonism is closely linked with the frame of mind responsible for the new technology. In the treatises of the Harvard Ramists nature was defined as the art (*techne*) of God, and the headings of their expositions bore the title *technologia*. 'Technology' then, in both philosophy and the mechanical arts, was a Platonic conception in which reality was symbolic or representational. In practice, of course, what was seen to work was 'real'. Nonetheless there was a continuous chain which linked idea and thing and *vice versa*. Facts were facts by virtue of their representational quality and they represented a conveniently forgotten but powerful notion of order. In printing, for example, the homogeneity of the letters lent plausibility to a linear process of thought. The all-pervasive image of the clock depicted the way in which particular parts depended for their identity on the harmonious working of the whole. The existence of repeatable homogenous objects, whether the divisions on a clock face or movable types, gave, as William Ivins has said of print-making, the individual fact a sense of an invariable ideal.[9] The ideal according to the commentators is visual. But it is visual in only the narrowest of senses. It is impossible by merely observing the natural world to infer homogeneity. The abstract visuality of Euclidian geometry, dialectical classification, perspective, the machine image, although initially necessary imaginative simplifications, came eventually to have the authoritative status of an invariable reality. When Newton wrote his *Principia* in 1686, the age of the purely visual even in simple diagrammatic form, was over as far as science was concerned. The followers of Descartes in France, for example, objected to Newton's system because it failed the proof

[9] William M. Ivins, Jr., *Prints and Visual Communication* (Cam., Mass., 1968 for London, 1953), p. 162.

of seeing is believing. McLuhan's view of the scientific renaissance
as a transition from an oral to a visual culture is an oversimplifica-
tion. All sense experience (including the visual) was abstracted from
scientific concern. It was necessary for its own development. The
problem arose when the view of the universe arrived at through
Newton's own idiosyncratic mathematical notation became an over-
simplified metaphor of human and social relations.

The importance of these issues from the American point of view
lies in the evolution of the theory and practice of the public drama of
representative democracy, both from the Congregational theory
of church government and from the imprint of technology on the
scientific renaissance. The new scientific method and the theory of
representation are intimately connected. By the beginning of the
eighteenth century, and in an increasingly secular world, the one
supplies the rationale for the other. It has been suggested that the
Globe Theatre of Shakespeare's time, itself a representative microcosm of the world, was ordered by the abstract mathematical geometries which structured Vitruvian architecture.[10] The religiopolitical
drama of public theatre or church was increasingly authorized not
by the visual iconography of ancient ritual but by the invisible
power of geometrical equations. Frances Yates suggests that the
public theatre of the Elizabethans was the nearest equivalent of the
neo-Classical churches of the continent.[11] The process is seen more
easily in the Puritan attitude to drama. The visual drama of the
traditional church and public theatre was felt not to have the same
authority as a drama which under their auspices was becoming more
and more nonvisual and abstract. Just as Ramus placed rhetoric
after logic, so the Puritans stripped the churches of images, and then
claimed that only the most abstract, logical and invisibly representative of theatres was real. Equally the movement from divine kingship to representative government, although clear theoretically
was often unclear in its actual political manifestations. The path
from rhetoric to logic as it affected the verbal discourse of propaganda was not a simple one.

The concept of dialectic is intimately related to theatre. Not
only is this true in structural terms (the actor needs an audience)
but also in the dualistic world on which the concept of representation insists. Geometry represents the real world in the same way as
Christian ritual, externalized as in Catholicism, or internalized as in
Puritanism, represents the real world. Representation is also wedded

[10] See Frances A. Yates, *Theatre of the World* (London, 1969).
[11] Ibid. p. 168.

to the idea of repetition. Just as scientific proof was thought to consist in the invariable repetition of the same result, so ritual represented an invariable ideal of truth and consistency.

The relation of the visible (content) to the invisible (form) by way of representation is the business of the rhetoric of political propaganda. The interpretation of abstract form is a priest-like function. The representation or description of form tends to become the universal form because its representational quality invests it with the authority of absolute truth. Where form and content are separate whoever has most power describes reality, and generally in terms of an infinitely receding ideal. In crude terms it is heaven at a distance and conflict on the home front engineered by king or representative.

Technology, in its important original sense (*techne*-grammar), like politics, was an art of representation which claimed an absolute objectivity. Although seemingly diverse in nature, the subjects and areas of knowledge created by the new technology had a certain similarity. In architecture, mining, navigation and military art the new emphasis was on use and control. Rossi has shown how the very logic of invention itself was comparable to a tool.

Since architecture, for example, represented popularly the totality of technological achievement, it is not surprising that, with the Vitruvian revival, it became a tool of understanding whether applied to theatre or church. Architecture consequent upon the application of Euclidian geometry to practical building, visibly embodied such concepts as geometry, musical harmony, perspective, astronomical abstraction and linear concepts of time and space. As a means of representation architecture organized man's relation to the cosmos and hence had an important religiopolitical function. From Palladio to the Palladian revival to the colonial houses of Virginia and the English colonies, the Vitruvian ideal of simplified rectilinear order befitted, in its abstract academicism, the ideal of imperial control.

In mining, too, the new technology showed itself to be the archetype of the new age, not only in the development of new machinery, but also as affecting social and ecological change. Agricola's famous mining treatise of 1556 *De Re Metallica* gives us a very clear idea of these events. Agricola's aim was to defend mining against its detractors, against their charges that it increased the distance between rich and poor, despoiled the evironment, and invaded the realms of Satan himself. In the long view of history we can see the superstitions of the detractors were scarcely improved on by new types of superstition: arguments from necessity, utility and the creation of abstract wealth.[12] Of all the arts mining was the most crucial to the new technology and its results. America itself was proposed as an ideal and as a fact in the name of its untold wealth in silver and gold. Mining practice was the embodiment of the machine process. New machines, such as pumps, financed by uninvolved owners, were operated in the nearest earthly equivalent of nonsensuous Newtonian space. The extraction of iron led to improvements in military machines, and the abstract wealth embodied in the product led to the disassociation of labour and wages and to the separation, in the primitive machine process, of the worker from the ends of production. It also involved a systematic despoilation of the environment.

Finally the eventual precision of navigational methods in military science and technology came about through increasingly sophisticated applications of geometry and time-keeping machines to astronomical observation. Thus the evolution of precise instruments for measuring the connections between earth and the solar system became the means of extending control over the globe in spatial terms. The maps produced are themselves simplifications for practical purposes, and they served as the chief visual link between geography and military technology. The end-product of the invasion of the machine consciousness into all areas of knowledge is the military industrial complex.[13]

This is the end of the process inherent in the philosophical view of a dualistic universe of ideal forms and particulars. The fact that a crude form of dialectic replaces syllogism, one vaguely Platonic and the other vaguely Aristotelian, does not fundamentally challenge this view. Now that we are beginning to revalue Bacon it also seems likely that 'Aristotelianism' will be found to play a far larger part in the scientific revolution than commonly thought. The syllogism provides as good a model for the machine as Ramian dialectic. Its chief characteristic after all is that subject and predicate are reversible logically about a verb which denotes use and connection innocently. It is not surprising that originally *technologia* meant a grammar of language. On the structure of the sentence depends a concept of a dualistic world, one part directing operations (subject), one part supplying the force (verb), and one part embodying the objective product (object). This primitive notion of language is

[12] There is a good recent reprint of this book which figures in all histories of technology, Gregorius Agricola, *De Re Metallica*; translated from the first Latin edition of 1556 . . . by Herbert Clark Hoover and Lou Henry Hoover (New York, 1950).
[13] These connections were first made by Lewis Mumford in his book *Technics and Civilization* (London, 1946), p. 68f.

paralleled by Marx's definition of the paleotechnic machine which has a similar tripartite structure:

> All fully developed machinery consists of three essentially different parts, the motor mechanism, the transmitting mechanism and finally the tool or working machine.[14]

The model of the machine thus defined reflects closely the reality of a linguistic inheritance derived from Greek culture. In his introduction to a collected edition of Benjamin Lee Worf's work on linguistics, Stuart Chase in fact connects the idea of the syllogism with not only an Aristotelian but also a Platonic view of language and continues:

> The Greeks took it for granted that back of language was a universal uncontaminated essence of reason, shared by all men, at least by all thinkers. Words, they believed, were but the medium in which this deeper effulgence found expression. It followed that a line of thought expressed in any language could be translated without loss of meaning into any other language.
> This view has persisted for 2,500 years, especially in academic groves.[15]

In fact language is not the dress of thought as Horace would have had it. The medium is the content, it does not represent reality. Where language is assumed to have this representational quality, truth is taken out of the public arena where it properly belongs. It is beyond question and beyond appeal. One effect is the attribution of the timeless authority of a Platonic ideal to repeatable facts. The other is a divorce of means and ends. Pragmatic action takes the place of radical thinking. Finally, in political terms, the insistence on a dualistic reality, with its ultimately invariable truth mirrored in the form of the sentence has, from the time of the Greeks, presented those in authority (academicians, bureaucrats, politicians and religious leaders) with an incontestable argument for maintaining the status quo. This insistence has also presented its challengers with an equally authoritarian claim to truth in the name of a scientific reality. The effect in either case is a continuation of conflict in the cause of an ultimately natural but never to be achieved destiny.

[14] Karl Marx, *Capital* (Chicago, 1912) I. p. 407.
[15] Benjamin Lee Whorf, *Language, Thought and Reality; Selected Writings of Benjamin Lee Whorf*, ed. John B. Carroll, forward Stuart Chase (Cam., Mass., 1970 for 1956) p. vii. For a major attack on 'Aristotelianism' as a mode of thought in all disciplines see A. Korsybzski's *Science and Sanity: An Introduction to Non-Aristotelian Systems and General Semantics* (Lancaster, Pennsylvania, 1933).

For our purposes this Renaissance inheritance in America had several important consequences. It is well known that the Ramian philosophy made headway first among the more pietistic sects in America in the late seventeenth and early eighteenth centuries. In the English Quaker Robert Barclay's *An Apology for the True Christian Divinity* (1st English Edition, 1678) the faithful were encouraged to undertake geometrical researches in their leisure hours. The change to an abstract belief in visuality in religion is best exemplified by the last American Puritan thinker to hold together the now conflicting demands of piety and practicality, faith and reason. In Jonathan Edwards's significantly titled manuscript notes, *Images and Shadows of Divine Things,* we see him reversing the traditional position of the church on the nature of visual proof. Already confronted with the mid-eighteenth century phenomenon of the Great Awakening (the first major American religious 'revival') Edwards had created a series of tests whereby he could distinguish the true from the false conversion. This unprecedented synthesis of Lockean empiricism and Calvinism was justified not by grace but by scientific proof.[16] In the following passage Edwards reverses the medieval church's distrust of sight as illusion (*non potest fieri scientia per visum solum*):[17]

> The late invention of telescopes, whereby heavenly objects are brought so much nearer and made so much plainer to sight and such wonderful discoveries have been made in the heavens, is a type and forerunner of the great increase in the knowledge of heavenly things that shall be in the approaching glorious times of the Christian church.[18]

Galileo of course had needed to convince the church authorities that what he saw through his telescope was true. Edwards's attempted synthesis had the effect of making religion dependent on visual proof and hence subservient to it. As Harriet Beecher Stowe shrewdly observed of him:

> He was the first man who began the disintegrating process of applying rationalistic methods to the accepted doctrines of religion . . . .. He sawed the great dam and let out the whole waters of discussion over all New England.[19]

[16] See the introduction to Jonathan Edwards, *A Treatise Concerning Religious Affections,* ed. J. E. Smith (New Haven and London, 1959).

[17] For an excellent discussion of changes in the science of optics during the Renaissance, see Vasco Ronchi, 'Complexities, Advances and Misconceptions in the Development of the Science of Vision: what is being discovered?' in *Scientific Change: historical studies in the intellectual, social and technological conditions for scientific discovery and technical invention, from antiquity to the present,* ed. A. C. Crombie, (London, 1963), pp. 542–61.

[18] Jonathan Edwards, *Images or Shadows of Divine Things,* ed. Perry Miller (New Haven, 1948), p. 102.

[19] Harriet Beecher Stowe, *Old Town Folks* (Boston, 1869) p. 229.

After Edwards, this shot-gun marriage of Locke and neo-Platonism became split up into a vague pietistic sentiment (the direct ancestor of the genteel tradition in late-Victorian America) and a pragmatic practicality, notable for its insistence on discipline and method, but separated from the questions of ends and purpose.

It was, however, in the 'democratic' theory of civil history that the consequences of the new scientific and technological conscious-ness were important. One of the earliest American political theorists, John Wise, in his important treatise *A Vindication of the Govern-ment of New England Churches* of 1717, argued in the now familiar dialectical manner:

> And in this essay I shall peculiarly confine the discourse to two heads, *viz.*:
> 1   Of the natural (in distinction to the civil) and then
> 2   Of the civil being of man.[20]

By the turn of the century Bacon's multifarious dialectical categories had been reduced to two simple ones interacting as theory (nature) and practice (history). It is the way Wise argues that is important, for his concern is with the method or condition of law:

> But more particularly in pursuing our condition for the discovery of the law of nature, this is very obvious to view, *viz.*:
> 1   A principle of self love, and self preservation . . .
> 2   A sociable disposition.
> 3   An affection or love to mankind in general.[21]

The argument could be worked back without apparent contradic-tion. In the God-given soul of man was a natural propensity to view obviously. This obviousness to view is the rationale of the confident statement of method and involves all the presuppositions about natural reality which Wise then went on to prove from natural law. Again it is noticeable how the three parts of the condition work in a kind of abstract harmony. The precise relations between them are, of course, never defined. They are assumed to be reconciled in a never-never world of ideality. The three parts of the condition operate according to the technological reality of the sentence. Self-love is the motor mechanism, a sociable disposition the transmitting mecha-nism and the love to mankind the object or result of the activity of the tool. The philosophy is highly individualistic, and of course was familiar through the writings of the English philosopher

---

[20] John Wise, 'A Vindication of the Government of New England Churches' in *Colonial American Writing*, ed. Roy Harvey Pearce (New York, Chicago, San Francisco, Toronto, London, 1962 for 1950), p. 319.

[21] Ibid., pp. 321–2.

Shaftesbury. Shaftesbury, arguing against Hobbes-style visions of external means of order, and working out of the arguments of the neo-Platonists, had declared that man was *naturally* social, that he *naturally* tended toward unity and proportion in his moral thinking, that he could naturally balance self-affection for himself against a natural affection which extended towards the public good.

But it was not only the theorists of civil history who were so determined. On the other side of the dialectic, the historians of nature were working out similar theories based on the more idealistic side of the great divide. The famous French natural historian, Buffon, who after Linnaeus was most influential in America, wrote:

> On pourroit donc diviser toutes les Sciences en deux classes Principales, qui contiendroient tout ce qu'il convient à l'homme de savior; la premier est l'Histoire Civile, & la second l'Histoire Naturelle, toutes deux fondées sur des faits qu'il est souvent important & toujours agréable de connoitre: ....[22]

Buffon's development of these ideas shows their antiquity. Civil history is the province of men who imitate the divine work of God. Natural history is a more spiritual and contemplative exercise which is the province of philosophers. Buffon's division comes at the end of a long process of dualistic thinking reactivated by Ramus and Bacon at a time when America itself was discovered.

One of the clearest summaries of this process is provided by Engels who was one of the few nineteenth-century thinkers really to challenge, not dialectic, of course, but the method of classificatory order and of visual separation:

> But this method of work has also left us as legacy the habit of observing natural objects and processes in isolation, apart from their connection with the vast whole; of observing them in repose, not in motion; as constants, not as essentially variables; in their death, not in their life. And when this way of looking at things was transferred by Bacon and Locke, from natural science to philosophy, it begot the narrow, metaphysical code of thought peculiar to the last century.[23]

It is, I believe, to the literary, visual and technological arts that we must turn in order to explore the fate of this inheritance in America. We look first at the hero because during the nineteenth century, writers from Carlyle to Nietzsche were, in the aftermath of the Romantic revolution, obsessed by them. In America it was thought that representative ideology had supplanted the social role of hero.

---

[22] M. de Buffon, *Théorie de la Terre, Oeuvres complètes,* I (Paris, 1774), pp. 28–9.
[23] *Karl Marx and Frederick Engels: Selected Works* (London, 1970), p. 406. This is referred to as the most easily available and best recent translation.

The next chapter shows that it did not. As we look at hero worship in the public biography, the portrait, the philosophies of history, and in fiction we shall chart an interaction, (sometimes challenging, often acquiescing in, the status quo) between public need, an ideology based on the need for security and the real or imagined public and private myths of an immanent and permanent doctrine of conflict.

2

The Hero as Representative

The intense and hysterical involvement of many Americans in the deposition of a recent president shows the continuance in American life of the politicopsychological phenomenon of hero worship. The need for heroes reflects a clamour for social identity and is deeply allied to thwarted social needs. From the initial deification of Washington to current demands for presidents with charisma, the phenomenon has held its place steadily in American life. The history of American democracy is a history of the nature of representative government, and its roots lie far back in the human past, in the primitive rituals of priesthood and in public tribal drama. Norman O. Brown goes back to Hobbes for the more modern origins of the representative hero and representative thought. Arguing from a wide range of sources, Brown's tone is unmistakeably urgent: 'Peaceful existence, existence without historical action, needs no kingship'.[1] At the same time he quotes Paine and John Quincy Adams to show how Americans and Englishmen were aware, at the time of the Revolution, of the need to resist such rituals:

> 'The putting of any individual as a figure for a nation is improper' (Paine).
> 'Democracy has no monuments. It strikes no medals. It bears the head of no man on a coin. Its very essence is iconoclastic' (John Quincy Adams).
> The old idea was that man must be governed by effigy and show; the new idea is—modern representative government. An end to idolatry is not so easy.[2]

The origin of that idolatry goes back to a synthesis in European thought created nearly a thousand years ago, to a time when the writings of Aristotle were beginning to be known to the medieval world. Representation depends on a conflict of interests and the creation of *law* which symbolizes dramatically that split between permanent piety and changing need. The twelfth-century medieval jurists created a double characterization of the law of nature from

---

[1] Norman O. Brown, *Love's Body* (New York 1966) p. 112.
[2] Ibid., p. 114.

Roman civil law (which they found chiefly in the writings of
Justinian) and from the Bible. The Dutch theologian and founder
of international law, Hugo Grotius (1583–1645) who was read and
cited by many eighteenth-century Americans, conveniently restated
that twelfth-century synthesis. He saw the law as existing independ-
ently of earthly sovereignty and operating in two parts: natural
law (*jus naturale*) and volitional law (*jus voluntarium*). The former
operated according to right reason which discovered the authority
of God, the latter was beyond human argument because it was simply
the will of God. On the model of the second was human volitional
law (*jus voluntarium humanum*) which, when applied to the law of
nations, denoted an invariable public will. Like the exponents of the
Ramian method we find Grotius proceeding intellectually by dicho-
tomies. Further, an Aristotelian bias toward classification led him
to convert into two Justinian's three categories of law, and also to
proceed by a method of dialectic:

> Thus a law either exists by nature or is laid down (by a law giver as
> positive law). That laid down is either law of nations or civil law. Law
> is public or private: that which is public relates to sacred or profane
> things.[3]

Law, in fact, according to Grotius exists by division. From division
comes category, and out of the conflict of interests comes the
necessity for law, permanence and heroes.

The metaphysics of hero and state depended upon an ideology of
conflict. When the travellers on the Mayflower compacted themselves,
in their famous declaration, into a 'civil Body Politick', they had
behind them an inhospitable ocean and before them the bleak and
menacing landscape of an unknown and hostile wilderness. Hannah
Arendt speculates that it would be interesting to know whether the
Pilgrims had been prompted to 'covenant' because of the bad
weather which prevented their landing farther south within the
jurisdiction of the Virginia Company that granted them their patent,
or whether they felt the need to 'combine themselves together'
because the London recruits were an 'undesirable lot', challenging
the jurisdiction of the Virginia Company, and threatening to 'use
their owne libertie'.[4] It was almost certainly both. The hostility of
nature paralleled, in an important analogical synthesis, the feared
natural state of man. Faced with an assault from within and without,

---

[3] Edward Dumbald, *The Life and Legal Writings of Hugo Grotius* (Norman, Oklahoma
1969) p. 172.
[4] Hannah Arendt, *On Revolution* (New York 1963) p. 166.

a man, according to compact theory, contracted for his security by
alienating his personal right.

Compact theory had always been argued from natural necessity,
whether from reason and nature as in Roman law, or from Christian
doctrine which saw nature as the art of God. It was most simply
stated, for our purposes, by the French political theorist, Vattel, in
his famous and influential *Law of Nations* (1760). After summing
up the history of the interaction of divine nature and historical
law-giving in its progress through Justinian, Grotius, Hobbes, Puffen-
dorf and Wolfius, he concluded that 'The Law of Nations is certainly
a natural law,' and that:

> It is essential to all civil society (*Civitatis*) that each member has given
> up his right to the body of the society, and that it has an authority of
> commanding all the members, of giving them laws, and of constraining
> those who refuse to obey.[5]

It was precisely in the conflict of individual and transferred power,
of man in his natural state and man in a state of civil society, which
occupied all the political theorists of the time. Most opposed power
to law, an unequal balance, but even in Montesquieu, with his more
politically realistic balance of powers as such, the problem remained
unsolved. In the place of individual gratification of passion,
Montesquieu supplied a love of country, the emotional aspects of
which came close to masochism:

> The less we are able to satisfy our private passions, the more we abandon
> ourselves to those of a general nature. How comes it that monks are so
> fond of their order? It is owing to the very cause that renders the order
> insupportable. Their rule debars them from all those things by which the
> ordinary passions are fed; there remains therefore only this passion for
> the very rule that torments them. The more austere it is, that is, the
> more it curbs their inclinations, the more force it gives to the only passion
> left them.[6]

As in Hobbes, civil society is a permanent state of war. The civil
state is held out as an alternative to the personal insecurity which
characterized the state of nature. According to Montesquieu this
alternative characterized all government of whatever kind, and each
found its own balance. Furthermore, each body politic had its own
character with its own spirit which guaranteed equilibrium. Hence
virtue was the spirit of democracies, moderation the spirit of mon-
archies and honour the spirit of despotic government. And so we go

---

[5] M. de Vattel, *The Law of the Nations* (London 1760) p. x.

[6] Baron de Montesquieu, *The Spirit of the Laws*: (1748), trans. Thomas Nuget
(New York 1949) vol. I pp. 40—41.

back to the old see-saw between religious and civil law, with actual
power separated from 'moral' power. In the second part of his treatise,
Montesquieu talks of the 'greater sublimity' of religious as opposed
to the 'greater extent' of civil law.[7]

Even where the power is totally invested in the whole people, as
in Rousseau's conception of the 'general will', on the practical level,
the gap between the theoretical locus of power and actual power
makes the idea of compact an imitative drama in which some individual authority is alienated. The pure republic, Rousseau admitted
to be impossible. Rousseau's metaphor of 'will' merely substitutes
a more abstract dynamic of the *persona ficta* of the state, than the
individual labour of Locke's self-owning political animal. In a sense
Hobbes's metaphor of the 'artificial person' gives a better view of
the state's role than Rousseau's 'moral person'.

But there was another view of nature in the late seventeenth and
eithteenth centuries. It was seen as a system of total and invariable
harmony, confirmed through analogies with the 'geometrical laws'
of physics. Given the inheritance of Hobbes's view of nature, the
reaction produced a desire for order which fathered the fact. In
revolutionary terms the desire proposed a superstition powerful
enough to negate the metaphysical doctrines of inherited authority
and divine right, but substituted an equally absolute and invariable
system. As the ingenious intellectual syntheses of James Otis's
well-known pamphlet, *Rights of the British Colonies Asserted and
Proved* (1764) showed:

> The same omniscient, omnipotent, infinitely good and gracious Creator
> of the universe who has been pleased to make it necessary that what we
> call matter should *gravitate* for the celestial bodies to roll round their
> axes, dance their orbits, and perform their various revolutions in that
> beautiful order and concert which we all admire has made it *equally*
> necessary that from *Adam* and *Eve* to these degenerate days the different
> sexes should sweetly *attract* each other, form societies of single families,
> of which *larger* bodies and communities are as naturally, mechanically,
> and necessarily combined as the dew of heaven and the soft distilling
> rain is collected by the all-enlivening heat of the sun. *Government* is
> therefore most evidently founded *on the necessities of our nature*. It is
> by no means an arbitrary thing depending merely on *compact* or *human
> will* for its existence.[8]

In such a system rights of individuals and states mystically accord.
The laws of physics reflect the harmony of sexual attraction, and

[7] Montesquieu, *The Spirit of the Laws*, vol. II, p. 65.
[8] *Pamphlets of the American Revolution, 1750—1776*, Bernard Bailyn, ed., (Cambridge,
Mass. 1965), I, p. 423.

the harmonies of families mirror the harmony of the state. Here Locke and Filmer are united, Rousseau's geometrical calculations anticipated, and the authority of Hobbes's Leviathan preserved, together with a Christian and scientific notion of a God-given natural state. All distinctions are obliterated in the assumption of harmony behind all things.

Such was the European inheritance, and from the evidence of the pamphleteering it was mulled over, argued about, digested and contradicted by virtually every individual from every political viewpoint. The possibilities were infinite, and at no time before in western history did so many men of all types and classes so actively engage in building their own constitutions. From the radical anti-authoritarianism still persisting in the creeds of Baptists and Quakers, to the intellectual middlemen like Jefferson, Madison and John Adams, to the intellectual radicalism of a Tom Paine, the question of the place of liberty in a duly constituted state was unceasingly discussed.

Eventually it was decided that the form of government was to presuppose conflict and hence to necessitate a permanent balance of interests and powers. The states were balanced against the national government, the house of representatives against the senate, the executive against the legislature, the judiciary against the states, the senate against the president, and the people against the government. The history of the making of constitutions in America is a history of political retrenchment. Bailyn talks of the 'contagion of liberty' most theorists feared. Permanent institutions could be the only defence against the continual threat of anarchy, actually demonstrated in the recently experienced Shays's Rebellion. This impluse was the same whether appearing in the arguments of James Otis who, while denying grace, force, compact or property as the basis of power in the state, yet saw a metaphysical law of nature guaranteeing institutions, or in the new type of politician, Alexander Hamilton, who, representing the businessmen, argued for constancy, necessity, utility, an habitual sense of obligation, force and influence as essential to the nature of good government.

In actual historical terms the political conception of representation for eighteenth-century Americans was a mixture of English theory and practice, modified by the very different conditions of the American Revolution. It was impossible to define the term representation clearly. Attempts to do so were frustrated in the face of the diversities of meaning and practice which claimed it as a descriptive term. By the middle of the eighteenth century one English radical pamphleteer noted that representation was one of

those words which 'acquire so many senses that they lose exactness'.[9]
Nonetheless historians like to see a kind of pragmatic evolution of
the term from the English notion of 'virtual representation' to the
American practice of 'representation by election'. The English
notion of 'virtual representation' was a means of propaganda to
maintain the status quo. The landed gentry employing lofty
benevolence and loftier common sense assumed homogeneity of
interests throughout 'the people'. *A priori* consent smoothed the
path of their actions and salved their consciences. In America where
interests were much more articulately diverse, representation by
election eventually brought property interests the more respectable
authority of majority rule. In America the Assemblies with their
public galleries and their members' Whiggish assumptions of 'majority
interest' (a term as elusive in practice as English 'virtual representation') and their insistence that legislative power was invested in
the people gradually toppled the authority of the Royal Councils,
only to set up major problems of representation within the States
themselves. Americans attacked England with the famous slogan,
'no taxation without representation' but at home they felt very
nervous about those strident demands for actual representation so
threatening to the power of American country landowners. The
passage from theoretical to actual consent, and the forms in which
consent could be given or withheld, was not an easy one. The
struggle between the towns and the state, and the state and the
federal government to some extent repeated the intellectual and
actual difficulties of the notion of representation in the struggle
with England. Without abandoning the notion altogether there was
in fact no way out of the dilemma. Who had a right to vote and on
what basis? Should persons or property be represented or a mixture
of both? Or should a person be considered to have sufficient property
in his own person? What binding force should instructions have on
the representative? How were those instructions to be represented
in debate without loss of sovereignty to their authors? What guarantee
did the represented have that they would in fact be represented?
Should the representative act for the good of the whole even if
party interest was threatened? What happened to minority interest
in majority rule? The Whigs' intellectual conviction of the 'good
of the whole', used in ways very similar to the English cry of
'virtual representation', paradoxically helped to stimulate demands
for actual representation, for representational accountability,

[9] Gordon S. Wood, *The Creation of the American Republic 1776–1787* (Chapel Hill,
N. Carolina 1969) p. 173.

for equal property qualifications, equal electoral districts, and hence finally worked against their own interests.

From the Carolinas to Vermont these issues were debated in the years following the Revolution. In spite of considerable variation of state and local conditions there was a broad swing away from philosophies of the people's interest and the popular voice to hard power struggles with shrill party division, a supression of local democracy, involving a rough and tumble political life enough to ruffle the most benevolent of eighteenth-century spirits. Indeed one historian states that the struggles of Americans to seek actual representation after the Revolution exposed 'the whole representational process for the fiction that it was'.[10] By the 1790s the radical spirit of the American Revolution had virtually disappeared. Theoretically power was in the hands of the people, but actually to assume that power was in the hands of the people was felt by many to destroy centralized government and law itself. In the growing reactionary atmosphere, there grew up a kind of good taste consensus that questioning of central authority was mob rule, and that deference was democracy. The ancient Roman ideal of virtue in a republic was in fact supression of personal sovereignty. The classical ideal of the republic itself, Wood remarks, was 'founded on decline and decadence'.[11] The liberty of the demagogues was not personal liberty but a fictional public liberty which served the interests of power. As Madison pointed out the Roman injunctive *'divida et impera'* was the working rule of representative democracy.[12]

Paralleling these discussions of representation and republics, the phenomenon in the visual and architectural arts of neo-Classicism provided both Europe and America with models of order, civic decency and progressive enlightened statesmanship. Neil Harris has shown that statesmen 'turned to visual forms as easily (though not so effectively) as words,' and uses the fact to demonstrate that the Americans needed a didactic justification for their interest in art.[13]

From the early years of the eighteenth century there evolved a concept of art as ideal representation which nonetheless had to be plausible in terms of a particular reality. Du Piles, the French art theorist, on the threshold of the neo-Classical movement, stated that allegory itself must be understandable by common usage rather

[10] Ibid., p. 188.

[11] Ibid., p. 55.

[12] Adrienne Koch, *Jefferson and Madison: the great collaboration* (New York 1964) p. 38.

[13] Neil Harris, *The Artist in American Society* (New York 1966) p. 19.

than by references to learned books on the subject, indicating that even the most extreme form of symbolic iconography had somehow to find its plausibility in general public comprehension. Political theory as we have seen placed great stress on the generalized representation of particulars, and in Sir Joshua Reynolds, the first president of the Royal Academy and perhaps the most influential theorist before Winckelmann, the artistic ideal had to be constructed out of particulars whose relation would express their own generality. In the writings of the Swiss theorist Winckelmann, (1717–68) however, we come close to a summary of the kinds of neo-Classicism that would appeal to the Americans. The official meeting of American painting and European neo-Classicism took place in Rome in 1760, when the young Philadelphia-born Benjamin West, who was to be the second president of the Royal Academy, made his legendary exclamation over the bust of the so-called Belvedere (Apollo), 'My God, how like it is to a Mohawk warrior!'. What the Americans found in neo-Classicism was its thoroughgoing Platonism which, when combined with Christian sentiment, helped to alleviate Puritan distrust of art in general. Winckelmann's description of ideal beauty in the human figure, with its emphasis on generality, unity and absence of blemishes or personal idiosyncrasy, pointed to a concept of a 'moral person' as abstract as Rousseau's characterization of the state. The semantics of generalization are so abstract that one may transfer meanings at will. For example, squeamishness about the state of nature could be countered by a desexualized and representative figure which was at once moral and beautiful. Wickelmann's rules for the representation of the 'ideal figure' is a case in point:

> From unity proceeds another attribute of lofty beauty, the absence of individuality; that is, the forms of it are described neither by points nor lines other than those which shape beauty merely, and consequently produce a figure which is neither peculiar to any particular individual, nor yet expresses any one state of mind or affection of the passions because these blend with its strange lines, and mar the unity.[14]

Accompanying the desire for beauty and virtue came a new emphasis on civic seriousness and public responsibility. It included a new patriotism of a nationalistic kind and a stress on public liberty as the condition of great art. As Mengs, Winckelmann's pupil, remarked:

> We see in fact that the polite arts began to flourish in Italy when *liberty* gave its impulse to the *republic of Venice.* Its traffic and the continual

[14] Johann Joachim Winckelmann, *History of Ancient Art* (1764), trans. G. Henry Lodge (New York 1968) vol. I, p. 201.

communication with Greece, made them conceive ideas worthy of its greatness . . . .[15]

Like Montesquieu, Winckelmann strongly believed in climate as giving direction to the spirit of a state. Unlike Montesquieu he was disposed in favour of republican government. But since republican governments could only operate by the virtue of its people, its art had therefore to be representative of a morally enobling ideal. Winckelmann was largely concerned with Greek sculpture which for him embodied the timeless ideal of the human form. Like the *persona ficta* of the state the ideal form represented the characteristics of all human bodies.

In Europe the neo-Classical impulse had thrown up a cult of busts of famous men variously adorning cathedrals, colleges and ornamental parks in order to perpetuate the memory of their achievements in some visible form. The most notable American instance of this cult, apart from cemetry sculpture, was the New England eccentric, Timothy Dexter, who employed Joseph Wilson, the figure-head sculptor, to set up life-size painted figures of his heroes both sacred and secular around his garden. The neo-Classical marriage of art with the service of the state goes back to an ultimately Roman civic ideal propounded by Cicero that statues of state heroes might induce morality, or rather a respect for law and order, among the people.

Two statements by John Adams take us into the earliest and most conservative treatments of the representative hero in the initial phase of an independent American culture. First there is his summarizing conclusion that 'The body politic cannot subsist any more than the animal body, without a head',[16] and secondly, speaking of the roles of the representative assembly, that '. . . the perfection of the portrait consists in its likeness'.[17] Our first example of the representative hero is George Washington. In the portraits and statues and then in the biographies we can form some idea of how the new republic squared its private democratic tendencies with a public figure, the aristocratic, land-owning, slave-holding ex-colonel of England's erstwhile Virginia regiment.

Samuel Morse, famous inventor of the telegraph who, beginning life as an extremely competent painter of the third generation of

---

[15] Anton Raphael Mengs, *Collected Works,* vol. II (London 1796) p. 21. Several works are bound haphazardly in this volume and differently paginated. This reference occurs in an essay entitled 'Fragment of a Discourse upon the means of making the polite arts flourish in Spain'.

[16] *The Selected Writings of John and John Quincy Adams,* Arienne Koch and William Peden, eds, (New York 1946) p. 91.

[17] Ibid., p. 80.

American painters living in England, summed up the ideology behind official portrait painting in this description of his portrait, not of Washington, but of Lafayette:

> It is a full-length, standing figure, the size of life. He is represented as standing at the top of a flight of steps, which he has just ascended upon a terrace, the figure coming against a glowing sunset sky, indicative of the glory of his own evening of life. Upon his right, if I remember, are three pedestals, one of which is vacant as if waiting for his bust, while the two others are surmounted by the busts of Washington and Franklin—the two associated eminent historical characters of his own time. In a vase on the other side is a flower—the helianthus—with its face towards the sun, in allusion to the characteristic stern, uncompromising consistency of Lafayette—a trait of character which I then considered, and still consider, the great prominent trait of that distinguished man.[18]

The life-size length gives a particular credibility to the figure in purely proportional terms and the flight of steps indicates the personal achievement. The glowing sunset indicates not the sun-king role of a Louis XIV, but a more personal life style naturally in alliance with the movements of nature. The vacant bust, surmounted by those of Washington and Franklin, proclaims his place as one of the architects of American nationhood, but even more pertinently suggests that the place is predestined, depicting an historical drama beyond the accidents of time and place. The virtuous statesman's public life becomes destiny. That two portraits are paintings of sculptures points to the commonplace that sculpture was more durable than painting and hence more befitting heroes. A specific allegorical note is recorded in the helianthus but it is much muted and needs the literary description to give it full effect. The portrait captures that moment between life and death where life already extinct is about to become a purely public fiction. The representative of the people becomes the representative of the abstract notion of the nation in the same way as symbolically the bust incorporates the man. Historical character therefore has this peculiar quality. It is actually dead, but alive insofar as it promotes public consciousness in favour of the past. Lafayette's lifetime 'consistency' becomes eternal and ensures the stability of the American state.

The major academic painters to portray Washington were Charles Willson Peale, John Trumbull, Gilbert Stuart and Charles Willson Peale's son, Rembrandt Peale. Charles Willson Peale, the father of

[18] *Samuel F. B. Morse. His Letters and Journals,* E. L. Morse, ed., (New York and Boston 1914) vol. I, p. 272.

a number of sons famous in painting and natural history, was himself one of the most interesting cultural figures of the revolutionary
and post-revolutionary era. His first influence was Copley and he
had studied in London with Benjamin West. Before returning to
America in 1767 he had completed a full-length portrait of William
Pitt (suitably berobed as a Roman senator). Peale represents that
polymath intellectual vigour and curiosity characteristic of the
period, which spilt over into most of the scientific, technological
and artistic concerns of his time.

Washington first sat for Peale at Mount Vernon in 1772 and the
mid-nineteenth-century art historian Tuckerman provided the
following commentary on the picture:

> The dress (Blue coat, scarlet facings and underclothes) . . . and the
> youthful face, make it suggestive of the first experience of the future
> commander, when, exchanging the surveyor's implements for the
> colonel's commission, he bivouacked in the wilderness of Ohio, the
> leader of a motley band of hunters, provincials, and savages to confront
> wily Frenchmen, cut forest roads, and encounter all the perils of Indian
> ambush, inclement skies, undisciplined followers, famine and woodland
> skirmish.[19]

There is, however, in the portrait **pl. 1** little to suggest the rough
leader of guerilla warfare. Tuckerman's literary reading of the picture
suggests the political iconography required of an American hero in
a later and more sentimentalizing time. Here we see Washington,
dressed in his new London outfit, as colonel of the Virginia regiment.
His right hand is stuck self-consciously into his waistcoat, the sash
fits awkwardly over his frame and the 'Wolfe hat', the silver gorget
and the 'Orders of the March' are conspicuous indications of first
promotion. Here is a young provincial aristocrat intent on display-
ing his new rank, and perhaps wondering whether the old-fashioned
style of the uniform looks sufficiently dignified. The slight turn of
the head so that the eyes look straight into the light source, hints
at a personal awareness of destiny, while the tightly-closed mouth
indicates firmness of will.

By 1776 Washington had become enough of a king figure for the
supreme executive council of Pennsylvania to order his portrait
from Peale for the council chamber. Peale painted many versions of
this type—known as the 'Princeton-type' portrait—and undertook to
visit the battlefields of Princeton and Trenton to obtain the particulars for the generalizing process. The Pennsylvania directive was

---

[19] Washington Irving, *Life of Washington, Works* vol. V (Philadelphia c. 1900)
p. 383.

carefully worded: '. . . contemplation of it may excite others to tread in the same glorious and disinterested steps which lead to public happiness and private honor'.[20] Although the language recapitulates the sentiments of a Locke or Montesquieu, the impulse is more aristocratic than democratic. One is reminded of Henry VIII

1 *George Washington* (1772) by Charles Willson Peale. (*Courtesy of Washington and Lee University, Lexington, Virginia.*)

commissioning Holbein to make replicas of his portraits for the major English castles, and indeed, in an ever increasing number of state rooms throughout America the portrait of Washington became a visual incitement to public virtue and private honour. If internally

[20] A. T. E. Gardner and S. P. Feld, *American Paintings*, vol. I (New York 1965) p. 62.

the gathering Washington cult became the psychological foundation
of legal order, externally it defined the country as a nation state to
other nations. Peale made replicas for the embassies of Spain, France
and Cuba. In the copy reproduced here **pl. 2**, Peale has substituted
a bare and desolate landscape for the usual Princeton battle scene.

2 *George Washington* by Charles Willson Peale. (*Courtesy of
the Metropolitan Museum of Art, New York, Gift of Collis P.
Huntington, 1896*)

Both artist and sitter have grown more confident in the years since
the Mount Vernon portrait. The insignia of war have become more
prominent, the right hand side of the background exhibiting a
European-inspired collection of military iconography: the captured
standards, cannon and gun carriage, the charger and colonial flag

surmounting the brick-a-brac of victory. Washington's pose is that
of an eighteenth-century military dandy. It has been suggested that
Mrs Washington had some influence here and indeed the cult of
sentiment surrounding the hero figure was, as it still is, supplied by
women. Women were the moral guardians of private honour, protected by the activity of men in active public life. But if the metic-
ulously-painted uniform, the pose and the national icons of war
depict an America retreating from democracy into nationalism, the
left hand side of the background with its war-ravaged landscape
still hints at some ambiguity in Peale's feelings. His own earlier,
first-hand experience of war had very much sickened him. This
portrait, then, reflects Peale's double view of war. The realities of
cruelty and desolation and the military pomp are juxtaposed here,
not ironically but factually. But for later commentators even this
socially-relaxed, drawing-room general was not morally steadfast
enough. The first major American art historian, William Dunlap may
have had some of these pictures in mind when painting his own
full-length Washington:

> I placed my hero on the field of battle at Princeton. I did not take the
> liberty to throw off his hat, or omit the black and white cockade [as
> Peale did] ; but in full uniform, booted and spurred, he stood most
> heroically alone—for the figures in the background I had thrown to a
> most convenient distance.[21]

Here the completeness of the uniform—the symbol of public dress—
is most emphasized and there is a further accent on the splendid
isolation of the public figure. The figures in the background are
reduced in size, not by some necessity of portrait convention, but
as a specific moral act.

John Trumbull is chiefly known for his monumentally dull pictures of American revolutionary scenes in the Rotunda of the
Capitol building. But in his earlier days he was a more than competent history and portrait painter. In 1792 he painted Washington
before the battle of Trenton, pl. 3. He claimed to give 'his military
character, in the most sublime moment of its exertion'.[22] At the
representative historical moment the public character is most typical
and hence most true and most invariable. Here the artificial life of
the hero is glimpsed as a morally instructive parable of state. As an
American, Trumbull had to give the symbols of public character a
private reference and to find local meaning in historical destiny.

[21] William Dunlap, *The History of the Arts of Design in the United States* (Boston
1918) vol. I, p. 301.
[22] Gardner and Feld, *American Paintings*, p. 103.

But particular and general had to be synthesized:

> In the countenance of the hero, the *likeness,* the mere map of the face, was not all that was attempted, but the features are animated, and exalted by the mighty thoughts revolving in the mind on that sublime occasion; *the high resolve,* stamping on the face and attitude its lofty purpose, to conquer or to perish.[23]

Likeness had to be representative therefore, and if we turn to the picture, the broken cannon can be seen both as signifying the fruits

3 *General George Washington before the Battle of Trenton* by John Trumbull. (*Courtesy of the Metropolitan Museum of Art, New York, Bequest of Grace Wilkes, 1922*)

[23] Ibid., p. 104.

of victory and as indicative of a moment of battle. Read in literary terms, as was then the mode, the horse, controlled by the aide, provides an exteriorization of the hero's will in conflict with forces that threaten to turn anarchic. Trumbull hoped he had also pictured this conflict in the features of the general. Internal and external landscapes had to harmonize through the public activity of the representative figure. The effect is helped by parallel planes moving diagonally back into the picture space. Washington is the focus of the forces of history and nature. The outstretched arm connects the general with the receding planes, and also links the dead tree at the top right-hand corner with the live growing plants at the bottom left-hand corner. The hero stands and serves to mediate the pattern of life and death in nature itself. Behind him man and nature, in the figures of the aide-de-camp and horse, structurally and icono-graphically link the private moment of decision. In the farthest plane is the battle proper, the physical counterpart of the mental activity of the foreground. The battle smoke links symbolically with the war clouds to reaffirm the identity of natural and historical analogy. The details of uniform and harness Trumbull copied faith-fully from the originals. But, with one hand clasping the spy-glass and the other the sword, these details represent a union of mental and actual foresight and the power of physically implementing destiny.

No one devoted himself more assiduously to portraiture than Gilbert Stuart, also of the first generation of American painters who went to London to study under West, and who in turn was studied for portrait technique by Trumbull. He painted Washington three times from life, once in 1795 and twice in 1796. Of all the 'Stuart types', the 'Atheneum type' is the best known and the art critic, John Neal, said of it in 1860 that, if Washington were to return, and were to be different, he would be taken for an imposter. The portrait is highly idealized, an archetype of the benign patrician, though experts agree that it could have resembled Washing-ton but little. Some critics complain of weakness around the lines of the mouth which Tuckerman graciously attributed, as do modern commentators, to false teeth. It is noticeable, however, that in many later replicas by Stuart, the lines of the mouth are hardened as if to counter such criticism and to stiffen the hero up a little. From Stuart, too, we get the most aristocratic version of an heroic portrait of Washington. For these who admitted that portraits had any value at all, the emphasis was on 'real' rather than symbolic or allegorical detail. Tuckerman in his commentaries thought that pictures such as David's *Napoleon* were not for those who 'spurned

a crown'.[24] Stuart's 'Lenox type' portrait, however, made few
concessions to democratic simplicity. Here Washington is painted
in full aristocratic paraphernalia which Stuart got straight from the
portrait of Bossuet by Rigaud, the official painter to the court of
Louis XIV. As Eisen points out the pillar and the curtain were
standard in this type of portrait, from Rubens's *Anton Triest, Von
Ghent* to Sir Henry Raeburn's *Adam Roland of Gask.*[25] The imperialist symbols of cloth and pillar are included in Stuart's
portrait **pl. 4** and, as if to emphasize the greater imperial power of
America, he changes the pagan mask on Rigaud's table to a pair of
eagle heads surmounted above legs shaped as fasces. On the table
lie the sword and the map, twin symbols of executive and legislative
power, and the picture-framed landscape of turbulent clouds show
the conflict of war, emblematically internalized in the hero's mind.

There is a well-known incident of the whole Peale family surrounding Washington for simultaneous portraits. Peale's son, Rembrandt,
painted one of the more famous portraits: the 'port-hole type', which
is chiefly distinguished by an oval frame of stone fretwork.
Rembrandt Peale's long account of how he constructed the picture
reveals what he, in theory, believed he was doing. His neo-Classical
language matches his quest to give timelessness to his attempt. He
studied details both from his father's sketches and from his own
memory and continually complained that the *beau ideal* of his hero
seemed continuously to retreat before him. Finally in a frenzy of effort
he thought he had succeeded just about well enough, 'although it was
not the perfect Washington to equal my insatiable desire I felt I
could do no more'.[26] This is a good example of how, at this time,
neo-Classical and Romantic explanations of the creative process,
lie in uneasy balance.

Artists made many copies of their own originals and they reached
a wider public through authorized and unauthorized engravings.
Rembrandt Peale himself did over eighty versions of the 'port-hole
type'. By the mid-century, there was little left of the restrained
soul-searching idealism of the earlier generations. The sentimentality
always latent in neo-Classicism became more widespread. The muted
symbolism of the hero operating amid discrete symbols of nature
and history turned into frank theatricality.

This Victorianism is accountable for by a reintroduction of
European values around the mid-century. When the Americans went
to Europe during the second half of the eighteenth century and the

[24] Irving, *Life of Washington, Works*, vol. V, p. 402.
[25] G. A. Eisen, *Portraits of Washington*, (New York 1932) vol. I, p. 78.
[26] Gardner and Feld, *American Paintings*, p. 139.

first years of the nineteenth, they went to England and found as
president of the Royal Academy a fellow American. When Leutze
went to Europe in the mid-nineteenth century, he went not to
London but to Düsseldorf where he found an heroic tradition of
history painting much modified by Christian piety. There the
emphasis was on line and draughtmanship—a technical correlative
of the neo-Classical belief in form. Purity was associated with line

4 *George Washington* after Gilbert Stuart. (*Courtesy of
the National Portrait Gallery, London.*)

and the moral analogies could be read endlessly, though in fact this
association of line with ideality was a result of the medium of engraved pictures such as illustrated the works of Winckelmann. The
Düsseldorfians modified the European heritage of historical
painting, by democratizing and sentimentalizing its impulse. Leutze's
Washington Crossing the Delaware (1851) **pl. 5** painted under this
influence, is undoubtedly the best-known historical picture with
Washington as a central character. The *Literary World* said of it in

1851 that 'It is incomparably the best painting yet executed of an American subject'.[27] Even now 100,000 people every year visit to the elaborate museum on the banks of the Delaware once built specially for it. Like the Trenton reception, the Braddock defeat, the leave-taking of his officers and the last address, this incident is part of the official iconography of Washington's career. The figure groupings are academic with their obvious Renaissance-like triangular forms. Washington's theatrical pose is implausibly secure in the overloaded boat, as he stands at the apex of the main figure

5 *Washington Crossing the Delaware* by Emanuel Leutze. (*Courtesy of the Metropolitan Museum of Art, New York, Gift of John S. Kennedy, 1897*)

group. Appropriately the flag takes the highest position in the overall design. Curiously the photographic detail is betrayed by the design and the disproportion of some of the figures. The care for detail does not imply that the relations of those details add up to photographic accuracy. It is interesting to note that, in spite of the parallelism of the poles or oars, not one man gives the impression of cooperating with a fellow crewsman. Each is engaged in a private struggle, or has his eyes fixed on some light of destiny ahead of him. In both thematic and technical terms, therefore, this frank picture of manifest destiny sums up the contradictions of private and public person. The relations are expressed in a rather crude pastiche of European Renaissance patterning. The proud upstanding average man in a fur trapper's hat supports the flag, and he is connected by

[27] *The Literary World*, IX (New York 1851) p. 311.

the line of his body with the head of state dressed in full and impeccable uniform. But the connection is merely formal and symbolic. In spite of Flexner's attribution of 'barbaric yawp' to this picture, there seems little possibility here of shedding blood. The action is metaphysical. Once more it is the forces of nature which suggest the continuity and permanence of the conflict, here symbolized by the ice through which the boat is progressing in true pioneering style, and in the dark storm clouds from which the general leads his troops into light and truth.

The new mass-produced lithograph did not neglect the subject of the president. In 1846 the firm of Currier and Ives published a lithograph called the *Death of Washington* drawn in full Victorian manner. Washington lies in bed surrounded by his family, with his black slaves standing respectfully behind the chair on which Washington's mother sits. Such a picture marks a complete change from emblematic symbols of representational psychology and turns the symbolic art into pictorially realistic theatre. We witness here the death of the state as symbolic family tragedy. The representation of the death of the 'father of his country' is a melodramatic inducement to hero worship, and a consequence of the need to perpetuate heroes. It also illustrates Christian eighteenth-century pieties of the perfect death, familiar in literary terms at least from novelists like Samuel Richardson.

The most obviously classical form of representation was the statue but there is a history of long resistance to public statues during the first 30 or so years of the republic's life. The predominantly ex-Puritan populace preferred to internalize in conscience their moral imperatives, rather than have them induced externally by artefacts all too easily connected with idolatry and popery. Nonetheless statues of Washington appeared early on and, on Jefferson's advice, a statue of Washington, Virginia's first commissioned public monument, was executed by the Italian, Canova. But already Ceracchi had made a bust which recalled the looks of a Roman senator, and there was Houdon's statue, also commissioned by Jefferson, for the state of Virginia in Paris. Washington himself insisted on modern dress, though Houdon's original intention to depict Washington as a farmer holding a plough, was superseded by the introduction of the fasces, sword and cloak, with the plough set behind the feet of the general. The statue sums up republican neo-Classicism. The obvious references to Cincinnatus are rejected, and the objects do not represent a particular classical event, but the theories of permanent nationhood as reworked by the seventeenth- and eighteenth-century theorists on the basis of nature and Roman law. The plough represents labour and agriculture indicating the political character of person and state. In its more private representational capacity the statue gains authority from Houdon's own knowledge of anatomy, his detailed examination of the face from sketches made at Mount Vernon and his technique of employing life masks. The contemporary dress democratizes the symbols of state to make the identification of private and public roles more obvious and the private and public citizen are also linked by the fact that one hand is placed on a walking cane, the other on the fasces.

The European with republican sympathies scored a greater success than the American sculptor, Horatio Greenough, who was much more an American with European and reactionary leanings. Houdon's statue was also a greater success than Canova's statue of Washington as a Roman senator which was copied after the antique statue of Mars in the Terme Museum at Rome where he is seated inscribing the laws on a table of stone. This unlikely combination of Moses and Mars does, however, point to the connection between law and conflict.

Greenough's ill-fated statue **pl.** 6 illustrates the divinity of the hero, since the sitting position and the upraised arm was borrowed from Phidias's Zeus in the temple of Olympia. Like the American philosopher Ralph Waldo Emerson, Greenough had a firm belief in great men and their public uses. In his *Travels, Observations and Experience of a Yankee Stonecutter* (1852) he declared, 'if a man say to other men that he is great, they will laugh him to scorn—if he say that he is God, they will take it into consideration'.[28]

The most lasting public monument to Washington was the federal capital itself. It was designed as a public theatre of state. L'Enfant's plan **pl.** 7 captures the visual mechanics of Paine's metaphor of the wheel, for the city had indeed 'a common centre, in which every radius meets'.[29]   Mixing his labour with nature, L'Enfant turned the muddy channel of Goose Creek into a canal worthy of Venice. But although L'Enfant spent weeks tramping round the swampy environment, the final plan was an abstract linear design worthy of the greatest baroque demagogues. The endless vistas secularized a religious impulse to contemplate infinity, and the landscape only

[28] Horatio Greenough, *Travels, Observations and Experience of a Yankee Stonecutter* (Boston 1852) p. 127.

[29] The change from body images to more abstract ones to characterize the state is no better illustrated than in the following passage by Paine: 'A nation is not a body, the figure of which is to be represented by the human body; but is like a body contained within a circle, having a common centre, in which every radius meets; and that centre is formed by representation'. Thomas Paine, *Collected Works* (New York 1954), vol. II, p. 203.

6 *George Washington* By Horatio Greenough. (*Courtesy of the
Smithsonian Institution, Washington, DC, Photo No. P6450.*)

made sense seen from the centre, the home of the invisible *persona
ficta* of the state—the White House. Dickens said the avenues were
splendid but went nowhere.[30] Looked at as a plan, the relations
between the different aspects of government and memorial found
a geometric order which symbolized the link between parts and
whole. Only from the centre do the relations of this homogenous and
uniform space take on meanings as an art of nature. In L'Enfant's
plan, Euclidian geometry hitherto applied to neo-Vitruvian architecture and the Globe Theatre now became embodied in a total

[30] Charles Dickens, *American Notes, Works* (London 1874) p. 135.

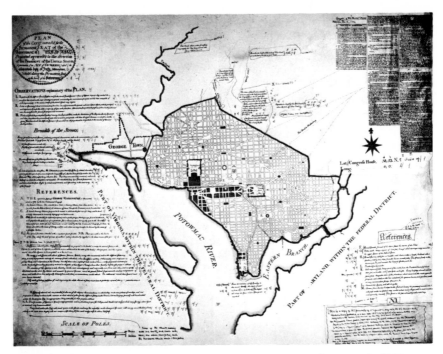

7 Detail from a copy by the United States Coast Guard and Geodetic Survey in 1887 of [L'Enfant's] plan for Washington, DC. (*Courtesy of the Library of Congress, Washington, DC.*)

representative urban theatre of a nation's life. The drama of representative democracy found in the city of Washington an official landscape which was the actual environment of the people. It is not only that, as Mumford says, 'its mechanical order makes no allowances for growth, change, adaptation, and creative renewal',[31] but also that anyone walking or living away from the centre has no concessions made to his point of view. And this is true politically and visually, for the visual representation of urban space involves important political assumptions.

The visual representations of Washington were paralleled by literary biographies. As with the portraits and statues, the developing biographical image traces the need for a social reassurance of America's public character. In terms of seventeenth- and eighteenth-century thought, with its multiform implications, we can see that the very

[31] Lewis Mumford, *The City in History* (London 1966) p. 461.

notion of 'character' is a product of the interrelations of society conceived of as individual and state. Public character is the artificial representation of the people, which authorizes external repression. In a similar way, private character is formed by internalizing repression. Republics were thought to be impossible by the European philosophers, since they believed that by nature the individual could not sufficiently repress himself to make the state survive.

It is not surprising that many biographies swiftly recast Washington into a timeless Christian hero. The moment of the hero's death becomes the moment of apotheosis—just as in the portraits. With the life complete, the canonization process could proceed without embarrassment. One of the earliest panegyrics was given only a year after Washington's death by David Tappan, the Harvard professor of divinity:

> Yet thy dying, as well as living greatness, has raised thee above the ordinary level. It has proclaimed thee a Christian conqueror. It has visibly exemplified and sealed thy future glory. It has consecrated thy character, instructed thy fellow-men, and honored thy God.[32]

The Virginian aristocratic land-owner, deist and slave-owner, a man singularly inept in politics, is transformed into a political hero and raised above the conflicts of ordinary mortals. Even the representative nature of the private-public contract is changed to the much older one of priest-king and worshipper, so that criticism of the state and controversial debate become totally irrelevant. 'Let us,' says Tappan, 'then deposit at the tomb of our common father all our political contentions'.[33] Half a century later these public characteristics would become even more explicit in a book by George Lippard (most poetic of writers on Washington) called *Washington and his Generals*[34] in which a mid-nineteenth-century synthesis of Christian mythology and Roman imperialist pretensions is made, drawing on the events of the lives of Christ and Julius Caesar, to make up Washington's own symbolic life.

Many commentators, articulating the commonplace assumption of portrait philosophy that outward physical character is the guide to inward grace, sought literally to find in the features of Washington clues to his greatness. 'It is natural, . . .' wrote Goodrich, quoting one Dr Thatch, 'to view with keen attention the countenance of an

---

[32] David Tappan, *Washington's Political Legacies* (Boston 1800) p. 277.
[33] Ibid., p. 291.
[34] George Lippard, *Washington and his Generals: or, Legends of the Revolution* (Philadelphia 1847). For a summary see W. A. Bryan *George Washington in American Literature* (New York 1952).

illustrious man, with a secret hope of discovering in his features some traces of excellence which distinguishes him from and elevates him above his fellow mortals'.[35] While living memory was fresh the comments were more cautious and probably truer:

> Though his eyes neither sparkled with striking vivacity, nor flashed with uncommon fire, their steady, firm and searching expression, bespoke the strength and activity of his intellect. He possessed a certain sublimity of person and aspect, calculated to absorb and over-awe the human faculties.[36]

In a biography some thirty years later, however, Paulding, commenting on Peale's Mount Vernon portrait of 1772, declared precisely the opposite: 'his eye is full of fire, and its expression rather gay than grave . . . .'[37]

Where a more scientific authority for these speculations was felt to be more directly needed, Coombe, the phrenologist, came up with the answers. After examining Washington's skull he declared, 'His temperament seems to have been sanguine bilious; his head large, and well adapted in every part—the moral sentiments and intellect reigning supreme'.[38] Many, however, rejected the idea of pictorial or literary portraiture to preserve Washington's memory and another biographer summed up a common feeling: 'his most enduring statue is in the hearts of a grateful people, and his noblest monument is in the liberty and prosperity of his country'.[39]

At the root of the interest in public character is the imposed psychological need for the perfect father. The most common as well as the most significant metaphor is 'father of his country'. All the biographies use it and most reverently write it in capital letters. In spite of Locke's refutation of Filmer, the literary biography seems to guarantee a psychology of primal family myths and ahistoric paternal power.

The many biographies written for children emphasize the respect owing to the law-giving father. These instructions took the form of psychological conditioning. In the preface to his *Life of Washington* Paulding made the point clearly:

> In a word addressed to the youth, and to the popular feeling of his country, it seemed allowable, if not absolutely necessary to the purposes of the writer, to place the actions of Washington before the reader in a

[35] Samuel Griswold Goodrich, *Life of George Washington* (Philadelphia 1844) p. 171.
[36] C. Caldwell, *Character of General Washington* (Philadelphia 1801) p. 5.
[37] James Kirke Paulding, *Life of Washington* (New York 1835) p. 121.
[38] Quoted from S. G. Arnold, *The Life of George Washington* (New York 1849) p. 222.
[39] Ibid., pp. 219–20.

manner the more strongly to affect his reason as well as his imagination, and co accompany them with reflections calculated to impress him deeply with the virtues and services of the Father of his Country. . . . The intention is to appeal . . . rather to the feelings of nature than to the judgement of criticism.[40]

Benson Lossing, America's first pictorial historian, perpetuated a similar philosophy in his widely popular books, and characterized the endless dream of success with the possibility of power in an ancient guise: 'Here every boy is heir-apparent to the throne of sovereignty, and every girl may become a queen-mother'.[41] Lossing hoped too, that 'germs of general information in the young mind . . . shall take root and never be forgotten; . . .'.[42]

One of the most ignored cultural events of American life is the public parade. A contemporary visitor to America is likely to find himself unprepared for their frequency, their length and devotion to symbolizing, in a kind of official public theatre, what are often bigoted nationalistic, military and sectarian goals. An early biographer, Aaron Bancroft, described one such early public drama— perhaps the most famous of many which greeted officially welcomed heroes of the state. Washington's reception at Trenton was modelled after the example of a Roman triumph:

> Gray's bridge over the Schuylkill was, with much taste and expression, embellished on the occasion. At each end arches were erected composed of laurel, in imitation of a Roman triumphal arch; and on each side was a laurel shrubbery. As the general passed, unperceived by him a youth by the aid of machinery let down upon his head a civick crown . . . . On the bridge over the creek which runs through this place, a triumphal arch was erected on thirteen pillars, these were entwined with laurel and decorated with flowers. On the front of the arch was the following inscription, in large gilt letters,
>
> THE DEFENDER OF THE MOTHERS
> WILL BE
> THE PROTECTOR OF THE DAUGHTERS[43]

This single public drama gives many examples of the relations of public and private character in this period. The neo-Classical aspects of the decoration emphasize the Roman rather than the Greek inheritance of that tradition: military victory and unity. The symbols of the arch, and the 13 pillars of state compel the federalist

---

[40] Paulding, p. vii.
[41] Benson Lossing, *Lives of the Presidents* (New York 1848) p. iii.
[42] Ibid.
[43] Aaron Bancroft, *An Essay on the Life of George Washington* (Worcester, Mass. 1807) p. 264.

interpretation of history. The ingenious mechanic literally employing a mechanical tool to confer public character was Charles
Willson Peale. The sexual basis of such hero-worship comes across
in the inscription. Since chastity or motherhood are the 'natural
alternatives', this rule of nature shows that an assumption of female
demands for security ensures the double role of male as protector
and woman as moral guide. Women are assumed to have no active
political role. Thus the patriarchal family structures the representative theatre of the state. This incident was a favourite one with the
biographers. One tells of how a 'number of beautiful young virgins,
robed in white met him with songs of gratulation—they strewed
laurel before the benign hero, who moved slowly on a white
charger,[44] and in Goodrich's *Life of George Washington* there is
a crude woodcut of the scene.

The implications of the psychology of power with all its contradictions, as outlined in the writings of the theorists of the American Revolution, become more explicit as one approaches the Civil
War, and they are more obviously apparent in the arguments of
right-wing writers. In a vicious and violently pro-slavery book called
Washington Our Example, one Mrs Searle wrote as a motto to her
work, 'Providence appointed Washington Childless that a Nation
might call him Father'. If power necessitates the protection of its
subjects' chastity and motherhood, the hero himself is made into
a sterile, desexualized cult object. Characteristically Mrs Searle
emphasizes the divine necessity for pure white fathers. 'No negro
or Indian ever sat in the councils of the nation, with the Fathers
of the American Republic . . ... But God selected that precious seed
from the Caucasian race alone.'[45] The law of nature could be invoked and extended to give authority to any racist attitude.
Obliquely, however, Mrs Searle made the connections between the
representative system and the psychology of power. In a paternalist
power situation, the people (especially women) must desexualize
themselves, either remaining conventional virgins or mothers, and
the hero, incapable of children himself, vicariously fathers the
whole society.

Two books published in the mid-century point to a new direction in
thinking about heroes and representative men. Whereas the seventeenth and eighteenth-century theorists attempted to justify their
claims in terms of society and political order, Carlyle and Emerson

[44] P. Potter, *Life of General George Washington* (Philadelphia 1812) p. 96.
[45] S. L. Searle, *Washington Our Example* (Philadelphia 1865) p. 10.

create a dialectical metaphysic out of history and the self. Carlyle,
the English Romantic historian, strongly aware of a German idealistic philosophical tradition, and Emerson, with a transcendentalist's
interest in German culture, continued the key debate about the
nature of authority and the self, using the barely secularized
language of Christian–Platonic thought for their metaphors of social
psychology. In contrast to Carlyle, Emerson tended to fight shy of
the concept of the 'divinity' of the hero, his representative men
emerged as less tyrannical and he omitted the values of worship,
externally imposed discipline and a sense of power to be found
everywhere in Carlyle.[46] The differences were at least great enough
for Emerson, in his vast correspondence with Carlyle, conspicuously
to avoid references to *Heroes and Hero Worship* (1841) published
some ten years before *Representative Men* (1850). Both books mark
a falling off from the radical political awareness exhibited by some
of their countrymen half a century earlier. For Carlyle the functions
and purposes of heroes are quite straightforward. History as such
is the personal history of great men. And these men or psycho-
historical types have developed historically as God, prophet, poet,
priest, man of letters and king. All his heroes have qualities in common.
They are the foci of an everlasting order of nature in a time of
historical chaos. Their characteristic metaphors vary. They are living
rocks, fixed points, portraits of time, sun heroes working order out
of the undifferentiated energy of darkness, lightning of heaven and
fountains of light. Carlyle's pursuit of the spirit of heroism relies
on a conception of psychological types divided into hierarchical
categories, but in fact, the types become archetypes and the arbitrary
categories take on the authority of a natural order. The character
types he creates in the course of the book thus reflect a need for
the personal reassurance of a natural social order he found lacking
everywhere about him.

With Emerson, who is our chief concern, the idea of the representative man was acquired fairly early in life and changed little.
Whereas Carlyle was always, in spite of his transcendental rhetoric,
very much alive to the social implications of his philosophy, Emerson
pushed the gap between representer and represented further apart
and also the distance between thought and action implicit in that
gap. 'Men,' he saw, 'have a pictorial or representative quality, and
serve us in the intellect.'[47] This 'reading' of men's actions makes

[46] I am indebted here to an unpublished Ph.D. dissertation: K. Kurtz, 'The Sources
and Development of Emerson's *Representative Men*', Yale University 1947.

[47] Ralph Waldo Emerson, *Representative Men, Works,* vol. IV (Centenary edition,
New York and Boston 1876) p. 8.

Emerson's synthesis of the split tradition of thought and action, and of practicality and piety, a purely semantic exercise. It has not been often enough noticed that Emerson's dynamic impulse towards synthesis is nearly always verbal, in the sense that a shifting of terms feeds a somewhat passive hope for reconciliation and change. For example, 'reason' always means 'instinct' in the essays, but, far from effecting a unity of body and mind, it merely turns passion and creativity into a more bloodless mental activity.

The same processes are to be observed in his treatment of representative men. As in much of his other work, the concept of representation depends on shifting and apparently conflicting theories of vision. At the outset Emerson sums up his own contradictions when he says that the eye 'repeats every day the first Eulogy of things—"He saw that they were good".'[48] To be sure, Emerson wanted a theory of creative vision. The suggestion here is that, like Coleridge at his most intellectually daring point in the twelfth chapter of the *Biographia Literaria,* Emerson believed that the imagination could imitate the divine mind in synthesizing its own vision. This characterization of the activity of the eye, in its very phrasing, in its sense of literary reference, and in its attempt to unite vision and religion, shows how Emerson tried to push together the elements of his divided world. But the belief in essences and forms undercuts whatever is critical and astringent in his thought. The parts of the sentence and the phrasing itself, merely point to an undefined eternity of things beyond language itself, belittling the unique and particular, and throwing a cloak of piety over the vitality of the changes he is describing. Here the sense of sight gives a hint of creativity but lapses into confirming, through repetition, a permanent and unstated idea. What is thus emphasized is a representative quality of vision. Sight, in a revolutionary *manner* only, reconfirms an original and predestined order. Because the connections between representation and what is being represented structure the relation of the past to the present, that imaginative way of seeing which crystallizes, in a particular moment, the whole field of our experience is despaired of and denied, Emerson[49] confuses, in a deliberate intellectual attempt at synthesis, what is seen with the invisible process of thought, but (as with his concept of reason), instead of endowing our sense of sight with new imaginative possibilities, he gives to sight the Platonic mysticisms of an unstated

---

[48] Ibid., p. 10.
[49] For a discussion of this see Sherman Paul, 'The Angle of Vision' in Milton R. Konvitz and Stephen E. Wicher, eds., *Emerson, A collection of critical essays* (Englewood Cliffs, N.J., 1962) pp. 158–78. See especially p. 175.

order. It is hardly surprising that for Emerson, Plato was a 'great-eyed' geometrician. The sense of vision denies therefore any quality but a representational one. Like the symbols of public polity, Emerson's geometry of the mind and morality points to and perpetually reaffirms an uncontaminated essence of reason. Even where he most advocates change and hints at new syntheses, there is a nagging sense that the new is always some kind of secular revelation. In a definition of the *Genius*, a popular activity of the time, he showed the ideal quality of the representative man:

> Genius is the *naturalist* or *geographer* of the super-sensible regions, and draws their map; and by acquainting us with new fields of activity, cools our affection for the old. These are at once accepted as the reality, of which the world we have conversed with is the show.[50]

Through his physical map-making activity, the geographer symbolizes a nonphysical reality in the linear and abstract representation of landscape. Emerson has stated an important truth here which many twentieth-century American poets have pursued. It is that any creative innovator redefines the fields of relationship and that the image of the geographer is a revolutionary one. But Emerson takes away with one hand what he gives with the other. The imaginative effort with its excitement and mystery is withdrawn from the activity of making and transferred to a sense of merely imitating the the 'super-sensible regions'. In what sense, we may ask, is this new 'reality' any less a representative theatre than the 'show' which is superseded? And what of Emerson's political sense here? Do we accept a new reality so readily?

The contradictions come out even more strongly when Emerson takes up the more traditional arguments of the representative debate. For Emerson the great man benevolently guards the hero-worshipping public against its own excesses of adulation and veneration. We are to suppose that a man of power has the will to reject that power when the people are too grateful to him. All the decisions about the suspension and continuity of sovereignty are therefore left in the hands of one individual. Emerson's reasoning is politically naive in the extreme, in its refusal to recognize the nature and effects of power. Nonetheless, in searching for an ideal representative man, and having to choose a representative example from history, he has to face the challenge that, historically, political leaders are prime-movers of perpetual and unprofitable human sacrifice:

> Why are the masses from the dawn of history down, food for knives

[50] Emerson, *Representative Men*, p. 16.

and powder? The idea dignifies a few leaders, who have sentiment, opinion, love, self-devotion; and they make war and death sacred; but what for the wretches whom they hire and kill?[51]

Here human sentiments are only accorded to the leaders or representatives who make death and war 'sacred', and yet Emerson is clearly concerned for the masses. His solution is a more abstract visuality which discovers the ultimately calm universal reason of the cosmos in which individuals as such are irrecoverably lost. From an imaginary point of view a panorama unfolds which reconciles all. The convolutions of the phrases become more and more desperate: 'The genius of humanity is the right point of view of history'.[52] That history is made in particulars, that conventional history is the point of view of the men in power, that the right point of view is not something universally agreed, that humanity and history are not so easily to be linked, never seem to have occurred to this unruffled spirit. The sense of panorama in Emerson sanctions the contradictions of representation of all kinds. The vision is simply enlarged until everything becomes reconcilable in terms of its opposite. History reveals the predetermined pattern of nature from a calm fixed point of view. Emerson is the natural heir to Jonathan Edwards. The representative drama of history and nature in Emerson's verbal gymnastics served to widen the split between thought and action, and to sanction whoever held enough power to persuade others that his was the right point of view of history.

If we take one example of Emerson's representative men, we can observe the contradictions working in a particular case. According to Emerson, Napoleon is the great modern representative man. The argument is, of course, conducted above the level of the realities of power in France during the 1790s and must therefore be discussed in terms of Emerson's own psychic need in creating, by means of an essay on Napoleon, a symbol relevant to his own society. Carlyle had already written on the subject. For him Napoleon was the last great man, but at the same time, in Carlyle's picture, he was a cynical manipulator of power and religious belief.

Emerson is less critical. He finds Napoleon modern because he is representative, and states that the common man 'finds him, like himself, by birth a citizen, who, by very intelligible merits, arrived at such a commanding position that he could indulge all those tastes which the common man possesses but is obliged to conceal and deny: good society, good books, fast travelling, dress, dinners,

---

[51] Ibid., pp. 30—31.
[52] Ibid., p. 33.

servers without number . . .'.[53] The self-repressing multitude hence satisfy their desires vicariously in their image of Napoleon. For Emerson, simply because the relationship is 'representational' it is justified, whether or not the effect is human. But Emerson is right to see Napoleon as a proper cult figure for American society. The image of the omnipotent bureaucrat was needed for the rapidly industrializing nation. Emerson continued, 'he is so largely receptive, and is so placed, that he comes to be a bureau for all the intelligence, wit and power, of the age and country'.[54] In Napoleon, Emerson celebrated the hero as bureaucratic machine, a simple variation on the old conception of government as an impersonal body existing outside the ebb and flow of human relations. Emerson's metaphysic of representation makes any radical criticism impossible. Nonetheless in the last sections of the essay, he does criticize Napoleon as a representative of the middle classes. Central here is his insight that the ownership of property is a conservative force which results in a property-defending representative as a political leader. But the only solution is to call for a better representative: 'The counter revolution, the counter-party still waits for its organ and representative, in a lover and a man of truly public and universal aims'.[55] Napoleon succeeded where he represented the modern, the rational, the scientific; he failed when he killed a million men to gain an objective. Emerson does not realize that the one is consequent upon the other, for the source of his power was the 'representative character which clothed him'.[56] Emerson calls for a more active and heroic representative in spite of the fact that according to representation theory he is supposed to have no private character at all.

It is instructive to compare Emerson's essay with that of an earlier transcendentalist, William Ellery Channing, whose review of Scott's *The Life of Napoleon Bonaparte* was published in 1827. In it Channing challenged the whole concept of hero-worship:

> We have here an explanation of the striking fact in the history of our revolution; we mean the want or absence of that description of great men, whom we meet in other countries; men, who, by their distinct and simple agency, and by their splendid deeds, determine a nation's fate. There was too much greatness in the American people to admit this over-shadowing greatness of leaders . . . . But Washington was not a hero in the common sense of that word . . . .

[53] Emerson, *Representative Men*, p. 225.
[54] Ibid., p. 227.
[55] Ibid., pp. 256–7.
[56] Ibid., p. 240.

By an instinct which is unswerving, we call Washington, with grateful reverence, the Father of his Country, but not its saviour. A people, which wants a saviour, which does not possess an earnest and pledge of freedom in its own heart, is not yet ready to be free.[57]

In the late twenties Channing still had a sense of the best revolutionary vigour. In the same essay, he inveighed against the pernicious influence of the dead, the public figures who execute deeds for which in private life they might be seriously punished. He complained, too, of the forcible extension (of the heroic personality) into every department of the individual's life so that his personality was but a shadow of the representative.

The contrast between Washington and Napoleon, between, in classical equivalents, Cinncinatus and Caesar, was obvious and frequently made. It was always made in terms of private character, although public characters, according to representation theory, left their personalities behind them in private life. By the mid-century, the weaknesses of representation theory were becoming seriously apparent, and for a change in the relationships of the field of the problem we must turn to Melville's greatest fictional hero, Captain Ahab.

The most complex and interesting insight into the representative hero's role is to be found in *Moby Dick* (1851). In the character of Ahab we find Melville attempting to probe and understand the nature of power against a backdrop of nature conceived as a treacherous double and inscrutable spirit imaged in the sea and whale itself. In creating his story, Melville takes on the whole of the western intellectual tradition—particularly that sense of doubleness, the inheritance of Platonism and Christianity—and uses it mythically to reaffirm the sovereignty of a natural evil, the existence of which is paradoxically still in doubt. This enabled him to criticize his hero's hubristic exploitation of man and nature. Nonetheless nature, in its totally destructive and savage revenge, still pointed up man's Promethean-like greatness in taking on so monumental a task. In one of the earliest, and still one of the most interesting critical works to be published as a result of the revival of Melville criticism in the 1920s, Lewis Mumford[58] spoke of Melville's ability to synthesize 'imagination' and 'science' into a conscious mythology of the actualities of mid-nineteenth-century American experience: exploration, concentration upon power and dominion, without the necessity for ancient symbols. He is, however, only half right, because

[57] *The Christian Examiner*, vol. IV (Boston 1827) p. 427.
[58] Lewis Mumford, *Herman Melville* (1929) (revised edn London 1963) p. 131f.

Melville in fact took the traditional symbols of power and made them analogous with the symbols of a new mythology based on money and scientific mastery of nature.

We have already seen how Carlyle attempted to create symbols (out of the heroic archetype) for a new social psychology. Melville read Carlyle carefully and like him explored the nature of traditional mythologies as models for understanding the nature of society. In *Moby Dick,* he continued that shift from the philosophers' view of society as a metaphysical machine to the mid-Victorian conception of it as a historical myth which gave a clue to the 'permanent' socio-psychology of man's relation to nature. But the theatre of an ancient hunt for the sea-monster had, in Melville's American mind, to be set as a theatre of normal life. The argument of the scholars over the realistic versus the symbolic *Moby Dick* is redundant because, given the cultural inheritance, the most matter-of-fact incident had a representative reference which, in the mid-nineteenth century, involved the complexities of human societal relations and a metaphysic of nature.

In Ahab then we are concerned with Melville's insights into an apparently demythologized democratic society in America in the mid-nineteenth century. First, in one of the shortest and yet most revealing chapters of the novel, 'The Cassock', Melville gives a complex picture of that point where the working rituals of the whaling ship are made analogous with a new kind of social ritual based on making an art of nature.[59]

On the face of it the chapter describes the moment after the capture of a whale before its blubber is turned over to the try-works. It is hence that moment between life and death which is the setting for heroic ritual. The 'mincer's' office is to chop the blubber into convenient pieces for the try-works. In order to protect himself in this somewhat messy process the mincer removes the skin from the penis of a freshly caught whale, turns it inside out, and cuts holes for his arms and head'. Thus he is robed in what Melville calls 'the full canonicals of his calling'. The images of priestly law are connected, in this phrase, with the sacred task of the Christian worker, and yet the nature of the protective covering indicates that this penis-embodied man has taken on the devilish power associated with the genitals in order to exploit the rest of the body of nature. The outcome of this inverted fertility ritual is not life but death. The penis is likened to a dead comrade borne off the

[59] Herman Melville, *Moby Dick: or The Whale* (1851) Luther S. Mansfield and Howard P. Vincent eds., (New York 1962) ch. XCV, pp. 417ff: All subsequent quotations are from this edition and page references are given in brackets following quotations.

field of battle. But dead nature is turned into live history when the mincer crawls into it. The dried-out, re-erected penis is the eternal form, the robe of power, investing the living with authority. In the process man and nature are turned into history, the state of conflict in which the hero holds the balance between life and death. Melville makes the connection between his character and the role of the politican when he describes how the thin leaves of blubber are cut into the wood trough 'with a capacious tub beneath it, into which the minced pieces drop, fast as the sheets from a rapt orator's desk'. The mincer's function is therefore to turn the dead-living oil into exploitable excrement, in an analogy with the orator's verbal diarrhoea. One is reminded of the right-hand part of Bosch's triptych, *The Garden of Earthly Delights*, where a devil sits on his throne eating the living bodies with gold coins and vomit being spewed into a capacious hole below. Melville's devil-priest is a totally genitalized being, a perpetual monument like a stiff, or a dead man among the living. He is a politician exercising oratorical persuasion in the interests of a false religion, for Melville observes that the sailors call the thin slips of blubber 'bible leaves'.

We might expect that Ahab, too, should be primarily the Devil's agent manipulating collective human energies in the interests of power, and himself more of a corpse than a human being. At least like his biblical counterpart he has the curse of doom upon him. He has his full complement of ancient symbols which take us back to the neo-Classical origins of representative thought. He first appears like Cellini's bronze of Perseus and other images belie his monumental character. He is compared to Danish kings on their seat of Narwhal, and to a Caryatid, the figured stone support of a Greek temple. The whaleman in general is compared to Perseus, St George, Hercules, Jonah, Vishnu and the Grand Lama and Melville's Wagnerian sense of these god-like mortals combines with a specifically American epithet of disappearing hero-gods when he describes Ahab as the 'last of the Grisly Bears'. Ahab is branded with lightning—at once the mark of the gods and the curse of Cain. In fact Ahab's progress becomes a life-death struggle between Ahab as private being and the public hero as man of power.

The ship and Ahab, the machine-like microcosm of society and its directing will, are held together in a mutually destroying dialectical relation. Ahab himself is composed of natural and artificial elements with one leg of whale bone, the other of flesh. Melville frequently refers to the auger hole in the wooden deck of the ship, which receives the ivory leg in a kind of symbolic interrelation

between man and machine to ensure stability of design and purpose: 'his bone leg steadied in that hole; one arm elevated, and
holding by a shroud; Captain Ahab stood erect, looking straight out
beyond the ship's ever-pitching prow' (121). With the *double
entendre* on shroud, we are scarcely sure whether it indicates a life
support or a premonition of death. The hero is introduced in a
suitably ambiguous manner. In the chapter called 'Ahab's Leg',
Melville continues to elaborate the sources and implications of this
symbolic mutilation. While in pain from his first wounding by a
whale, Ahab soliloquizes on the vulnerability of the natural man,
as understood in the religiopolitical mythology by which he inter-
prets the world:

> For not to hint of this: that it is an inference from certain canonic
> teachings, that while some natural enjoyments here shall have no
> children born to them for the other world, but, on the contrary, shall
> be followed by the joy-childlessness of all hell's despair: whereas some
> guilty mortal miseries shall still fertilely beget to themselves an eternally
> progressive progeny of griefs beyond the grave. (460)

Obliquely referring to the Calvinistic doctrine of predestination
(canonic teachings), Melville suggests that 'natural enjoyments'
(sexual pleasure) produce children in nature but not in the cosmic
view of history, where reality is determined by an acceptance into
some eternal heavenly life. Misery, or the acceptance of nature as a
vale of tears, the appropriate sentiment for the individual caught
in a mythology of power-mongering, may 'fertilely beget' by contrast.
In a typically savage Melvillian note, however, the reward for this
stance is still 'an eternally progressive progeny of griefs beyond the
grave'. The wound appears like some symbol of original sin secularized as a flaw in nature itself. Continuing his sexual and political
images, Ahab reflects on the sources of this permanent conflict:

> To trail the genealogies of these high mortal miseries, carries us at least
> among the sourceless primogenitures of the gods; so that it is the face
> of all the glad, haymaking suns, and soft symbolically round harvest
> moons, we must needs give into this; that the gods themselves are not
> for ever glad. (461)

The natural fertility in fruition which the harvest indicates pales
before the monstrousness of the 'sourceless primogenitures' of the
original chaos. The aristocratic line of the first born to which the
hero belongs has no originating father. The disappearance of the
cosmic father, who once conferred meaning on the heroic destiny,
is part of Melville's specifically mid-nineteenth-century agony from
which he never escaped. For Ahab, the wound and its meaning lead

him to hide himself away in temporary exclusiveness before the voyage, 'and for that one interval sought speechless refuge, as it were, among the marble senate of the dead' (461). In a sense this is the traditional journey of the hero to the underworld. It is also a parody of the emergence to a new life after the moment of desolation and despair which characterizes the conversion experience. The phrase 'the marble senate of the dead' sums up the connection of the symbolic importance of monuments with the processes of Roman law and with the cult of death which crowns that process.

In the figure of the carpenter, the man who literally reconstructs Ahab, Melville outlines the nature of the man who, as a technical aide, becomes the tool by which the ends of power are achieved. Consequently he has no political nature. He is merely a transmitting mechanism in the machinery of state. Melville defines him in a series of uncompromising images:

> He was a stripped abstract; an unfractioned integral; uncompromised as a new-born babe; living without premeditated reference to this world or the next. You might almost say, that this strange uncompromisedness in him involved a sort of unintelligence; for in his numerous trades, he did not seem to work so much by reason or by instinct, or simply because he had been tutored to it, or by any inter-mixture of all these, even or uneven; but merely by a kind of deaf and dumb, spontaneous literal process. He was pure manipulator; his brain if ever he had one, must have early oozed along into the muscles of his fingers. He was like one of those unreasoning but still highly useful multum in parvo, Sheffield contrivances, assuming the exterior—though a little swelled—of a common pocket knife; but containing, not only blades of various sizes, but also screw drivers, corkscrews, tweezers, awls, pens, rulers, nail-filers, counter sinkers. So, if his superiors wanted to use the carpenter for a screw-driver, all they had to do was to open that part of him, and the screw was fast; or if for tweezers, take him up by the legs and there they were. (464)

The carpenter helps turn Ahab into an inanimate object and there follows a series of dirty jokes between them which suggests that Ahab's wound may be in some sense sexual. 'Canst thou not drive that old Adam away?' asks Ahab, to which the carpenter replies, 'Yes, I have heard something serious on that score, sir; how that a dismasted man never entirely loses the feeling of his old spar, but that it will be still pricking him at times' (467). The carpenter reflects that Stubb, the whale boat chief, says that Ahab is queer, 'Nothing but that one sufficient little word queer . . .. Yes, now that I think of it, here's his bedfellow! has a stick of whale's jawbone for a wife' (468). The implications of the images are virulent. The hero dismasted of natural enjoyments can never quite forget them as in the moving scene towards the end of the book where Ahab recollects his wife and child. The whale's jawbone reminds us of that verbal sterility of the rapt orator, and one recalls too (what would have been more familiar to Melville's contemporaries) Sampson's jawbone of an ass with which he slew a thousand men and Sampson also the destroyer of the temple of Dagon.

Like Shakespeare's fools, the carpenter speaks more truly than it at first appears. The more Ahab's monomania increases, the more he becomes the public monument. His sterility scarcely means impotence, for his power is never in doubt. But that energy is redirected, deflected until the body politic which he directs becomes a pure reflex of his own ego. 'Unconsciously' he uses 'the musket for a staff' (471). He becomes 'an iron statue' (478) with the iron harpoon symbolizing the man. Dedicating his iron penis to the devil, and holding the lightning rods, by a species of black magic he genitalizes the whole crew; 'in various enchanted attitudes, like the standing, or stopping, or running skeletons in Herculaneum, others remained rooted to the decks; but all their eyes upcast' (499). The neo-Classical images come back into play. The audience of the political theatre are literally turned into stone, transfixed as living-dead men by the magical display of the hero. As Ahab receives no answer to his final agonized plea for love, he takes on a frigidly masculine role. Rejecting the feminine side of his nature, he becomes an object of terror to his crew who merely visualize the drama from the sidelines. They are turned into stone, 'Petrified by his aspect' (501). For the crew have literally surrendered their sovereignty, before the form of the sovereign, (no accidental pun) which Ahab has nailed to the mast as a reward for the first person to see Moby-Dick. As Hamilton said the life-blood of the body politic is money.[60] The mast is the stiff (the puns are already there in the carpenter's words) later lit up by the demoniac fire, and the gold nailed to it is the 'image of the rounder globe' (428). This image defines the relationship of crew to hero in the representative theatre of political power. As Starbuck, the first mate, says such intercourse can never be natural: 'No fairy fingers can have pressed the gold, but devil's claws must have left their mouldings there since yesterday' (428).

Visualization of action in the representative drama reveals the old separation of passivity and activity inherent in the lying

---

[60] 'Money is with propriety, considered as the vital principle of the body politic; as that which sustains its life and motion, and enables it to perform its most essential functions,' quoted from H. W. Schneider, *A History of American Philosophy* (New York 1963) p. 81.

contraries of that drama. The little black boy, Pip, at the moment of total impotence, when he is left behind by the whale boat, sees into the heart of things. And his comment afterwards, 'I look, you look, he looks, we look, ye look, they look', (432) not only means that to visualize the drama without participating in it is a lesson in subordination and death, but also points to the grammar of political division in which men as a body are yet divided. The implicit passivity of this division permits the rise of heroes and leaders who claim eternally unresolvable struggle as the basis of their inherently destructive roles. In this novel Melville adds the literal machine process to the old mechanics of state. The result is a concentration of power at the top with those below specialized into their respective roles (as tools of the machine) from first mate downwards. The increasing powers of money, together with the new industrial processes, are re-interpreted by Melville in terms of the old organization of society which made history out of a fear of nature. Melville could not have been expected to see an alternative to that sense of permanent conflict. But he knew all the same that its dialectic leads to the extinction of all society and human life.

3

The Arts of Peace

The closing lines of *Moby Dick* show Ishmael, the eternal wanderer, revolving with lessening speed on the outer and upper edge of the vortex which has consumed Ahab and his crew. As this movement is lost in the homogenous and infinite space of the sea Ishmael experiences that utter solitude in which all referents of time, space and society have been lost. Ahab's earlier rejection of log, line and compass, and the embracing of an instinctive and tragic course reflect that distrust of abstract theories of control which lies at the heart of American consciousness, although such control in common-sense life, is felt to be necessary in the face of an hostile and threatening nature.

We have seen how the European hero re-emerged in American consciousness as the representative man. The mild and politically innocent Emerson celebrated, quite unconscious of the irony, the image of Napoleon as the new American representative man. In the popular consciousness Washington became a mythic father, while Melville's masterpiece, delineating the obscenities of such a social need, was to remain hidden and obscure for more than 70 years. In this chapter we look at ideas of peace and civilization which were all too often defined by the new heroes as insurance against the constant threat of social anarchy. Peace is defined as a bulwark against war. War is fought for future peace. Americans saw the arts of peace as consonant with the need to establish a stable political and social order. Republics were risky institutions according to the theorists, and virtually impossible in practice without a high level of public education. In America the initial impulse towards public education on a vast scale was less a result of benevolence than a fear of anarchy. The function of education was to establish public order. We move in this chapter from late eighteenth-century symbolizations of cosmic social order to Whitman's celebration of the private self in conflict with a society on the verge of the worst disaster in American history. Beginning with the Philadelphia astronomer David Rittenhouse and his clockwork model of the universe, we come back to earth with Bowditch's *The New American Practical Navigator*, followed by an examination of two cultural phenomena which attempt to demonstrate order in architectural terms: Jefferson's design for his home at Monticello and for the University of Virginia, and Charles Willson Peale's Philadelphia museum. Following a line from abstract to actual space, from theoretical physics to navigation and architecture, we next turn to actual machines invented or improved on by Americans which they particularly felt served the needs of national 'artistic' pride. Parallel to this is the modification of more conventional artistic legacies. The phenomenon of genre painting, though inherited from Europe, particularly served the artistic needs of the rising American middle classes. The Americans generally reserved the grand tradition of history painting for their battle scenes. Genre painting served the purposes of domestic peace, as opposed to public conflict. Finally these general issues are looked at together in the single phenomenon of Whitman's poetry which deals with the problem of the private and public self, the national implications of the new technology and science, as well as certain aspects of the genre tradition.

In the early years of the republic's life, order and law were thought to be synonymous with civilization. Civilization was an art of peace, its chief occupation, the pursuit of happiness. And yet the years following the Revolution saw continuous domestic battles against Indians and un-American immigrants, slavery continued as an institution in the South, in the North the industrial revolution began to enslave the masses, and, in a rising crescendo of official imperialistic violence, there followed the War of 1812, the Mexican War, and the bloodbath of the Civil War. By 1865 the failure of the ideology of 1776 was all too apparent. Nonetheless this was also the period when American culture made its first great contributions to science, literature, painting and poetry with an energy and skill which rarely simply copied European achievements, and which occasionally achieved an originality which came to be appreciated only by later generations. In the cultural artefacts of this period we can see the start of a vital tradition which, in the best American sense, constantly challenged the European inheritance. Here too we can find the origins of failure. From pure science to technology, from painting to poetry, the need is to define a new space and a new time theoretically and politically. Traditional arts such as painting and poetry were at first felt to be too aristocratic ever to admit of their practice in a republic. Since nature was the model for representative democracy, the scientist became more

important than the artist as an expounder of the nation's consciousness. He had access to truth in a way denied to the writer or
painter and early American culture heroes were Franklin, Rittenhouse and Bartram rather than Trumbull, Vanderlyn or Charles
Brockden Brown. Science was not only an art of peace, it supremely
characterized nationalistic claims to greatness reserved hitherto for
more traditional artists.

With the inheritance of Baconian attitudes, the Platonic belief
in the reality of geometry and a conviction of the appropriateness
of such mathematical speculation to Puritan right-living, it is
scarcely surprising that the hero of most educated Americans
towards the close of the eighteenth century should be Isaac Newton.
As in England he was better known through his very able explicators
like Desaguliers, Ferguson and Martin.[1] Through the writings of
these men even the most nonmathematical minds could form some
idea of the classic Newtonian synthesis. Leaving aside for one moment Franklin's work in electricity, the man who most fulfilled
American scientific aspirations was a Philadelphia clockmaker called
David Rittenhouse (1732—96). His two orreries provided, according
to one recent historian of American science, 'the best concrete
representation of Newton's mechanical world'.[2] An orrery is a
clockwork model of the cosmos. They were made in Europe but
in America Rittenhouse's models occupy a unique place in the
cultural consciousness. For here is an important visual representation of a theoretical space from which speculative assumptions
about man's place in the universe could be deduced, and by implication his role in it. That Rittenhouse should have been a clockmaker
is important. For machines operating by clockwork which purport
to represent the movements of the planets, sun and moon, have an
ancient history. In fact as Derek de Solla Price has shown, the most
continuous of all scientific traditions is mathematical astronomy,
and his essay on Greek and Chinese clockwork indicates the equal
continuity of the technical tradition involved in its representation.[3]

In order thoroughly to understand Rittenhouse's work we must

[1] See, for example, J. T. Desaguliers, *A Course of Experimental Philosophy*, 2 vols
(London 1734—44); James Ferguson, *Astronomy explained upon Sir Isaac Newton's
Principles, And made easy to those who have not studied Mathematics . . . A New Edition,
corrected* (London 1773) [note, frontispiece has an engraving of Ferguson's orrery] ;
Benjamin Martin, *Philosophia Britannica: or, A New and Comprehensive System of the
Newtonian Philosophy, Astronomy, and Geography . . .* 4th edn. 3 vols (London 1788).
[2] Brooke Hindle, *The Pursuit of Science in Revolutionary America, 1735—1789*
(Chapel Hill, N. Carolina 1956) p. 170. For an excellent account of Rittenhouse's
Princeton orrery and the history of orreries in Europe and America, see Howard C. Rice,
Jr, *The Rittenhouse Orrery* (Princeton, N.J. 1954).
[3] Derek de Solla Price, *Science since Babylon* (New Haven and London 1961) p. 5.

briefly recapitulate the history of mathematical astronomy, for
Rittenhouse draws on many of the styles of cosmic representation
employed throughout human history. We can begin with that
conjunction of Greek geometry and Babylonian quantificatory
arithmetic leading to the great Ptolemaic system which, for nearly
a thousand years, gave a satisfactory account of the planets and the
'fixed' stars. By the time of Ptolemy (AD 100–178) a complex
system of deferents, epicycles and equants could be used to account
for a great many unevennesses of planetary motion upon which
observation insisted.[4] Perfect circles could be combined to account
for irregularity. By centring epicycles on the deferent, on or inside
the circumference, the visual illusion of planetary irregularity could
be accounted for. Pure circles could give the illusion of flattened ones,
and the speed and tilt of the epicycle could account for such
phenomena as retrogression and temporal variation. Copernicus
used these insights, and they undoubtedly helped to continue the
belief that clockwork (which is none other than the representation
of space-time relations through circular wheel work) and plane
geometry were complementary. In less empirical terms, however,
the mathematics of the circle, as propounded by Archimedes who
said that an infinite number of straight lines make up a circumference,
began a train of thought which eventually led to the infinitesimal
calculus of Leibnitz and Newton. On the purely theoretical side
of the question one may pursue the metaphysics of infinity-thinking
through the writings of Cardinal Nicholas of Cusa in the late
Middle Ages, who speculated that infinite speed coincides with
infinite rest, that in infinity the tangent coincides with the circumference and the centre with the circumference. The Renaissance
philosopher Giordano Bruno based his own work on this forgotten
figure, and, as is well known, went to the stake for proclaiming
the infinite universe.

Technically and theoretically, therefore, clockwork and astromathematics are linked. Indeed the clock as we know it was a
relatively late development from more generalized planetary
machines. That Rittenhouse should make clockwork models of
the cosmos is therefore scarcely surprising. The early nineteenth-
century *Rees' Cyclopaedia,* which is the most comprehensive source
available for eighteenth-century orreries and their construction,
makes the important point (while giving some rather questionable
genealogies for the machines) that 'the histories of astronomy, and
of astronomical instruments, are so intimately united, that they

---

[4] See Thomas S. Kuhn, *The Copernican Revolution: Planetary Astronomy in the Development of Western Thought* (Cambridge, Mass. 1957) pp. 59–72.

cannot be separated, but throw mutual light on each other'.[5] Already by the middle of the fourteenth century, as Giovanni de Dondi's Padua astronomical machine shows, mechanical representations of the heavens had reached a highly sophisticated degree of complexity.[6]

The first machine which could be said to be the direct ancestor of eighteenth-century orreries, and hence of Rittenhouse's, and which placed the sun rather than the earth at the centre of the planetary system, was made by Christian Huygens (1629–95), the famous Dutch astronomer and instrument maker. Assuming, like Copernicus, planetary orbits to be circles, but, like Ptolemy, considering them to be off-centre to account for irregularity, Huygens showed that a continuous attractive force from the sun, operating by Kepler's law of inverse squares, could account for the motions of the planets. The way in which Huygens made his own planetary machine gives us a good idea of both the theory and the practice of orrery making and has the additional advantage that we know that Rittenhouse himself read an account of this work in a book by Benjamin Martin.[7] Martin also reprints a woodcut of Huygens's pendulum clock and gives equations appropriate to the calculation of forces involved in both pendulums and clock springs. Martin proceeds from first principles of velocity, gravity, acceleration and time and uses the latest form of 'fluxions' (calculus) to explain his results. Huygens had used a pendulum clock for his machine's prime-mover, and Martin also clearly prefers 'those *Automata* which are regulated more by *Nature* than *Art, viz.* by the Power of Gravity governing the Oscillations of *Pendulums.* But here the Artist must follow pretty closely the Dictates of the omniscient Mechanic, and work, if he proposes to merit Applause, by the Rules of divine Geometry'.[8] Martin himself postulates a 'universal pendulum' for measuring accurately the times of solar, lunar and planetary days operating with such accuracy as to be a visual demonstration of Newtonian time moving like an ever flowing stream. Even so Martin is obliged to take mean times for planetary revolutions and he omits such considerations as air-resistance to the pendulum, the unequal centrifugal force of the earth owing to its

[5] Alexander Rees, *The Cyclopoedia; or Universal Dictionary of Arts, Sciences, and Literature* (London 1819) see under Planetary Machines, unpaginated.

[6] Price, *Science since Babylon,* p. 29.

[7] Rittenhouse's biographer reports from a letter to his brother: 'I am glad you took the pains to transcribe, and send me, Martin's Account of Orreries'. William Barton, *Memoirs of the Life of David Rittenhouse, LLD, FRS* (Philadelphia 1813) p. 193. Barton assumes the work is *Philosophia Britannica,* see above note 1.

[8] Benjamin Martin, *A New and Comprehensive System of Mathematical Institutions, Agreeable to the Present State of the Newtonian Mathesis,* 3 vols (London 1764) vol. II, p. 400.

spheroidal shape and irregular gravitational pull, both operating on the pendulum's weight. Huygens's planetary machine, however, provides us with a sufficient archetype. It uses a clock movement as prime-mover, regulated by both pendulum and balance spring. The wheel-work is calculated by a series of multiple fractions, the drive wheel teeth providing the number for the denominator, and the connecting wheels attached to the same axis providing the numerator. These fractions which describe the number of teeth in any given wheel were always calculated pragmatically from the latest planetary tables available. One example from *Rees' Cyclopaedia* will serve to make it clear. From the most recent almanac one found that the solar year was 365 days, 5 hours, 48 minutes and 48 seconds. In order to calculate the wheel work necessary to express the relation between the earth day and the solar year, and to carry the earth round the sun once in the above time, one proceeded as in the following example:

Train for the Earth's annual and diurnal Motions.—The earth's diurnal rotation and annual revolution, taken jointly, constitute the standard of our measure of time, and is always referred to, not only when we speak of historical facts, but when we describe the revolutions and rotations of all the other planets; it is therefore of the utmost importance, in an astronomical instrument, that the train, which consists of the ratio between a day and a year, be accurate. The solar year, as we have seen, consists of 365d 5h 48m 48s, or, in another form, of 365·24222; the nearest fraction to represent the decimal portion 24222 exactly is $\frac{109}{450}$, and $365\frac{100}{450} = \frac{164359}{450}$ are divisible into $\frac{269}{10} \times \frac{47}{9} \times \frac{13}{5}$ which numbers constitute a movement for the *truth itself*. If, however, we wish to substitute an approximate ratio of as nearly an equal value as we can obtain for smaller numbers than 269; the small fraction suitable to approximate from is $\frac{8}{33}$ = 2424, and the nearest multiplier is 35; for $365\frac{8 \times 35}{33 \times 35 \times 1} = \frac{1156}{422220}$ is reducible into $\frac{4}{227} \times \frac{17}{60} \times \frac{7}{31}$ the time corresponding to which is 365d 5h 48m 47s which will be allowed to be exact enough for the nicest purposes, as the error in a year does not amount to three quarters of a second.

   The numerator 4, it will be observed, is too small a number for a pinion to consist of, for which reason let it be doubled, and also the 31 among the denominators or drivers, by which alteration we shall have a practical train of $\frac{8}{227} \times \frac{17}{62} \times \frac{17}{60}$. Here the large wheel of 227 will be suitable for the fixed wheel in an orrery or tellurian, where the rest of the train is placed on the annual arm, and carried round it; or for what is called the annual wheel in any orrery where all the wheels revolve in fixed situations.[9]

This, one of the simplest examples, is taken to show the incredibly lengthy and boring rather than complicated work involved in setting up an orrery. What was necessary was the patience to do endless primitive long division sums, and ratio calculations. Even so the most gifted made mistakes. For his machine Huygens had calculated periods in fractions of a solar year, yet had his prime-mover make a revolution in a civil year of 365 days. For all his 'fluxions' a machine which Martin himself proposed building in the second volume of his *A New and Comprehensive System of Mathematical Institutions Agreeable to the present State of the Newtonian Mathesis* (1764) contained even larger errors.[10] For example he calculated the relation of the diurnal to the annual train of the earth and sun on the basis of 365 days exactly, so that in the space of four years the calculations become inaccurate by a whole day. In addition the earth's parallelism was inexact by one hundredth in each revolution. Martin was striving for simplicity by having two wheels common to the two trains of earth parallelism and annual-diurnal rotation. As a result the same mechanism which correctly accounted for the parallelism bar moving backward once in a year, also caused the diurnal mechanism to run backward once with the resultant loss of an earth day. Also since the earth's rotation is from east to west and the annual revolution from west to east, one annual day must be deducted from the solar transit. To compensate, earth rotations should be calculated on a 366 day basis (omitting fractions) in order to even out the difference between years calculated by earth revolution round the sun and round its own axis. Martin's machine, therefore, would have had an eventual earth year of 363 days.

We may summarize the problems faced by David Rittenhouse before turning to his orreries, and seeing whether or not they deserve the title, 'the best concrete representation of Newton's mechanical world'. First he had to decide what kind of prime-mover he would have, whether pendulum, pendulum clock or simple crank. Martin had preferred the former because it approximated more nearly to nature than art. Gravity could be the driving force and regulator in the wound up weight and in the regulating pendulum. A glance at Martin's work shows that this involved calculations of

[9] Rees, *Cyclopoedia,* under Numbers Planetary.
[10] Martin, *A New and Comprehensive System . . .* vol. II, p. 480. The slip occurs thus; 'In $365\frac{1}{2}$ Days there are 730 Half-days of 12 Hours. This Number is produced by the Factors $18\frac{1}{4}$, 8, 5; for $5 \times 8 \times 18\frac{1}{4} = 730$'. Martin omits consideration of the $\frac{1}{2}$ day.

a high mathematical order.[11] The relating of time to wheel-work involved in a machine of this nature was enormously complex. Rees's contributor stated that 'the fifteen theorems of Martin . . . have deterred the instrument maker'.[12] Rittenhouse also had to choose what data he would take as the basis of his calculations. Would he, for example, take mean times for planetary revolution? Would he represent the elliptical movements of the planets as circles? What of the overall organization of his machine, would he attempt to combine solar, lunar and 'tellurian' cycles in one complex structure? Would he be able to resolve the discrepancy between the solar and the earth year? Would he take the Julian or Gregorian calender as his basis? Finally is there anything specifically Newtonian about the machine in the sense that his enthusiastic contemporary eulogizers claimed?

David Rittenhouse's own 'Description of a New Orrery' (i.e. the first Princeton Orrery), originally enclosed in a letter to his brother-in-law, Thomas Barton, on 27 March 1769, stated that, 'If it shall be thought proper, the whole is to be adapted to, and kept in motion by, a strong pendulum clock; nevertheless, at liberty to be turned by the winch, and adjusted to any time, past or future'.[13] As far as we know no such pendulum was ever made. The same 'Description' printed in the *Proceedings* of the American Philosophical Society adds that the 'clock part of it may be contrived to play a great variety of *Music*'.[14] This like the previous scheme was obviously abandoned, but its very consideration takes us back to the great clocks of the Middle Ages, and to the clock of Su Sung, and shows Rittenhouse sharing the ancient musicomathematical concepts of celestial harmony. As for astronomical data, Rittenhouse was already an accomplished almanac calculator, and we know that he made his own calculations, finding existing ones not accurate enough. For these he may have used 'fluxions', for, although he never produced any original work in mathematics, it has been demonstrated that he understood the necessary processes.[15] Nonetheless when it came to the point, he did use mean times for planetary orbits, and although he also varied the orbit time by irregular cutting of the wheel teeth, from observing the machine, it is clear that he did not use an extra radius arm at the end of the main one to complete the illusion. The *Rees* contributor pointed out that the irregular cutting of teeth

[11] See Martin, *A New and Comprehensive System* . . ., vol. II pp. 459–64
[12] Rees, *Cyclopoedia*, under Numbers Planetary.
[13] Barton, *Memoirs*, p. 202
[14] Rice, *The Rittenhouse Orrery*, p. 84, n. 7.
[15] See W. Carl Rufus, 'David Rittenhouse, as a Newtonian philosopher and defender', *Popular Astronomy*, 56 (1948) pp. 122–30.

produced only half the illusion required, but that, working on the
ancient Ptolemaic principle of epicycle, a weight-operated extra
arm revolving in a retrograde direction could produce the effect of
the other half of the illusion and incidentally help to maintain the
parallelism of each planet about its axis. The radius of this extra
arm plus the eccentricity was equal to the aphelion distance. The
radius minus the eccentricity was equal to the perihelion distance.
The problem of the ellipse itself Rittenhouse solved, not by a
Newtonian, but by a pre-Keplerian device. Although Rittenhouse
stated that the planets 'are to move in elliptical orbits, having the
central ball in one focus, and their motions to be sometimes swifter,
and sometimes slower, as nearly according to the true law of an
equable description of areas as possible, without too great complica-
tion of wheelwork',[16] he in fact produced the effect of an ellipse
by the ancient device of off-centring circles. The same statement
shows that he is following Keplerian rather than Newtonian law.
However much the principle of the circle had been abandoned
in theory, the necessities of clockwork demanded its use in practice.
In the overall design of his machines, Rittenhouse followed Martin's
innovation of splitting his representation of the heavens into three
sections. He rejected the idea of a spherical case, 'what has a Sphere,
consisting of a great number of metaline Circles, to do with the
true System of the World. Is there one real, or so much as apparent
Circle, in it? (the bodies of the Sun and Planets excepted.) Are
they not all merely imaginary lines, contrived for the purposes of
calculation'.[17] In that last sentence Rittenhouse shows himself a
Newtonian by conviction and instinct. He rejected naive visual
representations such as the old armillary sphere which he probably
had in mind here. He also rejected the popular half sphere—like
Martin's orrery in the Harvard University Library—which he considered as 'unnatural and imperfect'.[18] His own solution was to
make his orreries stand with vertical faces, like clocks. The representation was hence more abstract than the European models, but
it had the disadvantage of making it more difficult to observe the
angles of rotation about the sun and individual axes. In his Princeton orrery only Mercury has unevenly cut teeth to give an indication
of varying speed, and, in spite of their complexity, the clockwork
trains of the moons of Saturn and Jupiter fail to give a proportion-
ately accurate number of rotations. In the recent restoration of this
machine, independent motors were installed because the friction

[16] Barton, *Memoirs*, p. 200.
[17] Ibid., p. 194.
[18] Ibid.

involved in their movement proved to exert too strong a pressure on the delicate structure of the smaller wheels. The length of time which may be demonstrated is 10,000 years, calculating piously from Archbishop Ussher's view of the date of creation. By using the Julian calender of $365\frac{1}{4}$ days for earth rotation, Rittenhouse did manage to get an accuracy within 3 days in 400 years. He also installed a correcting device though it has been pointed out, in view of other accumulating errors, it was doubtful whether it could have been of much advantage.

Even in his first letter to his friend Barton on the subject, Rittenhouse knew he would have to compromise, and it is this realization of the imperfection of the machine which makes the modest Rittenhouse so attractive a character. For in absolute terms, Newton's universe was not open to concrete representation. Descartes's followers accused this English mind of occultism. Rittenhouse was really illustrating a combination of Keplerian and Copernican systems, and in broad terms he did that rather well, though the difficulties of clockwork made a true representation impossible. Newton's explanation or assumption of invisible gravitational forces could be paralleled with observable space-time interactions but could scarcely be expressed in terms of them.

The most important aspect of Rittenhouse's orrery was its place in the general cultural consciousness. Clockwork models of the universe have always been used as socioreligious artefacts. From Su Sung to Louis XIV the claims to complete systems of truth which they suggest have always been used to dramatize omniscience. There is a history of kings and emperors laying out large sums of money for such machines, and Thomas Jefferson, in the earliest days of American democracy, sought to purchase Rittenhouse's own machine for Louis XVI as a reward for France's help in the War of Independence. To gain some clearer idea of the functions (other than astronomical) Rittenhouse's orrery was expected to perform we can conveniently turn to his famous *Oration* delivered to the Philadelphia Philosophical Society in 1775.[19]

This *Oration* gives early American astronomical interests a philosophical and cultural context as important as the scientific achievement itself. For his sources, Rittenhouse drew on Bacon's *Advancement of Learning,* Pierre Bayle's *Historical and Critical Dictionary*, Newton's *Principia* and *Optics,* the *Encyclopaedia Britannica*—published in Scotland— and *Chambers' Universal Dictionary of Arts and Sciences.* Although the sources are European,

[19] David Rittenhouse, *An Oration delivered February 24, 1775, before the American Philosophical Society* (Philadelphia 1775) and for subsequent quotations.

the selection indicates an American direction of thought which was
to become central. Dictionaries, a distinctly European Enlightenment phenomenon, by their linear design and lay-out both broke
down hierarchical conventions of knowledge and made the result
available to the highly literate American democrat, who in turn
made his own synthesis. As we have already seen Bacon is an
obvious hero, and Newton's own amalgam of mystical, religious
and scientific work was known and cited as a defence against foreign
atheists, and against the general free-thinking tendencies of scientific
thought. Most of the statements in the *Oration* could be paralleled in
European work. But there is a difference of emphasis, a Puritan
fervour behind the Enlightenment commonplaces, a separation of
emotional from intellectual concern, and, in spite of the contrary
opinion of the few other commentators on this work, a willingness
to let theory push facts into coherence.[20] There is praise for the
Greek invention of geometry, a regret that Tycho Brahe 'mangled
the beautiful system of Copernicus', and an identification of religion
and astronomy in terms of the great issues of the questions of
boundary and infinite extent. Further one senses an almost medieval
distrust of observation when he discusses the discovery of the
circular figure of the earth, and there is praise for Kepler whose
'love of harmony' encouraged him 'to continue his pursuits, in spite
of the most mortifying disappointments'. Rittenhouse's account of
the historical progress of astronomy takes on an almost Manichean
sense of the conflict of light and dark, truth and error. The triumphant sense of light over darkness only serves to underwrite the
threatening sense of opposing forces. This cosmic sense turns
naturally into social sense. The religious sense of light triumphing
over darkness paradoxically emphasized its opposite; the sense of
threat to the operation of light. This led in turn to a need to control
those fears of a world more and more out of harmony. It is but a
short step to a full scale misanthropy, characteristic of the progress
neurosis, which projects a dream of impossible utopia. He is quick
to defend himself against misanthropy and hatred, but one suspects
here an American impulse to Puritan perfection which quickly turns
to a prurient interest in its opposite. He imagines a utopia without
slavery, without government and without error. He continues, 'I am
ready to wish—vain wish!—that nature would raise her everlasting
bars between the new and old world, and make a voyage to Europe

[20] Commentators seem to follow Boorstin's theoretically weak characterization of all
American science of the period as 'empirical'. See Daniel Boorstin, *The Americans: The
Colonial Experience* (New York 1958) pp. 246—51. Brooke Hindle's (op. cit.) discussion
is good, see chapter VIII 'Confession of Faith 1775'.

as impracticable as one to the moon'. The later part of the work
surveys the imperfections of astronomical knowledge. The
universe contains for Rittenhouse, and here he is less radical than
Bruno, infinite variety but not infinite extent. The paradox is that
of a world of uniform, infinite variety which is also bounded. The
oration ends with an impassioned testimony to his belief in eternal
life, and 'eternal improvement in knowledge and happiness'.
Rittenhouse's training and beliefs made him one of the most
efficient and valuable men of his time. His habits of thought
enabled him to perform technical tasks which required skill but
not too much speculation about end results. He was an excellent
surveyor (here the metaphysics of boundary making have a practical
value), he worked with Charles Willson Peale on rifle improvement,
he held high financial positions, and worked in the Mint for a
while. In the range of his intellectual and practical pursuits he is
an archetype of one kind of American character.

Apart from a general metaphysic, astromathematics had important
practical applications. The two outstanding experimental achievements in the field in late eighteenth-century America came with
John Winthrop's and David Rittenhouse's observations of the
transit of Venus in 1761 and 1769 respectively. The story is well-
known of how Rittenhouse, after months of preparation when he
made, with his own hands, an equal altitude instrument, a transit
telescope, and an extremely accurate pendulum clock, was so overcome by excitement that he fainted at the crucial point when Venus
appeared to touch the sun's perimeter. At the request of Neville
Maskelyne, the British Astronomer Royal, observations were carried
out in Norrington and Pennsylvania. In order to compute exactly
the distance between the two places, two men set out to survey the
country complete with 'chains' and instruments. It took them two
days to walk and measure the distance physically. The final computations (the first issue of the *Transactions* of the Philadelphia Philosophical Society gives the details), whether by luck or judgement,
were extremely accurate by the European standards of the day. The
importance of the transit of Venus may be accounted for in many
ways. From the point of view of pure astrocosmology, it helped
to determine, by trigonometrical calculations, the relationships of
interplanetary distances on the basis of an accurate knowledge of
the sun's parallax—that is, the angle subtended at the sun by the
earth's radius. The Venus transit could therefore serve as a practical
confirmation of Newtonian and Keplerian theory.[21] But even more

[21] Bernard Cohen, *Some Early Tools of American Science* (Cambridge, Mass. 1950)
p. 38.

important was its practical application to navigation. One hundred years before the method was ever used at sea, the vexed question of determining longitude had been theoretically solved. The importance of viewing eclipses at different places enabled longitude to be computed with accuracy in relation to Greenwich time.

The purely practical application of astromathematics to navigation, in a form simple and democratic enough to be used by an ordinary seaman with some smattering of literacy and persistence, received its classic expression in the work of an American, Nathaniel Bowditch (1773—1838). Robert Elton Berry's popular account of Bowditch, *Yankee Stargazer,* makes the telling point that while Emerson complained that no great work of literature had been produced in Massachussets between 1790 and 1820, hundreds of young men in the eastern seaports had mastered Bowditch's *The New American Practical Navigator* (1802) which opened up new worlds in a way Emerson's directives scarcely could. Bowditch's popular handbook for seamen is itself a masterpiece of explication outlining theory and practice to illustrate practical ways of exploring the earth itself in the most literal way possible. It is the first American 'whole earth catalogue'.

For most practical purposes theoretical navigation depended not so much on a Bruno-like conception of an infinite universe, nor on a Copernican sun-centred cosmos, but on the Ptolemaic assumption of the earth centred within a larger sphere. The first to suggest longitude measurement by measuring the angle between the moon and the fixed stars was John Werner of Nuremberg (1468—1528). Even more than theoretical astrophysics, the history of navigation is dependent upon the development of scientific instruments. Huygens's pendulum clock is again important here, for exact time-keeping enabled a comparison to be made between a fixed point (Greenwich) and any other point on the earth's surface. Chrono-meters of sufficient accuracy were not obtainable for land use until the middle of the seventeenth century, and for navigational purposes, until the middle of the eighteenth century. 1732 saw the first successful trial of Hadley's quadrant which theoretically employed Newton's laws of refracted light practically to line up, on a moving ship's deck, the horizon and the observed astronomical body in a simultaneous view.[22] The problems for navigation were again largely geometrical, and the immense calculations involved were

[22] This discussion relies greatly on Charles H. Cotter's excellent, *A History of Nautical Astronomy* (New York 1968).

speeded up by a series of mathematical advances. Sine tables were invented in the fifteenth century by Rubach (1423—1501) and Müller (1436—76). Tables of trigonometrical functions simplifying computations of unknown parts of triangles, tables of the sun's declination and amplitude and right ascensions of stars were in general use by the end of the seventeenth century. In the mid-eighteenth century the reflecting circle, a further refinement on Hadley's quadrant, was especially useful for taking lunar distances.

The extent to which astronomers were involved in navigational problems can be seen from the composition of the Committee of Longitude in Great Britain which at one time included Newton, John Flamstead and Edmund Halley. In 1765 *The Nautical Almanac* gave tables of lunar position for 1767 of sufficient accuracy to be used for navigational purposes. Years before, similar calculations had given Newton the only mathematical headache he is said to have suffered. The most tedious part of the process in the computation of longitude by the moon was known as 'clearing the distance'— that is a series of calculations to find the true as opposed to the apparent position of the moon. By the end of the eighteenth century, there were, according to a paper published in the *Philosophical Transactions of the Royal Society,* over 40 methods for 'clearing the distance'.

In Salem, Massachussets, however, by the end of the eighteenth century, few ships computed longitude by anything other than dead reckoning. In 1802, Nathaniel Bowditch published his *New American Practical Navigator.* It was modelled on the Englishman John Hamilton Moore's *The Practical Navigator* with tables calculated by Neville Maskelyne. After attempting to revise it for his American publisher's pirated edition, Bowditch had discovered so many mistakes that he decided to write his own.

Bowditch added his own tables for lunar distance and a proportional table to correct lunar altitude. He was not original in this impulse as we have seen, rather his originality lay in his devotion to the experimental correction of existing information. Traditionally there had always been a wide gulf between the supercilious mathematician (whose computations often obscured as much as they revealed) and the very conservative seaman. Bowditch's book is a teaching manual designed to democratize the art of theoretical navigation, and to dethrone the priesthood of astonomers royal all over the world. The book was a utilitarian encylopaedia of communications and direction finding. And it began by assuming nothing. Bowditch's book turned the whole world into a learning space with simple geometrical rules for its comprehension. The rationale

of this intellectual and physical cosmos is geometry and Bowditch
properly begins there. Axioms are explained and problems appended
so that the novitiate could learn the rules more easily. Plane, right-
angled and oblique geometry are explained in single stages. Age-old
theoretical problems are but lightly touched on, and it is the first
stage of implication, rather than first principles, which is
brought to the seaman's attention:

> The earth is not a pefect globe or sphere, but a little flattened at the
> poles, being really of the figure of an oblate spheroid, the equatorial
> diameter being about 34 miles longer than the polar; but since this
> difference bears but a small comparison to the whole diametre, we may,
> for the practical purposes of navigation, consider the earth as a sphere.[23]

The general introduction to astronomy and geography gives the
seaman just sufficient context for the mathematics: 'The common
opinion of astronomers of the present day is, that the universe is
composed of an infinite number of systems . . .'.[24] One senses a
difference of the generations between Bowditch and Rittenhouse
here. Bowditch clearly felt no compulsion to square his calculations
with a more general system of belief. Bowditch intersperses his
explanations of parallax, refraction and dip with practical instructions on the handling of log and quadrant. The lengthy calculations
of longitude are set out neatly with a dividing line between 'clearing
the distance' calculations and final calculations. Examples and
example problems are set out. And in the later parts of the book,
sea terms and rigging terms are given in tables. Here too the seaman
could find information on marine insurance, bills of exchange, and
nautical law relating to owners, master, agents and factors, and on
freight and chartering—all drawn from the first-hand experience of
Bowditch himself. In its day the book was known as the 'seaman's
bible'. Whereas earlier Quakers had studied geometry in their leisure
hours, and devoted their best working hours to the Bible, now geometry itself became a surer guide to the universe and showed the
budding New England capitalist the wherewithal of worldly success.
The world of *The New American Practical Navigator* is a microcosm
of one kind of American consciousness. The spheres of the geometrical calculations reflect a view of stability and graduated progress
in which accident and loss are insured against. Bowditch himself
became president of a marine insurance company. Money and geometry are both abstract guides to position whether geographical or

[23] Nathaniel Bowditch, *The New American Practical Navigator* (Newberryport, Mass.
1802) p. 74.
[24] Ibid., p. 73.

social. Bowditch's book, however, is a guide to a whole system, and looking at it as a cultural artefact, we must revise our idea that the American empire simply moved in a straight line 'Westward'. Bowditch's book opened up the whole system of the earth to an individual with sufficient time and patience. The key half-truth of the achievement is that the context of learning was democratized, and that the earth, turned into a large learning space, became secularized and removed from the sole province of educated elites. The instinct of the popular anecdote, however limited in actual fact, was American and sure: when the German aristocrat, Baron von Zach asked a black cook on an American ship by what method he calculated lunar distances, the reply was prompt: 'I use sometimes the method of Maskelyne, Lyon or Bowditch, but I prefer that of Dunthorne, as I am more accustomed to it'.[25] The supreme irony in Bowditch's life was that his greatest work was not *The New American Practical Navigator*, but his translation of Laplace and a critical commentary on his work.[26] But as yet there was no audience for such an achievement, as there was to be little audience later for Melville or Willard Gibbs.

In the popular consciousness, however, the cosmos was regarded as an orderly structure upon which, given the appropriate instructions, a navigator could locate himself at one point, with reference to other known points. Given correct judgement and a little luck, one could find one's position within a longitudinal error of between 20 and 30 miles. This correspondence between heaven and earth with its combined practical and educational value led to an early American desire to create miniature learning spaces for the demonstration of natural law. It was aided by an assimilation of Scottish and French instinct for encyclopaedias, and the notion that education in a republic was the only defence against anarchy. The identification of civilization and natural law led two key early figures, the American president Thomas Jefferson, and a great early American painter, naturalist, mechanic and inventor, Charles Willson Peale, to create architectural, three-dimensional learning spaces which reflected, in complex physical detail, powerful metaphysical notions of the cosmos.

Thomas Jefferson's own home at Monticello and the University of Virginia present, spatially, a complex web of meanings which extended into every presupposition about public and private life current for an educated American (or European) of the time. We

---

[25] Berry, *Yankee Stargazer*, (New York 1941) p. 120.
[26] Pierre Simon Laplace, *Mecanique celeste. By the Marquis de la Place . . . Translated, with a commentary by Nathaniel Bowditch . . .* (Boston 1829–39).

have already looked at some of the assumptions of the neo-Vitruvianism of the Palladian revival, and these serve as a starting point for Jefferson's own total system. From Europe Jefferson especially ordered a copy of Leoni's translation (c. 1721) of Palladio's *Four Books of Architecture*.[27] It was the English country gentleman's architectural bible, and Jefferson's thought, in spite of those who insist on the variations he used in practice (Palladio encouraged local variations within the bounds of decorum and individual taste) is that of an American country gentleman. In England Palladianism had already reached its apogee by the mid-eighteenth century. From Inigo Jones's Banqueting Hall at Whitehall (1619–22) to the crescents and circles of Bath set in the magnificent Somersetshire hills, it captured a desire for neo-Classical virtue, especially the Roman variety. Stemming from the clear lines of architectural engravings of Jones to the publications of Lord Burlington, a marriage of purism and monumentality was arranged, dear to the ambitions of the country oligarchy.

The centre of inspiration for Palladio was the architecture of the Rome of the Augustan era. The spaces created reflect the philosophy of the *res publica* as the result of the division assumed between public and private life. They embodied the sense of the permanence of law, the division between public and private character, a sense of linear and visual stability, the mechanical interdependence of a balance of public functions, the bureaucratization of government, centralized control of transport, military control of the state, and a formalization of the concept of the city. We may imagine what struck Jefferson in his reading and reinterpret his reaction for ourselves.

First for Palladio there is the absolute division between public and private activity: 'I shall therefore in the first place treat of private Houses, and next of Public Edifices'.[28] Having made the distinction there follows the need to connect the parts in some way. For Jefferson there is the twin reality of Monticello and the University of Virginia. The public place is in fact an architectural detail in a private landscape. Then there is the problem of proportion. For the republican no less than for the geometrician, the total space must be seen as the sum of uniform parts. For Palladio as for Jefferson, the diameter of the column, or the 'module', divided into 60 parts became the standard unit for the proportions involved. This 'circu-

---

[27] Andrea Palladio, *The Architecture of Andrea Palladio* [in four books] *revised, designed and published by Giacomo Leoni. Trans. from Italian original J. Watts* (London ?1715).

[28] Palladio, vol. I, preface.

lar' philosophy which Palladio took out of Vitruvius ensured for republican and architect that a fine structure would 'appear as an entire and perfect body, wherein every member agrees with its fellow . . .'.[29] By this means all the proportions were calculated; the relation of the diameter to height of column, of wall to floor and ceiling, and the height of a wall to the arch of its dome. In fact the square and circle construct the public place and its buildings. The square is favoured for the public space, the circle for the most important building. Palladio appeals to both geometry and Christianity for his concept of separateness and interdependence. In this context he quotes St Paul's metaphor of the church as one body with many members and speaks of the geometrical form of the circle:

> . . . in which neither end nor beginning can be found nor distinguish'd from each other, and having all parts like one another, and that each of 'em partakes of the figure of the whole: and finally the extreme of every part being equally distant from the centre . . . is therefore the most proper figure to show the Unity, infinite Essence, the Uniformity, and Justice of God.[30]

To give his theories substance he adduces the somewhat dubious historical evidence that the early Christians met in private houses (which he calls Basilicas) anyway. The argument is ingenious. Its effect is to endow the public space—a Roman concept—with the authoritative backing of medieval Christianity and to dignify the body politic as a metaphysically ordained institution. Each part of Palladio's system reflects the other. Like the city the private house must have its public space designed to confer dignity on its owner. In addition the point of view is from country to city. The sober point of view of the country engages the values of sobriety, chastity, individuality and gardening. But Palladio also speaks of the things that threaten this perfect state, for circle and square presuppose the concepts of outside and inside. We learn that the Romans placed inside their city circle the gods of chastity, peace and the useful arts, while without the boundaries they ordered temples to Venus, Mars and Vulcan as the powers that excite men's minds to lasciviousness, wars and burnings. Nature is thus doubly characterized as an area of anarchy and refuge.

When we come to the private house we find that some parts of the body are more harmonious than others. Here up and down seems to mirror inside and outside. One must construct a building in such a way 'that the finest and most noble parts of it be the most expos'd

---

[29] Ibid., vol. I, p. 1.
[30] Palladio, vol. IV, p. 6.

to public view, and the disagreeable dispos'd in by-places, and
remov'd from sight as much as possible; because thither ought to
be conveyed the refuse of the house, and whatever may produce
any ill effect or embarrassment'.[31] Things like cooking, washing,
heating and servants 'should be placed in the lower part of the
Building, and which I commonly order a little underground'.[32]
Refuse and those subject to human dominance were relegated to
this area. So in Monticello, as in hundreds of English country houses,
concealed passages and back stairs served the needs of the master.
As Palladio had advised, Jefferson built his house on an 'eminence'
and combined square and circle as main structural units. The sense,
too, of a single homogenous space for the main areas is achieved by
the concealment, within and without, of the second storey by a
judicious arrangement of windows and interior staircases. From the
main hall by ingenious wind dials, thermometers and a pendulum
clock of his own construction, Jefferson observed and measured the
vagaries of nature.

The layout of the University of Virginia is again a microcosm of
Jefferson's philosophical and social principles. Many as such were
admirable. His attempt to get faculty and students mixing in the
public areas was excellent, his arguments for abolishing censorship
sound (though his practice varied), and his efforts to create religious
toleration and a public system of education in Virginia, against the
anti-intellectuals and private enterprise mongers, were little short
of heroic. The most admirable thing about Jefferson was his insatiable and untiring energy in every area of learning and public life.
And yet every public statement gives one an uneasy feeling of its
opposite like the back stairs to the open spaces of his own house.

The space enclosed by the University of Virginia is formed into
an open-ended oblong by a series of porticoes and pavilions. The
most interesting feature is observable from the library, placed at
one end. Jefferson compensated for the tendency of parallel lines
to converge when admiring the prospect from this point, by
lengthening the spacing between the several parallel pavilions. He
also compensated for the apparent rise in the horizontal plane by
successively lowering the levels of the lawn. Here the laws for
diminishing the diameter of a column are applied to a rectilinear
space. The public square is hence preserved as a stable space by
abstractly compensating for the visual irregularity. But of course
the illusion only preserves itself from a single viewpoint.

As a plan, the layout reminds one of a Palladian neo-Classical

[31] Palladio, vol. II, p. 2.
[32] Ibid.

church with choir and side chapels in appropriate positions. Behind the public space the private yards of the professors are bounded by serpentine walls after the model of Hogarth's line of beauty. Like contemporary American suburbia, the fronts are completely open but nobody goes there, and the back yard is where one is entertained, and that is carefully enclosed. The houses of the teachers are themselves points in the definition of regularity—strung out like a series of forts along a battlement. The utilitarian reason for the porticoes was that they were supposed to keep the students dry while changing classes. The fact that they might have to *cross* the square doesn't seem to have been considered. Each pavilion preserves the general homogeneity of the 'Greek' styles, though the columns are varied according to Palladio's 'Five orders'. The 10 pavilions eventually built (16 had been proposed at first) coincide neatly with the 10 branches of learning Jefferson proposed for the curriculum.

At the head of the public space stands the library in the form of a rotunda. It was built in imitation of the Parthenon. Palladio had explained:

> This temple was called the *Parthenon,* either because, after Jupiter, it was consecrated to all the Gods; or, as others will have it, because it bears the figure of the World, or is round. The height of it from floor to the opening at the top, (whence it receives all its light) is the Diameter of its breadth from one wall to the other. [33]

As Palladio had explained, the forms of the basilica were indifferently used for courts of justice and churches. With Jefferson's own conviction that power was knowledge, the circle conceived within the square made the perfect abstract form for the metaphysics of infinite reality. The plan of the Rotunda bears a family resemblance to Ledoux's proposed monument to Newton. It is scarcely surprising that a page from Jefferson's notes shows a plan for adapting the inside of the dome to the purpose of teaching astronomy. The roof inside was to be painted dark blue like the face of Rittenhouse's orrery, with the fixed stars in gilt, 'copied from any selected hemisphere of our latitude'. [34] The operator, slung on a boom and seated on a saddle with stirrups, was hoisted from point to point within the hemisphere. The horizontal diameter plane was graduated and supplied with a movable radius, and a movable meridian, pivoted

[33] Palladio, vol. IV. p. 1.
[34] These notes and drawings are reproduced in William Alexander Lambeth and Warren H. Manning, *Thomas Jefferson, as an Architect and a Designer of Landscapes* (Boston and New York 1913), plate VII.

at the zenith with a movable chord, was also graduated. The kinds
of calculation proposed were strictly of the navigational kind,
depending less on reality than on the concept of the perfect
hemisphere.

Hence Jefferson's university reflected an ancient power structure
founded on astrophysics. Knowledge is here dignified by use, and
its categorizations represent reality itself. The line of authority is
exact. It proceeded from the country mansion to the object mirrored
in its own landscape, and from the Rotunda, the high church of
authority and learning, to the square of knowledge made stable by
compensation in nature for the requirements of a single viewpoint.
And yet this ancient religioarchitectural space is here for the first
time applied to a public university where the audience is paradoxically encouraged to develop active participation in the theatre of
knowledge. However aristocratic the space, designed as it was from
a single viewpoint, its adaptation to a university lay bare the faint
possibility of the development of individual and conflicting points
of view.

For Charles Willson Peale, whom we have already seen as a painter
and a mechanic, the whole world was 'a museum in which all men
are destined to be employed and amused . . .'.[35] Peale's actual
museum in Philadelphia is yet another learning space which reflects
a precise metaphysical conception of the earth. Peale is, however,
less concerned with the cosmos than the earth itself. The secularization of an ancient heresy that God is knowable only through his
works makes Peale's space, like Jefferson's, a teaching area in which
the symbols of divine wisdom are visually observed for practical
use; 'for, indeed he who knows it not from observation of nature,
can scarcely learn it from another source'.[36] A famous self-portrait
of Peale, shows the painter raising the curtain on his theatre of the
universe. The total space is box-like, enclosed and defined linearly
by the floor boards. Here we see Peale as the author of his own
nature. But there is a new element in Peale. If for Jefferson and
Rittenhouse, the prime-mover was God and Newton was his prophet,
for Peale Newton had to share the honours with the Swedish natural
historian Linnaeus 'to whom I am infinitely indebted for the perfect
arrangement of my museum'.[37] In a late manuscript of a lecture
Peale wrote:

> *Linnaeus stands before me shrouded in splendour—that great and good*

[35] Charles Willson Peale, *Introduction to a Course of Lectures delivered in the
University of Pennsylvania, November 16, 1799* (Philadelphia 1800) p. 19.
[36] Ibid., p. 9.
[37] Ibid., p. 19.

man was *beloved* and *honored* by *all civilized nations;* He opened the
book of nature to a wondering world; he travelled into frozen regions
under so many privations to acquire knowledge, *that* knowledge he
defused into classical arrangement, which will be admired for ages: . . . .[38]

We shall see later how Linnaeus's classification of species gives a
model of scientific stability as important and with as far-reaching
effects as the popular conception of Newton's cosmology. A watercolour of the long room by Peale's son, Titian R. Peale, in 1822,
emphasises the sense of order even more pl. 8. Here is the mystical

8 *Interior of Peale's Museum* (1822); watercolour, by Titian Ramsay Peale (1799–1885).
(*Courtesy of the Detroit Institute of Arts, Purchase, Directors' Fund.*)

perfection of rational order. Above the cases of dead birds are the
portraits painted by Charles Willson Peale of the revolutionary
leaders, and the busts of great representative men surmount the cases
to the right. The museum was symbolically sited on the second
floor of Independence Hall and provided an education fit for
democrats:

> Since it is by our being well informed and by a virtuous education that
> our republican government and the liberties of the People will be secured,

---

[38] Manuscript lecture, 'A Walk through the Philadelphia Museum', in Peale Papers,
Archives of American Art, Detroit.

trained, and perfected, therefore Policy should encourage such Institutions as have a tendency to improve the march of the people.[39]

The sentiments are unimpeachable and the greatest result of Peale's example is still seen in the high premium set on education by Americans to this day. But the intellectual curiosity, remarkable though it is, is founded on the visual categorization of a conservative world order. The portraits of the dead men, the stuffed animals, the Indian antiquities, and the bones and rocks of extinct ages articulate a view of time as progressing uniformly within a stable structure. Here the dead point to unchanging truth. The past controls the future.

For the contemporary visitor to the museum, however, here was a brave and exciting new world. We have a late description of 1818 from a broadsheet of that year. At the entrance democrats could emulate the great by having their portraits taken by a silhouette maker 'who attends every day'. The quadruped rooms contained over 200 animals including a 'cow with five legs and a large and powerful Electrifying Machine'.[40] One of the most outstanding features of the museum was the depiction of animals and birds, so far as their sizes would permit, in three-dimensional cases depicting their natural habitat. In this way Peale predates both Alexander Wilson's and Audubon's use of landscape in their bird paintings. In the long room there were cases of minerals and fossils, and although they are difficult to make out from the picture, 'various optical amusements, and Lukens's model of perpetual motions'.[41] But if these rooms pointed to the light and clarity of scientific achievement, the Mammoth Room gives an early romantic sense of sublimity and gloom. In his *Introduction to a Course of Lectures* at the University of Pennsylvania in 1799, Peale had quoted the following lines, which belie his sense of a dark and dream-like world which always appeared to lay seige to the scientific world of order:

> Without thy ray divine, one dreary gloom,
> Where lurk the monsters of fantastic brains,
> Order bereft of thought, uncaused effects,
> Fate freely acting, and unerring chance.[42]

The Mammoth Room showed just this side of the picture. Here were the Indians modelled with correct ethnic costume, and also a picture of the 'harbour of Gloucester representing the Great Sea Serpent'.[43]

[39] Ibid.
[40] Broadsheet advertising museum (Philadelphia, April 1818).
[41] Ibid.
[42] Peale, *Introduction . . .* , p. 9.
[43] Broadsheet advertising Mammoth Room, undated.

The principal exhibits were the huge bones of the mammoth Peale had dug up in 1801. An accompanying broadsheet gave the visitor, who paid his fifty cents, some idea of what he might expect. The description was 'delivered in the very terms of a Shawnee Indian'.

> Three thousand moons ago, when nought but gloomy forests covered this land of the sleeping Sun, long before the pole men, with thunder and fire at their command, rushed on the wings of the wind to ruin this garden of nature . . . when nought but the untamed wanderers of the woods, and men as unrestrained as they, were the lords of the soil . . . a race of animals was in being, huge as the frowning Precipice, cruel as the bloody Panther, swift as the descending Eagle, and terrible as the Angel of Night.[44]

This drama of the tragedy of time was illuminated every evening by lamp light (except Sunday nights), and accompanied by organ music, somewhat ironically symbolizing the harmony of nature.

Peale's famous picture the *Exhuming the . . . Mastodon* **pl. 9** showing the digging up of the mammoth's bones, throws yet more light on this strange cultural happening of the turn of the century.

9 *Exhuming the First American Mastodon* (1806–1808) by Charles Willson Peale. (*Courtesy of the Peale Museum, Baltimore, Gift of Mrs Henry White in Memory of her Husband.*)

[44] Ibid.

After a preliminary examination of some bones unearthed by a farmer of the name John Maston, and with the Philadelphia Philosophical Society underwriting the costs, America's first organized scientific expedition began. After five months, bones belonging to three skeletons had been discovered and the best one was exhibited. The wood sculptor, William Rush, after making a careful comparative study of the skeletons, filled in the missing parts. The publicity was spectacular and the Peales encouraged it. On one occasion, before going to Europe to exhibit the second skeleton, Rembrandt Peale entertained friends to dinner with a patent portable piano inside the huge thorax. The picture Peale painted between 1806 and 1808 of the actual exhuming of the mastodon, however, sums up attitudes towards scientific events in the early republic. Dominating the picture is a huge wheel and its supporting frame—a primitive kind of pump. Iconographically it may remind us of Leonardo's sketches of men hoisting cannon. The figures in the picture are organized in terms of the work they are performing, but there seems to be little actual human interaction. It might just be that Peale was primarily a portrait painter, or that he lacked the necessary skill, but the relations between men here have to be read in a literary way. The figures perform separate tasks along the production line of this primitive machine. The individual buckets on the wheel scarcely seem too fanciful a metaphor for the relations of the humans in the rest of the picture. There is a keen sense of theatre here too. The museum consciousness is taken outdoors and the world is divided into active and passive. Peale used the spectacular nature of his wheel to obtain free labour from the curious. Peale himself, with his family, is principal spectator expounding the wonders of nature. The family stands awkwardly in line as if on view to some further spectator who is overlooking the whole scene. To the left stands Alexander Wilson, the ornithologist, with his arms folded. The picture is a news picture giving a sense of the arbitrariness and informality of the photograph and yet following a line of history painting which gives formality to certain kinds of figure grouping. The dramatic use of light adds a metaphysical dimension to the historical situation. For although in almost journalistic fashion the picture recounts an actual event, this same event is also symbolically an account of the discovery of time in the face of the oblivion-creating forces of nature. Although Peale feared that rain would ruin his enterprise, he had fine weather throughout. But here we see in the far right-hand corner approaching rain clouds, a flash of lightning and horses running wild. The effect is to give us an almost gothic sense of the struggles of the scientific spirit against the powers of darkness. The dark pit is luridly lit by the last of the sunlight from the vanishing blue sky. In the *Book of Sentiments,* placed in the entrance to the museum, Peale had written, 'I love the study of Nature for it teacheth benevolence'. This engaging early American picture hints, however, at a more Manichean world in which the opposite of benevolence lies behind the world of endeavour, industry and public spectacle. The picture transfers the museum into the open air, with nature as the text of the learning space and machines for use and pleasure.

For the Americans of the post-revolutionary period, machines of all kinds were felt to be a better indication of national character than the conservative arts of literature and painting. Up until the Civil War there was also very little distinction made between pure sciences and technology. A machine like Rittenhouse's orrery represented scientific truth. Traditional arts were also felt to have too firm a basis in aristocratic cultures. 'The ghost of books, however,' said one early commentator, 'shall not continually haunt us. Do we need stimuli? Avert ye rising candidates for glory, to the American sun and those other shining orbs that irradiate our Columbian world.'[45] Others like the governor of New York, De Witt Clinton, gave elaborate reasons for the lack of a national literature and pointed to the sciences and technology where rising natural genius might profitably distinguish itself. Hume's remark was often repeated that 'a republic is most favourable to the growth of the sciences, a civilized monarchy to those of the polite arts'.[46] Many early American scientists and technicians began life in more traditional ways. Robert Fulton who pioneered steamships began life as a painter, and so did Samuel Morse who is chiefly remembered for his electric telegraph. In 1794 Charles Willson Peale stopped naming his sons after painters (Rubens, Raffaelle, Titian) and gave them names like Linnaeus and Franklin. Nonetheless the European inheritance of painting and literature developed alongside more republican interests, and it is worth remembering that in the Great Exhibition of 1851 in England, the American sculptor Hiram Powers exhibited his sensational 'Greek Slave' a naked girl carved in white marble in the neo-Classical manner, chained to her post and with her eyes upcast, alongside McCormick's reaper, the first really practical combine harvester.

By the mid-nineteenth century the earlier energy and considerable

[45] *Monthly Anthology* (1803) vol. I, p. 439.
[46] See, for example, *North American Review* (1815) vol. I, p. 400.

erudition of a Peale had become much more diffusely focused. The
later stages of his museum as taken over by his sons dwindled into
mere eclecticism and showmanship and prepared a taste out of
which an entrepreneur showman like P. T. Barnum was to make a
fortune. In 1853 a writer for *Putnam's Monthly Magazine* objected
to the idea of any kind of museum because the whole continent he
felt should be regarded as such:

> . . . the industry which best illustrates our national life, which is best fitted
> to declare what we have done, and what we are, is on too gigantic a scale
> to appear even in a crystal palace. Yachts like the North Star, steamboats
> like the Francis Skiddy, clipper ships like the Flying Cloud, hotels like
> the St Nicholas, canals like the Erie, the thirteen thousand miles of rail-
> road, the endless reaches of the electric telegraph . . . cannot be shown
> in expositions. . . . Let him take his position on a spur of the Alleghanies,
> and sweep with the telescope of his fancy the populous plains that
> stretch from the Atlantic to the Mississippi; . . .'[47]

The intellectual shift from the enclosed museum to the museum
without walls has several important significances. First the continent
itself becomes visualized as a work of art which makes the spectator's
viewpoint practically rather a difficult one. For in fact the simple
linear, three-dimensional form of the interior of Peale's museum
suddenly encompasses a whole continent and the very American
dream of infinite space becomes allied to the concept of Manifest
Destiny. Carried over are the values of use and control, which, in
spite of more creative impulses to relate to a space in its entirety,
effectively wrecked by the end of the century, the country and its
native inhabitants.

Before moving on to look at some of the more traditional arts we
can follow how the machine consciousness developed in a country
committed to developing vast space under the aegis of pragmatism
and utilitarian values, by looking at three actual machines: the combine harvester, the locomotive and the electric telegraph. Throughout
the century Americans made great contributions to mechanical
innovations in farming. Behind Washington, in Houdon's statue,
was a plough which illustrated command in peace no less than did the
sword in time of war. We shall see later how 'agriculture' was in
fact a synonym for 'civilization' in the early years of the republic.
But in actual farming Americans were early innovators. Jefferson
himself had invented a flat-breasted plough, and by the mid-century,

[47] *Putnam's Monthly Magazine,* new series (1853) vol. II, p. 126.

there were over 60 different kinds generally made of cast iron. Many were for specifically American purposes as the nature of the new land dictated. There were rootbreakers, self-sharpening ploughs, ploughs for subsoil and hillside land, ploughs for prairie and meadow, and ploughs for specific crops such as corn, cotton, rice and sugar cane. Physically, historically, socially and even psychologically the whole of the development of the Middle West depended on these inventions.[48] The most famous, and the one cited most frequently in 'great men' orations was McCormick's reaper. Quite apart from its actual usefulness and the vast new wealth it opened up, this particular machine gave a severe jolt to normal concepts of land-scape. The vast prairies themselves, by presenting the same space continuously, seemed to eliminate the concept of time. Only the machine could create this sense of timelessness just as earlier astronomical machines represented cosmic space. A McCormick reaper was exhibited in the Great Exhibition of 1851 and the *Illustrated London News* carried a picture, and described it in detail, adding this comment from the *Cultivator*, an American journal:

> The machine cuts all the grain; and if the raker is careful, none is scattered; and if the binders carry a rake and use it, none need be lost. Fields harvested by these machines have a beautiful appearance. The stubble is uniform in height, while no prostrate, scattering straws speak of waste. If the binders have felt at all interested in doing their work well, there is nothing to glean with the sickle, bagging-hook, or rake. Weeds, brush, pitchforks, rakes, if standing in the way, or even horses' legs are all cut smooth alike.[49]

Here was a way of literally shaping the continent. The *Cultivator*'s comment is somewhat ambiguous about the ruthlessness of the machine's operation, but surely here was an instance where the elimination of irregularity, and the appearance of uniformity was indeed beautiful. Later the nagging sense of ruthlessness was to be amply justified in the devastations and dust bowls of the latter half of the nineteenth century.

More dramatic than these innovations in agricultural engineering, however, was the steam engine. In 1830 Peale's son, Franklin, decided to boost the publicity for his museum and resolved to 'gratify public curiosity concerning railroads by introducing into his establishment a small working locomotive and train of cars'.[50]

[48] For a good account see Siegfried Giedion, *Mechanization Takes Command* (New York 1948) p. 149.

[49] *The Illustrated London News* (19 July 1851) pp. 89—90.

[50] Angus Sinclair, *Development of the Locomotive Engine* (1907) (Cambridge, Mass. 1970) p. 15. This work is the great rambling classic of early locomotive development.

The work was carried out with the engine and two small passenger cars running round a circular track inside the museum. By 1838, only eight years later, a writer in the New York *Knickerbocker*, reviewing Parker's *Journal of an Exploring Tour beyond the Rocky Mountains* (1838), exulted in the prospect of a railroad from the Atlantic to the Pacific:

> The granite mountain will melt before the hand of enterprise; valleys will be raised, and the unwearying fire-steed will spout his hot, white breath where silence has reigned since the morning hymn of young Creation was pealed over mountain, flood, and field. The mammoth's bone and bison's horn, buried for centuries, and long since turned to stone, will be bared to the day by the laborers of the Atlantic and Pacific Railway Company; rocks which stand now as on the night when Noah's deluge first dried, will heave beneath the action of 'villainous saltpetre;' and where the prairie stretches away 'like the round ocean,' girded with the sky, with its wood-fringed streams, its flower-enamelled turf, and its herds of startled buffaloes, shall sweep the long hissing train of cars, crowded with passengers for the Pacific seaboard. The very realms of Chaos and Old Night will be invaded; while in place of the roar of wild beasts, or the howl of wild Indians, will be heard the lowing of herds, the bleating of flocks; the plough will cleave the sods of many a rich valley and fruitful hill, while from many a dark bosom shall go up the pure prayer to the Great Spirit.[51]

With the steam engine liberated from the tight circle of the track of the museum, the whole countryside became visualized as an open theatre of the rites of scientific progress. From the moving train the country was at once accessible and removed. The booster-like passage above brings out strongly, with its pastiche of biblical language and Miltonic echoes, the popular conceptions of the invasion of Eden, the sense of trespass, the uncontrollable desire to remake everything, the sense of the dark secrets of natural history, and the idea of the invasion of historical time as well as space. There is an overall belief in the ability of the machine, characterized itself as a fiery angel, to bring the desired haven of light, agriculture, property, a flat landscape and hymn-singing Indians. The locomotive pitted natural power (steam) against natural power (landscape, animals and Indians). From the beginning its speed was thought of consciously as a protection against robbers and Indians in rather the same way that, for the contemporary American, the automobile provides immunity from contemporary urban jungles. We shall see later just how important the locomotive was in introducing a new

[51] Quoted in William H. Brown, *The History of the First Locomotives in America* (New York 1874) pp. 219–20. For the train as an image in the literature of the period see Leo Marx, *The Machine in the Garden . . ..*

panoramic sense of the American landscape. But the mechanics of the machine as well as its effects are of importance. The steam engine as a model for machine conscious Americans was very different from Rittenhouse's orrery. The steam engine produced new connotations of efficiency, work, regularity and precision rather than harmony and theoretical elegance.

The theories of thermodynamics were being worked out in Germany, Holland and England. It was not until the second half of the nineteenth century that Willard Gibbs made the first great American contribution. As it was the steam engine as technology presented problems enough in efficiency and organization. Watt's initial difficulty had been how to avoid wasting heat, and his invention of the separate condenser, enabled a perfect vacuum to be maintained in the cylinder after the steam had been discharged. The problem was also one of control, and standardization of speed. In one of his most elegant inventions, Watt produced the 'governor' which was described by Samuel Smiles in the following manner:

> Two balls are fixed to the ends of arms connected with the engine by a movable socket, which plays up and down a vertical rod revolving by a band placed upon the axis or spindle of the fly-wheel. According to the centrifugal force with which the balls revolve, they diverge more or less from the central fixed point, and push up or draw down the movable collar; which, being connected by a crank with the throttle-valve, thereby regulates with the most perfect precision the passage of the steam between the boiler and the cylinder.[52]

Steam was uncontrollable energy directed to the ends of work. Stephenson improved efficiency by directing the steam escape into the smoke chimney thus stimulating the draught and hence the heat intensity of the furnace. He also directed hot air round the boiler with copper tubes. This mechanical control of forces was quickly seen as a metaphor for human work. 'The Rocket,' said Smiles, 'showed that a new power had been born into the world, full of activity and strength, with a boundless capability of work.'[53]

In strictly historical terms the Americans introduced no fundamental revision of the principles of a Watt or Stephenson. But in modification of design and in piecemeal improvement, they showed an ingenuity and originality unsurpassed in Europe. From the first, imported English locomotives were useless. They were too heavy, too rigid and too complex. They were also built for heavy-duty

[52] Samuel Smiles, *Lives of the Engineers* (London 1874) vol. IV, p. 266.
[53] Smiles, *Lives*, vol. V, p. 219.

straight iron rails which were simply too expensive for American
requirements. The *Lion* whose boiler front was 'ornamented with a
large, fierce-looking face of a lion, in bold relief . . .',[54] built in
Stourbridge near Birmingham, proved a failure for just these reasons.
American locomotives were lighter, wood-burning, and designed to
take much sharper turns and gradients. Tunnels, embankments and
steep gradients were simply too expensive in a labour-short
economy. The American landscape created a unique design. The
most important prototype of the 'American type' locomotive was
invented by one J. B. Jervis and it was explained by his chief mechanic David Matthew in the following letter;

> American locomotive No. 1, second series, was built at the West Point
> Foundary Works, for the Mohawk and Hudson Railroad, from plans
> sent by John B. Jervis, Esq., chief engineer of that road. I left New York
> in August, 1832, with the engine in charge to place on the road and run
> it. This was the first bogie engine or truck used under the front part,
> ever built in this country or any other. The engine had nine and a half
> inch cylinders, sixteen-inch stroke, and had two pairs of driving-wheels
> five feet in diameter, and set aft the furnace; had four wheels, thirty
> inches diameter in the truck. This truck was placed under the front end
> of the boiler for support, attached by a strong pin, and worked upon
> friction-rollers so as easily to follow the curves of the road, as the fore-
> wheels of a carriage upon common wheels.[55]

The front truck mounted on a central pin enabled the locomotive
to negotiate very tight bends, and Baldwin, one of the most famous
locomotive builders in America, adopted this engine in his 'E. L.
Miller' for the South Carolina railroad in 1834. Baldwin's own
works produced a series of important modifications in design,
although he was by turns progressive and conservative to the extent
that it becomes impossible to generalize too dogmatically, even
about the so-called American type with a 4-4-0 wheel pattern. He
was reluctant to adopt the latter variety which had been patented by
Henry R. Cambell in 1836. Baldwin's less visually obvious invention
of the flexible beam truck engine which had three pairs of connected wheels, the front two of which could move laterally, surmounted the same problem. Some, like Ross Winans's *Camel* for the
Baltimore and Ohio railroad, had no leading truck, however, and
seemed as inflexible as anything produced in Britain. The general
point holds, nonetheless, that for simplicity, lightness and ability
to negotiate curves and gradients the Americans had no equals.

[54] Brown, *History of the First Locomotives in America*, p. 86.
[55] Ibid., pp. 207–8.

Delicate and complex craftmanship was not called for. Some more tradition-oriented craftsmen, especially Philadelphian watchmakers, found that their machinery was too complex when it came to harnessing it to steam power. If one can imagine an orrery driven by steam one can easily realize what a significant replacement the steam engine was in terms of what Americans thought of as a machine. But in Philadelphia, too, the firm of Garrett and Eastwick, later Eastwick and Harrison (Harrison invented the driving-wheel equalizer, thereby immensely improving traction), turned out magnificent 4-4-0 types. These were so suitable for rugged pioneering conditions that the firm later emigrated to Russia where they established the Alexandroffsky Head Mechanical Works. In production techniques the Americans were also early advanced. Rogers, another early railway boss, followed Eli Whitney's example in fire-arms and began making interchangable standardized components for locomotives as early as 1838.

Visually these early locomotives summed up a culture still imbued with faith in the rightness of mechanical elegance. Overall, form followed function and yet elaborate scroll-like work in iron fastened lamp to boiler, flag staff to 'cow driver', or ornamented some part of the frame. The engines were brightly coloured with exotic landscape scenes painted on the cab and along the tender, continuing a powerful native tradition of sign painting. The eclectic nature of the effect is important, making these engines an important and significant example of American popular art of the period. The very materials of iron and paint ensured success. The ornamentation on the early engines, or indeed on the bowsprits of the clippers, is not somehow un-American as organic'-oriented critics seem to think, just as the ornamental work of a Sullivan is no less American than the 'organicism' of a Frank Lloyd Wright. At the same time the steam was seen as a monster, an overriding power which threatened at any time to get out of control. Actual accident rates were very high and there were many casualities. A picture by Currier and Ives much later in the century sums up the rather nervous humour of the earlier response pl. 10. Belching fire, steam and smoke the 'Jas R. Pitcher' screams to an emergency stop with 'United States Mutual Accident Assn' prominently figured on the tender. It sums up much of the popular capitalist attitude where risk is at once a virtue and thing to be avoided, and where security and enterprise lie in uneasy balance.

If the steam engine had revolutionized the concept of the machine, the invention and wide use of the electric telegraph made even that change seem insignificant by comparison. One of the famous 'queries'

10 *The Danger Signal* (Engine 'Jas R. Pitcher'). Advertisement for US Mutual Accident Association, Currier and Ives lithograph, 1884. (*Courtesy of the Harry T. Peter's Collection, Museum of the City of New York.*)

which Newton posited at the end of the widely-read *Optics* concerned the nature of 'electric' forces. It was enough to stir up intense scientific activity, for here was a field not charted by the master, and its exploration hence assured equal fame to anyone who might take up the challenge successfully. We have seen how, somewhat erroneously, the image of a clockwork cosmos was thought to represent Newton's system. It is equally important to realize that, at the very time that the image of a stable, fixed, linear universe was being taken for granted, work in electricity had begun a chain of investigation which was to lead to the end of the Newtonian world view and to the sub proton and nuclear world of contemporary physics. In America from the beginning there is a persistent interest in electrical phenomena, chiefly the result of Benjamin Franklin's work which made him famous on both sides of the Atlantic. In 1838 Poe's prose poem, *Eureka,* which attempted to synthesize Newtonian and Laplacian cosmology with certain electrical and magnetic phenomena, was perfectly comprehensible to the lay audiences of the lecture circuits, and we shall see below how Whitman's finest poetry depended on his vision of the new world of research into electricity and magnetism.

Unusually, we must begin with a pure scientist who was also an American. Contrary to prevailing cultural characterizations Franklin was first and foremost a theoretical scientist. His most important contributions were his persistence in his theory of a single electric fluid (which, although rejected in the mid-nineteenth century, proved an important working theory at the time), his discovery of the equal positive and negative charges of a Leyden Jar, his assumption of the conservation of charge, and of course his identification of lightning with electricity. The famous kite experiment does not prove Franklin an empiricist, for he had already convinced himself of the identification with pointed conductors in his own laboratory. He had also already proved the variously negatively and positively charged nature of thunder clouds when a French follower D'Alibard with Buffon and De Luc carried out his *sentry box* experiment in France.[56] Although these researches concerned the nature of static electricity, and not of electromagnetic induction of the later telegraph, they did further the idea of communicating over long distances by 'electricity' and created a climate of interest in which further research was stimulated and its results eagerly awaited. As early as 1727 the Englishman Stephen Grey observed electrification from rubbed glass through a wire 700 feet long. In 1748 Watson, the greatest of early English electrical pioneers, who promoted Franklin's work in England, extended a wire across old Westminster Bridge from a Leyden Jar and used the Thames as a returning conductor. In the same year he conducted a charge through two miles of wire on Shooters Hill. In 1748 Franklin made a similar experiment across the Schuylkill, as did Du Luc across Lake Geneva. In 1744 with the aid of two suspended pith balls (the first type of electrometer) the Frenchman Lasage conceived the idea of sending simple messages for many miles. Some of Franklin's most elegant experiments, such as the one he described in Number 14 of *Opinions and Conjectures*, to explain the shape of electrical atmospheres, were performed with such a pith ball electrometer.[57] In the 1790s a Spaniard, Don Silva, sent messages 24 miles by a wire charge which was read by the divergence of pith balls.

If we ignore telegraphs based on the galvanic pile, the next important step is Gauss and Weber's telegraph of 1833 based on important theoretical advances in the intervening period, especially the discovery of electromagnetism by Oersted and Ampère, and above all Faraday's discovery of electromagnetic induction in 1831.

---

[56] For these passages I am indebted to I. Bernard Cohen, *Franklin and Newton, an Inquiry into Speculative Newtonian Experimental Science and Franklin's Work in Electricity as an Example thereof* (Philadelphia 1956).

[57] See I. Bernard Cohen, ed., *Benjamin Franklin's Experiments* (Cambridge, Mass. 1941) p. 215.

Steinheil's improvement of Gauss and Weber virtually created the modern form of telegraph consisting of an inductor, a line and receiving apparatus. Messages were printed out on a strip moved by clockwork, permanent magnets checked the needles when not under strain from induction currents. With Wheatstone and Cooke's telegraph of 1834, using five pointers deflecting left to right or right to left by a series of small 'multipliers' of wound copper wire, the telegraph came of age. Wheatstone and Cooke's instrument was a product of Wheatstone's research into the velocity of electrical waves in solid conductors.[58]

As with the steam engine, the main theoretical positions had been worked out before the Americans took up the problem. Morse first began working on the problem in 1832. A sketch of that time shows how he was working on similar lines to Gauss and Weber, and it contains the germ of the standard design he was later to create. A metal rod is projected onto a moving coil of paper by a charged electromagnet, and lifted back by a weak permanent magnet when the poles are disconnected. Morse's first machine of 1837 is interesting enough to look at in detail. It was made with a picture frame and parts of a clock, showing how a new form evolves out of the preconceptions of an old one with almost symbolic fitness. As with many other designs the clockwork in Morse's machine was confined to the system which unrolled the paper on which the marks of the message were produced. The most interesting feature of this machine is the metallic abstract letters which Morse stereotyped for the transmitting board. Each letter had a different number of projecting teeth differently spaced to guide the operator. Morse explained:

> At the time of the construction of this first telegraphic instrument, I had not conceived the idea of the present *key manipulator,* dependent on the skill of the operator, but I presumed that the *accuracy* of the imprinting of signs could only be secured by mechanical mathematical arrangements and by *automatic process.* Hence, the first conception . . . of embodying the signs in type mathematically divided into *points* and *spaces.*[59]

This description is especially revealing. Morse is thinking in terms of linear fixities and of human work as being more efficient when most like a machine. He is also thinking that the most natural type of

---

[58] The foregoing short history is derived factually from an excellent mid-nineteenth-century work, which is, however, rather biased in favour of European developments: Robert Sabine, *The Electric Telegraph* (London 1867).

[59] James D. Reid, *The Telegraph in America, and Morse Memorial* (New York 1886) p. 57.

communication is visual. In fact, as he subsequently realized, instead of 'printing characters at a distance'[60] (the phraseology shows how naturally he is thinking in terms of the press and printing) his invention worked much better using the manual dexterity of the human operator, and on *aural* not visual signs. It is also interesting to note that the electromagnet is suspended with a triangular frame pivoted at the apex to swing backwards and forwards from the soft iron beneath it. It is almost a visual reminder of Franklin's diverging pith balls. Leaving aside the cut-throat struggle Morse had in order to get his instrument patented and accepted, which required all the endurance his Calvinistic nature could summon, we can say his success depended on the elegance and simplicity of his basic design. At rest the key made the contact for the returning message, cutting out one of the two power suppliers at either end and sending the charge through the earths in order to complete the circuit. The process was a simple reversible one. In addition Morse's idea of repeating circuits facilitated long distance communication with underground cables. The remarkable thing is that Morse was not a theoretical scientist like a Franklin or a Wheatstone. Through a friend, Morse gained enough information from an article he never read by an American professor, Joseph Henry of Princeton, about needing more voltage rather than current to make his invention work. He was actually ignorant of the fact that the necessary voltage could be obtained by increasing battery cells and the number of turns of wire about the electromagnet.

Nonetheless, this erstwhile painter had succeeded in making practicable an invention which was to revolutionize space-time relations. The art historian Tuckerman summed up his career when he wrote, 'He has put his artist fire into locomotive shape, and writes with electric fluid instead of painting in oil'.[61] Electricity was mistakenly shown to have the same power-work-transmission effect of the conventional steam engine. A couplet by James Alger stated, 'T'was Franklin's hand that caught the horse,/T'was harnessed by Professor Morse'.[62] But Morse's invention was not of the machine age at all, it belonged to the one which was to follow. Samuel Smiles talked of the electric telegraph as the 'nervous system of the railway',[63] and Morse himself commented, 'it is not visionary to

[60] Ibid., p. 58.
[61] Henry T. Tuckerman, *Book of the Artists: American Artist Life* (New York and London 1870) p. 169.
[62] E. L. Morse, ed., *Samuel F. B. Morse, His Letters and Journals* (New York and Boston 1914) vol. II, p. 246.
[63] Smiles, *Lives*, vol. VI, p. xv.

suppose that it would not be long ere the whole surface of this country would be channelled for those *nerves* which are diffuse, with the speed of thought, a knowledge of all that is occuring throughout in the land, making, in fact, one *neighbourhood* of the whole country'.[64] Thoreau's backward-looking literary view was stated in *Walden*: 'We are in great haste to construct a magnetic telegraph from Maine to Texas; but Maine and Texas, it may be, have nothing important to communicate'.[65] The telegraph *line* was deceptive, electricity did not move *through* it, it instantaneously set up what Faraday called strain. The fact that Maine and Texas became part of the same space-time landscape was more important than communication through space in time. McLuhan connects this sense of interdependence with de Chardin's view that the discovery of electromagnetism should be regarded as a biological event.[66] It is the externalization of the nervous system into a total field of interplaying information as electric strain which was the most significant innovation. Popular prints of America as progressive angel leading mankind into the far west with coils of wire under her arm were, in literary fashion, depicting advancement in one direction. In fact there was now no backward or forward as the instantaneous news from the Mexican war showed. Only four years after the implementation of the telegraph, major press organizations began to spring up. Newspapers rechannelled in visually mosaic forms the total field opened up by the electronic media.

Some inkling of the importance of the discovery was given at the unveiling of a statue to Morse in Central Park by John T. Hoffmann, the governor of New York: 'If the inventor of the alphabet be deserving of the highest honours, so is he whose great achievement marks this epoch in the history of language . . .'.[67] The mass instantaneousness of impulse and response seemed to create a magic new sense of social awareness. McLuhan links the new phenomenon of the best-seller and sensational news story with the corporate sense brought about by the telegraph. Harriet Beecher Stowe and Morse reacted in the same way to the success of their respective achievements, turning to their Calvinistic inheritances for a suitable epigram. When Harriet Beecher Stowe was asked about *Uncle Tom's Cabin* she replied, 'God wrote it', and Morse consulted his friends to relay, over the Washington-Baltimore line, this text to mark its

[64] E. L. Morse, ed., *Samuel F. B. Morse*, vol. II, p. 85.
[65] Brooks Atkinson, ed., *Walden and Other Writings of Henry David Thoreau* (New York 1937) p. 47.
[66] Marshall McLuhan, *Understanding Media* (London 1964) p. 247.
[67] E. L. Morse, ed., *Samuel F. B. Morse*, vol. II, p. 483.

opening, 'What God hath wrought'. The potentials for democracy and autocracy were immense. In our own time the political battle has to be fought out still in technological terms. On the one hand we have Buckminster Fuller's vision of a new space-time world with total democratic access to total information and on the other the actual horror of computers which can store police information on every member of the democracy.

The more conservative way

It was American painters who first gave traditional arts in America an international reputation. In London, from the mid-eighteenth century, the Philadelphia-born Quaker, Benjamin West, painted huge 'historical' canvasses for his patron George III. As successor to Sir Joshua Reynolds at the Royal Academy, West encouraged successive generations of American expatriate painters from Copley to Samuel Morse. In the next chapter we shall see how Americans coming to London, with their own peculiar mixture of piety and nationalism, found the history painting tradition of the Reynolds-West school particularly appropriate as a model for their own desire to paint the pride of their own country in terms of battle, honour, sacrifice and victory. And yet Americans, to describe their country in peace, sought cautiously for models and were sensitive to the need to find sources in Europe which could be felt as democratic.

At the opposite end of the painting spectrum from history paint-ing was the art of Dutch genre, in which domestic not heroic sub-jects were chosen and which appealed to the rich middle classes of Holland. England exhibited many of the features of Dutch society, and partly mediating this source and creating an original art were the engravings of Hogarth. The bourgeois morality, the availability of these first mass-produced prints for the people, the skill with which the caricaturing dramas captured the neuroses of an unstable, emerging capitalist society, made his popularity some 50 to 100 years later in America inevitable. Similarly the eclecticism of his sources, his shunning of formality in design (though figure group-ings were often taken from Baroque-Renaissance masters), and above all what critics mistakenly call his pictorial realism, accounted for his reception in America as the most important source for American genre. After all here was the real prisoner dying in the real dungeon that Paine had called for, instead of the aristocratic shows of heroic drama which provided subjects for history painting.

Hogarth's work makes explicit the connection between theatre and pictorial representation which was to be so important for his

successors in Europe and America. Strangely the same principles
of theatrical pictorialism which Hogarth developed take their origin
in sources similar to those of Jefferson's university and his home in
Monticello. Hogarth's early association with actual theatre is well
known. He illustrated the frontispiece to Fielding's *Tom Thumb*
in 1731 (a play which burlesqued Dryden's heroic tragedies) and
many of his print dramas were reconverted back into actual dramas
as in Cibber's *The Harlot's Progress; or, ridotto al'fresco, a grotesque
pantomime entertainment* in 1733. The conception of space in
Hogarth's prints derives from the so-called realistic space of early
eighteenth-century theatre. And this space in turn came from two
sources synthesized in the Renaissance; Roman theatre and the
invention of perspective. In Serlio's famous treatise of 1545 the
seating of the spectators was arranged according to the Roman
cavea. The long narrow stage which formed the diameter of the
circle was retained. Behind this, however, was a perspective scene
giving depth to the once absolute barrier of the *scaena fons*.
Palladio's *Teatro Olympico* at Vicenza employed, in a more classical
and conservative way, a heavy architectural *scaena fons* but pierced
it with a central arch which had a passage taking the eye straight
back, and two smaller side-arches, complete with more oblique
passages. With the sophistication of mathematical techniques relating to the rules of perspective it became possible to dispense with
heavy architectural sets and create the same illusion with side screens.
Set parallel to each other, and diminishing in size as they receded
from the edge of the stage, they solved the same visual problems
as Jefferson's variously spaced pavilions. The *proscenium arch* framed
the front end of the box. Whether this arch developed from archways
in pictorical art, or from triumphal arches, or from the ubiquity of
the box-like city square in early Italian scene painting, or from the
conception of giving depth to the *scaena fons,* can be left to the
scholars. Any and all of these possibilities are germane to the present
argument.

The implications of this brief account are important. The Roman
origins (revived through Vitruvius and Palladio) of theatre point to
the convention of public representation and passive audience. The
illusion of perspective as Kernodle pointed out long ago,[68] is
effective only from a single viewpoint. Scene painters used to work
from the point-of-view of the royal box. The mathematicoreligious
principle of infinity authorizes the reality of the illusion. The

[68] George R. Kernodle, *From Art to Theatre, Form and Convention in the Renaissance*
(Chicago 1944) pp. 178–9.

combination of Roman *cavea* and Renaissance perspective makes
the theatre experience one of simultaneous rejection and expulsion.
The spectator is drawn in by the illusion of depth, and expelled by
the passive nature of his relation to it, through his physical situation.
On the dividing line is the *proscenium arch* enforcing this paradox
of contradictory command. The appearance of city squares on early
backcloths demonstrating perspective skill, shows how close the
connections are between theatrical illusion and the spaces created
by the city state.

We may look at our notions of tragedy and comedy in the same
light. How often is tragedy concerned with the fate of the individual
in terms of secular or divine fate? Is not the Aristotelian *flaw* of the
man of power a demonstration of the individual's frailty confronted
by the need for superior stability in the public persona of the state?
How often, on the other hand, does comedy relate to purely
private concerns of sexuality and domestic intrigue. Two plates in
Serlio's treatise show us the same severe box-like structure for
tragedy and comedy. The main difference is that for the tragedy
there is a door left open in the back-cloth to indicate the infiniteness
appropriate to destined failure. For the comedy the door is shut
giving us the sense of a more cosy, unthreatened space, with infinite
authority shut out, but, nonetheless still governing the rules of space.

Hogarth makes the connection between theatre and painting in
a convenient manner. Pictorial realism is a theatrical realism dependent on a precise historical development with its own kind of permitted action. History painting and genre balance the notions of
comedy and tragedy. Hogarth did not do away with these categories,
(indeed he painted purely comic and purely heroic pictures)
rather he synthesized them in a satiric genre which Aristotle had
claimed as the third category of drama. In a real sense Hogarth's
pictures dramatize the war inside a peaceful society. Hogarth used
the high historical style to structure the relations of his far from
heroic characters. Quite conscious of his innovations, he wrote,
'Subjects I considered as writers do my Picture was my stage and
men and women my actors who were by Means of certain Actions
and Express[ions] to exhibit a dumb show'.[69] Drawing
indifferently on Bosch and Callot, on Dutch genre, and on the
compositions of the Old Masters, Hogarth set his moral satires
within a box-like theatrical setting which became a visual stage of
the fears and hopes of the rising bourgeoisie. When Lamb wrote
his famous comment that one 'reads' a Hogarth print he implied

[69] Joseph Burke, ed., *Hogarth's Analysis of Beauty* (London 1955) p. xiv.

that from the literary genre of the theatre one was to interpret
successive actions as indicative of 'character', as well as interpreting
the details in a morally emblematic way. The bad apprentice, the
rake and the harlot are recognizable, in their claustrophobic
atmospheres, at the end of their careers because they have affronted
the common sense morality of prudence—the key virtue of that
illusionary vision of a stable and unchanging world. All Hogarth's
settings, indoor or out, have the same sense of enclosure and
theatricality. Hogarth's relation to his characters is cynical and no
alternative reality threatens the mirror-like image of the real
world. Leigh Hunt, whose father was a staunch Tory in the American
colonies, saw in Hogarth's work qualities of American life which he
characterized as 'one great shop counter . . . all down their coast
from Massachussetts to Mexico'.[70] Commenting on some children's
books he saw in the United States, Hunt wrote, 'They were the consequences of an altogether unintellectual state of trade, aided and
abetted by such helps to morality as Hogarth's Good and Bad
Apprentice which identified virtue with prosperity'.[71] In a similar
manner Hunt called the moralizings of Franklin's *Poor Richard's
Almanack,* 'scoundrel maxims'.[72]

Another English artist at the end of the century whose life and
works provide many parallels with American painters is Benjamin
Robert Haydon. There are many similarities between Haydon's
circle of painters and poets (Keats, Wordsworth, Lamb, Leigh Hunt)
and American Knickerbocker artists, not in terms of their quality,
but in terms of their interests, activities and interconnected discussions of literature and painting. Haydon and Washington Allston,
the Boston painter and friend of Coleridge, are almost identical
in their search for an ever-illusive ideal of historical painting. For
an Englishman working in the historical style, Haydon was also
fiercely democratic and anti-establishment. In almost the last year
of his life he remonstrated with Wordsworth for going to court. His
best-known achievements are, however, in genre, the supposedly
democratic form, and his best-known painting is *The Mock Election*
which is especially interesting for our purposes. Election themes
were popular from Hogarth's engravings and in England were
scarcely treated from a democratic point of view. Haydon conceived
the idea of his picture while in prison for debt; and (the tone is
reminiscent of Gay's *Beggar's Opera*) wrote of his vision in the

---

[70] Leigh Hunt, *The Autobiography of Leigh Hunt* (London 1850) vol. II, p. 175.
[71] Leigh Hunt, *The Autobiography,* vol. I, p. 87.
[72] Ibid., vol. I, p. 196.

following terms:

> . . . baronets and barbers; authors and merchants; painters and poets; dandies of rank in silk and velvet, and dandies of no rank in rags and tatters; idiotism and insanity; poverty and affliction mingled in indiscriminate merriment, with a spiked wall, twenty feet high, above their heads! I saw in an instant the capacity there existed in this scene of being morally instructive and interesting to the public, by the help of an episode in assistance.[73]

The symbolic effect is religious and aristocratic. The figures in the drama, brilliantly coloured, become icons, not of social oppression, but of fate, whether characterized by death or imprisonment. This democracy of misfortune relies on the distinctions of rank and class still being made. The characters' pretensions are mocked by the 20-foot high wall. The moral instruction does not extend to questioning the authority and permanence of this theatrical back drop. If it had, George IV would never have bought the picture. Haydon's sense of colour and grouping, with his democratic sentiment and conservative piety are elements which will be found in most American genre. Like Emerson, Haydon believed in the greatness of great men. The heroic sentiment complements the belief in the domestic theatre of genre.

It is impossible to chart exactly the precise effect the European genre tradition, stemming from Dutch painting and Hogarthian caricature, had in America. One of the most important innovations of Hogarth was his use of engravings for a 'mass' production of his work by which he freed himself from the necessities of aristocratic patronage. From the beginning of the nineteenth century, engravings of Hogarth and 'Old Masters' flooded the American booksellers. Washington Allston along with many others, made his *Buck's Progress* in deliberate imitation of Hogarth, and his leaning toward Dutch genre can be seen in his picture now existing only in a print: *Wouter Van Twiller's Decision in the Case of Wandle Schoonhoven and Barent Bleeker* (1817).

The interest in Dutch domestic comedy was principally stimulated by the novelist Washington Irving, whose *Sketch Book* and *Knickerbocker History of New York* provided subjects for aspiring illustrators. His most famous story in the style was, of course, *Rip Van Winkle.* Artists like John Quidor and F. O. C. Darley profusely illustrated the works of Washington Irving and James Fenimore Cooper. Quidor's illustration of a story from Washington Irving's

---

[73] Benjamin Robert Haydon, *The Autobiography and Memoirs* (London 1950) vol. II, p. 430.

Tales of a Traveller (1824) is one of the outstanding genre pieces
of this artist. The last story in *The Money Diggers,* 'Wolfert
Webber'[74] is a classic instance of what literary critics would call a
transference of the 'gothic' to an American story. Leaving aside such
confusing terms we may note that the chief character, Wolfert
Webber, is a good Dutch bourgeois householder who, despairing of
finding buried buccaneer treasure in his cabbage patch, becomes
insane with miserly greed. He enlists the help of one Dr Kipperhausen, a sub-Faustian magician, to seek out a black man, Sam, who
is alleged to have seen treasure buried by pirates somewhere off
Long Island Sound many years previously. The black man, Sam, is
one of nature's sons and knows the whole territory from 'Hell Gate
even into the Devil's Stepping Stones'.[75] Magician, miser, and black
man find the spot but are surprised by the ghostly re-appearance of
the buccaneer whence all is confusion as Quidor's picture shows.
Later Webber makes a remarkable recovery from the point of death
when he hears (in a splendidly American dénouement) that the city
council of New York want to run a main street through his cabbage
patch, and that therefore the new value of his real estate makes him
a rich man. The story is an adaptation of Harz mountain mining
legend to America and illustrates humourously the guilts of capitalist
psychology. The connections are made even clearer when in a note
on Dr Kipperhausen's magic tricks, Irving actually quotes Agricola's
De Re Metallica. The desire for wealth alternates with fears of
exploiting the earth. Quidor had brilliantly captured the essence of
the story in his picture *The Money Diggers* pl. 11. The details have
symbolic significance; the pick-axe is the tool of enterprise, the
bottle of 'Dutch' courage shows the intoxication of the nightmare
world and the divining rod illustrates the metaphysic of direction-
finding. The figures seem halfway between the kind of caricature
associated with engraving and the kind associated with genre.
Theatrically the light falls on Webber. The black man, not a Harz
mountain goblin, is naturally 'the miner' and in the process of
climbing out of the pit. He is the 'body' as opposed to the 'mind'
of the pseudo-intellectual magician. Webber is the entrepreneur
who exploits both. The buccaneer is the real hero. He is an outlaw
combining physical strength with cunning and hence a culture hero
appropriate to an incipient capitalist country. The dark central pit
symbolizes the dark fears of the mining enterprise; the fear of burial
alive and of trespass in Hell. The treatment is uniquely American

---

[74] Washington Irving, *Tales of a Traveller* (Philadelphia 1824) part IV.
[75] Ibid., part IV, pp. 122–3.

11   *The Money Diggers* by John Quidor. (*Courtesy of the Brooklyn Museum, Gift of Mr and Mrs Alastair Bradley Martin.*)

in style; a kind of soap opera comedy where the actors joke round the edge of their own neuroses.

The dénoument of 'Wolfert Webber' depends on recounting the urbanization of an erstwhile rural society. More and more genre itself became a lament for a lost world of agriculture and farm life. Lamb remarked that Hogarth took the traditional rural figures out of the country and placed them in the city. Americans countrified them again. William Sidney Mount (1807−68), the 'American Wilkie', was perhaps the first to make American genre a distinctive style. At first he painted 'histories' after the manner of West, but then turned to the complementary domestic world and was urged by Washington Allston to study the genre painting of Jan Steen. He is also known to have been interested in Hogarth. The theatrical nature of his pictures is at once apparent. Many of them depict the interior of a barn with a spectator, usually a black man, watching from the outside. The viewpoint is mediated by this figure. The barn is a theatre-in-the-country showing a half-way stage between European urban stage and country as an open theatre of American landscape. This is an American quality of compromise as if the

reality of either as theatre could not quite be taken for granted.
Nonetheless the interest in perspective is clearly there in more traditional ways as can be seen in the meticulously drawn floorboards
and in the hard edges of the box-like interiors. We know he
studied Edward Edwards's *Practical Treatise of Perspective . . .*
(London 1806) from his perspective notebook. The impeccable
sense of linear space, and colours standing out in their own light
are the American aspect of this style, and give painterly confirmation to a remark once made by Gilmor Simms, the Southern
literary critic, that the republic was a 'day perfect from the beginning'.[76] Absence of dramatic chiaroscuro is also absence of hierarchical emphasis. Mount refused to be sent to Europe for training
and consequently his work avoids the laboriousness of those
American artists who went to Düsseldorf in the mid-century. Mount
read and ignored Chevreul's book on colour which was to influence
the Impressionists, though he may have been alerted to some aspects
of Dutch colour through his reading of Frank Howard's *Color as a
Means of Art.*[77] He also made notes from Hogarth's drawings on
the variety of facial expression as a key to character, though he
really failed to differentiate substantially any of his own characters'
faces.

Mount's subjects are simple adaptations of the growing American
and European taste for sentimental anecdote. Mount painted at an
average of $200 a picture for a new class of wealthy art patrons in
New York. The kinds of subject which appealed to their taste can
be seen from a list he himself wrote out:

> Two lovers walking out. Walking out after marriage, one after the other—
> after the manner of Jude and Sam. A husband two months after marriage,
> with a bag of grain on his shoulder going to mill. A Whig after the
> Election [this doubtless inspired by Hogarth]. A Clergyman looking for
> a sermon at the bottom of his barrel. A Negro fiddleing [sic] on the
> crossroads on Sunday . . .[78]

The earliest of his pictures in the genre manner, *The Rustic Dance
after A Sleigh Ride* is interesting not only in itself but for an incident
which the painter describes connected with its composition.
Apparently his grandmother had just brought in some live coals in
an iron kettle to warm his studio:

> My thoughts were busy with the fingers in my picture, when presently

---

[76] William Gilmor Simms, *Views and Reviews in American History, Literature and
Fiction* (New York 1845) p. 45.
[77] Oliver W. Larkin, *Art and Life in America* (revised edn., New York 1966) p. 217.
[78] Alfred Frankenstein, *Painter of Rural America: William Sidney Mount 1807–1868*
(Washington, DC 1968) p. 48.

I began to yawn, to feel sleepy, but I roused[?] up in my chair & worked on. All at once I felt still more heavy & stupid—my hand and brush, pallette and maulstick caught the infection. My chin settled upon my bosom like on going to sleep—There before me on the easel stood a group moving in the dance full of mirth and hilarity while death stood over my chair ready to grasp the painter—but my good spirit whispered in my ear and my eyes moved slowly round the room. The cause of my strange feelings struck me like a ray of light. I saw the door and opened it with difficulty and I was save [sic]. Elliott the painter was caught in the same trap.[79]

The 'scientific' explanation is that live coals burn up all the air and suffocate the inhabitant, but the mode of telling is interesting. The claustrophobic atmosphere, the difficulty of opening the door, the sense of the dance coming alive in the dream while the painter's own life is threatened suggests the mutually exclusive nature of art and life which carries such sinister overtones in Poe and Hawthorne.[80] The picture of death hovering over the gaiety of the dance points to almost Puritan guilts about pleasure and art. Mount's theatre of representative life is not the every-day realism commentators seem to find in every genre painter. It is also claimed that Mount's handling of black people is not stereotyped, though the black man of the 'Banjo Players' appears as if straight from some European metropolitan opera. It was in fact engraved and became very popular in Paris. *Farmer's Nooning* shows a small white boy tickling the nose of a sleeping black man, a species of practical joking which Twain was to criticize severely in *Huckleberry Finn*. Today one of Mount's most admired pictures is *Eel Spearing at Setauket* where the sparse landscape details give a sense of transparent light mirrored in the clear water. The only shadows are reflections in the water which seem to depict a world without ambiguity as if the whole of nature were a 'day perfect'. It is a world like the one a Harriet Beecher Stowe or an Oliver Wendell Holmes were to write about in their more sentimental moments. Mount wrote to Charles Lanman on 17 November 1847, about his first lesson in eel-spearing given him as a boy by a black man named Hector—'no young Master step this way. I will learn you to see and catch flat-fish—'.[81] The narrative mythology is strongly American; the initiation into the secrets of nature given by the black man to the white boy. One recalls that in 'Wolfert Webber', Sam knew the Christian names of all the fish in Long Island Sound.

[79] Alfred Frankenstein, *Painter of Rural America*, pp. 14—15.
[80] See Nathaniel Hawthorne, *The Artist of the Beautiful* (1844) and Edgar Allan Poe, *The Oval Portrait* (1842).
[81] Alfred Frankenstein, *Painter of Rural America*, p. 37.

George Caleb Bingham (1811–79) continued and modified distinctively the tradition extending from Hogarth through Haydon and Wilkie and seventeenth-century Dutch genre. He knew of the works of the Europeans through engravings and was acquainted with the rules of perspective through John Burnet's *An Essay on the Education of the Eye,* which gave an uncomplicated nonmathematical account of perspective in relation to simple geometrical figures. And perhaps it is through this work as well as through the study of the 'Renaissance-Baroque Masters' that he obtained his rather formal ideas about figure grouping. Burnet said:

> Geometric forms in composition are found to give order and regularity to an assemblage of figures, for, in fact, we can have no idea of form without a portion of distinct shape, which being arranged so as to make one part of the composition dependent on another for its completion or extension produces an harmonious assemblage of lines, independent of the aid of light and shade or color.[82]

It is also interesting that Burnet quotes Priestly's *Opticks,* where Priestly traces the rise of perspective from painting particularly 'that branch of it which was employed in the decoration of the theatre . . .'.[83] Like Hogarth before him Bingham went straight to the compositions of the Renaissance masters for his figure groupings. Critics differ as to the nature of his *realism.* Some talk of the 'rhythms of common life', others state that he never seemed to paint directly from nature or from human models.[84]

If we look at his three main political paintings we see the end of the line of election subjects. In Bingham they are taken seriously though the sets are still theatrical. Election subjects (the representation of representation) are connected with the theatre in painting from Hogarth to Bingham. The three paintings of this subject exhibit similar features. In all three are to be found foreground seated figures, a mid-way horizontal division of the picture emphasized by a line of people in shadow, a completely formal use of light and dark (it can scarcely be called chiaroscuro) to handle the problem of mass figure painting, a light distant landscape, the standing orator vividly outlined in light against a dark stagey set of either buildings or trees, a formal triangle of people in the foreground with the orator at the apex picked out as if by spotlight. In addition many of the characters reappear in each picture. There is

[82] John Burnet, *An Essay on the Education of the Eye with Reference to Painting* (London 1837) p. 41.

[83] Ibid., p. 5.

[84] See Vergil Barker, *American Painting* (New York 1950) p. 477 and James Thomas Flexner, *That Wilder Image* (New York 1952) p. 147.

always a fat figure, in two there are a black man, a drunk, and a cross-legged seated figure. Most of the figures are in groups of three and there is a singular absence of women in all of them.

Bingham's finest painting is undoubtedly the *Verdict of the People* **pl. 12.** Whereas in Hogarth's political engravings the point is

12 *Verdict of the People (No. 2)* (After 1855) by George Caleb Bingham. (*Courtesy of the R. W. Norton Art Gallery, Shreveport, Louisiana.*)

always antidemocratic—the politicians are knaves, the people fools in the shapes of pimps, prostitutes, thieves and beggars— Bingham's canvases portray the people generally as sober upright citizens, standing or sitting in unextravagent poses. But already in England Wilkie had taken the sting out of Hogarthian genre. The connections between Wilkie's *The Blind Fiddler* and *The Jolly Flatboat Men* have been suggested already,[85] but there are many general similarities in their paintings. If one compares Wilkie's *Chelsea Pensioners Reading the Waterloo Dispatch* with Bingham's political paintings, the same use is made of the crowd around the reading figure who focuses the attention of a busy street upon himself.[86] The reading-

[85] See John Francis McDermott, *George Caleb Bingham, River Portraitist* (Norman, Oklahoma 1959).

[86] E. Maurice Bloch makes the same connections in *George Caleb Bingham, the Evolution of an Artist* (Berkeley and Los Angeles 1967) pp. 148–9.

of-the-newspaper motif is to become more common during the
nineteenth century, reflecting a new public response to the speeded-
up communications network. Common to Wilkie and Bingham is
the use of the lineally defined street scene with buildings clearly
articulating a sharp three-dimensional stage-like set, and both
have the almost statutory black man. Technically Wilkie is much
more skilful in the deployment of his figures over the canvas, and
in the reaction of the spectators to the news he manages to create
a much more unified response. Critics lamented the lack of unified
response in Bingham's pictures, for each character seems to share
little dramatic connection with his neighbour. But this is the
American charm of the picture. The connections in society are taken
for granted through the representational process depicted and we
are left with the democratic individualism of the represented. In
the *Verdict of the People,* unlike with Wilkie, the people loom
larger than the buildings, and seem stolidly indifferent to the pompous light-bathed figure reading the result. The absence of unity of
focus among the figures is only apparent, for the formalities of
geometric grouping form the invisible connections in this society.
The middle space of the picture is left empty and attention is drawn
first to the immediate foreground occupied by black man and drunk,
then to the laughing figure by the pump and finally to the group of
three men below the speaker. This empty 'corridor' gives an impression of a stage moving back and rising to meet the requirements of
conventional perspective. In colour, Bingham is more adventurous.
A comment by the *Literary World* on the now lost *Stump Orator*
is indicative of East Coast reactions to Bingham's use of light in
general:

> All the laws of chiar'oscuro are set at defiance, so that the eye is dis-
> tracted and carried all over the canvass, without a single resting-place.
> He evidently has no idea of the value of light, and how sparingly it
> should be used in a picture. In color it is unmistakably bad; its only
> merit is in the broad exaggerated character of the heads, which look as
> if painted from daguerreotypes.[87]

The uniquely American quality of this Mid-Western picture is just
this failure observed by the supercilious East Coast critic. The totally
arbitrary bands of dark and light moving horizontally across the
picture dispense with the necessity for hierarchical emphasis implicit in chiaroscuro of the conventional kind. Again the effect is to
make the picture less theatrical. The figures seem constructed on a

[87] Quoted from John Francis McDermott, 'George Caleb Bingham's "Stump Orator"',
Art Quarterly, 20, No. 4 (Winter, 1957) pp. 388–9.

flatter plane. The effect of deep perspective is also cut off by the band of dark figures across the middle distance. An engraving of this by one Prout interestingly breaks this dark band to give a much more conventional perspective to the background.[88]

Bingham did not go to Europe until 1856 so he avoided in his early career the worst effects of the Düsseldorf school in Germany. For an example of what happens in America under this European influence we can turn to Eastman Johnston's (1824–1906) *Old Kentucky Home* (1859). Early in his career Johnston had done drawings of Longfellow, Emerson and Hawthorne, and he went to Düsseldorf in 1849 where he stayed in Leutze's studio. While he was there his father had a copy of Washington's uniform made for Leutze, to be used in his painting of *Washington Crossing the Delaware*. The *Old Kentucky Home* is very different from the genre painting he did in the 1870s where, at times, he comes close to the style of the young Winslow Homer whom he helped and encouraged. In this picture the iconography of people at play is transferred to the black man with his music making, love making and playing with children. Whereas in Mount the spectator had been the black man here the spectator is the prepubescent white girl, so that here one image of fantasy watches another. The point of view is aristocratic, and it is but one year to the Civil War and eight years after the publication of *Uncle Tom's Cabin.* It is an ugly picture in the handling of paint and in the claustrophobic manipulation of light. The excessive draughtsmanship and awkward pose of the figures, over-theatrical in their groupings, show how Düsseldorf emphasized the worst tendencies in the American inheritance. Here the inconography of servant life,—the dark mirror of established life—provides the comic undertone to the serious life of order and work.

But the most popular medium for 'genre' about the mid-century was not the oil painting but the lithograph. The firm of Currier and Ives created in their mass-produced lithographs a whole iconography of national life. Many of the artists were in fact European and the firm ransacked America's very respectable artistic tradition for subjects. They popularized the historical paintings of West, Trumbull and Leutze, Catlin's Indian *Portfolio,* and shrunk Bingham's *Jolly Flatboat Men* into details of panoramas of the Mississippi. Theirs was the first commercial exploitation of lithography. Using limestone imported from Bavaria, and employing the wives and daughters of German immigrants, they eventually had a production line process, and mail-order circulars complete with coupons and post office

[88] Reproduced in E. Maurice Bloch, *George Caleb Bingham.*

box number.[89] Currier had sprung to fame with a print of the
Lexington disaster, a steamboat tragedy of the late thirties. Their
subjects reflected the whole scope of American Victorian society.
Works of a subhistorical and subgenre nature became further separated into sensation and sentiment. Currier and Ives are virtually a
unique American cultural phenomenon. They catered for an explicit
cultural thirst and give a near complete indication of the psychology
of the emerging urban society. A Currier and Ives print, in spite of
its size, was the direct precursor of the photograph in its mass-pro-
ducibleness, its three-dimensional realism, its sense of immediate
journalistic relevance. At the same time it inherited most of its
subjects from a more aristocratic art. Within the broad and quite
distinct categories of history and genre most of the subjects may
be accounted for. From the first, pictures of war and disasters
were popular, following the many accidents of early technology, and
the successive wars of Independence, of 1812, of the Mexican War
and Civil War. Equally popular were the religious scenes. Following
West's and Haydon's example, many early American painters used
to tour round with huge religious canvases which would be exhibited
to an audience for a fee. Now every American could have his own
religious experience in his own home. Public pride was celebrated in
the prints of the clippers and the steam-engines, public aspiration
in the many prints of sporting and country life, as the dream of the
English squirearchy embodied, as it did for the English middle classes,
the *summum bonum* of the good life. The passion for heroes, the
inheritance of Carlyle and Emerson, was gratified in the prints of
Washington and Ulysses S. Grant. The range was comprehensive
with the *Death of Calvin* ranged alongside *Queen Victoria* and
Beatrice Cenci. Similarly illustrations from literature indicate precise bourgeois taste. Byron and Longfellow are the most popular
authors, representing respectively the heroic and the sentimental.
Uncle Tom's Cabin and *Robinson Crusoe* are among the more
popular titles, the one a sacred, the other a profane, bourgeois
masterpiece. With the strict separation of male and female activity
in the public and private sectors, prints assumed to appeal to women
were poured out in their thousands. Travelling salesmen haunted
the doorsteps of the housewives with such gems as *No, no Fido,
Will he bite?* and *My Highland Boy*. If the subject matter follows a
debased tradition, the total experience was new and American. In
an important sense the fact of the large, brightly coloured lithograph,

<hr/>

[89] There is an excellent short history of the firm in Roy King and Burke Davies, *The
World of Currier and Ives* (New York 1968).

the production line, the power of the controller of the medium (for example, firms paid to have their railroads represented) catered to the fantasy world of the middle classes with an exuberance and energy scarcely matchable even in Victorian England. The eclecticism of the process re-introduced European values to American culture and yet the result was an original American art.

There is not space to look at more than a few of the prints in detail. If we compare a lithograph of 1847 by the Baltimore firm of E. Weber and Co. **pl. 13** with a famous Currier and Ives lithograph of

13 *Elements of National Thrift and Empire* by J. G. Bruff, Lithograph of E. Weber and Co., Baltimore, 1847 (*Courtesy of the Library of Congress, Washington, DC.*)

1868, *Across the Continent* **pl. 14**, we can find evidence of an important shift in American consciousness. The title of the first, *Elements of National Thrift and Empire*, points to a sense of order which goes back to the Revolution. That order belongs to a static and unchanging universe here exemplified by the not quite three-dimensional setting. The items have a symbolic two-dimensional structure and relationship. Ancient symbols stand by new ones. Liberty, seated like Britannia, holds Gilbert Stewart's portrait of Washington. The liberty pole and Jacobin cap replace shield and sceptre. Underneath the portrait stand the plough, sickle and broad-axe, underlined by the sword. Following the bottom of the print to the right are scrolls: 'PATRIOTISM, the highest object of Public

14 *Across the Continent,* 'Westward the Course of Empire Takes its Way' (1869) Currier and Ives Lithograph. (*Courtesy of the Harry T. Peters Collection, Museum of the City of New York.*)

gratitude', and 'Agriculture, Manufactures & Mechanical Arts'. Their emblems can be seen in the cog-wheels, ploughs and millstones. The role of science and art is shown in the next scroll, 'SCIENCE & ART Parents of Emulation & Enterprise', and such sentiments seem to be given public blessing by the final scroll which is a charter of the Smithsonian Institution. To the left stands the goddess of agriculture with the symbols of her business about her; sickle, plough, sheaves of corn with fruit and vegetables overflowing from a basket. To the left of this again are two scrolls, 'Rail Roads, Canals, Rivers and Harbours', and 'PUBLIC LANDS, Primitive Partition [Formation?] of new States'. The centre of attention is a gigantic obelisk which seems visually to centralize and stabilize the picture, and which towers over the gothic church, neo-Classical banks and public buildings. In prints such as these the arts of self-denial and material prosperity occur within a stable, paternalistic framework. Order is maintained on the principle of ancestor worship, visualized in monument and portrait. This empire is based on conservation and thrift, and a more static view of the world in which the contradictions of capitalism were resolved harmoniously.

The Currier and Ives lithograph, on the other hand, shows a significant shift in the conception of empire. It was drawn by Fanny Palmer, an indefatigable English woman who worked for the firm, and James Ives. With the railroad track leading to infinity, the rites of Manifest Destiny have an appropriately structured theatre. Parallel with it is the wagon trail and the telegraph line in process of construction. To the left of the line we find a drama of incipient civilization, in which trees are cut down, log cabins erected, public schools opened and churches built. Behind these, and, if read correctly, in literary fashion as further on in time, the wagons start out for the West and the new lands. To the left of the line, then, is history in the making. On the other side of the tracks is the dream of nature with a winding river measuring out more leisurely its own vanishing point which is cut off by the mountains. Here we see mountains, rivers and trees already being turned into a sport area (that is an area controlled and policed for people to *play* in). The Indians are about to be engulfed in steam, the buffalo are scarcely discernible on the horizon. The double and diverging perspective, each with its respective iconography of history and nature sum up the inheritance of the view of the earth as theatre and museum, conceived as in a single viewpoint with eternally diverging vanishing points, creating division actually and psychically.

Whitman's poetry has its roots in both the early American delight in science, and in the more conservative types of literary and painterly art. It also bears witness to a fascinating struggle in the poet's mind with all the dramatic complexities of the European inheritance. Whitman's poetry was long ago linked with the 'genre' tradition,[90] though the criticism which uses words like realism and accuracy of vision in relation to that tradition, scarcely brings out the uniquenesses of Whitman's work and misses the complications of his dramatic relation to the reality of mid-nineteenth-century American life. As the poet of America's democratic consciousness, Whitman attempted to preserve an early vision of America's life with a full awareness of its contradictions and imminent failure.

As a poet of the self with a commitment to the notion of democracy *en masse,* Whitman takes on the full range of the paradoxes of representative reality. The split between public and private life, between the demands of the body and the body politic constitute the heart of Whitman's concern. In *Democratic Vistas* (1871) he invented two dialectical categories of human response which he called 'separateness' and 'adhesiveness': 'Not that half only, individualism which isolates . . ... There is another half, which is adhesiveness or love, that fuses, ties, and aggregates, making the races

[90] See F. O. Matthiessen, *American Renaissance* (New York 1941) p. 597ff.

comrades, and fraternizing all'.[91] Again and again in the poetry this
sense of separateness is achieved through visual images giving the
sense of a spectator watching the drama of American life. The sense
of adhesiveness, on the other hand, is achieved through images of
touching, and frequently through images of the new sciences like
electricity and magnetism.

But the sense of separateness is not a simple one. The point of
view of Whitman's very American *panoramic* vision engages the
whole spectrum of emotional response. Although the long and famous
lists of the republic's multifarious activities in *Song of Myself* can
be likened to a portfolio of Currier and Ives' lithographs, the experience of reading them gives one a sense of having to shift one's
viewpoint actively to engage in responding to them. Whitman
alternately bullies and cajoles, encourages and rejects, pleads with
or rages against the reader. Our identification with the scenes he
describes, for all the genre-like quality of their subject matter,
cannot be that of the passivity of a spectator in a traditional linear
theatre. In the poem (especially sections 10 and 15), the so-called
categories of national life become subsumed as part of Whitman's
own complex and contradictory poetic self. The democratic faith
of *likeness* is here simply expressed, and the problems of vicarious
identification left for a moment in abeyance: 'And of these one and
all I weave the song of myself'.[92] It is Whitman's panoramic viewpoint where the spectator, not the scene, shifts that enables him to
experience the body politic as a whole. So his own motion imparts
motion to the body politic. There is a revealing passage early in
Specimen Days where Whitman describes his sense of the city. New
York becomes the theatre of society, and the Staten Island Ferry
a moving, dynamic and shifting viewpoint which makes the spectator's
experience of it an active not a passive one:

> Almost daily, later, ('50 to '60,) I cross'd on the boats often up in the
> pilot-houses where I could get a full sweep, absorbing shows, accomp-
> animents, surroundings. What oceanic currents, eddies, underneath—the
> great tides of humanity also, with ever-shifting movements. Indeed, I
> have always had a passion for ferries; to me they afford inimitable, stream-
> ing never-failing, living poems. The river and bay scenery, all about New
> York island, any time of a fine day—the hurrying, splashing sea-tides—
> the changing panorama of steamers, all sizes, . . .—the prospect off
> towards Staten island, or down the Narrows, or the other way up the
> Hudson—what refreshment of spirit such sights and experiences gave me

[91] Walt Whitman, *Prose Works*, vol. II, Floyd Stovall ed. (New York 1963) p. 381.
[92] Walt Whitman, *Leaves of Grass*, H. W. Blodgett and S. Bradley, eds. (New York
1965) p. 44.

years ago (and many a time since). My old pilot friends, the Balsirs,
Johnny Cole, Ira Smith, William White, and my young friend, Tom Gere
—how well I remember them all.[93]

It is the same with the omnibus drivers '—riding the whole length
of Broadway—'[94] and Whitman comments in parenthesis, 'I suppose
the critics will laugh heartily, but the influence of those Broadway
omnibus jaunts and drivers and declamations and escapades undoubtedly enter'd into the gestation of "Leaves of Grass".'[95]

Perhaps the most crucial passage of *Song of Myself* is the middle
section (from 27 to 37) where Whitman cautiously explores the
possibility of unity, not through sight but through touch. It is
precisely the anarchic sense of touch which brings on a major crisis
in the poem, 'To touch my person to some one else's is about as
much as I can stand'.[96] He cannot relate sensuously to humanity as
a whole in terms characterized by visual models of oneness. Nevertheless he does provide, at points in the poem's rhythmic pattern,
intensified verbal syntheses which incorporate these contradictions
as a single impulse.

Whitman has a continual problem of whether to look at things
in representative terms, or in relational terms. For the moment,
however, at this point in the poem, he sees any detail of nature
equal in importance to any other thing in spite of traditional
hierarchies:

I believe a leaf of grass is no less than the journey-work of the stars . . .[97]

The interrelatedness of nature here democratizes traditional notions
of the chain of being, or the sense of organic or inorganic matter.
Whitman now extends his vision through time, so that the poet
conscious of his world can penetrate the secrets of earth history
and the elusive sources of animal behaviour. With the vision of a
magnificent stallion, which acts as a catalyst to his own erotic
sureness of himself, he describes a superbly detailed vision of America
where nature and history seem to rest in balance with each other.
The parallelisms of the lines unite the traditionally split worlds of
technology and nature, and confer the warmth of animal sexuality
on the farther reaches of space itself;

Where the she-whale swims with her calf and never forsakes it
Where the steam ship trails hind-ways its long pennant of smoke . . .

[93] Walt Whitman, *Prose Works*, vol. I, p. 16.
[94] Ibid., vol. I, p. 18.
[95] Ibid., vol. I, p. 19.
[96] Walt Whitman, *Leaves of Grass*, p. 57.
[97] Ibid., p. 59.

> Speeding with tail'd meteors, throwing fire-balls like the rest,
> Carrying the crescent child that carries its own full mother in its belly.
> Storming, enjoying, planning, loving, cautioning
> Brawling and filling, appearing and disappearing,
> I tread day and night such roads.[98]

Then, as he has done before, Whitman attempts to assimilate the contrary evidences of cosmic interrelatedness, so that he can identify himself with that, too. In strongly patriotic tones he recalls the 1836 massacre of the Americans by the Mexicans, and John Paul Jones's fight with the *Serapis*. But in spite of the need to identify with these heroic Americans, Whitman is in fact stongly repelled by the horror and bloodiness:

> I discover myself on the verge of a usual mistake . . .
> That I could look with a separate look on my own crucifixion and bloody
> crowning.[99]

At moments like these Whitman's desire to be 'Both in and out of the game'[100] cannot be sustained. His double vision of man as the ubiquitous centre of the universe and man as spectator cannot be reconciled. Evasive and mystificatory lines follow:

> I remember now,
> I resume the overstaid fraction,
> The grave of rock multiplies what has been confided to it, or to any graves,
> Corpses rise, gashes heal, fastenings roll from me.[101]

It seems too simple, this image of death unifying the factions of the republic in order to accomplish a kind of resurrection. Is the rock (*petros*) seen as a kind of secular basis for the church of state? Does the state become alive by virtue of the corpses entrusted to it? The anarchistic Whitman could not go so far. Representation emphasizes the whole. Whitman's panoramic sense could fruitfully compromise that fact by insisting on the dynamic relation of the viewer to the social scene. But where institutions are greater than the individual, where the hero (as Whitman here) claims the power of life and death, man is reduced to a spectator at his own funeral. Faced with war, death and disease, easy visualizations of identity with the state became impossible for Whitman, and too often he fell, as here, into a rhetoric of faith which fails to convince.

If Whitman's sense of the changing and active self broke up the immovable and hierarchical notions of static viewpoint, this sense

[98] Ibid., p. 64–5.
[99] Ibid., p. 72.
[100] Ibid., p. 32.
[101] Ibid., p. 72.

of panorama could not really break down the gulf between personal, sensuous experience and the sense of the whole society. Whitman is the poet of American nationalism and with the abstract presuppositions of the national group having a human identity, personal feeling vicariously related to it turns quickly into nightmare. But there is another range of experience in Whitman which celebrates the body as never before in western poetry. Here relationships between people are imaged not in terms of the mechanics of state, but in terms of the newer discoveries of the sciences of electricity and magnetism. Here the poet is less concerned with representing human activity in terms of an abstract model, than with seeing relationships subtly interpenetrating as the forces within an electric field. In some measure this enables Whitman to overcome that old sense of self *and* society which was the visual and linear inheritance. We have already seen how the instantaneousness of the electric telegraph gave people the sense of a biological event. As a poet Whitman instinctively knew that the inheritance of Gutenberg had created a world of characters and types, separate in their own space and artificially reunited into abstract wholes:

> This is unfinished business with me—How is it with you?
> (I was chill'd with the cold types, cylinder, wet paper between us.)
>
> Male and Female!
> I pass so poorly with paper and types, I must pass with the contest of body and souls.[102]

Joseph Beaver, one of Whitman's most perceptive critics, long ago noticed how, in *Leaves of Grass,* Whitman uses his knowledge of electricity and magnetism to equate male and female with negative and positive poles of electrical discharge. He also pointed out parallels in Whitman with the kinds of synthesis made by Faraday and Maxwell in their search for a unified explanation of electrical phenomena, light and magnetism. These parallels have been substantiated by recent work on Faraday. Whitman is connected through Emerson to Coleridge, and to the new sense of a cosmos of interpenetrating forces in a dynamic of attraction and repulsion which was philosophically formulated by Kant. Through Coleridge these ideas of so-called 'transcendental idealism' passed not only to the English-speaking world of the American writers but also to English scientists like Humphrey Davy and Faraday. In Coleridge, the images used to demonstrate this field of interpenetrating forces are from nature, from plants and from metaphors of the seed as a

---

[102] Ibid., p. 628. This poem is excluded from *Song of Myself.*

matrix of relationship and potentiality.[103] The crocus in its form, the pattern of its leaves, its interpenetration with light, air and water demonstrates this fact more clearly than the abstract world of Newtonian imponderables. It is not surprising that the same complex of ideas led the scientists to investigate the phenomena of electricity and magnetism, and poets to explore the sense of what Coleridge called 'organic nature'.[104] Whitman is the heir to both, and in the farewell poem of *Leaves of Grass* all these themes are brought into a single, passionate poetic movement. The polarizations of life and death, soul and body, man and woman are bridged in a life-enhancing moment of recreation. Whitman imagines his own death as a poet, and the moment of departure is also a new beginning. He recalls his poems and his work:

> I have sung the body and soul, war and peace have I sung,
>   and the songs of life and death.[105]

He announces his faith in the Union but slowly the rising crescendo of assertions begins to overreach itself to a very Whitmanesque point of vulnerability. It is the point where the sensual man attempts to relate to the visual *en masse* of the representative system. The lines move rhythmically to a danger point, to Whitman's sense of being caught naked in a crowd. But for once he moves beyond this point to a vision of a world unstructured by the mechanics of time and space, and all it has implied in human organization:

> Screaming electric, the atmosphere using,
> At random glancing, each as I notice absorbing,
> Swiftly on, but a little while alighting,
> Curious envelop'd messages delivering,
> Sparkles hot, seed ethereal, down in the dirt dropping,
> My self unknowing, my commission obeying, to question it never
>   daring,
> To ages and ages yet the growth of the seed leaving,
> To troops out of the war arising, they the tasks I have set promul-
>   gating,

---

[103] See Leslie Pearce Williams, *Michael Faraday; a biography* (London 1965) p. 64.
[104] This kind of perception about the universe is frequent in the early Coleridge.
One might note the famous lines in *The Eolian Harp* (1795):

> And what if all of animated nature
> Be but organic Harps diversely fram'd
> That tremble into thought, as o'er them sweeps
> Plastic and vast, one intellectual breeze,
> At once the Soul of each, and God of all.

[105] Walt Whitman, *Leaves of Grass*, p. 503.

To women certain whispers of myself bequeathing, their affection
    me more clearly explaining,
To young men my problems offering,—no dallier I—I the muscle
    of their brains trying,
So I pass, a little time vocal, visibly, contrary,
Afterward a melodious echo, passionately bent for, (death making
    me really undying,)
The best of me then when no longer visible, for toward that I
    have been inseasonably preparing.[106]

As Beaver shows, the initial images of the passage parallel Maxwell's
work on electric forces operating through ether, and the problems
of the undulating or vibratory nature of light itself. 'The random
glancing' also suggests the corpuscular theory of light, and the 'seed
etheral' may refer the particles which transmit the force through the
ether. So Whitman's world points to the world which is to replace
the conventionalities of linear space and the dualistic thinking which
was the inheritance of the Revolution. The prodigious biological
events which the passage celebrates reflect a new world of instantaneousness, of invisible events which may be trusted, a confidence
in abstract thought which is sensuous at the same time, and a complete synthesis of physical and mental activity. Images of electric
discharge point to physical communion and fertility, uncannily
anticipating the work of Wilhelm Reich in our own time. There is
a sense of consciousness recovering from the contraries of physical
and mental, man and woman, peace and war, visible and invisible.
Here earth and heaven are reunited in the electrified seed mingling
with the dirt, the soldier finding worthier work, the *affection* of
women *explaining,* the brain characterized as a muscle, and death
itself becoming a contrary movement of undying. The 'single farewell' is impossible and the poet advances 'from behind the Screen'
to announce:

Camerado, this is no book,
Who touches this, touches a man.[107]

The screen is the mask of the writer, like a book in its distancing
and separating qualities. The imagination of a sexual encounter with
the reader in the lines that follow is intensely moving and indicates
that the poet's sense of himself and his audience is for once in accord.
The poem ends with a vision of light 'from an unknown sphere more
real than I dream'd . . .', difficult to understand but sure in its relation of dream and reality. Here, for a moment, Whitman challenges

[106] Ibid., p. 505.
[107] Ibid.

the very nature of mid-nineteenth-century American reality; that mass psychosis of pragmatism and sentimentality. Whitman's achievement was to be able to bridge the gulf between poetry and science, and to reconceive time and space outside the representational reality he inherited. To be sure, this new reality interacts with the older one. It represents the central drama of the poems, but nonetheless Whitman's poems do challenge in a very fundamental way inherited assumptions.

Whitman's insight that all principles are rooted in love, and that metaphysical satisfaction is in inverse proportion to an erotic sense of life, remains in spite of the fact that he failed to work it out in social terms. On the threshold of the Civil War, Whitman pointed the way out of the impasse of the contradictions of state representative identity. In other areas too, Americans were beginning to seek out ways of particularizing even the most unpromising legacies. The movement towards understanding the total field of a man's experience is seen equally in Peale and in the results of the electric telegraph. Even in Mount the assumptions of a single viewpoint, and conventional linear perspective are almost intuitively modified. The peacetime artefacts in painting, literature and technology bear witness not simply to vitality but to actual achievement.

4

The Arts of War

In this chapter we take up many themes relating to the problem of war in American theory and practice which in many ways reflect *ab verso* the patterns and structures of the notions of peace. We have seen how Jefferson and Peale fortified the individual against himself, now we shall examine the public fortifications of the West Point academy: a public learning space with more overt military implications. In Samuel Colt's Hartford factory we investigate the apparent paradox of peacetime production of firearms, and in the layout of industrial space, and the private space of the industrial boss's home and pleasure gardens we can draw some conclusions about the use and theory of land and labour in the new republic. In the successive wars of Independence, 1812, 1845 and 1860—5 we shall chart the literary and painterly reactions to these progressive retreats from the finest ideas of the Independence movement. The emphasis will be on the few who resist public fashion and public hysteria. Thoreau's famous essay on Civil Disobedience is at least one masterpiece to emerge from the wars of this period and we shall conclude with Whitman's elegy to Lincoln which, while stimulated by private and personal senses of loss, is in fact an elegy to the failure of that great dream of public and private identity which lay at the heart of American representative democracy.

In defining a country for themselves, and by participating in the cult of nationalism, Americans created an armed society like any other built on the same premises. In practice the conflict of individual and central view-points was decided in favour of the latter. The sentiment of equality sanctioned the practice of autocracy. As we have seen, the technologies of perspective, printing, and mining, the philosophy of scientific method combined with the conception of the permanent state provided enough tension and conflict to make the notion of a metaphysic of hostile nature perfectly credible.[1]

[1] McLuhan connects nationalism with the rise of printing and the fixed point of view in perspective. See *The Gutenberg Galaxy*, pp. 218—22.

The years between 1776 and 1860 see the progressive failure of a
popular antimilitarism (the individualist sentiment) and the proportional growth of a centralizing, military-aggressive, state bureaucracy.[2] We can trace this failure through the development of the
mechanical arts of war, the poetry and painting of the successive
conflicts. First, however, it is important to look specifically at an
important learning space which is the military equivalent of
Jefferson's University of Virginia. In the history and growth of the
military academy of West Point we find a model of a complete system
fulfilling every requirement of the eighteenth-century political
philosophers. As one shrewd commentator put it: 'Indeed to use a
homely figure, it is the great city clock by which all the smaller
clocks and watches are regulated'.[3]

Historically the military academy is the result of the War of
Independence. In geographical terms its site was the most important
strategic location of the war. It was fortified by two of those many
military engineers from Europe who were the essential tools of
American success. Fort Arnold at West Point, later called Fort
Clinton, was built and designed by de la Radière and the Polish
patriot Kosciuszko. Kosciuszko, who is the more important of the
two, had been trained in French military academies at a time when
French military thinking, as a result of the reversals of the Seven
Years' War, was undergoing a theoretical revolution which was to
lead eventually to the military victories of the Napoleonic Era. He
is said to have studied with the great French architect and engineer
Perronet,[4] who under Louis XVI had designed bridges and canals
in an attempt to rival the engineering achievements of imperial
Rome.[5] The art of permanent fortification, growing somewhat
obsolescent by the end of the eighteenth century, had become a
highly complex geometrical exercise. Fortification was an attempt
to provide a maximum security area by mingling art (geometry) and
nature (landscape). It was an effort to create a literal boundary, and
thus, the evolution of boundary styles (the military term is trace), in
response to the invention of gunpowder and the increasing proficiency
of the line of fire, became an important aspect of military art. From
simple 'star' traces to 'tenaille' and 'bastion' traces there was a con-

---

[2] See Marcus Cunliffe, *Soldiers and Civilians; the Martial Spirit in America, 1775–
1865* (Boston 1968).

[3] Ibid., p. 171.

[4] See Jean Rudolfe Perronet, *Description des projets et la construction des ponts. . . .,*
2 vols (Paris 1782).

[5] Ibid. The *Discours préliminaire* is a panegyric on Roman architecture: 'Nous trouvons
dans la plupart des édifices élevés par ce Peuple célèbre des modèles propre a former notre
goût'.

tinuous attempt to minimize the area of 'dead space' (i.e. space where one might remain alive) in the cross-fire area outside the boundary. Sebastian de Vauban, under Louis XIV, invented methods of raising a siege which involved a counter-geometry of assault based on the nature of the complex bastion traces of the fort under siege. In the most complicated of these late seventeenth-century forts, central authority was protected by a projection of a seemingly infinite number of straight lines with various angles about a hypothetical circumference. In addition each part could be individually self-sustaining, or tactically abandoned without weakening the whole. As such it was the perfect model for the eighteenth-century state. In practice, even in military terms, such forts were too geometrically complex to organize efficiently, not to mention the loss of morale in tactically abandoning one point in the system.

The site of Fort Clinton, on a large bend of the Hudson, forms an almost perfect bastion trace. From Kosciuszko's own plan we can see its shape even more clearly than on a good modern map, for by judiciously highlighting selected points in heavier ink Kosciuszko has given it a more regular geometric appearance than it in fact possesses. The fort itself adapts the geometries of its traces appropriately to the surrounding landscape. To the west, furthest from the river, is an almost perfect 'ace of spades' bastion, a trace originally designed in the late fifteenth century to minimize the effects of direct gunfire. The north river side is defended by a half ace of spades and half trenaille traces and two 'cremaillère' (triangular projections with one side longer than the other) traces give maximum open fire area to that important stretch of river. On the east side is a straightforward bastion trace. Other sketches by Kosciuszko show plans and elevations of hexagonal redoubts.

For the military engineer there were but two ways of visually representing a space. Representing 'relief' on a map was a very difficult procedure until sophisticated processes of colour printing had been developed towards the end of the nineteenth century.[6] Either, therefore, one could represent the country in two dimensional terms on a map, or in three dimensional terms as in a conventional painting using perspective techniques. The choice was roughly between geometry and topography. Following a Renaissance tradition the military engineer was called upon to be both artist and scientist. The first two artists who also wrote military treatises were Dürer and Leonardo da Vinci. The double vision of abstraction

---

[6] See a very important article on the development of surveying and cartographical signs: R. A. Skelton, 'Cartography, 1750–1850', in C. Singer *et al.*, *A History of Technology* (Oxford, 1957–8) vol. IV, pp. 596–628.

(as on a map) and representation continues right through the nineteenth century. F. O. C. Darley and James McNeil Whistler were both West Point products. Interestingly enough, as well as Kosciuszko's map, we have a topographical panorama of West Point by l'Enfant **pl. 15** made the year the fortifications were finished.

15 Detail from *Copy of L'Enfant's View of West Point* by Lt Richard S. Smith [Assistant Professor of Drawing at West Point]. (*Courtesy of the United States Military Academy Library, West Point, New York.*)

It had both practical and painterly value. It enabled relief to be demonstrated to acquaint the defender with the vertical relations of the landscape. In painterly terms the somewhat exaggerated slopes, the simplified architectural stone masses, the regularized and exaggerated stratigraphy, the almost figurative rows of trees, and the raised foreground with its two gentlemen contemplating nature take us back to a European watercolour tradition and the *a priori* visual assumptions of the eighteenth-century landscape painter. The misty river provides a convenient vanishing point, giving the landscape a certain ambiguity. The multiple vanishing points of the panorama are combined with the single vanishing point of the conventional representational scene. These early military topographical panoramas are a much neglected source of early land-scape painting. These maps and representational pictures, stemming from similar sources in the visual abstractions of geometrical space, were both means of controlling space for specific purposes. The map enabled the military planners to exercise their training in geometric direction finding for the purposes of conducting war. It fed the fantasies of abstract control at a distance over large groups of men and machines. The topographical representation, however, which appeared to give a more human cast to the landscape, was less practical in strategic terms, though more practical one imagines in more immediate fighting terms. The two modes of representation were in fact complementary. One appeared more scientific, the other more artistic. The one seemed more useful the other more ornamental. In fact, however, like the concepts of work and leisure in our own time, their apparent differentiation, their apparent status as altern-atives, points to a notion of nature and society not open to real change, and not amenable to a resolution of the conflict between war and peace of which they constitute the poles. The art of nation-making then was an act which mixed nature and art in a literal act of fortification and boundary making. Like the concept of the state as social deterrent, Fort Clinton was never called upon to show its strength, but acted as a quasi-invisible deterrent itself.[7] The so-called 'revolutionary chain' which as every American schoolboy knows was stretched across the river to prevent the British from sailing up it was a psychological rather than a military barrier. The British had cut the previous chain relatively easily in 1777.[8] Even now it figures prominently in the sacred relics of the nation and a visitor to West Point can see sections of it on display at Trophy Point.

The military academy itself was founded in 1802, the same year as the British equivalent at Sandhurst. In spite of popular public sentiment against standing armies and the general ridicule of the militia prevalent in the early years,[9] the academy grew stronger as the republic's life wore on. After some early danger of extinction, the academy thrived on the wars of 1812, 1845 and the Civil War.

[7] One historian of fortification disarmingly concludes his work: 'In fact, of both land and sea fortifications, it may be said that fortifications have most usefully accom-plished the purpose for which they were intended when by their very existence they have deterred the enemy from making an attack and therefore have actually never been called into use'. US Engineer School, United States Army, Pamphlet on the Evolution of the Art of Fortification, prepared under the personal direction of Major General William M. Black, Chief of Engineers, US Army (Government Printing Office, Washington, DC 1919), p. 107.

[8] Duportail in a letter to Washington, 27 August 1778, details the weaknesses of the defences of Fort Clinton. The letter is reproduced in Elizabeth S. Kite, *Brigadier-General Louis Lebegue Duportail . . ..* (London 1933) p. 100.

[9] See Cunliffe, *Soldiers and Civilians.*

The organization of the figures in this fortified landscape is of especial interest. During the War of Independence, another foreign advisor, Baron von Steuben, published a small book on army organization and military practice which 'except the Bible, was held in the highest estimation'.[10] Recalling memories of his Prussian military past, von Steuben set out clear simplifed rules for the cultivation of his somewhat raw recruits. There were slight differences from customary practice. Von Steuben's insistence on care of the sick marks him out as more humane than many theorists, and equally there is an emphasis on tutoring the individual soldier before corporate drill. The parts of the republican army were cultivated for the better operation of the whole. The 3,000 copies of the book demystified the art of drill to a certain extent and insisted on comprehending rather than on uncomprehending obedience. Throughout the emphasis is on simplicity. From Plates II and VI of the work one can see that von Steuben employs the great military theorist Guibert's method of forming a line from a column by deployment. A recent historian has declared this to be the most important military advance of the century.[11] Other plates show the emphasis placed on simple geometric rules for obtaining 'points of view' to steer an army in the direction it should go. Plate II combines representational landscape and geometric lines to indicate how to find the direction of the march.[12] Von Steuben's work towards the creation of a standing army, however, ran counter to popular sentiment. In an address of 1782, von Steuben stressed the insecure position of the independent states. There were Indians to the West, Canada to the north and largely undefended seaports along the east coast. He advocated obliteration of state identity in a permanent federal 'Legion', and stressed the importance of a teaching school of military art. Here a recruit would learn military mathematics, surveying and civil engineering. By the Civil War his arguments would have made sense to most Americans:

> If we examine mankind under the impression of property and interest, we will find that to make any art a study it should not only be a passion but a business.—The Merchant may read Marshal Saxe, the Mathematician Monsieur Vauban, but it is the soldier alone who regards their lessons

---

[10] Joseph B. Doyle. *Frederick William Steuben and the American Revolution* (Steubenville, Ohio 1913) p. 136.

[11] Robert S. Quimby, *The Background of Napoleonic Warfare* (1957; reprinted New York 1968) p. 123.

[12] Baron von Steuben, *Regulations for the Order and Discipline of the Troops of the United States* (Hartford, Conn. 1779), plate II.

and takes up the sword; not as the hasty avenger of a sudden wrong, but as his companion for life, that will study and digest them.[13]

The man who, more than any other, carried these principles over to permanent institutionalized practice was Sylvanus Thayer, president of the academy from 1817—33. It was the graduates from West Point who surveyed and measured the whole continent. They received the best education in mathematics and technology that it was possible to obtain at the time. The early curriculum instituted by Sylvanus Thayer was impressive: first year—French, geometry, trigonometry, mensuration; second year— the same with the addition of analytical geometry and fluxions; third year—topographical drawing, natural philosophy (physics) and chemistry; fourth year—engineering (mostly civil), mineralogy, rhetoric, and moral and political science.[14] But the context of learning was the military academy. As important for practical purposes as such a curriculum was, it developed expertise without regard for final consequences, or the relationship of that expertise to the general culture. The men who developed America were men trained in military obedience to orders from above. They were literally the tools of the machine of state. For it is really the surveyor, highly trained at West Point, who is the true folk hero of the developing West, the man who creates boundary, not the man like a Daniel Boone, or a Kit Carson, or a Natty Bumppo who operates in the undifferentiated space of a psychically pure wilderness. As we shall see later, in the work of another West Point graduate, Seth Eastman, these men seemed more at home with landscape than with people. Eastman was excellent in delineating topographical landscape but very poor at figures. Significantly Whistler failed chemistry, and became one of the outstanding artists of the century. West Point, therefore, was in itself a miniature society indicating some of the most fundamental aspects of representative democratic life. The technology developed there was a literal extension of the mechanical philosophy of democracy where the individual voluntarily suppressed his individuality in the interests of the corps. Here academic objectivity was unquestioningly accepted as a prerequisite of understanding the law of nature.

Although the military authorities grumbled at the large loss of their graduates to civilian life, to the canal and railroad builders,

[13] *A letter on the Subject of an Established Militia, and Military Arrangements, addressed to the Inhabitants of the United States, by Baron de Steuben* (New York 1784) p. 3.

[14] S. E. Ambrose, *Duty, Honor, Country: a history of West Point* (Baltimore 1966) p. 90.

their graduates were in fact carrying their peculiar knowledge and training into the nation at large. Contrary to the myth of the un-lettered and homespun philosopher of the Leatherstocking kind, these men often came from wealthy New England families who had given them enough pre-academy education to surmount its very rigorous academic demands. Once at the school the cadet was subjected to a rigorous daily, weekly and bi-annual testing. A com-plex system of grading meant that Thayer could instantly assess any cadet's position in his class at any moment of the week. The academy was the fulfilment of the liberal dream of education. Merit was the only guide to progress and advancement. Since the study of nature through mathematics rendered a view of the cosmos perfectly in accordance with the notions of law and order, the compatability of obedience and learning could not seriously be questioned.

The army was itself the perfect model for a capitalist as opposed to a democratic society. This was early noted by de Tocqueville whose chapters on the role of an army in the republic provide still a fitting conclusion to this discussion of West Point as an early American cultural artefact. While de Tocqueville has been proved wrong that among civilized peoples war becomes scarce, that civil wars in a democracy are brief, that soldiers in a democracy have necessarily better public relations than those in aristocratic countries, that aristocratic military manners are better than democratic ones, nonetheless many of his remarks hold good, and even where he is wrong there is often evidence which supports the bolder generaliza-tion.

At the heart of de Tocqueville's analysis is his unwavering belief that the structure of the whole society is reflected in the kind of army it has, and further that a society which needs an army is an armed society. For de Tocqueville the contradictions of represent-ative democracy emerge in a grotesque form in the army. In civil democracy success is won by risk and individual enterprise, the prospect for promotion for a democratic soldier is thin without an actual war. The spirit of capitalistic enterprise is transferred to the private soldier who desires a war to better his position. Further, de Tocqueville argues, because his social rank depends upon his army rank, 'Ce qui était l'accessoire de l'existence dans les armées aristocratiques est ainsi devenu le principal, le tout, l'existence elle-même'.[15] So in spite of the fact that democratic societies wish for peace, the absence of the traditional inequalities commits the

---

[15] Alexis de Tocqueville, *Oeuvres complètes,* Tome I, vol. 2 (Paris 1961) p. 271.

individual far more thoroughly to war. Amply proved by history is
de Tocqueville's assertion that Americans find wars difficult to
begin and end. Even more important, however, is the fact that the
very political structure of representative society serves to make wars
more hideous. For the army in war serves as a representative body
which has all 'les attributions du gouvernement civil; elle centralise
presque forcement dans les mains de celui-ci la direction de tous les
hommes et l'usage de toutes les choses'.[16] The 'restlessness' of
capitalistic democracy, together with what de Tocqueville calls
'un amour viril de l'ordre'[17] characterizes the army no less than the
civil polity. Seven years before Marx's first writings, de Tocqueville
identified capitalist competition with eventual total war:

> La guerre, après avoir détruit toutes les industries, devient elle-même
> la grande et unique industrie, et c'est vers elle seule que se dirigent alors
> de toutes parts les ardents et ambitieux désirs que l'égalité a fait naître.[18]

As a centre West Point became a basis for the encroaching power
of the state and the military machine. It was a suprapersonal icon
of a nation founded on the nationalistic principles of boundary, with
the magical texts of physical science as its bible. But the great
principles it embodied of uniformity, security, predictability and
progress were equally observable in the type and manufacture of
machines of war, and these are among the most important of the
'mechanical arts' during the first years of independence.

The theoretical text for the production of machinery of war is
not so much the *Principia,* nor books dealing with the laws of
nations and the structure of government. The most important text
is again European and relates to the laws of money and business.
It is an ironic coincidence that Adam Smith's *Wealth of Nations*
was first published in 1776. In that year America was freed from
British rule and shackled by this Scottish bible of natural capitalism.
The principles underlying the book are very similar to those principles we have already seen in Palladio or in Locke or in Vattel. The
laws of money proposed a system of reality, however, which struck
deeper than the elegant systems of the architects or theorists of
law. Founded on the dualistic philosophy of *private* self-interest
and *public* natural liberty, Smith's system was the most powerful
articulation of the dream of reason. Men trained in Lockean philosophy would have quickly understood the value of labour as an
exchange commodity, all would have understood the urban-rural

[16] Ibid., p. 274.
[17] Ibid., p. 275.
[18] Ibid., p. 283.

dialectic, the concept of natural balance between wages and prices, distinctions in the market of agricultural and mining produce. Like the structure of government itself, exchange and mart regulate human relations. It is the sense of a total system which appealed undoubtedly to the Americans. Smith sought to reduce to order every aspect of private and public life. Man is valued, like Locke's labourer, only insofar as he is a producer; servants, the lazy, clergymen, entertainers and all men of letters are irrelevant to the process. Smith readmits most of them through the back door, however, for they are seen as valuable as educators, and myth-providers in the cause of the industrial utopia.

Not surprisingly the highest achievement of art for Smith is the art of war. Like commerce and manufacture, the army is the model of good order and government essential to the liberty and security of individuals. Even more important, a standing army illustrates the divine principles of the division of labour and its presence symbolizes a civilized state. Whereas in Roman times barbarians invaded civilized states, in modern times with correct division of labour and the production of firearms, civilized nations can take upon themselves the civilization of barbarians. 'The invention of firearms, an invention which at first appears to be so pernicious, is certainly favourable both to the permanency and to the extension of civilization.'[19] Smith shared with the other European philosophers a deep respect for the Roman model of state and its legal system. To the charge that his division of labour produced masses of illiterate and stupid workers, Smith replied that it is the employers' duty to set up schools for children (where excellence is rewarded by 'little badges of distinction'),[20] and to provide some kind of religious education, as well as public entertainment. The magistrate in Smith's kingdom is an important person for he upholds the law founded on the possession of property. Smith admits that:

> Civil government supposes a certain subordination. But as the necessity of civil government gradually grows up with the acquisition of valuable property, so the principle causes which naturally introduce subordination gradually grow up with the growth of that valuable property.[21]

As Mumford pointed out long ago the operations of war and the army are perfect models for a state identified with the workings

[19] Adam Smith, *The Wealth of Nations. . . .* (1776; reprinted London 1962) vol. II, p. 198.
[20] Ibid., vol. II, p. 267
[21] Ibid., vol. II, p. 198.

of a machine.[22] Quoting from Sombart's work, he observed that
the production of armaments rather than 'pins' in Smith's famous
example, would have been a better model for division of labour
principles. The Americans, beginning a new society unhampered by
traditional power structures such as class or religion, were able to
fulfil Smith's dream to the letter. By 1860 American production of
armaments was on a scale unsurpassed by previous European efforts.
During the Civil War new machines were used for the first time as a
practical demonstration of Yankee ingenuity. There were ironclads
and repeating rifles with metallic cartridges. The telegraph and
railways 'improved' strategy and logistics. Submarine warfare claimed
its first victims, sharpshooters more effectively isolated their objects
in space by the use of telescopic sights. Artillery using balloons for
observational purposes became accurate to a hitherto unheard of
degree.[23] The death toll was greater than in any previous war in
history. The Civil War was the triumph of the American industrial
and political machine, with the inefficient rather than immoral
slaveocracy of the South superseded by a more progressive civilization.

Two quite distinct and yet interdependent features of the production of American war machines are important. The first is the
concept of uniform production and the interchangeability of parts.
The second is the division of labour and mass production. The nature
of means and ends is identical. The notion of the division of labour
presupposes an *a priori* concept of the whole. It is directed to the
efficiency, permanence and stability of the whole. Early arms makers
frequently used the example of firearms damaged in battle. Whole
guns could be speedily made up from the interchangeable parts.
Turned into a commodity by the nature of his task, the man making
a single part all the days of his life was as replaceable as his product.
War and peace like the fluctuations of wages and prices tended
towards natural balance.

This version of the machine philosophy affected the means of
production more than the actual machines it produced. Our primary
example is the life and work of Samuel Colt, the maker of the famous
Colt revolver, but his work came at the end of a long period of
experimentation with types of armament and production methods
which can be traced historically to the war scare with France in the
late 1790s. Like the steam engine, the firearm was a very different
machine from the machine ideas of the cosmos. The Connecticut

[22] Lewis Mumford, *Technics and Civilization* (London 1946) pp. 89–101.
[23] J. Coggin, *Arms and Equipment of the Civil War* (New York 1962) pp. 6–7.

arms manufacturer Eli Whitney once remarked:

> A good musket is a complicated engine and difficult to make—difficult
> of execution because the conformation of most of its parts corresponds
> with no geometrical figure.[24]

Mumford compared it with a combustion engine, but unlike the
combustion engine its output cannot be measured in terms of work.
Its effective working demanded a knowledge of a variety of
sciences—on chemistry for efficient gun-powder and on metallurgy
for strengths of materials, on geometry for computing line of fire,
on a consciousness of perspective for the ability to isolate objects
in space. Improvements in firearms fostered that dream of the safe
kill at a distance. It reduced the necessity for physical courage or
bravery in proportion as it isolated victim from attacker. With this
separation, fantasies of total manipulation and total control were
realizable in concrete form.

Two Americans are responsible for setting up the technological
context for Colt. It was Eli Whitney (1765–1825) who, during the
years of the war fever with France, received an order for 10,000
rifles from the United States government. He never fulfilled the
order, neither did he ever succeed in his ambition to make rifles with
interchangeable parts. Hand forging, hand filing and 'fitting soft'
were the age old methods perfected by Whitney. What he did achieve
however is best set out in this contemporary account:

> Thus Mr Whitney reduced a complex business, embracing many
> ramifications, almost to a mere succession of simple processes, and was
> thereby enabled to make a division of labor among his workmen, on a
> principle which was not only more extensive but altogether more philo-
> sophical, than that pursued in the English method. In England, the labor
> of making a musket was divided by making the different workmen the
> manufacturers of different limbs, while in Mr Whitney's system, the work
> was divided with reference to its nature, and several workmen performed
> different operations on the same limb.[25]

It is precisely this 'philosophical' approach to production which is
important. Whitney based his rifle of 1798 on the French Charlesville
of 1763, and his second rifle was modelled on the French musket of
1777 which Jefferson had thoughtfully sent over during his ambas-
sadorship in Paris. From the arguments of contemporaries on
Whitney's system, it is obvious that there is a wide awareness of
Smith's principles. They argued that although it was clear that the

---

[24] Claud E. Fuller, *The Whitney Firearms* (Huntington, West Virginia 1946) p. xvi.
[25] Ibid., p. 65.

artistic development of the workmen was somewhat retarded, there were new 'beauties' of uniformity, and of increased growth rate. The latter increased general wealth so that even people with artistic instinct would benefit.

If Whitney was the father of mass production methods, it was John J. Hall, also working with water power and child and unskilled labour, who seems to have achieved genuine interchangeability of parts around 1827. He also succeeded in inventing machines for making parts (as Whitney had tried to do). He had a drop and forging machine, a machine for cutting off surplus metal, and machines for drilling and milling. A nineteenth-century industrial historian quotes:

> In 1827 a hundred of Hall's guns, which had been sent to Springfield in 1824, were brought back to Harper's Ferry, and placed with a hundred guns of current make. The whole two hundred were taken apart, the pieces thoroughly mingled and the guns then remounted from pieces picked up at random. The whole two hundred fitted perfectly.[26]

It is, however, in the work of Samuel Colt (1814–62) that we can sum up the relation of a whole society to war. Colt was one of the first spectacular operators of the American industrial system, manipulating popular superstition and the ambiguities of the cultural inheritance to make a personal fortune on a scale more in line with those of the second half of the nineteenth century than of the first. He perfected that tradition of pragmatism and sentimentality in terms of personal profit making. This paternalist industrial boss, lover of women, children and animals, was also a cynical manipulator of mass extermination, innocently providing the tools of murder to the capitalist industrial machines of Europe and America. As a child he had had to live by his wits in the jungle of Jacksonian democracy, suffering the mortification of a family in reduced straits. He survived better than most of the other children. His sister committed suicide, and his brother, an ex-marine who adored military discipline, committed suicide in jail after being convicted of a murder in which he had hacked the body of his victim to pieces and crammed the body, salted, into a packing case. Colt, perhaps craving affection denied as a child, turned showman, and he appeared first in the public eye as Dr Coult, supplying the seemingly inexhaustible appetite of the republic for sensation at a time when anything from phrenology to animal magnetism could provide a nine day wonder. Like Peale and his sons he capitalized especially on magical

[26] A. S. Bolles, *Industrial History of the United States* (1881; reprinted New York 1966) p. 255.

displays of popular science. At one point in his career, Colt's brother John managed the Cincinnati museum, and here Colt, with the sculptor Hiram Powers, put on nightly a firework spectacle called 'the infernal regions',—Colt providing the fireworks and Powers the puppets. Dr Coult's own speciality was a 'gas act' in which he invited volunteers to inhale nitrous oxide (laughing gas) which is an addictive hallucinatory drug. Between stage and audience he placed a rope net, a more formidable barrier than the proscenium arch in its power to separate audience from actor, and reality from dream. But with the additional illusion of security, the dream too could be nearer the crazy heart of the fantasies of the audience. Once he gave laughing gas to six Indians, while his audience clutched pocket derringers in vicarious excitement. The Indians went peacefully to sleep, however, and it was left to an hallucinating blacksmith to knock the Indians off their chairs, chase Colt round the edge of his own safety net and provide the evening's excitement.[27]

Colt understood very clearly the psychology of action at a distance. The showman-salesman's technique, like that of the politician, is to rouse fears, exaggerate them, and then provide reassurance at the critical moment. As well as knowing Hiram Powers the sculptor, Colt was also the friend of Samuel Morse. In the late forties Dr Coult turned into Colonel Colt (thus demonstrating the easy interchangeability of academic and military titles as icons of popular status) and he provided Morse with waterproof underground cable of his own invention. Colt was also one of the first to suggest that the telegraph would make war operations more efficient. Putting together his knowledge of the galvanic battery and of gunpowder, Colonel Colt created a name in military circles for himself by successfully blowing up ships with 'submarine' batteries. It was the perfect kill at a distance and a great public spectacle for the crowds who lined the New Jersey and New York shore lines. After such a display of pragmatic action came sentiment, and on one occasion Colt was invited into President Tyler's yacht to be presented with a bouquet of flowers by the president's small daughter. The flowers were found pressed in a scrapbook after his death.

Colt's real achievement, however, was not to provide public fantasies of security, but possibilities for self-defence and private murder. An American named Shaw had thought of the percussion cap in 1817, and Colt put this idea together with the Whitney and Hall innovations of machine-turned, interchangeable parts and mass

---

[27] For most of this information I am indebted to Jack Rohan, *Yankee Arms Maker; the incredible career of Samuel Colt* (New York and London 1935).

production to ensure the success of his revolver. He had whittled a model of it on a sea voyage as far back as 1835 in wood, and like many another inventor of the industrial revolution, sought means to turn his wooden artefact into iron. The gun itself is essentially an assembly line of bullets in the round, with a regular and consistent output. It was first used against Seminole Indians in 1837, and frontier-hardened Texans were among the first buyers. Colt was in deep financial trouble when the Mexican War broke out giving him his first order from the government. Colt had no plant, so he contracted with Eli Whitney, Jr, to turn out most of the parts, cheating him fairly substantially in the process. By 1859, however, just before the Civil War, he had his own plant worth over a million dollars, and was manufacturing 60,000 weapons a year. His factory was the perfect model of an Adam Smith dream, with every workman handling one part of the production process only. Machines stamped out interchangeable parts with accuracy, and benevolent paternalism bribed employees into the business and kept them there. He provided pensions, a ten hour day, washing facilities, entertainment and a community centre with books and visiting lecturers. Colt was fond of music but his own workmen, strangely, had little talent for it. Consequently he imported a whole community of willow workers from a village near Potsdam in Germany, recreated their village, persuaded them to abandon their traditional crafts for more modern methods and was soon underselling the cane chair market as far away as the Mississippi. The German workers were musical and Colt's band soon became famous. Colt had imported not genre pictures but a 'genre happening' to satisfy desires for 'art' and rural peace in his private industrial city. The great fantasy reward for the years of labour and self-sacrifice was his home and the industrial estate itself. Like Jefferson's university, like West Point, Colt's home at Armsmear (the very word a conjunction of war and peace, industry and rural dream) is an important cultural artefact of the young American republic.

The way Colt laid out and created his private world is best read in a rare memorial volume of 1866, by one Henry Barnard, *Armsmear: the House, the arm and the armory of Samuel Colt*. The gardens round the house are a compendium of many styles. Contrary to the stiff linear lay-out of factory and workers' houses, there is not a single straight line to be observed here. The house itself was, appropriately, like a modern city, constantly being torn down and rebuilt, illustrating a life devoted to constant progress and productivity rather than satisfaction and stable achievement. Since all cultures could be bought, the result was an homogenization of effect through infinite purchasing power. Italian towers competed with oriental domes and glass conservatories. Every available wooden eave or overhang was pretentiously ornamented. Octagon, square and circle lay in uneasy mid-Victorian balance. At the entrance to the house, and guarding the gateway were two Uffizzi dogs copied in Carrara marble. In what Barnard calls 'pleasure gardens' were scattered Grecian urns, rustic bridges, statues of Hebe and Apollo, and a monstrous artefact by a German sculptor called 'Kiss's Amazon' [sic]. There were huge greenhouses and hothouses in which grapes, figs and other fruit were grown in enormous quantities. Colt was especially proud that he could have strawberries in February. The conservatory, which Barnard likens to Kubla Khan's pleasure dome, is best presented in the original to give some flavour of the breathlessly sycophantic style:

> It is composed of glass panels—each usually two yards long, set in frames of iron fashioned into foliate arches. Some of them are red, yellow, and violet. At each corner is a sort of minaret, while the centre rises in a dome capped with a golden pine-apple, as well as flanked on each side by two domelets.
>
> Beneath the central dome and in the midst of the central front, a bronze Triton, upward man and downward fish, blows up a triple waterjet on high, which sparkles into rainbows in the sun beams, and drops in diamonds into an ample laver, freshening it for the gold fish who gambol on the gravel or lurk beneath the sea-god.[28]

As we shall see in the final chapter, the dream of the pleasure garden complements the dream of the war outside the boundary. Even Kosciusko had one made for himself inside Fort Clinton. As Barnard comments, 'in the process of civilization, originated the art of pleasure gardening'.[29] From his home, Colt could survey the whole of his Gatsby-like dream. The garden sculpture is entirely academic, most of it was reproduction of classical sculpture. Kiss's Amazon depicts the barebreasted Amazon hurling a javelin at 'a panther that has caught her steed's neck in his massive jaws'.[30] The phallic-mother, as Brown has shown,[31] is the supreme icon of state power, but also, in the art of sentiment, power is symbolically given to those who are most denied it. The panther, too, symbolizes the forces of barbarism; horse, rider and *arm*, represent the progress of civilization. At the heart of the landscape was the 'grove of graves' where Colt

---

[28] Henry Barnard, *Armsmear: the home, the arm and the armory of Samuel Colt* (New York 1866) p. 88.
[29] Ibid., p. 90.
[30] Ibid., p. 164.
[31] See Norman O. Brown, *Love's Body*, chapter VII, 'Head'.

himself was buried, and which contained the lavish memorials to Colt's prematurely dead offspring. In the house, as if in counter-balance, are the memorials of his industrial offspring; gifts from the sultan of Turkey, from the czars of Russia, from King Albert of Sardinia, medals of honour from the London Institute of Engineers, from the American Institute, from the Great Exhibition of 1851, from the French exposition of 1855, from Victor Emmanuel and from the kings of Siam.

For the site of his factory Colt even made his own land, by build-ing a dyke against the flooding of the Connecticut river. The severe lay-out of the factory is ornamented by a dome in 'moorish manner . . . on which a colt is rampant, as it were triumphing over the world'.[32] The lower portion of the building is 'not unlike the lower story [sic] of the Pitti palace, in Florence'.[33] Power was supplied by a steam engine with a wheel 100 feet in circumference. Barnard further comments that the organization of the shops exhibited 'one of the best illustrations a political economist could desire of the division of labour'.[34] He continues to enumerate the advantages, drawing heavily on Mill and Adam Smith, and concludes:

> We may perhaps add, as a fifth advantage of dividing labour, that it opens a door of occupation to all. If all members in the body politic have not the same office, yet all members have an office, and that the best one suited to them. The hand cannot say to the foot, 'I have no need of thee'.[35]

As in Palladio, the doctrines of St Paul are dragged in to sanction the form of civil space. Barnard also pushes Palladio's philosophy of the circle (which complemented the New Testament texts in the architect's theories) to extravagant lengths. Circular movement becomes a figure of work out-put:

> Rotation is the law, and the law of its production. From the huge fly-wheel of the engine, rolling half a mile in a minute, to the tiniest circlet of leather for polishing; in all apartments even in the attics; beneath all ceilings, in all machines, you are reminded of Eziekiel's vision of wheel on wheel, and wheel in the middle of a wheel. Rotation pervades the products and the producing processes, as in certain monasteries the cross is repeated till you behold it on every bell-pull, the panels and handles of every door . . ... Amid so many wheels, all revolving, and that to produce revolvers, what a maddening position were it for the conservative

---

[32] Barnard, *Armsmear*, p. 210.
[33] Ibid.
[34] Ibid., p. 215.
[35] Ibid., p. 218.

Italian, who had such a horror of political revolutions that he refused to believe in the revolution of the earth.[36]

This is the philosophy of the material heaven of the mid-nineteenth-century industrialist. The law of nature disguised as a revolutionary law in the most absurd sense, masks the destructive nature of the product and process, and is literally turned into a metaphysical principle. Colt's career, his factory and his product show the active extension into reality of every principle of the American Revolution; order at the expense of dissent, law at the expense of freedom, stability at the expense of imagination and risk, a classical tradition at the expense of new forms of social living, a worship of the machine at the expense of society, a grotesque sentimentality at the expense of genuine life forms and a worship of death as an overall sanctioning metaphysic.

And yet there was not wanting in mid-nineteenth-century America criticism of the very processes Barnard describes in Colt's factory. Melville uses similar types of images in his own work, but they are directed to very different ends. As a convenient illustration of the receiving end of the war production process, we have in *Israel Potter* Melville's own description of the split functions of men organized about a war machine. The sociometaphysical implications are critical, however, not eulogistic:

> Stooping low and intent, with one braced leg thrust behind, and one arm thrust forward, curling round toward the muzzel of the gun, there was seen the *loader,* performing his allotted part; on the other side of the carriage in the same stooping posture, but with both hands holding his long black pole, pike-wise, ready for instant use, stood the eager *rammer-and-sponger;* while at the breech, crouched the wary *captain of the gun,* his keen eye, like the watching leopard's burning along the range; and behind all, tall and erect, the Egyptian symbol of death, stood the *match-man,* immovable for the moment, his long-handled match reversed. Up to their two long, death dealing batteries, the trained men of the *Serapis* stood and toiled in mechanical magic of discipline. They tended those rows of guns, as Lowell girls the rows of looms in a cotton factory. The Parcae were not more methodical; Atropos not more fatal; the automaton chess player not more irresponsible.[37]

Melville was to write a few years later about the Lowell factory girls in his short story, *The Tartarus of Maids,* where he used the model of gestation and birth as an ironic framework for parodying the inhumanities of machine production. In spite of the fact that the description quoted above occurs in the middle of a battle, the

[36] Ibid., pp. 220–1.
[37] Herman Melville, *Israel Potter, Works* (London 1921–2) pp. 168–9.

overall movement of the figures seem as static as a mid-Victorian diorama. The abased positions of loader, rammer-and-sponger, and captain of the gun gives a clue to their religious functions in the performance of a ritual with specialized and therefore dehumanized roles. Their uncomfortable positions show the effect on a human body required to conform to the totality of the body of the machine. The references to the 'Egyptian symbol of death', the Parcae and Atropos show how the new gods of the machine serve the old socioreligious functions. Melville is clearly aware that they have essentially magical functions. Of the numerous Egyptian gods of death (Anubis, Khent-Amentin, Sed, Wepwawet, Osiris) Melville is probably thinking of Osiris who, in the nineteenth century, was popularly known as the Egyptian god of death. The long-handled match which Melville describes, in Egyptian pictures symbolizes fertility. The irony is obvious. In terms of the war machine images of fertility turn into images of death. The reference to the Lowell girls reminds Melville of the spinning fates, and of Atropos, one of the three daughters of night, representing, according to Hesiod, the fate that cannot be avoided. In his famous *Dictionary of Greek and Roman Biography and Mythology* (London 1846), William Smith states that these three 'were represented by the earliest artists with staffs or sceptres . . .'.[38] Edgar Allan Poe provides a comment on Melville's reference to the 'automaton chess player' when he observes in his short story of that name that it was '*a pure machine*, unconnected with human agency in its movements, and consequently, beyond all comparison, the most astonishing of the inventions of mankind'.[39] Melville's gun, with its religious attendants, articulates the hell of what he calls the 'mechanical magic of discipline'.

The reaction to war in literature and in the visual arts is a complex one. In literature, whenever writers felt the need to create an *American* literature they were exposed to the ambiguities of nationalist sentiment, and few stepped back from the expansionist fever of these early decades. In the visual arts, the inheritance was extremely conservative, but photography was fully developed before the Civil War, and its effect was rapidly to sober enthusiasm for the old values of military glory and fantasies of combat. In the successive official wars, however, writer and illustrator alike give us some

[38] William Smith, *Dictionary of Greek and Roman Biography and Mythology* (London 1846) p. 1110.
[39] Edgar Allan Poe, *Works* (London 1895) vol. VI, p. 1.

understanding of the way Americans reacted to 'the art of war'—
the other half of the cultural dialectic.

The moment of success was celebrated by poet and painter alike.
In England, Blake, in a vision which defined revolution as personal
and sexual liberation, prophesied the end of priesthood and law. In
his *America: A Prophecy* (1793) boundaries dissolved for ever, and
the delights of uninhibited sexuality burst the 'stony roof' of the
Ten Commandments. Blake's hopes for the true American revolution, however, remain unfulfilled. But in Europe, in the nineties,
the American, and erstwhile poet in the 'Connecticut Wit' circle,
Joel Barlow (1754—1812) was rapidly assimilating the ideas of the
English radicals such as William Godwin and Thomas Paine. His
writing in the famous *Advice to the Privileged Orders* (1792—3)
is one of those few American syntheses of revolutionary thought
which assimilated the ideas of the early years of the French
Revolution. He adapted the metaphor of the planetary system to the
dispersal of power equally throughout the social system: 'We
perceive no exertion of power in the motion of the planetary system,
but a very strong one in the movement of a whirlwind; it is because
we see obstructions to the latter, but none to the former'.[40] For
Barlow war was the disease of aristocracy; and it was an opinion
shared by many Americans at this time:

> . . . the nobility of Europe, are always fed upon human gore. They
> originated in war, they live by war, and without war it would be impos-
> sible to keep them from starving.[41]

The whole nationalist war game of calculating success by comparison
of losses revolted him and was 'a stratagem of government, a
calculation of cabinet arithmetic'.[42] Barlow attempts to get to the
roots of conflict in human psychology. He understands the presence
of 'political superstition' as well as the religious variety.[43] In this
connection he speaks of the desire for property as a psychological
illness. It is substituted for the development of personal talents, it is
the origin of violence, it becomes an engine to be manipulated in the
hands of government, and the exterior pomp of its possession replaces a real enjoyment of life. In addition he attacks new developments in economic life. The 'funding system' (the creation of arti-

---

[40] Joel Barlow, *Advice to the Privileged Orders. . . .* (New York, part I, 1792, part II,
1793) part I, p. 25. See William K. Bottkorff and Arthur L. Ford, eds, *The works of Joel
Barlow* (Gainesville, Fla. 1970), vol. I, p. 117. Page numbers of this edition are hereafter
parenthesized, following page number of the original edition.

[41] Ibid., part I, p. 61 (vol. I, p. 153).

[42] Ibid., part I, p. 65 (vol. I, p. 157).

[43] Ibid., part I, p. 74 (vol. I, p. 166).

ficial debt to stimulate trade, with the development of the stocks and shares system) he claims 'has converted commerce into a weapon of war'.[44] The kinds of emotions engendered by its operations he says have 'taken [the] place of religious enthusiasm'.[45] Barlow's Jeffersonian agrarianism was not proof against the new money systems being rapidly developed in the new republic. Nonetheless he understood the political implications of the changes as few others did. He fought hard to avoid war with France in the late nineties and he campaigned against 'the rage for a navy'.[46] He was loathed by Washington and Hamilton and his *National Gazette* (1791—3) vigorously opposed the conservative *Gazette of the United States* which represented the business interests.

Barlow's poem *The Columbiad* (final version published in 1825) is the first of many attempts in American poetry, to create a total poetic system of national life and history. His first attempt at the poem was published in 1787 and dedicated to Louis XVI. It was called *The Vision of Columbus*. In terms of literary form it attempts to adapt Miltonic epic to the exigencies of the rhyming couplet, with often disastrous results. Its place historically is interesting, and its development follows the changing ideas of Barlow from the elegant littérateur of the Connecticut Wit to the radical of later life.[47] Just as the Archangel Michael shows Adam the future of the world in book XI of *Paradise Lost*, so Columbus is shown the future prospects of the discovery and settlement of America. The form follows the pattern of current political geographies, beginning with natural description, then the effect of climate on character, then the history of a representative hero (here Manco Capac giving laws to the Incas) and ends with a brief history of the Renaissance and the wars of the Revolution. The final vision, after the battles, is one of permanent peace founded upon government established according to nature.

In the preface to the final version, Barlow attacked the eulogies to martial exploits which he found in the work of the traditional epic writers such as Homer and Vergil. The balance of the poem's interest has shifted to the goal of liberty and to a condemnation of violence and war. Barlow has the nearly impossible task of trying to recreate poetry outside the political assumptions of the literary inheritance. Modern warfare, he writes, does not supply instances of single armed combat, though it has the 'advantage' of more

[44] Ibid., part II, p. 79 (vol. I, p. 289).
[45] Ibid., part II, p. 88 (vol. I, p. 298).
[46] Joel Barlow, *Two Letters to the Citizens of the United States. . . .* (New Haven, Conn. 1806) p. 28 (vol. I, p. 386).
[47] See introduction to Bottkorff and Ford, *The Works of Joel Barlow*, vol. I, p. xiv.

generalized shock, 'more sonorous and more discoloring to the face of nature, than the ancient could have been'.[48] Barlow explains, however, his poetic licence with some of the facts of the conflicts he describes 'being meant to increase our natural horror for the havoc and miseries of war in general'.[49]

It is interesting to compare two versions of one of the battle scenes, the one composed for the 1787 edition, the second in the final version. The fight described is the battle between two warships, beginning a tradition of describing these fighting machines at sea which is the single most important kind of warfare in the public imagination up to and including the Civil War. The first version is quite short, and ends.

> Here, shatter'd barks in squadrons move afar,
> Lead thro the smoke, armed struggling from the war;
> While hulls half-seen, beneath a gaping wave,
> And plunging heroes fill the watery grave.

and the second version:

> Hither two hostile ships to contact run,
> Both grappling, board to board and gun to gun;
> Each thro the adverse ports their contents pour,
> Rake the lower decks, the interior timbers bare,
> Drive into chinks the illumined wads unseen,
> Whose flames approach the ungarded magazine.
> Above with shrouds afoul and gunwales mann'd,
> Thick halberds clash; and closing hand to hand,
> The huddling troops infuriate from despair
> Try at the toils of death and perish there;
> Grenados, carcasses their fragments spread,
> And pikes and pistols strew the decks with dead.[50]

The first version draws on the stock imagery of eighteenth-century poetry. Here are the kinds of double epithets which Wordsworth was to condemn in the *Preface to the Lyrical Ballads*; gaping wave, plunging heroes, watery grave. The action is also removed to the distance, and generalized, fulfilling more the requirements of the heroic simile than the more visually detailed needs of the second version. Paine's call for a more realistic drama has been partially answered in the second version. The description is still generalized

---

[48] Joel Barlow, *The Columbiad* (Washington City [sic] 1825), preface p. xvi (vol. II p. 386).

[49] Ibid., p. xiv, (vol. II, p. 384).

[50] First version, *The Vision of Columbus*, Bk VI, p. 193 (vol. II, p. 293). Second version, *The Columbiad*, Bk VII, pp. 248–9 (vol. I, pp. 666–7).

but in a different way. The first passage seeks to realize an effect
by relying on conventional connotations, the second builds more
out of particulars, particularly those of a factual detailed kind, to
establish general credibility. To be sure there is no radical change in
the pattern, indeed there could not be, given the strict form of the
heroic couplet, but there are a few changes which indicate a shift
of direction in the revised passage. Here *barks* are replaced by
ships, heroes replaced by *troops.* There is a suggestion of new
clarity, both visual and philosophical. The details create the sense
of overriding destiny. 'The illumined wads' are of human manufacture
and intimate the sense of final destruction. There is a grim irony in
the equation of fragments from a grenade with human fragments
and a specialized knowledge of naval warfare makes the movement
of the description more credible.

Again in the 1790s another American poet, Philip Freneau, was
questioning the role of war in a democratic society. In England in
the same decade anti-war poems began to be produced in greater
numbers. Coleridge wrote *Fears in Solitude* and on a more popular
level Charles Dibdin wrote *Jack's Gratitude* which described, among
other things his experiences in a French prison. During the Revolutionary War, Freneau had been imprisoned in an English prison ship.
His biographer records that it was an experience which made a
profound impression on him. He was one of the few poets to have
actual first-hand experience of battle, and of the horrors of
imprisonment.

> . . . the sick were deluged with every shower of rain. Between decks they
> lay along struggling in the agonies of death; dying with putrid and bilious
> fevers; lamenting their hard fate to die at such a fatal distance from their
> friends; others, totally insensible, and yielding their last breath in all the
> horrors of light-headed frenzy.[51]

Like Barlow, Freneau contemplated with horror the rising anti-
French war fever. In a poem called the *War Patrons,* he contemplated
the failing belief in war as an aristocratic prerogative:

> Ye rising race, consider well
> What has been read, or what we tell.
> From Wars all regal mischiefs flow,
> And Kings make wars a raree-sho,
> A business to their post assign'd
> To torture, damn, enslave mankind.
> For this, of old, did priests anoint'em,
> Be ours the task to disappoint them.[52]

[51] Lewis Leary, *That Rascal Freneau, A Study in Literary Failure* (New York 1964) p. 83.
[52] *Poems of Philip Freneau* (Princeton, N.J. 1907) vol. III, p. 210.

Here, however, the old oppressors are recalled in order to revive a sense of disappearing radicalism.

In spite of the fact that popular sentiment was opposed to 'Battle Pieces', the first well-known achievements of American painting were in precisely this genre. In London, the Philadelphia-born Quaker, Benjamin West, created a new type of battle piece. Drawing on the French artists of the late seventeenth century, particularly Poussin, West selected incidents from recent history, instead of from the classics, to create a style which was to reach its apogee in the canvases of David and Géricault. West's early picture *The Death of Wolfe*, (1771–2) **pl. 16** widely reproduced in engravings, became the archetype for thousands of imitators in every visual medium.

16 *The Death of Wolfe* by Benjamin West (*Courtesy of the National Gallery of Canada, Ottawa, Gift of the Duke of Westminster, 1918.*)

The iconography is interesting, for the force of the picture is essentially literary, and in spite of the apparent realism—the contemporary uniforms and the drawing in of the Indian for the seated figure—the effect is that of a kind of natural symbolism. Instead of extraterrestrial angels, the division of the skyscape into light and dark gives the picture a metaphysical reference. Victory is pre-

destined, as the dark clouds give way to the light. The figure groupings follow Renaissance geometrical patterns, and the pose of the
dying Wolfe is akin to that of a *Deposition from the Cross* position.
The effects of war are simply to provide a background, illustrating
the reasons for the death of the hero. The sun acts as theatrical
spotlight to pick out the chief actor. In literary terms, the Indian is
the new classical figure, the stoic contemplating, with equal serenity,
life and death. The pose is the guide to the political intention. The
details of costume, of equipment and even tattooing were carefully
studied by West, and generalized into the total structure. The way
they are painted follows more the conventions of indoor portraiture
than of a representation of real battles so the 'realism' is a combination of classical and Christian iconography. Wolfe's death is a
sacred one, a kind of atonement in which the leader figure offers
his life sacrificially for the sake of the people.

Such themes in academic art were taken up by American painters
visiting West's studio in London. John Trumbull (1756—1843)
arrived in London first in 1780 where he was arrested as a reprisal
for the hanging of Major André, and then in 1784 became an apt
pupil of West's in following the 'historical style'. He particularly
wanted to create a historical record of the American Revolution
and actually consulted both Jefferson and John Adams on the kinds
of subjects he should paint. One of Trumbull's best historical paintings of war is *The Battle of Bunker's Hill*, pl. 17 painted in London
in 1786. It is a small canvas 25 by 34 inches, and in order to bring
out some of its more individual characteristics, it is instructive to
compare it with another ex-patriot American painting, the enormous
The Death of Major Peirson (1783) pl. 18 by Copley. The difference
in size is important. Trumbull wanted his paintings to be engraved
immediately and the small picture is more easily transferable.
Copley's picture needed a public gallery or Palladian country house
to hang in. By comparing the result of loyalist and revolutionary
attitudes to war as exhibited by these paintings there are some
interesting conclusions to be drawn.

Apart from the theme the two pictures have certain elements in
common. In both the main body of the troops is defined in a loosely
formed parallelogram. In both there is a side group which offsets it,
and a black figure. The differences are, however, even more important.
In Copley's picture the fighting takes place within a civil context
defined by the theatrical set of elegant eighteenth-century houses
with their connotations of order, restraint and civic decency. The
conflict therefore poses a threat to that order. In addition the painting of the group of figures around the fallen hero exhibits a collec-

17 *The Battle of Bunker's Hill,* 1786, by John Trumbull. (*Courtesy of Yale University Art Gallery, New Haven, Connecticut.*)

18 *The Death of Major Peirson,* 1783, by John Singleton Copley. (*Courtesy of the Tate Gallery, London.*)

tive response to the death. Much more skilfully than Trumbull, Copley shows tension inside the group. In spite of the common and approved sentimentality of the drummer boy's farewell to his dying hero, there are, in this picture of war, elements which point to the futility of conflict. The opposing force also experiences the death of a leader showing a kind of ironic balance in fortunes. The main light falls not on the wounded hero but on the family group, specifically on the baby. Copley's masterly technique in family portraits takes a new direction here. The superb handling of their costumes and the soldiers' uniforms points to an assumption implicit in the contrast of absolute divisions of war and peace, played off against each other for dramatic effect. The pose of the older girl is also suitably theatrical, but the gaze of the small child directed right out of the picture at the hypothetical painter gives an immediacy of effect one would associate more with a contemporary news picture than an act in the conventional theatre. The overall sense of uncertainty is increased by the sharply rising hill in the background as the town is destroyed from without as well as from within. In spite of the conventions, and the sense of threat to order keenly felt by this expatriate loyalist, Copley's picture manipulates that sense of three-dimensional linear theatricality, the perceptual mode of the middle classes, into perhaps the best analysis of war that is possible within the confines of this particular style.

Whereas Copley's picture has that large confident sense of the eternal verities inherent in the politically conservative character, Trumbull's small canvas gives us a sense of a tight introspective, almost psychological intuition of destiny. Trumbull has taken the conventions out of the theatre with the intention of making them more real. Hence there is no civil reference and the main light falls again on the dying hero. The figures are painted less distinctly, and form a more homogenous movement with the movement of the flags and the whirl of the clouds. There is far more of a suggestion of the convergence of history and nature in one destiny. Although his situation in London caused Trumbull to paint this picture of American reversals, the Americans retreat with gestures of defiance. The Americans are nearly all in civil dress. Lieutenant Grosvenor with his black servant threatens with the elegant gestures of a French fencing master, complete with lace and feathered hat. Major Knowlton, on the other hand is much more representative of the average upstanding American, bareheaded, coatless, and with his carbine still in his hand. Although the death of the hero theme is common to both pictures, there seems less overall attention focused on General Warren, than on Major Peirson in the respective pictures.

There is more a sense of superhuman forces in Trumbull's picture where a corporate destiny overrides individual fates. Trumbull's picture seems more American, there seems less distinction between civil and military action, he has taken the action out of doors in a way which seems more significant than the actual fact of the situation. Conflict is at once more personal and more general, and yet the distinction is not to be seen in conventional leader and corps terms as it is in Copley's picture. This seems all the more remarkable for these pictures were generally seen as an opportunity to gather portraits of famous soldiers into one representative action.

First-hand accounts of the battles of the Revolution and of the succeeding years are rare. But in military-academy style there are a number of panoramas and topographical views of not very distinguished quality. Christian Rennich painted panoramas in watercolour of the arrival of British troops in Boston harbour, Amos Doolittle, a well-known map maker, made engravings of the Battle of Lexington and views of the troops in Concord; Bernard Romans, the Dutch natural historian, painted a view of the Battle of Charleston. English and French watercolourists painted panoramic views of military deployments.

There were many reasons why the Americans went to war with England in 1812. Historians talk of the legacy of hatred from the War of Independence, the mismanagement of actual diplomatic relations, the Indian problems of the Northwest, the restless energies of the men who became known as 'war hawks', second generation politicians like Henry Clay and his followers who, removed from the necessities of establishing national security, bent their energies to exploit American resources to the full. Early in the century, as we have seen, it did not seem obvious that the values of trade were inextricably linked with those of empire, though the naivety on this score was not so rare as this might imply, as some of the speeches of the time show:

> But it is asked, will you go to war for commerce? . . . It is answered, England has been at war for commerce the greatest part of two-hundred years; and shall not the United States protect their commerce, in which is involved the safety of their seamen and the rights of the people?[53]

Expansionist fever was already running high, some twenty years before the official dates set on the phenomenon of Manifest Destiny. In 1812 the editor of the Nashville *Clarion* (28 April 1812) wrote, 'Where is it written in the book of fate that the American republic shall not stretch her limits from the Cape of the Chesapeake to

[53] R. Horsman, *The Causes of the War of 1812* (Philadelphia 1962) p. 231.

Nootka sound, from the isthmus of Panama to Hudson Bay?'[54] A war for commerce meant simply a naval war with Britain. The war ship at the time was the most sophisticated fighting machine devised. It could carry the heaviest guns, its organization exemplified precisely a hierarchical division of labour, it was a society of men subject to the most intense discipline. In action unremitting broadsides by entangled ships took a horrific toll in killed and maimed.

From Barlow to Melville, the sea fight is one of the most popular of literary subjects. In 1850 Melville wrote in his novel *White Jacket* of the relations between military organization and democratic thought, but without, however, describing a single battle. The book specifically attacks the hierarchical nature of power in the navy, as contrasted with civilian rights in America, and the degradation of the individual morally, sexually and physically in what Melville called 'wooden-walled Gomorrahs of the deeps'. We have already seen, in Barlow's revised poem, how the poet moves from a some-what generalized panoramic view of battle to one more personalized and detailed. The same claim is made for James Fenimore Cooper by his critics, and it is suggested that in, for example, *Afloat and Ashore* (1844), a more involved personal view of battle by a partici-pating actor substitutes for the panoramic sense.[55] While this is to some extent true, Cooper never loses sight of his overall, almost Manichean view of nature, alternately and endlessly in states of war and peace. Also the frequent indefiniteness of the action distances the literary spectator. Whether consciously or unconsciously, Burke's association of indefiniteness with sublimity is followed to the letter. Just as the details of Trumbull's battle scenes become fused in one natural historical action, so Cooper's battle scenes suggest a war in nature. In the earlier *Red Rover* (1827), Cooper describes a sea battle between the *Dart* and the *Dolphin.* It begins 'in the midst of a scene of broad and bright tranquility', [56] and ends with a terrifying squall. The particulars of the main action are deliberately indistinct:

> Hulls, spars, and sails were alike enveloped in the curling wreaths which wrapped heaven, air, vessels, and ocean, alike, in one white, obscure, foggy mantle. Even the persons of the crew were merely seen at instants, laboring at the guns, through brief and varying openings.[57]

Hence Cooper uses nature in two ways. First to point out its in-

---

[54] Quoted in J. W. Pratt, *Expansionists of 1812* (Gloucester, Mass, 1957) p. 14.

[55] See Thomas Philbrick, *Cooper and the Development of American Sea Fiction* (Cambridge, Mass. 1961) p. 149.

[56] James Fenimore Cooper, *The Red Rover* (1827; reprinted New York 1895–6) p. 435.

[57] Ibid., p. 436.

difference in the traditional sense to the affairs of history (rejecting the pathetic fallacy) and second to suggest, like the landscape in the traditional Romantic portrait, a permanent conflict in nature which becomes an extension of a similar conflict in society. The critics' claim that Cooper moves from *romance* to *realism* is so general as scarcely to give a good account of the distinction preferred, and nowhere in Cooper's novels does the point of view of the victim refute the generalized purposes of a superior class or an overriding destiny. The Boston painter Washington Allston felt himself unable to vie in painting with Cooper's battle scenes and gave this as his reason, unlike Trumbull, for not undertaking commissions offered to him for the Rotunda. In fact, however, he felt them to be immoral. In Cooper's fictional battles, visual distinctness, light, individually observed objects and the near view are played off dramatically against obscurity, darkness and the panoramic view-point, and effect is both to show futility and the sense of a per-manent division in nature. Even in his writing Cooper was divided. On the one hand he could write a competent factual history of the United States navy, and on the other, fictional accounts of battle.[58] The fact that one was fiction and the other was fact enabled him to separate reality from moral judgement and keep the separate prov-inces from impingeing on each other.

It is interesting to compare with Cooper's sea battles the work of an outstanding American marine painter who illustrated some of the naval events of the War of 1812. The chief subject for Thomas Birch (1779–1851) was the duel between frigates at sea in which the Americans, apart from the *Shannon-Chesapeake* fight, had been very successful. Birch overcame the limitations of a painting's ability to show only one moment in time by, like Hogarth, creating a num-ber of canvases of the same event at different times. Birch's pictures had news value and were widely reproduced in engravings. The originals, however, are most interesting. Unlike his contem-poraries who, for the most part, etched elegant ships in mathemati-cally precise waves against clear wash skies, Birch outlined the hulks of the defeated vessels, black and awkward against dark, troubled seas. In the example reproduced pl. 19, the artist delineates two ships, with their rigging above, their hulls below the horizon, mediating sky and ocean. Birch exploits the dualism of light and dark, order and chaos in the contrast of sea and sky, rounding out the details of his subject with a more general metaphysic. The sails of the ships reflect light from the sky, and the hulls of the vessels take on the colour of the darker water.

[58] James Fenimore Cooper, *History of the Navy of the United States* (1834).

19 *The 'Wasp' and the 'Frolic'*, 1820, by Thomas Birch. (*Courtesy of the Museum of Fine Arts, Boston, M. and M. Karolik Collection.*)

The most complex treatment of the duel of ships at sea, drawing on the descriptive devices of panorama and near view, the paradoxes of traditional and democratic military attitudes, the problems of generalization and detail, the chivalric and commercial ethics of war, and the metaphysicoliterary contrasts of clarity and indistinctness, is to be found in Melville's fictional reconstruction of the fight between the *Serapis* and the *Richard* during the battle of the Revolution, in his short and minor novel *Israel Potter* (1855). The description is intended to counter that 'rage for a navy' which Barlow talked about and which received such an impetus in the War of 1812. Like Cooper, Melville begins with the landscape and gradually narrows his field of vision. First however he establishes ironically the popular attitudes to such conflicts:

> All is clear, open fluent. The very element which sustains the combatants, yields at the stroke of a feather. One wind and one tide at one time operate upon all who here engage. This simplicity renders a battle between two men-of-war, with their huge white wings, more akin to the Miltonic contests of archangels than to the *comparatively* squalid tussels of earth.[59]

The contradictory connotations of the conventional dualism serve

---

[59] Melville, *Israel Potter*, p. 161.

to criticize their absoluteness. Clarity is as dangerous as obscurity and is associated paradoxically not with reason but with religion. The panoramic view and the oneness of nature so observed threatens death rather than wholeness of life. Having begun with an ironic metaphysic, Melville describes a landscape which turns quickly into a dark, and threatening nightmare:

> It is in course of incessant decay. Every year the isle which repulses nearly all other foes, succumbs to the Attila assaults of the deep. Here and there the base of the cliffs is strewn with masses of rock, undermined by the waves, and tumbled headlong below, where, sometimes, the water completely surrounds them, showing in shattered confusion detached rocks, pyramids and obelisks, rising half-revealed from the surf—the Tadmores of the wasteful desert of the sea.[60]

Whereas the new vision of open clarity turns out to have the deceptive connotations of ancient religion, the older darker vision here parodies the concept of stable civilization which was the dream of the eighteenth-century philosophers. The cult of ruins accompanied the progressive ethic of civilization. Here nature is compared with the barbarian without the walls of the Roman state, and in an analogy we shall become more familiar with below, the ruined rocks of the natural landscape are equated with the ruins of the architecture of civilization. This is the landscape which illustrates the unconscious mentality of the men engaged in combat on both sides. Melville also makes much of the change of name of the American ship from the *Duras* to *Bon Homme Richard*. In the traditional Melvillian way the ship becomes the microcosm of American society. Here it is endowed with Franklinesque values: '*Poor Richard* shall be the name, in honour to the saying, that "God helps them that helps themselves" . . .'.[61] The captain, the famous pirate, John Paul Jones, as the head of the society, takes on a national character, 'civilized in externals but a savage at heart, America is, or may yet be, the Paul Jones of nations'.[62] As the fight progresses the original clarity of the scene gives way to mist and fog. Melville's main achievement is to parody those violently maintained boundaries which make for national distinctions. Again and again in the description he emphasizes the indistinguishableness of the two ships with the common grave between:

> It was a co-partnership and joint-stock combustion-company of both ships—yet divided, even in participation. The two vessels were as two

---

[60] Ibid., p. 159.
[61] Ibid., p. 153.
[62] Ibid., p. 158.

houses, through whose party-wall doors have been cut; one family (the Guelphs) occupying the whole lower story; another family (the Ghibelines) the whole upper story.[63]

Melville's image of the two-family house engaged in business articulates the origins of war psychologically and economically. Melville instinctively saw that incorporation was a death-like process, that family boundary was family feud. The smoke of battle created by the civilizations at war parallels the mist of the natural landscape. It indicates the secrecy involved in the authoritarian process of division. That such a process is hell-fired is evident in the typical Melvillian description. In the end it is the smoke which prevents the cease-fire being immediate. The upper decks are at peace, the lower maintain fire. This parallels the actual misunderstanding of diplomatic exchanges when the War of 1812 was declared. The boundaries have all become mixed up in the smoke, so have friends and allies. Melville ends the chapter with a question about division: 'What separates the enlightened man from the savage? Is civilization a thing distinct, or is it an advanced stage of barbarism?'[64] The answer is rhetorically no. The official divisions are ways of killing people. Between the two ships 'that boundary abyss was the jaws of death to both sides'.[65] Although Melville's instinct, as a man living in the nineteenth century, was to see the cultural process as a religiocosmic one, his own images indicate a personal dissent from the war-sick fantasies of normal civilization in which formation of character through boundary sanctions violently maintained power. The duel of ships at sea is not for Melville, as it was perhaps more simply for Cooper and Birch, an illustration of some eternal fact of human nature, but rather a result of a precise social and cultural condition.

With the Mexican War (1846–8) Americans found themselves engaged in the biggest military operations since the War of Independence. It was, perhaps, the first popular war which employed all the mass-psychological means of persuasion we are accustomed to in our own time. The popular press, aided by the telegraph, kept public fever at boiling point, magazine articles and popular prints sanctioned the naked aggression. Although historians assign numerous causes to the war such as the conspiracy of the slaveocracy, the commercial interests of the New England merchants, 'Manifest Destiny', or the 'character of Polk', many Americans felt, generally proudly, that it

[63] Ibid., p. 167.
[64] Ibid., p. 173.
[65] Ibid., p. 165.

was inevitable, and that it was a 'logical' extension of American interests. H. H. Bancroft, in his famous *History of Mexico* (1824—61), however, had few doubts: 'It was a premeditated and predetermined affair, the war of the United States on Mexico; it was the result of a deliberately calculated scheme of robber on the part of the superior power'.[66] After the war a new phenomenon of large, lavish pictorial histories appeared, following the original example of America's first patriot, pictorial historian Benson Lossing.[67] As visual and literary justifications they show how far, at the popular level, the principles of Adam Smith had superseded those of a Volney, a Rousseau, or even an Adams or Jefferson. Typical works are John Frost's *Pictorial History of Mexico* (Philadelphia 1848) and George Wilkins Kendall's *The War Between the United States and Mexico Illustrated* (1851). The preface of the former sets the typical 4th of July tone:

> Such a glorious career of successful valour seldom presents itself to the notice of the historian. In many respects this contest is unparalleled in the annals of the world's affairs; and it will for ever hold a conspicuous place on that pillar of glory where the deeds of American freemen are emblazoned for the admiration of mankind.[68]

Frost insets woodcuts on most pages and the frontispiece is a huge fold-out picture of the *Landing of the Troops at Vera Cruz,* indifferently designed and gaudily coloured. The woodcuts, taken as a whole, illustrate a whole range of popular images which define public fantasy about war, and quite racist attitudes toward the Mexicans themselves. Pictures of Mexican human sacrifice, and 'gladitorial sacrifices' articulate the American view of the enemy as savages in need of civilization. The titles of insets in the genre tradition explain themselves: *Drilling for Raw Recruits,* a *Texas Prayer.* Illustrations of more emblematic design appear frequently. In one an American eagle feeds off a dead Mexican, in another America appears as a woman weeping over a shield on which is a portrait of General Walker. Frost's whole career was spent churning out books of like kind (many for children) which fed the most mindless kind of American patriotism. But not all post-war accounts were so inclined to justification of this nature. A. A. Livermore, whose *The War with Mexico Reviewed* came out in 1850, attacked

[66] Quoted in R. E. Ruiz, ed., *The Mexican War: Was it Manifest Destiny?* (New York 1963) p. 85.
[67] See Alexander Davidson Jr, 'How Benson J. Lossing wrote his "Field Books" of the Revolution, the War of 1812 and the Civil War', *Papers of the Bibliographical Society of America,* 32 (1938) pp. 57—64.
[68] John Frost, *Pictorial History of Mexico and the Mexican War* (Philadelphia 1848) p. iv.

the semantics of linear progression and mechanical cause-effect relations which were used to justify exploitation and empire building: 'For history is not so much a chain, as a net work. Its transactions do not obey a law of simple succession, but of intricate combination'.[69] From this point of view, Livermore denounced the concept of destiny and showed up the real motives of greed for land. 'The god Terminus,' he said, 'is an unknown deity in America.'[70] Above all Livermore attacked the semantics of martial rhetoric; those corporate generalizations which are inherent in representational theory of government, which alienate the individual from political involvement and subsume him in the interests of the corps:

> We are accustomed to speak of the late war between Mexico and the United States, as if it were the conflict of two souless generalizations, two historical or geographical bodies, that picked their camp and arrayed their battle one against the other. The terms are *corporate, political,* and *insensible.* Happy indeed were it, if it were the meeting of names on paper, and not of living men in the bloody field.[71]

Throughout his book, Livermore insisted on the relation of the nation's peace-time ideology to war; that relentless drive for land and gold and the fact that 'there is not, probably, a house in the country unless it belong to a Quaker or a Non-resistant, without its sword, pistol, musket, or rifle'.[72] Clearly well read in his own culture Livermore laments that he has not the talent of an Irving 'to picture scenes that would distress you'.[73] And he is a good enough Bostonian to quote Allston's aversion to battle-pieces. Also of interest, for our purposes, is his attack on the visual and literary images of war as they appear in the increasingly powerful mass media:

> This war-literature has circulated through the newspapers and cheap works over the whole land. The lives of victorious generals, the bloody feats of prowess, the histories of battles and sieges, have formed a good part of the reading of the mass of the people, and especially of many young persons, during the three past years . . ... The fine arts have been employed to pamper the love of war, and by pictures and panoramas, to set on fire the blood of youth with the intoxicating passion of martial achievements. The country is full of these things. Every village has its 'views' of battles, and the siege at Vera Cruz, or the charge at Bueno Vista. The eye of youth is taught to sparkle at the sight of a battle piece, before it knows what war is.[74]

[69] A. A. Livermore, *The War with Mexico Reviewed* (Boston 1850) p. 5.
[70] Ibid., p. 12.
[71] Ibid., p. 104.
[72] Ibid., p. 7.
[73] Ibid., p. 119.
[74] Ibid., pp. 227–8.

The panorama, originally used to demonstrate topographical views with correct perspective while avoiding the rigidities of the single vanishing point, and drawn to facilitate geophysical understanding of an area for military purposes, is now used as an agent of propaganda.

The literary record as far as the views of well-known writers of the period are concerned is not noticeably radical, with the exception of Melville and Thoreau. Whittier's *The Angels of Buena Vista* was ostensibly opposed to the war, but, in the poem, old Mexican women give succour to Northern troops, and battle is described with a succinct sense of Northern superiority. The blessings of American civilization are appropriately summed up in a relevant agricultural simile:

> Like a ploughshare in the fallow,
> Through them ploughs the Northern ball.[75]

Although Lowell wrote against the war in *The Biglow Papers* (1848 and 1867), like many others, he saw it primarily as an attempt to extend the slave states. He had no objection to extension as such, and merely thought that the concept of the religious fate of America had been abused, 'it is the manifest destiny of the English race to occupy the whole continent ...'.[76] The albeit somewhat young Whitman was more direct:

> Yes: Mexico must be thoroughly chastized! ... What has miserable, inefficient Mexico—with her superstition, her burlesque against freedom, her actual tyranny by the few over the many—What has she to do with the great vision of peopling the New World with a noble race?[77]

In Charleston, the Southern literary critic, William Gilmore Simms, had an ode printed on a press mounted on a moving car as part of welcoming home celebrations for the Palmetto regiment, and in the same year he published *Lays of the Palmetto: A tribute to the South Carolina Regiment, in the War with Mexico.* The year before he had written to his friend Hammond:

> You must not dilate against military glory. War is the greatest element of modern civilization, and our destiny is conquest. Indeed the moment a nation ceases to extend its sway it falls a prey to an inferior but more energetic neighbour. The Mexicans are in the condition of those whom God seeks to destroy having first made mad.[78]

[75] John Greenleaf Whittier, *Works* (London 1920) p. 37.
[76] C. E. Norton, ed., *Letters of James Russell Lowell* (London 1894) vol. I, p. 330.
[77] Quoted in H. S. Canby, *Walt Whitman, an American* (Boston 1943) p. 53.
[78] M. C. S. Oliphant, A. T. Odell, and T. C. D. Eaves, eds, *The Letters of William Gilmore Simms* (Columbia, S. Carolina 1953) vol. II, p. 322.

And although Emerson believed that in modern society war was 'on its last legs',[79] in an essay on the subject he wrote:

> War educates the sense, calls into action the will, perfects the physical constitution, brings men into such swift and close collision in critical moments that man measures man.[80]

In a letter to his cousin, Gansvoort Melville, Melville wrote:

> People here are all in a state of delirium about the Mexican War. A military ardor pervades all ranks—Militia Colonels wax red in their coat facings—a'prentice boys are running off to the wars by scores.—Nothing is talked of but the 'Halls of the Montezumas' . . .. Lord, the day is at hand, when we will be able to talk of our killed & wounded like some of the old Eastern conquerors reckoning them by thousands.[81]

And yet it is an American response to the war which has become one of the most famous of all anti-war documents, and which has been a bible of creative resistence to men as far apart as Gandhi and Martin Luther King. Thoreau's essay, *On the Duty of Civil Disobedience,* strikes at the heart of the contradictions of representative government. Like de Tocqueville, Thoreau identified government and war, 'The standing army is only an arm of the standing government'.[82] Thoreau saw accurately that the American government was an eternal history maker, 'endeavoring to transmit itself unimpaired to posterity, but each moment losing some of its integrity'.[83] Neither did Thoreau share Melville's uncertain respect for law. Slavish legality is identified in no uncertain terms with organized violence. The process of legal historical government is a process of war:

> A common and natural result of an undue respect for law is, that you may see a file of soldiers, colonel, captain, corporal, privates, powder-monkeys, and all, marching in admirable order over hill and dale to the wars, against their wills, aye, against their common sense and consciences, which makes it very steep marching indeed, and produces a palpitation of the heart . . .. Now, what are they? Men at all? or small moveable forts and magazines, at the service of some unscrupulous man in power. Visit the Navy Yard, and behold a marine such a man as an American government can make, or such as it can make a man with its black arts—a mere shadow and reminiscence of humanity, a man laid out alive and stand-

---

[79] Ralph Waldo Emerson, *Works* (Boston and New York 1876) vol. XI, p. 161.

[80] Ibid., vol. XI, p. 132.

[81] M. R. Davies and W. H. Gilman, eds, *The Letters of Herman Melville* (New Haven, Conn. and London 1960) p. 29.

[82] Brooks Atkinson, ed., *Walden and Other Writings of Henry David Thoreau* (New York 1937) p. 635.

[83] Ibid., p. 635.

ing . . .. The mass of men serve the State thus, not as men mainly, but as machines, with their bodies.[84]

By associating slavish respect for war and law, Thoreau demonstrates that both cater for the needs of dehumanized people who have turned themselves into machines. A soldier is a man already dead by the magical control of the state, a representative of death-in-life: 'a man laid out alive and standing'.

No war in history was so thoroughly visually documented as the American Civil War. The newspapers' demand for material set up a whole new industry of artists whose on-the-spot sketches could be quickly turned into engravings for the particular story, and then reproduced in their thousands. Men like Alfred R. Waud of *Harpers Magazine* were among the more distinguished, and the young Winslow Homer was also among the more prolific. Currier and Ives had a field day and once more their hundreds of prints covering the war articulated the popular image, for propaganda purposes, to their Northern audience. The most important new development was, however, the photograph and it was of such revolutionary implication that its appearance will be dealt with in the next chapter.

In the more traditional media, some indication of the scope of visual record could be seen at the National Gallery of Art's exhibition of 1961 *The Civil War: the Artists' Record*.[85] Scarcely a picture takes up a critical attitude to the war. The priest-king organization of war which Freneau had condemned is often openly avowed, and the compilers of the exhibition's catalogue quote one Augustus Woodberry:

> I can scarcely imagine a righteous battle better prepared for, than by
> the closing hymn that was sung after the prayer, accompanied with the
> music of the military band.[86]

The war gave ample scope, too, for the full flowering of the Victorian genre painting such as, for example, Edwin Forbes' *Drummer Boy Cooling his Coffee* and George C. Lambdin's *The Consecration* pl. 20. In the latter picture we find the characteristics of the chivalric ethic transferred to the mid-Victorian drawing room. It describes a magical ritual of 'consecration' in which the man kisses the rose and the woman the sword. The sword which the woman holds is the male image of phallic violence in the literary tradition, and similarly the rose is the literary vagina of the courtly love allegory. Separately

---

[84] Ibid., p. 637.
[85] H. W. Williams, *The Civil War: the Artists' Record* (Washington, DC 1961).
[86] Ibid., p. 38.

20 *The Consecration, 1861,* by George C. Lambdin (1865). (*Photograph Courtesy of Berry—Hill Galleries, New York.*)

from each other (for the theme is separation and non-fulfilment owing to the war) they kiss the symbols of each others' sexuality. The implications of the obscenities of chivalry are clear and capture the essential features of the myth; that love and war exhibit similar features, that war is fought for love, and love is war, and that the gift of her body to the man by the woman is a reward for valour. So love and war form an endless dialectic; Venus and Mars in eternal symbolic (not actual) copulation in the interests of nation-building. Lambdin has also reduced the background, realistic as it appears, to essential elements. The flowers balance the statue and both are on pedastals indicating the separable themes of nature and history. Like the sword, the statue is on the woman's side, and the flowers, like the rose, are on the man's side. The implication is that after the necessary war when peace is restored, he will be a hero (hence the statue) and she will cultivate the arts of peace. The abstractness of the symbolism seems emphasized by the books which line the shelves, and the gauntlet on the table shows that the boy has accepted the challenge of manhood, duty, honour, and nation building in the presence of the goddess.

The symbolism of Lambdin's picture was typical of one major way in which the war was visually represented. Similar scenes and images found their way into poetry albums and keepsakes, aided and abetted by the myth-making propensities of poets such as Longfellow. According to one recent historian both sides in the war 'delighted in images of gallantry and chivalry'.[87] Both sides were hence seduced into conflict by similar visual propaganda.

Panoramic views of battle were again popular. Generally speaking the wider the point of view, the more insignificant the figures and the more glorious the presentation of mass slaughter. But one picture in the academic tradition which combines aspects of both genre and panorama, and transcends the sum of the parts is Winslow Homer's *Defiance: Inviting a Shot before St Petersburg, Virginia,* (1866) pl. 21. The conventions of genre are there in the figure of the banjo-playing black man, and in the use of the visual anecdote as news. The wide panoramic sweep of the landscape which cuts the picture in half is like a land version of Thomas Birch's seascapes with their dark water and light skies. The land itself is desolate and ominous with flashes from snipers threatening in the black lower half of the picture. This first major picture of trench warfare is characterized by a landscape in which cut-off stumps of trees and upended bayonettes bear witness to a death in nature itself. An Englishman,

---

[87] Cunliffe, *Soldiers and Civilians,* p. 404.

21 *Defiance: Inviting a Shot before Petersburg, Va. 1864* by Winslow Homer (1836–1910). (*Courtesy of the Detroit Institute of Arts, Gift of Dexter M. Ferry Jr.*)

G. A. de Sala, described one such landscape in his diary when he was shown over the Bull Run battleground, and it is a precise literary counterpart to Homer's picture:

> The scene was simply a waste; houses, farms, wayside taverns, had disappeared bodily. Whole plantations of trees had been hewn down; and in many instances their very stumps grubbed up. The traces of turnpike roads had quite disappeared. There were no hedges, no fences, no gates, no signposts. There was nothing—absolutely nothing but the abomination of desolation . . . and yet I saw no skeleton, no grisly finger pointing from the earth, no half buried cannon, no rusted sabres, no dinted shakoes, no shreds of clothing scattered about. What marked this place as a shambles, as an Aceldama, as a Potter's Field, as a Valley of the Shadow of Death, was its entire nakedness and desolation, and the knowledge that Man not Nature, had made the waste.[88]

Like Homer, de Sala bears witness to the absence of the traditional symbols of war. For this was a new kind of conflict in which there were no trophies for the victors and where men disappeared without trace. Here the moment of daring, the traditional heroic moment, is an occasion for irony. The hero is clearly an idiot to expose himself

[88] G. A. de Sala, *My Diary in America in the Midst of War* (London 1865) vol. I, p. 266 and p. 268.

at long range to a death without honour. The figure stands out dark against the sky, not illumined by it. His act is therefore not sanctioned by the light of divine glory but cuts ironically across it. He is an intruder caught between heaven and earth in the impersonal mechanics of war. Working in the same academic tradition as West and Trumbull, Homer reverses the implications of the historical painting.

On the popular level, the contribution made by Currier and Ives to the cause of Northern propaganda was considerable. These mass-produced prints conceded no defeats, and turned reversals and stalemates into tactical victories. The mud, the trenches, the protracted destructive inertia of the reality were transformed into fantasies of Napoleonic strategies of bayonet charge and leader-directed heroic combat. Flags wave amid the smoke, and Southern troops retire in confusion. The print reproduced is called (somewhat optimistically for 1862) *The Battle of Malvern Hill, terrific bayonet charge of the federal troops and the final repulse of the rebel army* pl. 22. In the foreground troops retire in confusion and the same artist employed the same poses for a picture of Gettysburg a year later. The Union soldiers are formed in a perfectly repeatable, immaculately dressed unit. There is no point of actual contact between the two sides. The Union soldiers do not even look at the

22 *The Battle of Malvern Hill, Terrific bayonet charge of the Federal troops and final repulse of the Rebel Army. July 1st, 1862.* Currier and Ives Lithograph. (*Courtesy of the Harry T. Peters Collection, Museum of the City of New York.*)

enemy. The opposition melts away through the sheer presence of embodied Manifest Destiny.

Better as visual icons of destiny were the new war machines. Two-act prints of Currier and Ives called *The Mississippi in Time of Peace,* and *The Mississippi in Time of War* **pls. 23 and 24 respectively** illustrate the change. These were drawn by Fanny Palmer and published in 1865. In the first print Bingham's *Jolly Flatboat Men* has been reduced to fit the lower left-hand quarter of the picture. To the left black men roll barrels onto the tied-up steamship, *The Express,* while to the right and behind the flatboat, two steamships sail down the centre of the river, the one with a star between its funnels, the other with an eagle—twin symbols of empire. On the right bank stands a prosperous colonial style wooden mansion and in the centre background the sun goes down over the river in a blaze of glory. It is a picture of the older type of civilization, based on peaceful trade: established landed gentry, prosperity and the steamboats themselves combine the mechanics of the steam and iron age within the wooden frame of an older craftsmanship with its implication of leisure and luxury. In the second print the point of view is switched round (subtly emphasizing the permanence of the natural scene) and the wooden mansion is now in flames, so is the steamship renamed *Belle* to provoke identification with the entire Southern culture. Black men leap for the river as the flames illuminate the trees in gaudy chiaroscuro. To the left the flatboat sinks and with it a whole river culture. Cause of all the havoc is a single ironclad, the irruption of a new and mechanized impersonal force in a more aristocratic, genteel, leisured society. These partisan prints, justifying war crimes, depend on the sense of history played out as alternating cycles of conflict and peace against a permanent nature.

Ironclad monitors such as the *Montauk* had an impact on public consciousness that is now difficult to recall. In London, *The Times* declared that it made the British navy obsolete, and in America it became the public symbol of mechanized omnipotence—the dream of the perfect kill in perfect safety. Since Robert Fulton's steamboat successes (Fulton was, incidentally, another erstwhile artist and pupil of Benjamin West) Americans had been steadily improving their steam technology. Fulton himself had designed a double-hulled floating fort with a central paddle wheel, complete with furnace for heating shot, water pumps to drench the enemy's powder and guns trained to fire below the water line of enemy ships, which he appropriately called *Demologos* or the voice of the people. It was John Ericsson, however, a Swede, who invented the monitor, which was accepted in North America, after it had been turned

23 *The Mississippi in Time of Peace* by F. F. Palmer. Currier and Ives lithograph, 1865. (*Courtesy of the Harry T. Peters Collection, Museum of the City of New York.*)

24 *The Mississippi in Time of War* by F. F. Palmer. Currier and Ives lithograph, 1865. (*Courtesy of the Harry T. Peters Collection, Museum of the City of New York.*)

down in England. The turret was built up of eight layers of iron
plates one inch thick bolted together, and the gun could be run
inside the turret. The steam engine was of the vibratory lever type
and paddles were replaced by a screw propeller. The box boilers
had return tubes for heating, and propellers inside created a primitive form of air conditioning. In the Currier and Ives print reproduced
pl. 25 no Romantic conventions of light skies and troubled seas
characterize the landscape the machine inhabits. The cleancut shapes
and the overall clarity of the lighting point to a new kind of warfare
where the battle is not between people but between technologies.

25 *The Union Iron Clad Monitor 'Montauk'. Destroying the Rebel Steamship 'Nashville'
in the Ogeeche River, near Savannah, Ga. Feb. 27th 1863.* Currier and Ives lithograph.
(*Courtesy of the Library of Congress, Washington, DC.*)

Or perhaps it would be more correct to say that the imbalance
created by technological development could be seen for the first
time to be a major cause of war. Nathaniel Hawthorne provided the
literary description, and articulated the public response:

> It could not be called a vessel at all; it was a machine— and I have seen
> one of somewhat similar appearance employed in clearing out the docks;
> or, for lack of a better similitude, it looked like a gigantic rat-trap. It was
> ugly, questionable, suspicious, evidently mischeveous—nay, I will allow
> myself to call it devilish; for this was the new war fiend, destined, along

with others of the same breed, to annihilate whole navies and batter down old supremacies.[89]

Most Civil War literature was of course written after the event. The description of war which marked a turning point in American literary attitudes was Stephen Crane's *Red Badge of Courage* which was written in 1895, and was entirely fictional, bearing no relation to an actual participant, scene or incident. Most other responses can be read in Edmund Wilson's compilation *Patriotic Gore.*[90] The poetry of Melville and Whitman, however, makes a fitting conclusion to this discussion of war in early American society, for it illustrates very clearly the attempt to understand and come to terms with the immense catastrophe of the Civil War as a dramatization of the eternal contradictions of the principles of American nationhood.

For the most part, Melville's *Battle Pieces* (1866) parallels the other mediocre poetic jingles which poets from Whittier to Lowell felt obliged to devote to the patriot cause. Nonetheless they are worth examining for the few that rise above the general level and, read in Hennig Cohen's splendid edition illustrated with pictures by Waud, they give a good idea of one literary reaction to the war.[91] Cohen points to the multiple contemporary sources, chiefly newspapers, which Melville drew on and also emphasizes their relation to both academic and popular pictures of the time. The poetry hence attempts to reformulate in conventional poetic guise the massive fallout of information, both visual and verbal, supplied by the new media. Cohen suggests that the unifying theme is the contemplation of death, order and the sanctity of law. What is more probably correct is that Melville remains very ambiguous throughout about the verities of law, force and death. It is as if the conventions of the poetic forms, here modes of hymnology and ballad, turn Melville from the more radical analyses of warfare to be found in the novels. Nonetheless it is difficult not to bring one's sense of Melville's ironies to the poems. The following short poem, for example, seems almost too neat and orthodox in its affirmation of time and measure as eternal absolutes, with ascertainable rules which deny chance and unpredictability in human affairs:

> In time and measure perfect moves
> All Art whose aim is sure;
> Evolving rhyme and stars divine
> Have rules, and they endure.

---

[89] Nathaniel Hawthorne, 'Chiefly about War-Matters. By a Peaceable Man', *Atlantic Monthly,* 10 (July–December, 1862) p. 58.

[90] Edmund Wilson, *Patriotic Gore* (New York 1960).

[91] H. Cohen, ed., *The Battle-Pieces of Herman Melville* (New York 1963).

> Nor less the Fleet that warred for Right,
>   And, warring so, prevailed,
> In geometric beauty curved,
>   And in an orbit sailed.
>
> The rebel at Port Royal felt
>   The Unity overawe,
> And rued the spell. A type was here,
>   And victory of LAW.[92]

The internal rhymes of rhyme and divine, the associations of geometry, Unity, and type, by comic suggestion and overemphasis
indicate a sarcastic, but helpless response to the iron inevitability
of American domination by eternal law. In another poem, in which
he alludes to the new iron dome of the Capitol which Lincoln insisted
on being continued in spite of the war, Melville is much less
ambiguous:

> Power unanointed may come—
> Dominion (unsought by the free)
>   And the Iron Dome,
> Stronger for stress and strain,
>   Fling her huge shadow athwart the main;
> But the Founder's dream shall flee.
> Age after age has been,
> (From man's changeless heart their way they win);
> And death be busy with all who strive—
> Death, with silent negative.[93]

Ostensibly the completion of the Capitol pointed to the realization
of the democratic dream, in fact it served as a symbolic focus of
power for war-shattered troops coming back into Washington after
fighting at the front. The elegant principles of the cosmos which
Jefferson's dome at the University of Virginia demonstrated have
turned into an iron symbol of control. Melville knew that, with the
disappearance of the original dream, such symbolism provided a
means for much more autocratic control to be exercised later. The
nation in Melville's poem emerges stronger, but its new strength
casts an ominous shadow. In the rest of the poem, however, Melville
falls back on an almost medieval personification of death whose
presence negates any possibility of change in the continuum of
history. From the point of view of the tomb he could reconcile law
and anarchy, dream and disillusion as endless cycles of conflict. In

---

[92] Ibid., p. 48.
[93] Ibid., p. 40.

many ways Melville's failure to create a new form was a failure to create new meaning.

Whitman faced many of the same problems but in a much more complex way. Lawrence remarked that 'Whitman is a very great poet, of the end of life. A very great post-mortem poet, of the transitions of the soul as it loses its integrity'.[94] Whitman is supremely the poet of death, not because he explores the loss of integrity of the self however, but because he wishes to preserve the integrity of the nation in spite of contrary evidence. Nowhere is this more apparent as in his commentaries on the Civil War, both in *Specimen Days* and in *Drum Taps*. The problems of representational democracy become very acute in war, and Whitman's continued difficulties in reconciling the individual experience with the inhumane requirements of the body politic became more insistent and intense. Like all wars, the Civil War was a drama of 'making history' in which the social body affirms and perpetuates its own identity coerced by fantasies of the future. Fantasies of the future are attempts to recapture, in psychoanalytical terms, the past. D. H. Lawrence, for example, was unable to see that movement among contraries with a return to the body as a point of sanity was at the heart of Whitman's poetry. His much more conservative and European vision led him to stabilize intellectually these contraries in what he called the mechanics of one identity.[95] The celebration of the body, as in the *Calamus* poems, shows Whitman at his finest, depicting unrepressed human sexuality able to differentiate its experiences, and particularize its responses. When Whitman comes to celebrate the state, however, there emerges an intellectual celebration of national unity, and an uncritical acceptance of private, individual death on a large scale as the condition of public incorporation.

The war was a war for unity, and it was achieved by massive slaughter and corporate death. And one side of Whitman attempted to find feelings and reasons to sanction this:

> It was not for what came to the surface merely—though that was important—but what it indicated below, which was of equal importance. Down in the abysms of New World humanity there had form'd and harden'd a primal hard-pan of national Union will, determin'd and in the majority, refusing to be tamper'd with or argued against, confronting all emergencies, and capable at any time of bursting all surface bonds, and breaking out like an earthquake.[96]

[94] D. H. Lawrence, *Studies in Classic American Literature* (1924; reprinted London 1964) p. 161.
[95] Ibid., pp. 154—5.
[96] F. Stovall, ed., *Walt Whitman, Prose Works, 1892*, vol. I (New York 1963) p. 25.

Whitman characterizes the drive for unity as a natural process, like the earth itself with its varied strata, its violence and earthquakes. Where nature and history serve as mutually reinforcing metaphors, a birth in nature is the same as the birth of a nation. When the *New York Weekly Graphic* first published this passage, the final simile was 'like a cosmical earthquake'. The functions of the earth as a geological body with a tendency to catastrophe are turned into symbols of nation-making. As Ahab forged his iron harpoon in the blast furnaces of his own microcosmos, so Whitman formed and hardened his national will in the bowels of the metaphorical earth of the New World. Logically, therefore, for Whitman, the state of war was a true moment of birth. To insist on destruction as creation is to substitute death-in-life for the process of life and death. For the movement of tension and release in fulfilled love are substituted orgasms of death in which only release from the horror is possible. As Whitman moved about the wards of Washington hospitals, caring for the sick, writing letters home for the wounded, closing the eyes of the dead, writing the last letter to a waiting family, keeping communications going where care had ceased to exist, he felt the 'convulsions' of the dead and wounded, and it is a word he uses again and again to describe the relation of the individual body to the body politic destroyed in the service of each other.

In perhaps his most famous poem, 'When lilacs last in the door-yard bloom'd',[97] an elegy on the death of Lincoln, Whitman writes the great American classic poem on the relation of the individual in a representative system to his heroes, and on the relation of the state to the individual. It is a poem of general and particular death, of the relation of an interior to an exterior landscape, of the shifting relations of the near and far view, and of waste and needless sacrifice. The emotion, deeply felt, is the emotion of betrayed historical idealism. Public and private feeling are interfused in a death-like geographicohistorical landscape of American identity. The newspapers, the electric telegraph, the railways made the whole continent an interacting organism where, almost uniquely at this time, public life and its events had a deep personal significance.

It is strange that it is with the death of a hero that Whitman is able, in this poem, to fuse so brilliantly the private emotion and the public event. The opening images of star and lilac bear witness to the public destiny of empire and the private, sexual, nature of the self. The sense of that imbalance of nature in public symbolism is caught as the declaration of mourning coincides with the spring.

[97] H. W. Blodgett and S. Bradley eds., *Walt Whitman, Leaves of Grass* (New York 1965) pp. 328–37.

But the death-in-life is not a permanent sense. It is part of a rhythm
of change. One mourns only for a season and then goes away. The
lilac is broken off, and the lines suggest a sharpness of motion, giving a particular, transitory image of grief, but the tree rooted in the
yard goes on:

> and from this bush in the dooryard,
> With delicate-color'd blossoms and heart-shaped leaves of rich green,
> A sprig with its flower I break.

The shy and hidden bird, singing in the swamp, indicates the poet
himself. A different Whitman this, overwhelmed with grief, creating
an art which saves life. For the accent is on life. The panoramic view
of the coffin moving through the spring landscape seems part of a
ritual in which the people and the landscape are emphasized, not
the funeral train. Those dualisms which are so much of the philosophy
of American life, the country and city, the public and private life
are celebrated here unhindered by fantasies of progress. They alternate factually. First the funeral train goes through the country, then
to the city, building up to a powerful public climax with the organs,
the thousand voices and the bells. And at that point, almost non-
chalantly and familiarly, Whitman addresses his tribute:

> Here, coffin that slowly passes,
> I give you my sprig of lilac.

Then the poet imagines the personal tribute generalized and the
rhythm swings back again to the public sense with the images of
lilac sprigs from many bushes to celebrate the many public deaths.
And then comes the mystic paean to the star itself with a sense of
familiarity and secrecy alternating through the images. Against this
overwhelming inertia, the song of the bird calls the poet back to
life again. The frustrated, contradictory impulses of grief are hinted
at as the bird's song edges him back to life, while the heroic memory
detains him in the contemplation of death. The panoramic vision of
the land itself, with the sea breezes coming in from both coasts to
the prairie heart of America, provides a corresponding metaphor to
the private landscape with its overmastering scent of the lilac and
overwhelming sense of sexual loss. Whitman contemplates the
totem-like pictures of national identity he will hang in the burial
chamber, but we soon forget the pictorial nature of these representational landscapes. They are boundless and cannot be so contained.
The interior landscape of the burial chamber breaks into an actual
picture of the life outside. The feeling of light changing makes the
landscape active, creating movement within the limits of vision:

> Lo, the most excellent sun so calm and haughty,
> The violet and purple morn with just-felt breezes,
> The gentle soft-born measureless light,
> The miracle spreading bathing all, the fulfill'd noon,
> The coming eve delicious, the welcome night and the stars,
> Over my cities shining all, enveloping man and land,

There is a carefulness and gentleness in the imagery and in the rhythms (not part of popular associations for American character) as Whitman tries to free himself, with intermittent success, from his feeling of loss. At the two poles of feeling, powerful erotic impulses push him backwards and forwards, the one towards life, the other towards death:

> O liquid and free and tender!
> O wild and loose to my soul—O wondrous singer!
> You only I hear—yet the star holds me, (but will soon depart,)
> Yet the lilac with mastering odor holds me.

Personifying death and the thought of death, a crucial and life-enhancing distinction, with himself in the middle, Whitman is ready for the blackest moment in the poem, as he moves figuratively to the heart of the swamp, experiencing loss as death itself yet still realizing that the distinction is there. After the song to death as a dark mother-goddess, giver of life and death, Whitman is able to return to contemplate the war, strengthened by the bird's song the 'tally' or correcting measure of his own voice. In long panoramas he sees battles in memory as silent dream. It is a kind of photographic preservation, a trace of action. Perhaps he even has in mind the photographs of the war with their lines of dead bodies. Unlike the general public, however, Whitman does not react to them as images of life-in-death. There is no sense of the state sentiment of the eternal moment. For these are completed actions and the poet turns away from them:

> But I saw they were not as was thought,
> They themselves were fully at rest, they suffer'd not,
> The living remain'd and suffer'd, the mother suffered,
> And the wife and the child and the musing comrade suffer'd,
> And the armies that remain'd suffered.

The concluding stanzas are a farewell, a celebration of loss and a passing onward with no false memorials. And in the last brilliant stanza where he brings the song of the bird, the correspondence of his own voice, and the star and lilac in one final movement together, the balance is perfect:

> Comrades mine and I in their midst, and their memory ever to keep, for
>   the dead I loved so well,
> For the sweetest, wisest soul of all my days and lands—and this for his
>   dear sake,
> Lilac and star and bird twined with the chant of my soul,
> There in the fragrant pines and the cedars dusk and dim.

The movement drops down onto 'There' in the last line as a completing gesture pushing the experience away from him as at last he
comes to terms with it and understands it.

Once again out of a near disastrous inheritance, and with all his
own contradictory feeling about the war, Whitman makes a synthesis
which transcends the given alternatives. In the next chapter we shall
see how the invention of the photograph appeared to confirm an
old reality, but in fact led to views of nature and society which
contradicted that reality and questioned the mechanical operation
of reason itself.

5

A Technological Challenge to the Dialectical Nature of Representative Reality: the Photograph

We have seen how, in many areas and various ways, the European vision of a politically stable space, with hierarchical perspectives and isolated objects, begins to be challenged in the new republic. We have also seen that where the notions of formal order are retained there is a simultaneous contradictory movement of anarchy which necessitates an ideology of permanent conflict characterized as natural order. In a society founded as self-consciously as America, there was, in this early period, a continual necessity to relate cultural achievement to the public representative drama. In many ways the photograph was a naturally democratic mode, or so it appeared to be. Every man was now capable of taking portraits, battle pieces, scenes of domestic life and landscape. In this chapter which concludes the civil history section of the book, we look at the impact of photography on prevailing conceptions of representative reality, and hence by implication, on the inherited notions of the hero, peace and war. We shall see that the intersection of cultural expectation and a radically new medium of vision caused confusion of prevailing values. The photograph provided a fantasy world of private violence and sexuality even more polarized than the old public vision of war and peace. At the same time it did challenge old public notions of heroism and warrior virtue. The 'battle-piece' became the news photograph of unmitigated disaster, and slowly began to erode the vision of the arts of war as any kind of alternative reality. Finally by looking at one highly sophisticated but conservative analysis of the new phenomenon, we summarize some of the issues of this first half of the book by isolating a moment of change in consciousness parallel to developments in the more traditional arts.

The photograph then had two precisely contradictory effects in America. It at once summed up that desire for linear depth representation as a mode of reality, the culminating gesture of visual aspirations for nearly a thousand years in western culture, and

simultaneously made it irrelevant.[1] The photograph as we learn
from the standard histories was a multidisciplinary achievement;
Niepce, and then Daguerre and Talbot put together knowledge about
the physical operations of light in the *camera obscura,* the chemical
darkening of silver salts when exposed to sunlight and the technical
development of lenses to produce the first retainable images of
reality.[2]

Like all other modes of representation the photograph, in its
origins at least, is intimately associated with the nature of perspective,
geometry and theatre. It is interesting that the first published account
of the *camera obscura* appears as a gloss on the word *spectaculum*
in an Italian translation of Vitruvius's *Treatise on Architecture*
(1521).[3] Giovanni Battista Porta's book *Magiae naturalis* (1558,
2nd edn, 1588) popularized the interest of the painter, the mathematician and the architect in the *camera obscura* and gives us clues,
in its two editions, to the public psychology of the response to the
new phenomenon. In chapter 6 of the second edition, Porta describes
an entertainment he devised, consisting of a darkened chamber
serving as a *camera obscura,* in which was erected a white screen.
In the sunlight outside, opposite the aperture, he constructed a stage
on which he arranged various spectacular shows with battle scenes
and wild animal models moved by children. The effect was a literal
internalization of reality, with an isolated and masked-off illusion of
the real world. This isolation of the representative slice of reality,
and its removal from traditional context, an achievement which
needs a literate spectator able and accustomed to isolate objects in
space, freed the illusion of reality from reality and indeed substituted
the one for the other. The psychological effect was so overwhelming
that Porta was accused of being a sorcerer. The title of the work
Natural Magic was an effort to distinguish it from connotations of
demonic magic.[4] Isolated from reality and having the effect of an
even greater reality than reality itself, the new phenomenon was a
powerful agent for extending and developing the dream world of the
private viewpoint. The shows devised were an effort to draw on an
iconography of fantasy which privately complemented the public
dream of reason, and stability of public life. The *camera obscura's*

[1] The Arabian scholar Ibn Al-Haitham (965–1038) described the *camera obscura.*
See Helmut Gernsheim and Alison Gernsheim, *The History of Photography, from the
earliest use of the camera obscura in the eleventh century up to 1914* (London 1955)
p. xxvii.

[2] Niepce is generally credited with the first successful 'photograph'.

[3] Gernsheim, *The History of Photography,* p. 4.

[4] See, for the best discussion of this subject, D. P. Walker, *Spiritual and demonic
magic from Ficino to Campanella* (London 1958).

way of working followed scientific law, but its effect was to reveal a world in which law did not exist, in which all was permitted. With the development of the portable box *camera obscura,* the original social view of the phenomena as public entertainment was abandoned. Robert Boyle showed the semantic lag of the transition when he refers to his own 'box camera' apparatus of 1669 as a 'portable darkened room'.[5] The sedan chair *camera obscura* was of course just that. The connotations of secrecy in the word *camera* are also important, referring not only to the privacy of the new world, but also to the sense of intruder and voyeur. The vogue for detective cameras at the end of the nineteenth century points to a voyeuristic trespass of the forces of law into the recesses of private life. Whereas Porta's public theatre required an environment as fixed and rigid as the foursquare building in which it was housed, the portable darkened room enabled the viewer to shift his ground and make a stage of the world. Spectator attitudes were thus transferred from the theatre to the world outside it. It is significant that the rage for *camera obscuras* reached great proportions in the eighteenth century among landscape artists as an aid to 'correct delineation'. The country house owner showed great interest in this new species of natural magic, lending authority as it did to the view from the library, with its perspective view of nature as theatre. It is interesting that Thomas Wedgewood, himself an important early pioneer in photography, begged a friend for the use of a *camera obscura* so that he could complete a series of scenes of English country houses for a set of china he was decorating for Catherine the Great of Russia. The *camera obscura* was literally its own message. What had started out as a gloss on *spectaculum* in a treatise on architecture by Vitruvius who was responsible in a large measure for the design of the English country house through the Palladian revival, confirmed in a circular manner its own reality by literally representing itself.

A brief look at Daguerre's early career shows how Renaissance attitudes survive very little changed right into the nineteenth century. Daguerre's career in fact sums up the history of geometric illusion as entertainment. He began life as an apprentice architect learning the rules of perspective and of linear representation. He then drifted into theatre proper, serving an apprenticeship with Degotti, the chief designer for the scenery at the Opéra. Then he became assistant to Pierre Prévost (1764—1823) who, like the inventor Robert Barker (1739—1806), entertained the public with large canvases of

[5] Gernsheim, *The History of Photography*, p. 12.

panoramic paintings. Robert Fulton had introduced the invention of these large circular paintings to France, selling his 'importation patent' to the Americans Mr and Mrs Thayer, and, with the profits, turning to the steamboat.[6]

The panorama is, like the *camera obscura*, another important precursor of the photograph at least in its effect. A recent work points to the combination of sources the panorama drew upon; the mechanization of representation produced by the *camera obscura*, the solving of difficult perspective problems, and the building, and fashionability, of the rotunda as an architectural form.[7] The religioscientific illusion of all-encircling space is brought down from the abstract vision of the cosmos Jefferson wanted to depict inside his rotunda, to confer a mystical reality on the landscape itself. Daguerre worked for nine years with Prévost. In the panorama the stage becomes the locus of the individual viewpoint. Baker's patent described how the whole should be lighted from the top and how the public platform in the centre should have a roof to frame the upward view. The downward view was to have been framed by some kind of wall or paling running continuously round the base of the platform. The entrance had to be from below to preserve the continuity of illusion, and Barker suggested that the stage could be raised or lowered, to show how, even when the point of view was altered, the scene could present a total reality.[8] Instead of the frame of reality being out there in the landscape, the spectator himself occupies a stage which itself controls the viewpoint. This difference is crucial. For in the landscape 'out there' objects could be hierarchically disposed by means of perspective to represent reality. The panoramic canvases were full of irrelevant detail to give the illusion of not being preselected as in the picture from a *camera obscura*. The stage itself was the eye which did the organizing. The mechanization of vision amenable to a shifting viewpoint democratized the old theatre. In the theatre, Dr Johnson said we are always aware of being in the theatre. The aim of the panorama was to make the illusion of theatre seem natural. In an important way the effect of the panorama anticipated the photograph. The emphasis is thrown more unobservably on the apparatus of perception while, simultaneously, the totality of the image,

---

[6] Helmut and Alison Gernsheim, *J. M. Daguerre, The History of the Diorama and the Daguerreotype* (London 1956) p. 5. I am indebted to this book for most of the information on Daguerre.

[7] Heinz Buddemeier, *Panorama, Diorama, Photographie, Entstehung und Wirkung neuer Medien im 19. Jahrhundert* (Munich 1970) p. 19.

[8] Gernsheim, *J. M. Daguerre*, pp. 163–4.

experienced in all its unorganized reality, effectively pulled the viewer's response away from the neat presuppositions of theatrical representation.

But there was one more important aspect of the panorama similar to the photograph and that was its inability to represent more than one second or moment in time. In a most searching discussion of the effect of the panorama, a French critic, Millin, called attention to the kind of landscape this mode favoured.

> La nature inanimée dans tout son ensemble est le véritable domaine du panorama; ses masses les plus considérables, ses formes les plus nobles, ses lumières les plus vives sont l'objet le plus relevé qu'il puisse se proposer, et son élément le plus pur. La nature vivante au contraire n'est de son domaine qu'autant qu'elle est en repos, ou qu'elle pourroit du moins l'etre pour aussi long-temps que les regards du spectateur sont fixés sur le tableau.[9]

Consequently the kind of landscape most accesible to this mode, and which best preserves the illusion of reality is at once majestic and peaceful. The combination of religious connotations of the circular vision and the fixity of the frozen moment of time turns live nature into a symbolic landscape of dead nature. We shall see, in the final chapter, just how important this fact is for American landscape.

Daguerre quickly became a celebrity with his stage designs in the 1820s after his apprenticeship with Prévost. Critics generally lamented the crudities of the drama on the Parisian stage at this time, but they were unanimous in praise of Daguerre's sets. The sets replaced the people in one sense. The drama of nature, for various reasons, became more real than representative actions between actors. Again and again Daguerre astounded his audiences with moonlight scenes, and on 22 February 1822, he drew the theatre-going world into ecstasy with the Opéra's production of *Aladdin* with its innovative use of gas lighting.[10]

It was but a step from the spectacular representation of nature in the theatre to the diorama which excluded human action altogether. For it was with his diorama that Daguerre first achieved general fame. It was a drama of landscape in which the audience were the figures. In a specially constructed building, the audience saw two spectacles, each lasting some 15 to 20 minutes. The auditorium, which was entirely circular, could be revolved through 73 degrees to line up with the proscenium arches of two stages set

---

[9] Buddemeier, *Panorama*, p. 171.
[10] Gernsheim, *J. M. Daguerre*, p. 11.

side by side on the circumference. The scenes, revealed down long
tunnels, and lit by daylight from behind and above, exploited
every device of stagecraft and perspective learnt since the Renaissance.
It was an improvement on the *panorama* in the sense, that with a
careful gradation of lighting effects in a more plausible manner, the
impression of the fixed moment could be broken down as morning
gave way to moonlight. The juxtaposition of the two sets equally
broke down the feeling of fixed space. The swift passage from one
area of fantasy to another provided the viewer with more of the
sensations of travel than the traveller could hope to have. Daguerre
was a showman and perfectly able to exploit any area of landscape
reality, particularly those developed and encouraged during the
Romantic movement which, in the 1820s, somewhat tardily
became a major force in French culture. Daguerre's most famous
scene, *A midnight mass at Sainte-Etienne-du-Mont*, exploited the
magicoreligious effect of the illusion to the full. In the kind of
space which was the latest child of the Vitruvian-Palladian revival,
the gothic church was seen as it were through neo-Classical spectacles. Daguerre's show revealed a dream world which had been
directly produced from experiments with illusion and perspective
and which in turn had come about as a result of the application of
a highly abstract geometry to the problems of visual space. Scientific
perspective produced a fantasy landscape which articulated the
fears of insecurity, the religious aspirations and romantic hopes of
the public. It helped to confirm that invisible control of showman or statesman manipulating wonder-working science for an
audience whose energies could be so easily diverted into a vicarious
enjoyment of its own deprivations. Although the spectator was
projected into the landscape, the landscape was all around him, and
its content was organized through a mathematical relationship to
which the individual appeared to give his assent involuntarily.
And yet such a structure and experience revealed a dream iconography upon which the scientific renaissance had turned its back
and which, articulating as it did the fears, terrors and tragedies
complemented by religion, the Romantic love ethic and comedy,
had to be domesticated and controlled if the architecture of state
was to stand.

That Daguerre should have been the most famous name
in *fixing* the image of reality as an eternal artefact after such an
initial career is axiomatic. For the daguerreotype, and later the first
rudimentary photographs seemed to confirm a kind of visual reality
long prepared for by the Renaissance conception of architecture
as a totally controlled space for every kind of religious, theatrical

and social activity. But as we have seen it was a dead space per-
petuating the divisive realities of the Roman model. The photograph,
like printing, like architecture, was seen to confer immortality
and stability on human affairs. The faded browning photographs on
the graves of Italian cemeteries are the direct descendants of the master
portraits of Dürer and Raphael. The first photographs were seen to
confirm the presuppositions of representative art. Their subjects
certainly were similar. In addition the first cameras required long
exposure times, and were unable to freeze movement like the
cameras of the second half of the nineteenth century which enabled gesture to be appreciated as part of a continuous motion. The
subject had to sit for the photographer as he had to sit for the
painter. Immobile objects were the most amenable to the photographer. Deserted city streets or a spectator clamped in a vice were
favourite subjects. People were posed, landscapes were composed.
The portrait took over from the death mask as a perpetuator of
life, death scenes realistically posed were a sensation, and on the
field at Gettysburg the corpses preserved rigid immobility for the
camera eye.

And yet the photograph did not continue the pictorial tradition
at all, for in every potential subject area, portrait, landscape, and
historical event, the presuppositions of the older painterly art existed
in tension with new effects which were at once enigmatic and
disturbing.

True to his inheritance the portrait photographer worked hardest
in the darkroom, removing blemishes, altering hairlines, adding to
busts, carving away from waists. People were both right and wrong
not to be able to face themselves. The portrait photograph with its
pitiless rendering of detail was unselective in basic composition.
Whereas the inclusion of detail in space was unselective, time was
shown in one arbitrary moment. It takes considerable metaphysical
effort to see the moment of time as representative of character.
No one ever sees a person as he appears in a photograph, for in
social intercourse no gesture is ever separated from another. In a
ruthless and devastating way the portrait photograph destroyed
the notion of character in a visual sense. For character implies
continuity through time. The painted portrait claimed character
truth through selecting and then generalizing detail. The public
expected the same from the portrait photographer, and frequently,
in spite of heroic efforts in the darkroom, the moment failed to be
representative of any moment but itself.

In the fifties, the rage for the *carte de visite* democratized the
portrait and made available to all the high-flown pretensions of the

aristocrats. But whereas the painter could suggest the turn of a column by a graceful manipulation of chiaroscuro, or the richness of a hanging by simplifying folds and painting the colour more thickly, the unsubordinated totality of detail turned similar effects in photography to parody. Alfred H. Wall, whose articles from the British *Journal of Photography* were frequently reprinted in the American *Humphrey's Journal,* scathingly attacked the excesses of the mode:

> First there is the inevitable column and pedastle. That is well enough. It is very proper sometimes to represent a person thoughtfully contemplating the ruins of Balbec or Ninevah, and the observing traveller is fitly exhibited leaning on the shaft of some stupendous ruins. But an ambitious photographer is not satisfied with that alone. There is room in the back ground to introduce a view of the Hudson, and hence it appears. But he is not yet content. A curtain with a long cord and tassels can be put in by the side of the column aforesaid and come within the narrower limits of the piece of board on which the picture is to be mounted. Should there by any possibility be any space left, our ingenious phot. [sic] is not without resources to fill it. A chair or table and panel work can be perhaps introduced spontaneously.[11]

As we have seen in portrait painting, the landscape gave a clue to the social character of the individual psyche. Through these backgrounds, social mobility, the evidences of conspicuous consumption and the prestige of the grand tour could be visually attributed to the figure posed in front of it. Any kind of deprivation, political, social, sexual and economic could be restored through the photograph. The American democrat posed like Napoleon in front of the Alps, the English middle classes assiduously collected photographs of the home life of their dear queen, the city dweller contemplated rural retreats, and as all deprivations are proportional to the impulse thwarted, there was a swift realization of the photograph's potentialities for what McLuhan has called 'the brothel without walls'.[12] The pimps of Broadway used the photograph to advertise their wares. Under the heading of *Girls don't you do it!,* a writer for *Humphrey's Journal* warned of a new institution:

> The Photographic Union is designed to become a gallery of the portraits of young females, to which will be attached the name and description of each young woman, for the avowed purpose of showing their pictures to young men, and afterwards bringing about an acquaintance with the girls whose portrait and description happen to please.[13]

[11] *Humphrey's Journal,* 13 (1861–2) p. 241.
[12] Marshall McLuhan, *Understanding Media* (London 1964) p. 188f.
[13] *Humphrey's Journal,* 15 (1863–4) p. 314.

With the invention of the stereograph a new dimension was added, and at the beginning of the Civil War one horrified commentator talking of the stereoscopic slides freely available on Broadway said, 'It is positively sacrilegious to prostitute the light of heaven to such debasing purposes'.[14] For the same writer, what was possible in painting was too unnervingly realistic in a photograph. For a generation whose supreme artistic sex-object was the immaculately white, nippleless, hairless corpse of Hiram Power's *White Captive,* the nude photograph, initially unretouched, destroyed the immaculate women of fantasy:

> I am not shocked at the sight of a Cupid without pantaloons, nor hypocritically fastidious about the pose of a Hercules or a Venus, I do not call for an investiture of figures with togas and fig leaves, but to see a too life-like representation in all its faithful hideousness, to picture tablets by photo-actinism, a very microcosm of impurity, this is one of the things we cannot look upon without disgust.[15]

Such attitudes were common and typical, as commentators felt the artistic conventions of the genteel tradition severely embattled.

American landscape photography did not really begin to flourish until the 1870s. Early photographers quickly found out that the details of a landscape captured by the photograph were not naturally represented in the same proportions, with the same light values, or with the same effects as similar details represented in landscape painting. A common first reaction was to include too much sky, for unlike human perception, the camera eye did not compensate through habit for the imagined horizon of normal consciousness. In perspective representation the conscious spacing of objects from near ground to background gives them a hierarchy of interest according to the painter's intention. There is no such order in nature. A tree, which an observer might imagine took up the middle distance, might in the photograph appear too far away. Also in a photograph, the light, especially in a wide landscape, is much more diffusely spread, and the effects of shadows and chiaroscuro are minimized. The problem of light distribution became instantly crucial, for linear perspective as such was simply not observable in an ordinary landscape. Some of these problems were taken up by Wall in a series of articles on landscape photography which appeared during the early years of the Civil War:

> The best thing some of our landscape photographers could do for the

---

[14] *Humphrey's Journal,* 11 (1859–60) p. 116.
[15] Ibid.

> improvement of their productions would be to join a rifle corps, and
> pay more than usual attention to the 'judging distance drill', as they
> would thus learn how, apart from diminution in size, distance is also
> indicated with equal force by the variety of appearance due to the
> character and the amount of intervening air; or, in other words they
> would see that *aerial* is of no less importance in securing truthfulness
> than *linear* perspective. . . . how essential is it that we should educate
> the eye to recognize the quality we are seeking for our pictures.[16]

It was right that Wall should use a military example to expound
theories of vision. His advice is an excellent illustration of McLuhan's
connection of gun-fire developments with the rise of literacy and
perspective.[17] Most early landscapes simply depict dull stretches of
ground because the eye had exaggerated the size of some object in
relation to the distance. Wall's articles also drew freely on current
painterly theory of landscape and on the poetic and literary tradition
of eighteenth and early nineteenth-century aesthetics. He quotes as
freely from Thomson's *Seasons* as from Hazlitt's work. As linear
representations of reality became difficult in the photograph, the
criterion of 'indefiniteness' became increasingly important.

The descriptive vocabulary sometimes masks the importance of
the changes. Commentators talked about 'spiritual truth' (aerial
perspective) superseding 'material realities of Form' (linear vision).
Certainly in the Impressionist revolution in France, the discoveries
of the photograph helped to contribute to realizing depth in a
picture by a more homogenous distribution of light and colour
gradation, at the same time letting the sharpness of objects in space,
a function of geometric conceptions of depth, blur into a more two-
dimensional sense of patterning and relationship.

The photography of war also dealt a severe, though not instantly
felt, blow to the conventions of history painting. Matthew Brady,
born in Ireland in 1823, came to New York as a small boy. Falling
under the eye of a favourably disposed business man he made a
trip to Europe again in 1838 with Samuel Morse, and actually visited
Daguerre's studio at the very moment of the daguerreotype's birth.
He began a daguerreotype business in America, and won a prize at
the English exhibition of 1851. He did not get a top prize mainly
because his pictures were not picturesque enough. He succeeded
well enough, however, in embellishing the American democrat, with
a prosperous portrait business, as the following lines from Bret
Harte's *Her Letter* show:

[16] *Humphrey's Journal*, 13 (1861–2) p. 214.
[17] McLuhan, *Understanding Media*, p. 341.

> If you saw papa's picture, as taken
>   By Brady, and tinted at that,—
> You'd never suspect he sold bacon
>   And flour at Poverty Flat.

Brady's photographs of the Civil War are the most renowned of many taken of that war. Federal and Confederate photographers constantly risked life and limb to procure excellent pictures. Brady invested his fortune in training 20 assistants to help him in covering the war. His studio manager, a Scotsman, Alexander Gardner, published 200 photographs in two volumes after the war, but Brady's work and his thousands of negatives were not properly presented until, after many visicissitudes, an edition of 1911 appeared. Brady himself died in a poor ward of a New York Hospital in 1896.

Brady used the colloidon wet process, an operation very far removed from any conception of instantaneous photography. The equipment was so bulky that Brady and his assistants equipped themselves with specially fitted-out wagons. The camera itself might weigh over 20 pounds, and chemicals needed to be carried in bulk. Colloidon (a sensitizing agent made up of a solution of gun-cotton in alcohol and ether, mixed with a solution of iodide and bromide of potassium) was spread thinly over a piece of glass and, before drying out, was dipped into a solution of nitrate of silver from one to four minutes. It was then placed, still wet, into the camera, exposed and washed with a solution of sulphate of iron. The result was a negative which still had to be given a final wash in hyposulphate of soda to remove soluble elements liable to decomposition. Then paper was dipped in brine and a solution of nitrate of silver poured over it. Negative and paper were then exposed together, and the paper was finally washed in hyposulphite of soda and water twice, the second time with chloride of gold added. Even so over 8,000 negatives were made by Brady and his team.[18] The sheer number was a staggering factor in the concept of pictorial representation.

The result was a devastating record of the war. The landscapes have a double iconography of production and waste. The war was a business of bridge building, of transports, of provisioning where the production of spades was as important as the production of rifles. We see many sights which would not have been considered worth painting by the old painters of war; for example, a line of men trundling wheelbarrows each containing an explosive mine. Owing to the clumsy equipment of the photographer the move-

---

[18] Gernsheim, *The History of Photography*, p. 208.

ment of troops is nearly always seen at a distance, long impersonal
lines forming human counterparts to lines of barracks or trenches.
closer views come only in moments before and after action. The
views of troops lying around during hours off, and of groups of
officers before their tents seated at tables illustrate the fact that
90 per cent of the soldier's life is sheer boredom. Groups of men
pose proudly round guns like Melville's sketch in *Israel Potter*—
their stiff postures answering the requirements of photography as
well as providing a secular symbol of straight-jacketed psyches. The
officers appear as if for a high school graduation class, for the form
and occasion transcend the participants. The landscapes are ugly,
unorganized, empty of recognizable picturesque values, maintaining
a stolid neutrality against which the lines and squares of men operate
with seeming irrelevance. There are photographs of Virginian houses
with the dead being buried in the foregound, of towns standing in
ruins which were hardly to be known again until the bombing-out
of urban centres in Europe in the Second World War. The rubble of
Charleston, Atlanta and Richmond prefigure Warsaw, Berlin,
London and Dresden. The subject suited photography, rubble lends
itself more easily than grass or leaves to detailed effect. In the
natural landscape, however, stumps of trees achieve similar results
and the countless windings of trenches and earthworks break up the
monotony of the scene. Gone are the stable houses of Copley's
picture and the dramatic skies of Trumbull. There is scarcely a flag
to be seen, or where it does fly, it is reduced to a tiny space in the
landscape. Above all one gets a sense of improvisation, of pioneer
spirit, doubtless from the lines of covered wagons serviceable equally
for westward enterprise and war. The pictures of prisoners of war
prefigure the totalitarian disasters of the twentieth century. Ander-
sonsville anticipated worse European camps. The journalistic impulse
toward disaster had a new ally in the photograph.

It was the pictures of the dead, however, which brought home
the horror. Lines of bodies wait for burial like so much merchandise
to be disposed of. A bayonetted fourteen-year-old boy lies bare-
footed in a sun-lit trench others lie with their hands clutched over a
fatal stomach wound, and yet others are swamped, half in, and half
out of the mud, in stiffened positions with drawn up knees, or with
rigid arms raised incongruously over their prone and twisted bodies.

It was in these photographic scenes of war that the historical
landscape, painted in the cause of a coercive nationality, finally
rebounded against itself. From now on it was simply more difficult
to dress up war with flags and tempestuous skies, nobly dying
drummer boys, and leaders expiring in the the light of heaven. The

26 *Dead at Gettysburg,* Photograph by Timothy H. O'Sullivan. (*Courtesy of the United States War Department General Staff, Photo no. 165—SB—36 in the National Archives.*)

high style of description and writing also became patently ironic with the new photographic revelations **pl. 26**:

> . . . a bleak landscape, on which the shadows of evening are rapidly falling, revealing, in its dim light, a singular spectacle. It is that of a row of dead bodies, stretching into the distance, in the form of an obtuse angle, and so mathematically regular that it looks as if a whole regiment were swept down in the act of performing some military evolution.[19]

The stereoscope and the stereograph went even further in completing the desire for depth illusion. To many it seemed that it was simply twice as true as the photograph. A commentator in the late fifties remarked, 'the mind is not prepared to admit that perception could be carried to the extent of the stereoscope',[20] and another exclaimed, 'It is mathematics demonstrated, and geometry an

[19] *Humphrey's Journal,* 13 (1961—2) p. 144.
[20] *The American Journal of Photography and the Allied Arts and Sciences* New Series (1858—9) p. 137.

abiding proof'.[21] The stereoscope was introduced into America in the fifties by the Langenheim brothers of Philadelphia, and the writer and physician, Oliver Wendell Holmes, invented the popular hand stereoscope. As early as 1855 Langenheim found Philadelphia businessmen to put up money for a series of stereoscopic views to be taken of American scenery.[22] Albert Bierstadt, the American painter, on his first western journey of 1859, reported: 'We have taken many stereoscopic views, but not so many of mountain scenery as I could wish, owing to various obstacles attached to the process'.[23]

The real vogue for the stereograph came after the Civil War in America. Nonetheless Oliver Wendell Holmes wrote a series of articles beginning in 1861 on the stereoscope and on photography in general. These writings articulate an overall cultural view of the impact of the new phenomenon after its first 20 years, and sum up for us many of the preoccupations of the preceding chapters. In 'The Stereoscope and the Stereograph',[24] Holmes describes the photograph as a mirror with a memory, a kind of philosophical rebuff to religious and metaphysical use of the mirror as an image of transient vision. The emphasis on memory is important for it soon becomes obvious that the real theme of Holmes's discourse is the question of time in relation to normality, permanence and stability. Holmes anticipates many of the questions which William James was to sum up in his *Principles of Psychology* at the end of the century; chief among these is the search for a physical basis for human psychology. For the photograph seemed to indicate more problems in these areas than it solved. Holmes also uses the negative and positive process as an image for speculating in a new guise on the old problems of a dualistic universe. The negative has connotations of diabolism, the positive print of a more stable reality. Together they *fix* the image of normality. Opposing contraries determine the basis of the real world. Yet Holmes continually uses examples to show how precarious such assumptions are. He admits that depth perception is a function of education—the result of a complicated chain of causes like the production of the stereograph. Like William James, Holmes has to rely on the concept of 'healthy' and 'sick' contraries. He stresses the need for a 'right condition' in understanding the nature of perceptual reality. With the example

[21] Ibid., p. 82.

[22] Robert Taft, *Photography and the American Scene* (New York 1942) p. 175.

[23] Quoted in Hendricks, G., 'The First Three Western Journeys of Albert Bierstadt', *Art Bulletin*, 46 (Summer 1964) pp. 333—65.

[24] Oliver Wendell Holmes, *Soundings from the Atlantic* (Boston 1866). 'The Stereoscope and the Stereograph', pp. 124—165; 'Sun Painting and Sun Sculpture', pp. 165—227.

of the stereoscope before him the relations of perception seem far from normal. He is correct to call the stereoscope a 'squint magnifier' for abnormality paradoxically reveals normality. In speaking of the details of his examples, he is again pulled two ways. He accepts the choice of subjects inherited from the evolution of the Grand Tour to the Cook's tour; the statue of Rameses, the Pyramid of Cheops, the wall of Baalbec, Rhenish vineyards, Roman arches, Alpine glaciers, the Mount of Olives. Like the people inside Porta's *camera obscura* he is able to look into the eyes of wild animals. At the same time he stresses the accidental detail which the nature of the technology makes of equal importance to the more literary subject. The arbitrary completeness of unselected objects creates an equality between a washing line and the Colisseum arranged as arbitrary patternings over a two-dimensional surface. The viewer has to be active in selecting points of interest.

Strangely, Holmes continues by asserting that the apparent smallness of certain objects in a stereograph should not be surprising, for the sizes are the same as those perceived in nature. His major weakness is to wish totally to identify perceptual experience with the results of the photograph while giving hints that compensation or distortion are the ways in which most people visually perceive reality. He wants it both ways. He needs a stable reality 'out there' in nature, at the same time he realizes that perception is an infinitely changeable quality. For a doctor, what is normal is what is pragmatic. But his attempt to equate photographic reality with human perception leads him to some strange conclusions. Because the reality of the photograph seems so much greater than the reality itself he declares that 'Form is henceforth divorced from matter'. What he means is that reality is now illusion, and that the only real things are shadows. Holmes, as his correspondence with Harriet Beecher Stowe shows, was an avid reader of Jonathan Edwards and his statement is a scientific corroboration of that philosopher's view of reality. The purely visual world together with a secularization of a Platonic world of forms triumphs with the invention of the photograph. He suggests we may burn up the pyramids, or destroy the Colisseum as long as we have its photograph. The scientific consciousness cannot comprehend the unique event. The endless reproduction of the same thing in a photograph, like a series of experiments coming up with the same result, confirms an incontrovertible reality—at least in the popular view. Almost inevitably his last two suggestions are a call for a standardization of camera lenses and the formation of a vast museum to collect the repeatable images of the real world; a secular temple of representative truth

confirming an inner religious need for a permanent reality. Fortunately, like his Calvinist forbears, Holmes was able to separate
theory from practice. He had a reputation as a wit and *bon viveur*
which seems to compensate for the coldly obscene vision of his
museum of forms.

In another essay, 'Sun-painting and Sun-sculpture', he pushes
these questions further. In a more leisurely fashion Holmes continues
his theme of immortality and the consolation of the record of the
dead. True to his principles of the pre-eminence of form, Holmes
rejects the importance of colour in illusion. Colour is not quantifiable arithmetically and is unstable:

> The color of a landscape varies perpetually, with the season, with the
> hour of the day, with the weather, and as seen by sunlight or moonlight;
> yet our home stirs us with its old associations, seen in any and every
> light.[25]

The philosophy of unchanging form articulates the psychology of
fixation to the past. In the middle of a guided tour of the world
Holmes again philosophizes on the relation of the photograph to
time with a complexity of allusion that reminds one of Emerson's
style:

> What if the sky is one great concave mirror, which reflects the picture
> of all our doings, and photographs every act on which it looks upon
> dead and living surfaces, so that to celestial eyes the stones which we
> tread are written with our deeds, and the leaves of the forest are but
> undeveloped negatives where our summers stand self-recorded for
> transfer into the imperishable record? and what a metaphysical puzzle
> we have here in this simple-looking paradox! Is motion but a succession
> of rests? All is still in this picture of universal movement. Take ten
> thousand instantaneous photographs of the great thoroughfare in a day;
> every one of them will be as still as the *tableau* in the 'Enchanted Beauty'.
> Yet the hurried day's life of Broadway will have been made up of just
> such stillnesses. Motion is as rigid as marble, if you only take a wink's
> worth of it at a time.[26]

Here a Calvinist view of the imperishability of deeds added up in an
eternal account is given authority by nature designated as a camera
eye of God. The old Parmenides and Zeno paradox that, if movement
is a succession of still moments, how do we tell one moment from
another, is given a new twist. The photograph seemed to lend
authority to a view of time as a succession of still moments. For
Holmes this moment is more real than the flux and change of

[25] Ibid., pp. 172–3.
[26] Ibid., pp. 183–4.

human intercourse. The simile 'rigid as marble' is an exact one, for in this view, the photograph is a monument of time, an icon of memory as a guide to consciousness. The other simile of 'Enchanted Beauty' takes us to the legend of the sleeping princess awaiting her lover. But there was no way of making the girls on the Broadway stereograph come alive. This imagery of statuary and beauty is reminiscent of Keats's *Ode on a Grecian Urn* with its 'still un-ravished bride of quietness'. Keats's pun illustrates the frustration of the neo-Classical conception of the eternal moment where the principle of no change balances against sexual passion for ever in tension. The social implications of this mode of reasoning with its image of the arrested moment are conservative. The simple perma-nence of fixed memory becomes a substitute for real life with its unpredictabilities, its necessary risks, and its complexities. Looking at photographs of the Civil War corpses, Holmes takes the next step of asserting that these moments, in the grotesque aftermath of the already reductive experience of war, show us the moral essence of things.

> It is a sad thought that there are truths which can be got out of life only by the *destructive analysis* of war. Statesmen deal in *proximate principles,* unstable compounds; but war reduces facts to their simple elements in its red-hot crucible, with its black flux of carbon and sulphur and nitre.[27]

The photograph with its equally bewitching array of chemical reactions was a parallel phenomenon, confirming once again the truths of representative reality which was the result of the Christian and classical inheritance. Although we have seen that in many ways the photograph gave this kind of reality its death-blow, Holmes's expectations of it and his reactions to it were intimately part of a consciousness which led over many centuries to its development and final perfection.

In part II we turn from the effects of the dream of reason in civil history to its effect in natural history. We have already seen how the concepts of civil society depend on a view of nature at once peaceful and hostile. With the discovery of America, the European paradoxes of nature as refuge and wilderness could be played out with an inexorable logic.

[27] Ibid., p. 185.

PART II   Natural History

L'Histoire Naturelle prise dans toute son étendue, est une Histoire immense, elle embrasse tous les objets que nous présent L'Univers. Cette multitude prodigieuse de Quadrupèds, d'Oiseaux, de Poissons, d'Insects, de Plantes, de Mineraux, &c. offre à la curiosité de l'esprit humaine un vaste spectacle dont l'ensemble est si grand, qu'il paroît & qu'il est en effet inépuisable dans les détails.
                                        Buffon.

   Humanity is far above
Sexual organisation.
                Blake

6

Origins of Natural History in America and First Syntheses

The discovery of the New World had an impact on the European imagination which it is now difficult to understand. It was as if the wilder reaches of contemporary science fiction were discovered to have an immediate and actual reality. The study of nature and society as complementary activities was the Renaissance inheritance, and we have already seen how the very concepts of 'culture' and civilization depended on a complex series of presuppositions about man's relation to the physical landscape. Whereas theories about social relations, however, in all their nonvisual complexity, could be discussed in terms of compact, or universal harmony, nature itself presented a bewildering variety of forms and manifestations, singularly resistant to theory and law. It was at once perfect, the handiwork of god, and, at the same time, it was a fallen world, distant in time from Eden and the Golden Age. It was colonized in the name of religious salvation and in the prospect of untold agricultural and mineral wealth. It was a fantasy area for every European dream of utopia for thousands of years, and it was an untamed wilderness in which every decency of human life was achieved at immense cost. Its savagery, its boundlessness, its feeling of terrifying limitlessness, its uncontaminated sense of space could be called on in turn as evidence for human activity and as excuses for social law. It is the intersection of the European consciousness with the stubbornly new realities of America, its indigenous peoples, its fauna and flora and the very landscape itself which forms the subject matter of the following pages. The theoretical religious and scientific models of the body politic serve as a reminder of universal law, of unity and stability. Nature becomes amenable to such a metaphysic through the 'scientific' phenomenon of 'classification'. To ensure order in the body politic, a concept of character was needed. Classification served much the same purpose in the corresponding world of natural history. As in the civil-history inheritance, the results were generally disastrous, threatening in our own time an ecological disaster which seriously affects the possibility of human survival. At the same time, the aim in part II is to show the creative pockets of response, the very real achievements of the writers and painters in a period when it was still possible to combine the larger issues of philosophic and social concern with a unique vision of the New World. In the subject of natural history, the painter and topographer are of paramount importance. What geometry was to physics, representational art was to natural history. In the human drama of history, we have seen how perspective gave a model for the concept of a man isolated in his own space, homogenized, and part of an alternating reality of comedy and tragedy which was sanctioned by the notion of infinity. We have already seen how classification and perspective are linked. In the early years of scientific medicine the anatomist was *ipso facto* an illustrator. Some of the greatest achievements of this period are in natural history illustration. Right up to the Civil War, we can perceive two contradictory impulses in Americans' reaction to the physical reality of their country. From Europe they inherit the impulse to divide, separate, classify, distrustful of any but the most pragmatic and empirical of philosophies. On the other hand, there is the peculiarly American desire to create a whole system, to unite the divided inheritance of science and art, and of civil and natural history.

First, in this chapter, we look at some of the earliest manifestations of interest in natural history, and three *literary* 'geographies', by Jefferson, Crèvecoeur and Bartram. Then in order to examine the the attitudes and preconceptions to be found in these writers, and elsewhere, in actual contact with the land, selected government expeditions are looked at in some detail for official reactions towards the major categorizations of 'geography': landscape, anthropology, fauna and flora. Two chapters follow on the Indian and on animals and birds respectively, as representative examples of these categories, and finally, in the development of attitudes to-wards landscape in painting and literature, the split vision of the dream of reason is drawn together as the European inheritance is seen to be modified in several unique ways.

From the beginning the sixteenth-century explorers, often accom-panied by artists, brought back visual and literary records of the New World. In Thomas Haket's translation of *The New Found World* by Thevet are to be found some of the first pictures of the American bison and pineapple. Theodore de Bry's 23 engravings from John White's watercolours illustrate Thomas Hariot's 1590 edition of

A Brief and True Report of the New Found Land of Virginia. John White, who remains still perhaps the most famous of all painters of Indians, made 65 watercolour paintings of American Indian life in an otherwise fairly obscure career. De Moyne, an artist who accompanied the French Huguenot expedition under Landonnière to Florida in 1564, also had his pictures engraved by De Bry, and published in 1609. De Moyne's actual narrative dwells much on Spanish rather than Indian atrocities, though the drawings have a different emphasis as Indian scalping and mutilation seem to form the main centre of interest.

Reports of the new lands rapidly multiplied, from Raleigh's account of the potato and tobacco, to writings of many European writers: Gonzalo Fernandez de Oviedo y Valdes, Jean de Levy, Joseph d'Acoste, William Strachey, Foncesco Hernandez (the first to describe the buffalo) and Captain John Smith. The first formal treatises on New England's fauna and flora were William Wood's *New England's Prospect* (London 1634) and Morton's *New English Canaan* (Amsterdam 1637). Throughout the century, treatises of every kind proliferate; some written to promote trade, others to present rare varieties and species for the contemplation of noblemen, and others, more ambitious, attempt to cover the whole vast range of natural history like John Josselyn's *New England's rarities discovered; in birds, beasts, fishes, serpents, and plants of that country* (London 1675). Many elaborated theses on plants for medicinal purposes, like William Hugh's, *The American Physician* (1672), and in the last half of the seventeenth century, American contributions to the *Philosophical Transactions* of the Royal Society grew in number. John Winthrop, Jr of Connecticut, whose collection of books formed the largest scientific library in the country until the eighteenth century, sent to the repository of the Royal Society a 'strange and curious fish'.[1] At the beginning of the eighteenth century, John Lawson wrote his *A New Voyage to Carolina* which freely mingled fact with fiction, though not to the same extent as a very rare book by one Ibrahim Effendi, in which 'the prize picture is the tree of the New World, called 'Wak-Wak', on which women grew, mostly ripe . . . one in bud; . . .' pl. 27.[2]

The first really outstanding work was Mark Catesby's two folio volumes, *The Natural History of Carolina, Florida and the Bahaman Islands . . .*, printed at the expense of the author between 1731 and

---

[1] See Max Meisel, *A Bibliography of American Natural History, The Pioneer Century, 1769–1865* (New York 1924) p. 333.

[2] W. M. and M. S. C. Smallwood, *Natural History and the American Mind* (New York 1941) p. 24.

27 *The Wak-Wak Tree*, from a Turkish history of the West Indies, Constantinople, 1730. From: C. G. Jung, *Symbols of Transformation*. (*Reproduced from the Collected Works of C. G. Jung, Vol. 5, by courtesy of Routledge and Kegan Paul Ltd, and by permission of Princeton University Press.*)

1743. In the preface to his work Catesby described how he employed an Indian to carry his box, 'in which, besides Paper and Materials for Painting, I put dry'd Specimens of Plants, Seed &c . . . as I gathered them'.[3] He took care to observe what he considered to be

[3] Mark Catesby, *The Natural History of Carolina, Florida and the Bahaman Islands etc.*, 2 vol (London 1731—43) vol. I, p. viii.

natural colouring, and he painted his birds, shrubs and fish live
wherever he could. Catesby considered pictures essential to an
accurate understanding of natural history. In addition he is the first
of a long line of self-taught amateurs leading up to Audubon. Like
Audubon he had difficulties with perspective, but the 'difficulties'
and 'amateurishness', in a typical American manner, turn out to be
more fruitful than the 'correctness' of the tradition. He wrote:

> As I was not bred a Painter I hope some faults in Perspective and other
> Niceties, may be more readily excused, for I humbly conceive Plants,
> and other things done in a Flat, tho' scant manner, may serve the
> Purpose of Natural History, better in some measure than in a more
> bold and Painter-like way.[4]

What Catesby wanted was a semiotic simplification adapted to
function. Both chiaroscuro and 'depth' representation would have
confused the 'characteristics' by which he wanted the bird to be
identified. Catesby's aim was to find a ready means by which to
classify a species and the advantages of his method are obvious.
Just as a contemporary airman is unable to identify the ground by
an aerial photograph yet finds it easy with a map with more specialized information,[5] so Catesby's work served a similar function.
What is at issue here is not whether the representation is realistic
or not but whether a strategy of signs elicits the maximum useful
information. Artistically Catesby's pictures lose in the sense that
they cannot render the moment of experience with nature in its
unique mood, implying change from moment to moment, but they
gain in the sense that the fine drawing and sense of colour render an
aristocratic feeling of ornament, like the birds and flowers in a
Gobelin tapestry or the decoration of Vincennes porcelain.
Scientifically, the specialization of information helps towards
identification and classification, but the variation of colour in
flower or plumage throughout the year cannot be shown, as the
still near-representational mode he uses has no means of showing
this information.

What Newton was to American physicists, Linnaeus and Buffon were
to the natural historians. American natural historians were often
pupils of Linnaeus. In America Linnaeus's system of classification
by sexual differentiation was early and swiftly adopted. From the
beginning he had many American correspondents; Garden, Colden,

---

[4] Ibid. p. xi.
[5] Norwood Russell Hanson, *What I do not believe, and other essays,* Stephen Toulmin
and Harry Woolf, eds, (Dordecht-Holland 1971) pp. 15–9.

Bartram, Mitchell, Clayton, and many of his pupils sent him specimens from America: Kalm (whose important *Travels into North America* was published in London, 1770–1), Alstroem, Loefling, Kuhn (first professor of botany in America) and Rolander. According to one historian of natural history in America the earliest botanist to adopt the Linnaean system was one John Reinhold Forster.[6] Linnaeus and Buffon were the doyens of natural history in the second half of the eighteenth century, and most serious writers on the subject defer to, or argue over, their statements. The classic example is Jefferson's patriotic dissent from Buffon's view that certain American quadrupeds which have European equivalents were smaller: 'It does not appear that Messieurs de Buffon and D'Aubenton have measured, weighed, or seen those of America'.[7]

This incident is often cited as evidence for American empirical emphasis in science, but we have seen that the framework of empiricism and pragmatism is heavily biased historically, philosophically and psychologically. While Linnaeus's system depended upon visual evidence, the kind of evidence which was felt to be relevant was of a highly specialized kind. Recent articles on Linnaeus have shown that throughout his career he consistently attempted to discover a monistic explanation for his classificatory system where the kinds were fixed, discrete, natural and stable, as created and made permanent in the mind of God.[8] Linnaeus's achievement, however, was to provide a system whereby the botanist could distinguish and particularize various species.

In social terms, however, the achievement was much more ambiguous. The concept of stable law, substantiated by visual classificatory evidence describing a hierarchy in nature from God to man to animal down to the lowest forms of life, was a thin secularization of ancient Christian cosmology. Grafted on to this was a simplistic psychology of vision, typical of eighteenth-century theorists, which considered perception in terms of impressions conveyed to an uncreative or at most vaguely quantitative imagination. Linnaeus himself describes the psychology of his 'objective' vision:

> [Man] . . . is able to reason justly upon whatever discovers itself to his sense; and to look with reverence and wonder, upon the works of Him who created all things.

[6] See W. M. and M. S. C. Smallwood, *Natural History and the American Mind.*

[7] Thomas Jefferson, *Notes on the State of Virginia* (1785) Thomas Perkins Abernethy, ed. (New York 1964) p. 49.

[8] See James L. Larson, 'The Species Concept of Linnaeus', *Isis,* 59 (1968) p. 299.

That existence is surely contemptible, which regards only the
gratification of instinctive wants, and the preservation of a body made
to perish. It is therefore the business of a thinking being to look
forward to the purposes of all things; and to remember that the end of
creation is, that God may be glorified in all his works.[9]

Linnaeus's cosmos is as stable as Ptolemy's. His *A General System of
Nature* (1st edn, 1735) begins with a reference to the whole cosmos,
proceeds down through the stars to man and animals, then to the
lowest forms of life, and from thence to the mineral world. Such a
system enabled Linnaeus to claim objectivity in his *basis* for classification. If we look at *homo sapiens* as a test case we shall see such
a basis is far from 'objective'. Man is classified according to four
criteria; colour of hair; look of face; disposition, character, clothes;
mode of government. It is almost as if Linnaeus had wilfully
chosen the most unstable of all human characteristics in order to
shape his system. It is easy to see why this kind of cosmology
appealed to the Americans. Like Newton, Linnaeus was a maker of
a whole system, he was fairly orthodoxly pious and his laws provided
a psychological confirmation of world order. One American example
of the extent to which the ideas of Linnaeus reached the general
public can be seen in Jedidiah Morse's (father of Samuel) *American
Geography* (1789).[10] Morse refers to both Linnaeus and Buffon,
and his system of geography follows the general outlines of Linnaeus's
own *General System*. This geography was one of the first of its
kind and had immense popular success. It incidentally began a
tradition of 'whole-earth' thinking which reaches down to the
followers of Buckminster Fuller in our own time. When Morse comes
to *homo sapiens,* he uses the authority of Linnaeus and Buffon to
discuss the black man as one of six natural types, outlining his
characteristics in such statements as the following: 'It is the genius of
a savage to act from the impulse of present passion'.[11] In purely
political terms Morse's system and its implications are important,
since it was under his supervision that the first official government
enquiry into the state of the Indians took place in 1826.

It is interesting to note, however, that Buffon was at pains to
contradict much of Linnaeus's categorizing, 'puisqu'il n'existe
réellement dans la nature que des individus, et que les genres, les
ordres et les classes n'existent que dans notre imagination'.[12] But

---

[9] Carl Linnaeus, trans. W. Turton, *A General System of Nature etc.*, 7 vols (London
1806), vol. I, preface.
[10] Jedidiah Morse, *The American Geography* (New York 1789).
[11] Ibid., p. 18.
[12] Jean Louis Le Clerk, Comte de Buffon, *Oeuvres Complètes,* (1749–1804; reprinted
Paris 1853–9) vol. I, p. 54.

his more sophisticated theoretical overview seems to get lost in
America. It may be that in practice the tentativeness of his own
system was forgotten in the face of the results which were elicited
from it. More likely, the separation of piety and practicality led to
related but distinct ideologies which served the interest of pragmatic
exploitation. Some of his comments on *homo sapiens* demonstrate
this clearly:

> [La nature] . . . n'a ni choses, ni genres, elle ne comprend que des
> individus; ces genres et ces classes sont l'ouvrage de notre esprit, ce ne
> sont que des idées de convention; et lorsque nous mettons l'homme
> dans l'une de ses classes, nous ne changeons pas la réalité de son être,
> nous ne dérangeons point à sa noblesse, nous n'alterons pas sa condition,
> enfin nous n'otons rien à la supériorité de la nature humaine sur celle
> des brutes, nous ne faisons que placer l'homme avec ce qui lui ressemble
> le plus, en donnant même à la partie matérielle de son être le premier
> rang.[13]

What is missed out is the relation between the convenient category
and the overreaching ideal. What is the precise import we may ask
of 'la réalité de son être' and 'sa noblesse'? It will be shown below
how the Indian, for example, was pursued across a continent with
his 'noblesse' intact. Buffon's concept of civilization overrode the
theoretical wisdom he, unusually for his time, displays here. In a
traditional manner he can condemn the sexual habits of the
Samoiedes or the negresses of Senegal, or exclaim against the
apparent indifference to 'beauty' of the natives of Sierra Leone.
The term Buffon used to describe the opposite of a 'nation sauvage'
was a 'nation policée'. We can see here just how close the natural
historians are to the historians of civilization in the complex of
their shared ideas. Unlike Humboldt, in the next century, Buffon
excepts nations like Mexico and Peru from savagery, for in these
civilizations are to be found, 'des hommes civilizés, des peuples
policés, soumis à des loix, gouvernés par des rois'.[14]

It is against this kind of background that the first classic writers
on American natural history must be seen. Three American writers
of the period stand out. Their work is an attempt to create a literary
geosocial synthesis of the landscape and society they inhabit.
Thomas Jefferson's *Notes on Virginia* (1781), Hector St John de
Crèvecoeur's *Letters from an American Farmer* (1782), and William
Bartram's *Travels through North and South Carolina, Georgia, East
& West Florida &c.* (1791) are books of very different scope and

[13] Ibid., vol. III, p. 160.
[14] Ibid., vol. III, p. 308.

purpose, but together they help to determine the effects of the inherited knowledge which Buffon saw subsumed under the title of natural history.

C. F. Volney, himself a prolific writer on the law of nature and empire,[15] said of Jefferson's *Notes on Virginia*: 'Mr Jefferson, whose work appeared in 1782, has the credit of first leading the way, and of surmounting the chief difficulty, in first tracing a design until then new'.[16] Volney was not quite correct for it could be argued that Jefferson's work was in a tradition of English county topographies and related works going back to Camden's *Britannia* of 1586. In this tradition a geographical area is used as a *locus classicus* for certain kinds of information about soil, agriculture, local manufactures, topography and mineral deposits. Certainly much of the first part of the work contains similar kinds of information: topography, mineral deposits, the navigability of rivers, types of land and supplies of fish. Full lists of plants and quadrupeds are provided, the former categorized under the four headings of medicinal, esculent, ornamental and useful for fabrication. Jefferson's work, however, differs from the English topographies in its more cosmopolitan cultural outlook. Aware that his information will be eagerly sought after by European savants he adds Linnaean names to convey more precise information. He is always more aware of the philosophy of his methodology. On any doubtful question, Jefferson always takes an empirical stance. Arguing, for example, against Buffon's contention that moisture is unfriendly to animal growth, he states:

> The truth of this is inscrutable to us by reasonings *a priori*. Nature has hidden from us her *modus agendi*. Our only appeal on such questions is to experience; and I think that experience is against the supposition.[17]

When he comes to *homo sapiens,* however, we see some of the implications of the appeal to experience. For the appeal to experience, to precedent, is an appeal to memory transmitted in a far from culturally innocent form. It is in fact an *a priori* judgement of the most literal kind, and Jefferson contradicts himself precisely:

> Will not a lover of natural history then one who views the gradations in all the races of animals with the eye of philosophy, excuse an effort to

[15] See C. F. Volney, *A View of the Soil and Climate of the United States of America* (Philadelphia 1804) and, *The Ruins: or, A Survey of the Revolution of Empires* (London 1760).

[16] Volney, *A View of the Soil and Climate. . . .,* p. 319.

[17] Jefferson, *Notes,* pp. 42–3.

keep those in the department of man as distinct as nature has formed them.[18]

This same 'eye of philosophy' perceives that the black man prefers white women, 'as uniformly as . . . the preface of the Oran-ootan for the black woman over those of his own species'.[19] By contrast Jefferson's defence of the Indian is the result of his own *a priori* assumptions drawn from his classical education. The Indian becomes a primitive republican, and consummate orator, a characterization common enough at the time but scarcely founded on empirical observation. The claim then to empirical objectivity (which some historians take so much at face value[20]) leads Jefferson on the one hand to racism and on the other to sentimentality.

Jefferson's topographical descriptions are equally revealing, as one might expect from one who designed the University of Virginia. He describes the passage of the Potomac through the Blue Ridge Mountains as follows:

> The first glance of this scene hurries our senses into the opinion, that this earth has been created in time, that the mountains were formed first, that the rivers began to flow afterwards, that in this place, particularly, they have been dammed up by the Blue Ridge of mountains, and have formed an ocean which filled the whole valley; that continuing to rise they have at length broken over at this spot, and have torn the mountain down from its summit to its base. The piles of rock on each hand, but particularly on the Shenandoah, the evident marks of their disrupture and avulsion from their beds by the most powerful agents of nature, corroborate the impression. But the distant finishing which nature has given to the picture, is of a very different character. It is a true contrast to the foreground. It is as placid and delightful as that is wild and tremendous. For the mountain being cloven assunder, she presents to your eye, through a cleft, a small catch of smooth blue horizon, at an infinite distance in the plain country, inviting you, as it were, from the riot and tumult roaring around, to pass through the breach and participate of the calm below. Here the eye ultimately composes itself; and that way, too, the road happens actually to lead.[21]

The structure of the description involves many levels of meaning. One might point to the theories of Neptunist and Plutonist versions of creation, prefiguring what was to become catastrophist geological hypothesis of earth formation. Alternatively we might see here an Americanization of Burke's theories of the sublime and beautiful.

---

[18] Ibid., p. 138.

[19] Ibid., p. 133.

[20] See especially Daniel Boorstin, *The Americans: The Colonial Experience* (1958; reprinted London 1965) p. 195.

[21] Jefferson, *Notes*, pp. 16–7.

Neither takes us very far, however, for the same reason as sources never 'explain' the synthesis. For this landscape shows Jefferson, as a politician, basing a natural landscape on his own unconscious political wishes. The *Notes on Virginia* were written at a time of immense political unrest, and at a crucial stage in Jefferson's own career.[22] The description relies on a double sense of time and space, which are nonetheless interlinked. The anarchic foregound (the present which actually shows the evidences of a past struggle) is contrasted with the peaceful background with its classic single vanishing point (the future). Since in Jefferson's ideology the metaphors of nature and history are interchangeable, both pointing to conflict against which the hero establishes temporary control, the landscape here goes far beyond mere topography. Jefferson contrasts the moment (the first glance) with eternity, and the near view with the far view which illustrate war and peace respectively. Peace is born through the cleft of the rock of ages, for the complex symbolism illustrates an overall view of the nature of life and death itself. The politician offers present riot and tumult for ultimate peace, albeit at an 'infinite distance'. The birth of a nation, Jefferson argues, is as natural as the birth of the earth itself. The last sentence thus becomes very significant and the coincidence not a little ironic: 'Here the eye ultimately composes itself; and that way, too, the road happens actually to lead'. The passive construction is intended to emphasise the objectivity of the eye, and with mock surprise Jefferson discovers that the 'road'—the way of truth—goes the same way.

Like Morse, some years later, Jefferson used the major categorizations (topography, anthropology, fauna, flora, icthyology, entymology and geology) which were to be the basis of the reports of government explorations in the future. Out of the categorizations of Buffon and Linnaeus he established the bounds of interest and a structure which was to serve as a guide to the exploration of a continent. These imaginative categorizations were taken as real, and helped to determine a pragmatic approach to the land. Natural history was seen to be a practical art to enable the prospective inhabitant of the landscape to know which rocks contained useful minerals, which rivers could be used for navigation, what kinds of landscape were amenable to railway and canal building, and what animals and plants were useful for trade or medicinal purposes. In contrast to this is the sense of landscape as something sublime and beautiful, with what implications we have seen, but the connec-

[22] There is a good account of the circumstances of the composition in Thomas Perkins Abernethy's introduction to his edition of the *Notes*.

tions between the sense of awe and impulse to quantification and exploitation were never stated. In fact Jefferson's landscape of conflict aided and abetted pragmatic exploitation.

Crèvecoeur is less a scientific naturalist than either Jefferson or Bartram. His letters to the Abbé Raynal show him interested in the whole complex of ideas which made up the new nation's consciousness. His famous definitions of the 'American', the 'new man', his attitudes to history, politics, and philosophy, his marvellous descriptions of Nantucket, and the account of his visit to America's most famous natural historian, the elder Bartram, make the work one of the most fascinating of all early American literary artefacts. And yet the work seems less 'American' than parallel texts by Jefferson or Bartram. It is in the tradition of travel accounts and its interest for us is its dramatic breaking down of a confident European categorization of things before an American reality. In the latter sections particularly, as Crèvecoeur found himself in one of the more active theatres of the war, the literary survival programme he proposed to himself counterbalances a quite radical analysis of conflict. His descriptions of nature have always appealed to Europeans. Hazlitt praised the book for the painterly exactness of these and D. H. Lawrence admired the description of the fight of bird and snake. The drama with which Crèvecoeur endowed both his landscapes and natural phenomena appealed especially to the European Romantic movement. The *Letters* were a source for Campbell, Byron, Southey, Coleridge and Chateaubriand, and contributed to projected schemes of literary utopias by European poets and savants. Crèvecoeur's later years were spent mainly in Paris where he pursued his interests in natural history through the medium of the learned societies. He visited Buffon twice a week and was introduced to Parisian literary society by Rousseau's mistress, Madame d'Houdetot. Towards the end of his life, he met Maximilian in Munich. Maximilian's own travels in America formed the basis for a literary classic, and his accompanying artist, Karl Bodmer, was to paint some of the finest pictures of the old American West

In *Letters from an American Farmer,* the metaphor of civilization as an equation of labour and soil equalling liberty and property is given classic eighteenth-century expression, as the following selected quotations show:

> . . . it is as we silently till the gound, and muse along the odiferous furrows of our low lands, uninterrupted either by stones or stumps; it is there that the salubrious effluvia of the earth animate our spirits and serve to inspire us; . . .

... the instant I enter on my own land, the bright idea of property, of exclusive right, of independence exalt my mind.

This formerly rude soil has been converted by my father into a pleasant farm, and in return it has established all our rights; on it are founded our rank, our freedom, our power as citizens, our importance as inhabitants of such a district.

The father thus ploughing with his child, and to feed his family, is inferior only to the emperor of China ploughing as an example to his kingdom.

Men are like plants; the goodness and flavour of the fruit proceeds from the peculiar soil and exposition in which they grow.[23]

History and social relations are based on the dream of the perfect task, and on a mystic communion with the 'effluvia' of the earth. Society is defined by its ability to transmit itself securely through time. The paternalist family is the mirror image of the paternalist state, for, as Crèvecoeur's example shows, the father ploughing with his child parallels the symbolic act of the emperor of China. Crèvecoeur secularizes the biblical text, 'No man, having put his hand to the plough, and looking back, is fit for the Kingdom of God', into an injunction to work for a more earthly kingdom.

Having supplied the metaphysic, Crèvecoeur next provides an example of his ideas in practice. He recounts the story of his treatment of the 'honest Hebredaian', a mute, obedient Scottish immigrant who, in contrast to the unruly Irish, is able to profit from his master's benevolence. Crèvecoeur instructs him to forget his old religion as a 'Barra' man for a newer, more simple, moral directive; 'Go thou and work and till; thou shalt prosper, provided thou be just, grateful, and industrious'.[24] And indeed the history of Andrew, whose rebirth is characterized in a profit of $640 (Pennsylvania currency), is strewn with thankful tears. The same values are current when Crèvecoeur changes the metaphor of the land for the sea, in his description of Nantucket: 'If these people are not famous for tracing the fragrant furrow on the plain, they plough the rougher ocean . . .'.[25] The harpoon, with the name of the town etched along its shaft, replaces the plough but serves the same history-making function. Strangely such an image obliterates the distinction of the hunting and agricultural states as sequential eras of civilization, commonly made by Crèvecoeur and his contemporaries, in the interests of a more morally pragmatic profit-making.

---

[23] Hector St John de Crevecoeur, *Letters from an American Farmer* (1782; reprinted London 1912) pp. 16–7, 24, 25, 25, 44–5 respectively.

[24] Ibid., p. 68.

[25] Ibid., p. 92.

Crèvecoeur's reaction to the war is split two ways. On the one hand he can offer an analysis close to a Barlow or a Paine:

> The innocent class are always the victim of the few; they are in all countries and at all times the inferior agents, on which the popular phantom is erected; they clamour, and must toil, and bleed, and are always sure of meeting with oppression and rebuke. It is for the sake of the great leaders on both sides, that so much blood must be spilt; that of the people is counted as nothing. Great events are not achieved for us, though it is *by* us that they are principally accomplished; by the arms, the sweat, the lives of the people.[26]

On the other hand he can retreat into a 'popular phantom' of his own making.

> I resemble, methinks, one of the stones of a ruined arch, still retaining that pristine form that anciently fitted the place I occupied but the centre is tumbled down; I can be nothing until I am replaced, either in the former circle, or in some stronger one. I see one on a smaller scale, and at a considerable distance, but it is within my power to reach it: and since I have ceased to consider myself as a member of the ancient state now convulsed, I willingly descend into an inferior one. I will revert into a state approaching nearer to that of nature, unencumbered either with voluminous laws, or contradictory codes, often galling the very necks of those whom they protect; and at the same time sufficiently remote from the brutality of unconnected savage nature.[27]

The ruined arch is an image of fallen society with Roman connotations. Crèvecoeur sees himself as the keystone to the stability of his own society in spite of the fact that circumstances of ruin have been beyond his control. Like Jefferson's foreground, Crèvecoeur's bears witness to a past struggle, and like his background, the distant prospect seems at once more natural and peaceful. But Crèvecoeur's future is more disenchanted than Jefferson's. He sees it more accurately as a reversion to the past. In Crèvecoeur's distress, the normal processes have inverted themselves, for the future state he proposes for himself is life with the Indians which traditionally precedes the civilization symbolized by the arch. What Crèvecoeur could not see was that such an escape carried with it all those eighteenth-century assumptions of civilization which had led to the situation he was trying to escape from. His own sense of civilization presupposed conflict and endless cycles of decline and resurrection. Quite apart from the practical ironies of Crèvecoeur's dream, he scarcely seems to realize that it begins the whole process over

---

[26] Ibid., p. 203.
[27] Ibid., p. 211.

again. He is thankful his daughter will not marry an Indian. He proposes to make his family's sustenance depend on agriculture, to read every night from the Decalogue, and finally, to teach the Indians themselves agriculture. Utopia becomes the re-establishment of the family and paternalist attitudes, which Crèvecoeur extends to all society, in an area where these assumptions are not likely to be threatened politically. That was, however, the literary dream. In practice, Crèvecoeur solved the problem quite satisfactorily for himself by going back to France.

The main subject of interest in Bartram's book was botany, the most popular subject for natural historians during this early period. In scientific terms there had been much interchange between European botanists and American collectors, almost from the time America itself was settled. The year before Bartram's *Travels* appeared, Robert John Thornton's magnificent *New Illustration of the Sexual System of Linnaeus* began publication, which was to botany what Audubon's *Birds of America* was to be to ornithology some 30 years later. Certainly botany was the first science in America to reach some kind of order. Benjamin Smith Barton's almost definitive handbook, *The Elements of Botany,* came out in 1803. Two years later the major botanical societies began their growth; Charleston, 1805, the Linnaean Society of Philadelphia, 1814, Washington, 1817, New York, 1818 and Pennsylvania, 1822.

For all the botanical interest, the imaginative scope of Bartram's work is not confined by it. Three journeys collecting specimens for Dr Fothergill of London, and covering 6,000 miles in three years define the formal structure of the book, and account for the wide range of its information on settlers, frontier sermons, rice machines, Indian antiquities, manners and customs. Carlyle's word 'biblical' gives some sense of the imaginative range of the work. It is more a successor to Gilbert White's *Natural History of Selborne* (1789), or Carver's *Travels* (1778) than to Linnaeus's *Systema Natura.* He himself said it was the last book, 'Written in the spirit of the old travellers'.[28] We can clearly see the lessening interest in the kind of work Bartram wrote by two remarks of his successors. In 1807 Benjamin Smith Barton wrote that 'lesser minds hang over romantic and visionary volumes', though he thought nevertheless that 'Natural History is not merely a science of Names and Arrangements, Higher objects should claim the attention of the philosophical naturalist'.[29]

[28] William Bartram, *Travels through North and South Carolina, Georgia, East & West Florida etc.* (1791; reprinted New York 1955) p. 5.
[29] Benjamin Smith Barton, *A Discourse on some of the principal desiderata in Natural History. . . .* (Philadelphia 1807) p. 55.

And some 20 years later again, John Godman said of Barton, 'Fortunately for mankind the reign of imagination is rapidly passing . . . and the conjectures of the highest authorities are "void, and of none effect" when opposed by facts, and subjected to the scrutiny of common sense'.[30]

Bartram's work is known for its scientific value and for its Arcadian descriptions of nature with 'its sooty sons of Afric, forgetting their bondage, in chorus [singing] the virtues of beneficence with Venus and Adonis in the shade'.[31] But, once again, perhaps the most outstanding features of the *Travels* are the large imaginative landscapes which articulate a whole philosophy of life. In Bartram's case the synthesis goes far beyond the simple nature and history dualisms of Crèvecoeur or Jefferson. Since Livingstone Lowes's classic work, *The Road to Xanadu* (1927) scholars have known of the role played by Bartram's description of the Great Sink in Coleridge's poem *Kubla Khan.* Lowes argues that Coleridge used his reading as he used other travel writers, like Bruce whose *Travels to Discover the Source of the Nile* appeared the year before Bartram's *Travels,* as some kind of undifferentiated raw material out of which the creative synthesis was made. The case is in fact quite the reverse. In *Kubla Khan,* Coleridge creates a landscape out of those features which have already been juxtaposed and synthesized in Bartram. Coleridge shares a common inheritance of landscape archetypes which reach back as far, at least, as Seneca's description of Mithraic nature worship:

> . . . we venerate the fountain-heads of great rivers, the secret eruption of a vast body of water from the secret places of the earth. . . .[32]

Coleridge's half-terrified celebration of the erotic processes of creation in *Kubla Khan* is paralleled by Bartram's apocalyptic description of the Great Sink where the almost gothic architecture of rock formations, as in Jefferson's description of the Blue Ridge Mountains in Virginia, take on connotations of life and death. Whereas in Jefferson's landscape, however, the emphasis is more social, a kind of heroic direction to progress, in Bartram the landscape is more private and more introspective.

Into the vast receptacle of the Great Sink pour the streams of the surrounding countryside: 'where they descend by slow degrees, through rocky caverns, into the bowels of the earth, whence they are carried by secret subterraneous channels into other receptacles

[30] John D. Godman, *American Natural History* (Philadelphia 1826) p. 251.
[31] Bartram, *Travels,* p. 257.
[32] Quoted from C. G. Jung, *Psychology of the Unconscious* (London 1922) p. 44.

and basons'.[33] Fish, in great numbers, pour into the Sink:

> ... where those who are so fortunate as to effect a retreat into the con-
> ductor, and escape the devouring jaws of the fearful alligator and armed
> gar descend into the earth through the wells and cavities or vast perfora-
> tions of the rocks, and from thence are conducted and carried away, by
> secret subterranean conduits and gloomy vaults to other distant lakes
> and rivers.[34]

In the Sink are three great doors or vent holes through the rocks,
'two near the centre and the other one near the rim'.[35] The landscape partakes of the nature of nightmare, and must be interpreted
as such. Bartram turns the landscape of the American South into a
quasi-symbolic private dream world where natural objects become
indices of ancient ritualized response. The vent holes become
equated with the orifices of the human body as psychological
symbolism, and we shall miss the force of Bartram's symbolism and
the reasons that Coleridge chose this particular passage for *Kubla
Khan,* if we ignore these factors. The subterranean tunnels are the
secret places of life and death, representative orifices in nature of
the woman's body: mouth (predatoriness), vagina (birth), anus
(rejection and false birth). The images, as in all religions and religious
mythologies which attempt to create patterns of security and
eternity, deliberately turn biological fact into cultural archetype.
Bartram, inheriting very similar assumptions about civilization and
nature as Jefferson and Crèvecoeur, gives us a psychological insight
into the fear of nature upon which those assumptions are built as
it effects the private, rather than the public consciousness. Bartram's
Sink and his alligators are to the secularized mythologies of the
natural civilization of the eighteenth-century philosophers, what the
medieval vision of Hell was to the Christian cosmos. Everywhere
Bartram goes, he speculates on founding cities, as again and again
the idea of a beneficent nature breaks down in his prose, and with
it the dictates of reason. The city-country debate is given a new
twist, as the country far from being the place of virtue and repose,
turns, by virtue of the confrontation with the American wilderness,
into an area of actual hostility:

> I found myself unable, notwithstanding the attentive admonitions and
> persuasive argument of reason, entirely to erase from my mind those
> impressions which I had received from the society of the amiable and
> polite inhabitants of Charleston; and I could not help comparing my

[33] Bartram, *Travels,* p. 177.
[34] Ibid., p. 178.
[35] Ibid., p. 179.

present situation in some degree to Nebuchadnezzar's, when expelled
from the society of men, and constrained to roam in the mountains and
wilderness, there to feed with the wild beasts of the forest.[36]

In a remarkable passage earlier in the *Travels,* Bartram gives us
insight into how the vision of reason involves not only a nightmare
at its centre, but a confusion between an earlier eighteenth-century
theory of vision in which the mind was passive and the senses stable,
and a newer, more 'Romantic' theory, more private and creative
and hence far less stable. Not only is the prose remarkable for its
magnificent dramatic qualities and its fine sense of climax, but here
too are anticipations of Melville's own landscape of dream and reality
with the devouring animal of nightmare at the centre:

> The pine groves passed, we immediately find ourselves on the entrance
> of the expansive airy pine forests, on parallel chains of low swelling
> mounds, called the Sands Hills; their ascent so easy, as to be almost
> imperceptible to the progressive traveller; yet at a distant view before
> us in some degree exhibit the appearance of the mountainous swell of
> the ocean immediately after a tempest; but yet, as we approach them,
> they insensibly disappear, and seem to be lost; and we should be ready
> to conclude all to be a visionary scene, were it not for the sparkling
> ponds and lakes, which at the same time gleam through the open forests,
> before us and on every side, retaining them in the eye, until we come up
> with them. And at last the imagination remains flattered and dubious,
> by their uniformity, being most circular or elliptical, and almost surroun-
> ded with expansive green meadows; and always a picturesque dark grove
> of live oak, magnolia, gordonia, and the fragrant orange, encircling
> rocky shaded grotto of transparent water, on some border of the pond
> or lake; which, without the aid of any poetic fable, one might naturally
> suppose to be the sacred abode or temporary residence of the guardian
> spirit; but is actually the possession and retreat of a thundering absolute
> crocodile.[37]

(The British Museum actually has a drawing of the 'thundering,
absolute crocodile. pl. 28.) Where Bartram's account differs from
Jefferson's is in the new sense of movement, and with it the sense
of a shifting viewpoint. The peace in the background is created by
the approach of the traveller and is itself characterized as the aftermath of tempest. The sand hills however, lose their characteristic
shape in the near view, and, for the traveller, their sense of reality
might have been lost altogether were it not for the lakes, which
provide, like the image in a *camera obscura* a picture less open to
the vagaries and deceptions of the human eye. The lake-mirror gives

---

[36] Ibid., p. 292.
[37] Ibid., pp. 155–6.

28 *The Alegator of St Johns,* drawing by William Bartram. (*Courtesy of the British Museum, London.*)

an objective sense of uniformity (circles and ellipses) and of picturesque security in the circular lake, groves and grottoes. But the final twist is that this very harmony is deceptive, for the centre of the landscape is occupied not by the deity of reason but by 'a thundering absolute crocodile'. The shifting backwards and forwards from a reasonable reality which yet deceives to a personal creative viewpoint which cannot be trusted, constitutes Bartram's reaction to the terms of the nature-history inheritance. His landscape descriptions give us honest and complex insights into the American male contemplating the formation of civilization from wilderness; a masculine dream of reason which characterizes nature as a woman's body with the power of life and death. It breaks down that theory of vision which renders an entirely dualistic and eternal landscape, and gives the personal viewpoint a new emphasis which, if not yet to be trusted, at least challenges the absoluteness of an older more authoritarian vision.

In the next chapter we shall see some of these assumptions as they are put into practice by the men who undertook officially to explore the continent for the United States government. The experience of exploration as written down in the offical reports between 1800 and 1860 is one of the most important cultural artefacts of the early republic's life.

7

Government Expeditions, 1800 to 1860

> One space official has called the Apollo 8 mission 'the triumph of the squares'—meaning 'the guys with crew-cuts and slide rules who read the Bible and get things done'.
>
> *The Times,* 10 January 1969, p. 8.

> Let Sea Discoverers to New Worlds have gone
> Let Maps to other, worlds on worlds have showne
> Let us possess one world, each hath one, and is one.
> Donne, *The Good Morrow*

On one of the latest of American government expeditions, the Apollo 8 flight to the moon, the astronauts cited Lewis and Clark as their historical forebears. When Lewis and Clark cast about for appropriate historical predecessors, they came up with Columbus and with Captain Cook:

> Our vessels consisted of six small canoes, and two large perogues. This little fleet altho' not quite so rispectable as those of Columbus or Captain Cook, were still viewed by us with as much pleasure as those deservedly famous adventurers ever beheld theirs.[1]

Columbus as the historical archetype takes us back to the very discovery of America itself. The explorations of Captain Cook in the Pacific, however, provided a practical recent example of three actual voyages in the second half of the eighteenth century. Cook's expeditions articulate that peculiar mixture of late eighteenth-century scientific curiosity, and covert governmental imperial ambition. So close are the features of Cook's expeditions to those of the Americans, that not to mention some of the shared presuppositions and experiences would be like trying to deal with Rittenhouse without mentioning Newton.

Like the American explorations, the British ones were made

---

[1] Reuben Gold Thwaites, ed., *Original Journals of the Lewis and Clark Expedition, 1804–1806* (1904–5; reprinted New York 1959) vol. I, p. 7. Hereafter referred to as *Journals.* The explorers' original spellings have been followed.

initially under the secret auspices of the War Department, and besides more obvious imperialistic designs, a large part of their energies and activities were scientific. Cook observed, like Rittenhouse, the transit of Venus, and made many notes on ethnology and natural history. Like Lewis and Clark's, the voyage was conducted with strict military discipline which did not rule out summary flogging to maintain order. Cook's journals, like Lewis and Clark's, were simply day-to-day accounts which fairly nonsystematically observed everything from the transit of Venus to cannibalism. The descriptions of the inhabitants of the South Seas follow the same stylized pattern of intellectual inquiry as Lewis and Clark's descriptions of the North American Indian which begin with such visual and empirical evidences as physical form, observations of clothing and tattooing, and conclude with much less quantifiable matters such as 'customs and manners' which include major topics of war, sex, death and religion. In scientific terms the mode of vision was partly determined by the categorizations of the eighteenth-century whole earth system such as we have already seen outlined in Linnaeus, Buffon and Morse. The scientists carefully briefed the explorers. Just as Benjamin Rush of the Philadelphia Philosophical Society was responsible for drawing up a questionnaire on the Indians for Lewis and Clark, so the president of the Royal Society, James Douglas, drew up a list of hints and questions for Cook, including such advice as that natives should not be frightened by loud noises but 'should be first entertained near the shore with a soft Air'.[2] The methodology of inquiry stemmed partly from a wish to test European institutions and manners against the new and unknown, often in terms of the concepts of savagery and civilization, and partly from a wish to give some kind of shape and order to a genuine scientific curiosity.

　　Another feature of Cook's expeditions which provided a model for the Lewis and Clark expedition and which lasted down to the expeditions for the Pacific railroad, was the inclusion of painters to execute the visual record. On Cook's first expedition, Sir Joseph Banks, aristocratic representative of Royal Society science, engaged Sydney Parkinson and Alexander Buchan as painters to the expedition. After Buchan's death, the greater part of the task fell to Parkinson who found himself, as did the American artists of the nineteenth century, alternating between, and combining strict *camera obscura*-like topographical drawing and the image of nature as picturesque natural ruin, torn between 'the needs of a scientist

---

[2] J. C. Beaglehole, ed., *The Journals of Captain Cook* (Cambridge 1955) vol. I, p. 515.

and the tastes of the Grand Tour'.[3] On the second expedition William Hodges's paintings, in the style of his teacher, Richard Wilson, depict Pacific landscape as a record of antiquity. When Wolletts engraved Hodges's pictures they underwent a further transformation as can be seen in the Easter Island monument pictures, where the monuments to history are depicted as terrifying images of the grotesque. The movement from the vision of classical ruined order to dream landscapes of nightmare is as obvious in the change of medium here, as it is in the different juxtaposed styles of Bartram's prose. Another artist, Joseph Gilbert, explored the artistic possibilities of rock formations (paralleled again in the architectural geology of Bartram's descriptions) which American artist proto-geologists were to revel in right up to the Civil War. On Cook's third expedition, John Webber was the official artist and his drawing of a white bear and the descriptions of bear fights in the actual journal, strangely anticipate the accounts of the grizzly bear which accompany nearly every American expedition. As a final note on this particularly important expedition which provided so many visual and literary precedents for the American explorations, attention must be drawn to the drawings of James Cleverley, the ship's carpenter. These sketches worked up by his brother John into paintings, were sold, transformed into coloured aquatints, as late as 1787−8: an early anticipation of the popular success of Currier and Ives in mid-nineteenth-century America.

In many ways the Lewis and Clark expedition was a kind of active extension into reality of the principles of Jefferson's *Notes on Virginia*: a conversion of nature into a nation. Crucial to this process was the practical use of direction-finding instruments reflecting, as we have already seen, a utilitarian relationship between theoretical geometry and the requirements of trade and empire. Rittenhouse had done the fieldwork on the western limits of Pennsylvania for the map of the *Notes on Virginia,* and Jefferson sought advice on obtaining proper instruments for 'ascertaining by celestial observations the geography of the country . . .'.[4] The compass, the sextant, the artificial horizon and the chronometer were the key instruments, and Andrew Ellicot recommended to Jefferson the British-made Arnold's chronometer. Lewis, after much discussion, wrote to the president summing up the advice he had received from distinguished surveyors and instrument makers like Robert Patterson and George

[3] Bernard Smith, 'European Vision and the South Pacific', *Journal of the Warburg and Courtauld Institutes,* 8 (1950), 69.

[4] Donald Jackson, ed., *Letters of the Lewis and Clark Expedition with related documents, 1783−1854* (Urbana, Illinois 1962) p. 48. Hereafter referred to as *Letters.*

Ellicot. They would need, 'two sextants (one of which must be constructed for the *back observation*) an artificial Horizon or two; a good Arnold's watch or Chronometer, a Surveyor's compass with a ball and socket and two pole chains, and a set of plotting instruments'.[5] Lewis was sent off to the Philadelphia Philosophical Society to learn how to survey.

While making these preparations and overseeing them with his usual practical energy, Jefferson allayed the fears of the Spanish by talking of 'filling up the canvas',[6] an aesthetic gloss on the more practical realities of scientific empire building. 'Very speculative and a lover of glory',[7] was how the Spanish *chargé d'affaires* described Jefferson a year before the Louisiana purchase, and the Spanish were not deceived by Jefferson's characterization of the expedition as a 'literary pursuit'.

If we look at Lewis and Clark's reactions, first to the landscape they were among the first white men to see, then to the indigenous peoples, and finally to the fauna and flora of the country, we can see how *a priori* ideas about the science of natural history affect their response to the virgin land. Their reactions to the landscape were, as we might expect from military men, split two ways. On the one hand they surveyed and measured it, creating continuous maps of the Mississippi-Missouri river, and on the other hand, somewhat lacking topographical skills, they sang its glories in long literary descriptions in the manner of Virginian gentlemen of sensibility. They dismissed Indian stories about striking landscape features somewhat arrogantly, and substituted the conventional rhetoric of the eighteenth-century sublime. Before the Great Falls of the Mississippi, however, Lewis is speechless:

> I wished for the pencil of a Salvator Rosa [a Titian] or the pen of Thomson, that I might be enabled to give to the enlightened world some just idea of this truly magnificent and sublimely grand object, which has from the commencement of time been concealed from the view of civilized man; but this was fruitless and vain. I most sincerely regretted that I had not brought a crimme [camera] obscura with me by the assistance of which even I could have hoped to have done better. . . .[8]

Lewis attempted to respond to the landscape through a very literary view of the visual arts which was common enough at the time.

[5] *Letters*, p. 48.
[6] *Letters*, p. 254.
[7] *Letters*, p. 4.
[8] *Journals*, vol. II, pp. 149–150.

Thomson's famous lines: 'Whate're Lorraine light touched with softening hue,/Or savage Rosa dashed, or learned Poussin drew', structures this pioneer's vision of the raw American landscape. The desire for the *camera obscura* to redress his own artistic imperfections is honest enough, however, and shows the faith in objective truth which he believed such an instrument would reveal. His description of the famous Mississippi bluffs, gives us an interesting variation of the double vision of nature and art we have already observed in Bartram and Jefferson himself:

> The water in the course of time in descending from those hills and plains on either side of the river has trickled down the soft sand clifts and woarn it into a thousand grotesque figures, which with the help of a little immagination and an oblique view, at a distance we made to represent eligant ranges of lofty freestone buildings, having their parapets well stocked with statuary; . . . some collumns standing and almost entire with their pedastles and capitals; others retaining their pedastles but deprived by time or accident of their capitals, some lying prostrate an broken othe[r]s in the form of vast pyramids of conic structure bearing a serees of other pyramids on their tops becoming less as they ascend and finally terminating in a sharp point.[9]

It is significant that Lewis, his vocabulary formed by the European cult of the ruins of time, should see in the virgin land the relics of antiquity. Rather more awkwardly than the highly stylized syntheses of a Jefferson and a Bartram, Lewis gives what he thinks is the scientific explanation first, then, admitting distance, an oblique view and imagination, gives us a wild, almost Piranesi-like architectural configuration, which is impossible to visualize and which pushes the linealities of architectural order to the point of breakdown and confusion. These architectural images become the formula for describing the bluffs for a century. The first actual pictorial representation of unusual American geological formations in exaggerated architectural and 'gothic' mode are to be found in Henry Schoolcraft's *A Narrative Journal etc.* of 1820 and they continue a fashion already extant in English engravings of travels to Switzerland and Scotland in the later years of the eighteenth century.

Jefferson's main object in his projected relations with Indians was to extend the fur trade and deprive the tribes, peacefully if possible, of their lands. His message to Congress, 18 January 1803, betrays his anxiety that Indians are beginning to refuse to sell their lands as readily as in the past. 'A very few tribes only are not yet obstinately in these dispositions.'[10] Their instant 'civilization' is

[9] *Journals*, vol. II, p. 101.
[10] *Letters*, p. 11.

therefore necessary. It is imperative that they leave off hunting and indulge in the civilized pursuits of agriculture and domestic manufacture. The philosophy of possession as articulated by a Locke or a Volney is given government approval. The Osages were informed thus of the Louisiana purchase:

> Never more will you have occasion to change your fathers. We are all now of one family, born in the same land & bound to live as brothers. . . . For this purpose I sent a beloved man, Capt. Lewis, one of my own household to learn something of the people with whom we are now united, to let you know that we are your friends, to invite you to come and see us, and to tell us how we can be useful to you . . . on your return tell your people that I shall take them all by the hand; that I become their father hereafter. . . .[11]

On one level the expedition becomes a family romance, with Lewis and Clark holding paternal authority from the absent deity (Jefferson). In case the pristine simplicity of these family arrangements did not devastate by its logic, the Indians, in the same speech, were reminded that the whites were 'all gun men'.

Lewis carried out the instructions of his spiritual father. To every Indian chief he presented an 'Indian Commission' with a blank for the chief's name, promising protection in return for peace. He also presented medals with the image of the father of the country engraved on one side. These medals were visible emblems of power, and hung like millstones round the necks of the obedient chiefs. But not all of them were willing converts. One, seeing very clearly the implications of the ritual, informed Lewis that 'he knew the white people were all *medicine* and that he was afraid of the medal or anything that white people gave to them'. A footnote from Alexander Henry's *Journal* gives a fair indication of white attitudes to such a refusal:

> The Big Bellies pretended to say that these ornaments conveyed bad medicine to them and their children. They are exceedingly superstitious, and therefore, supposed they could not better dispense of these articles than by giving them to the nations with whom they frequently warred, in the hope the ill-luck would be conveyed to them. They were disgusted at the high-sounding language the American captains bestowed upon themselves and their own nation . . . these haughty savages, who have too high an opinion of themselves to entertain the least idea of acknowledging any race to be their superiors.[12]

The Indians were correct in imagining the medals to be magical, for they were a visual inducement to white ancestor worship. To

[11] *Letters*, p. 200.
[12] *Journals*, vol. V, p. 353.

give Jefferson's image to their enemies was the perfect comment.

We get some idea of how the ordinary men on the expedition viewed possible contact with the Indians from Patrick Gass, whose account of the whole expedition was the first to reach print:

> The best authenticated accounts informed us, that we were to pass through a country possessed by numerous, powerful and warlike nations of savages, of gigantic stature, fierce, treacherous and cruel; and particularly hostile to white men.[13]

Such rumours were not discouraged by the two captains who throughout the expedition proceeded with as much caution as though they were still fighting the Indian wars of the nineties. To play on such fears beyond sensible precaution was a strict inducement to discipline. More learned anxieties are inherent in the scientific questionaires which the expedition was supposed to answer. It was from a list initially prepared by Benjamin Rush that Clark made his final draft of questions which the expedition was to answer. This questionnaire was drawn up under ten headings: physical history, morals, religion, traditions, agriculture and domestic economy, fishing and hunting, war, amusements, dress, customs and manners. Although the continuous narrative of the journals allowed more scope for more uncategorizable responses, these divisions do highlight the patterns of interest within the written observations.

On the expedition, actual contact with the Indians varied from the pompous medal giving and official speeches to the quite open sexual relations of the men with Indian squaws. Gass laments in his journal that he does not have space to entertain his readers with 'narratives of feats of love as well as of arms'.[14] The split between business and pleasure, officialdom and life, science and nature, public and private reveals itself ingenuously in Gass's comments: 'Though we could furnish a sufficient number of entertaining stories and pleasant anecdotes, we do not think it prudent to swell our journal with them; as our views are directed to more useful information'.[15] Several of the men contracted various forms of venereal disease and were attended to by Lewis who acted as doctor. Wherever this miniature army went, the effects of civilization followed, and Gass commented, 'An old bawd with her punks,

---

[13] Patrick Gass, *Journal of the Voyages and Travels of a Corps of Discovery, Under the command of Capt. Lewis and Capt. Clarke of the army of the United States, from the mouth of the river Missouri through the interior parts of North America to the Pacific Ocean, During the Years, 1804, 1805 and 1806.* (4th edn. Philadelphia 1812) p. 12.

[14] Ibid., p. 74.

[15] Ibid., p. 74.

may also be found in some of the villages of the Missouri, as well as in the large cities of polished nations'.[16]

Wintering at Fort Clatsop presented certain problems. As long as the expedition remained on the move, the day-to-day unexpected experiences could be dealt with, and discipline, because of the naturally active and interdependent responsibilities of such an endeavour, was somewhat more relaxed. As soon as the microscopic society was founded, however, the fort built, and the boundaries established, full military discipline was instantly reinstated. Lewis complained that it was difficult to impress on the minds of the men, 'the necessity of always being on our guard with respect to them [Indians]. This confidence on our part we know to have been the effect of a series of friendly and uninterrupted intercourse'.[17]

For the more educated captains, the response to the Indians is almost entirely visual. It is as if the objects surrounding and belonging to their way of life were being continuously looked at through a *camera obscura.* It is another variant of the museum mentality, and indeed the iconography of burial mounds, Indian ball games, cooking implements, utensils, canoes, dress and wigwams was to continue in carefully preserved lifelessness through the pages of Schoolcraft's mammoth work of the mid-century to the photographs of Indians in the late nineteenth-century *Proceedings* of the Smithsonian Institution and to the glossy pages of the *National Geographic* in the twentieth century. This coldly objective visual distancing broke down somewhat comically in the Captains' repeated comments on Indian female dress. Of the Columbia river Indians, Lewis remarked that they dressed, 'so as barely to hide those parts which are so sacredly hid and secured by our women'.[18] Clark, always the blunter, remarked that one female garment, 'barely covers the mons veneris, to which it is drawn so close that the whole shape is plainly perseived'.[19] Perhaps such remarks are fitting illustrations of that substitution of the eye for the body inherent in the training given to a topographer.

Although many animals and birds were given lengthy descriptions in the *Journals* and in what is now called *Codex N,* Lewis and Clark discovered no new varieties of animals, and but three new species of birds. However two American natural historians, Rafinesque and George Ord (who was a rival and enemy of Audubon) derived some benefit from the descriptions, and the three new birds appeared in

[16] Ibid., p. 74.
[17] *Journals,* vol. V, p. 91.
[18] *Journals,* vol. III, p. 125.
[19] *Journals,* vol. IV, p. 222.

plate 20, vol. III of Alexander Wilson's pioneering *American Ornithology* (1808–14). At Fort Clatsop, Lewis had leisure to write extensive descriptions of the local fauna: mountain sheep, sea otters, racoons, silver fox, fox squirrel, large brown wolf, tiger cat, antelope, panther [sic] and pole cat as well as of the more striking examples of grizzly bear and buffalo which had both already been encountered. Nonscientific description was brief, a note on the value of the fur, the taste of a certain fish and perhaps a general remark on the beauty of the specimen. The California condor whose quills were used to store gold dust during the 49 rush, and was now almost extinct, is described, and there is even a crude drawing in the journal. From these journals as well as all the many hundreds of other travel accounts, official and private, one gets a breathtaking sense of the teeming wild life of the almost virgin American wilderness. Lewis commented, 'We eat an immense amount of meat, it requires 4 deer, an Elk and a deer, or one buffalo, to supply us plentifully 24 hours'.[20]

Apart from the necessities of life, hunting was clearly indulged in for the thrill. A strange incident is reported in Gass's account in which a grizzly bear, like Bartram's 'absolute crocodile', an absolute force at the centre of its own universe, becomes an occasion for the indulgence of weird boyish games:

> In the evening, most of the corps crossed over to an island to attack and rout its monarch, a large brown bear that held possession and seemed to defy all that would beseige him there. Our troops, however, stormed the place, gave no quarter, and its commander fell. Our army returned the same evening to the camp without haveing suffered any loss on their side.[21]

Unlike Bartram's account, however, the animal is no longer part of a dream landscape but of an actual one to which the fantasies of the dream are transferred. The bear is a *possessor* which the military detachment must ritually attack in order to become possessors themselves. Killing thus becomes a ritual of expiation for the guilt repressed in taking possession. The militaristic terminology embodies fantasies of killing without consequences and illustrates the need to impose order on a seemingly hostile nature.

Other expeditions followed and among the more interesting were those made by Major Long some 20 years after Lewis and Clark. Stephen Harriman Long's first expedition to the upper reaches of the Missouri was made under the auspices of the War Department

[20] *Journals,* vol. II, p. 227.
[21] Gass, *Journal,* p. 105.

in 1817. His most famous expedition was made shortly after, and an account of it published in Philadelphia by Edwin James in 1822–3. A third expedition (1824) to the sources of the St Peter's River completed the first stage of Long's extended activities. Thereafter he turned to surveying for the railroads. Long became an authority on railroad engineering, starting out with the Ohio railroad in 1828. He made a complicated chart of tables which eliminated the necessity for making computations of grades and curvatures in the field. Originally an assistant mathematics professor at West Point, Long thus united the theorizing of mathematics and physical geographical analysis.

Edwin James, who was botanist and geologist to the second expedition, compiled his two volume work from the notes of Long, Thomas Say (whose own work on American insects became a classic of the genre),[22] and 'other gentlemen of the party'. For the first time scientific interest became the special concern of expert individuals. Dr Baldwin was chief botanist, Say, zoologist and one Mr Jessup, geologist. Charles Willson Peale's son, Titian, was 'assistant naturalist' whose task it was to collect specimens suitable for preserving, and who was to occupy himself in 'drafting and delineating them . . . and in sketching the stratifications of rocks, earths, etc. as present in the declivities of precipices'.[23] The expedition also included a landscape painter, Samuel Seymour, and his instructions were explicit. He had to:

> . . . furnish sketches of landscapes, wherever we meet with any distinguished for their beauty and grandeur. He will also paint miniature likenesses, or portraits, if required, of distinguished Indians, and exhibit groups of savages engaged in celebrating their festivals, or sitting in council, and in general illustrate any subject, that may be deemed appropriate in his art.[24]

Seymour was the first American to paint the landscape of the upper Missouri, and the two frontispieces of the two volumes are outstandingly good.

The first of these pl. 29 which is of the Rocky Mountains, seen at a distance over the prairie, transfers certain aspects of eighteenth-century vision to the far west of America. They can be seen in the

---

[22] Thomas Say, *American Entomology, or Descriptions of the Insects of North America. Illustrated by Colored Figures From Original Drawings Executed from Nature* (Philadelphia 1824).

[23] Edwin James, *Account of an Expedition from Pittsburgh to the Rocky Mountains, performed in the Years, 1819, 1820. By Order of the Hon. J. C. Calhoun, Secretary of War, under the Command of Maj. S. H. Long of the U.S. Top. Engineers* (London 1823) p. 3.

[24] Ibid., vol. I, p. 3.

29 *Distant View of the Rocky Mountains (1823),* by S. Seymore, del. in Edwin James, Account of an Expedition . . . to the Rocky Mountains. (*Courtesy of the Newberry Library, Chicago.*)

raised foreground, an old painterly device for coping with the relation of the foreground to the middle distance, with its contemplative figures, and the low horizon. The details of the immediate foreground also demonstrate that interest in exact and detailed delineation of flora even in a comparatively huge landscape which continues in American landscape painting through the visionary landscapes of Cole and Church. This is a picture in which scientific detail has been generalized into symbolic order. The foreground is occupied by huge white bones, perhaps memories of Say's and Peale's earlier interest in the burial mounds near St Louis, and hence illustrates that sense of the past which we have seen appropriate to the foregrounds of Jefferson and Crèvecoeur. The hallucinatory feeling of space, obtained even in a frontispiece as small as this, is achieved by the large empty plain at the centre of the picture and bounded by the abruptly-rising range of dazzling white mountains in the background. The solitary gigantic tree to the right startlingly out of proportion adds to this sense of space which is peculiarly American, and there is a slightly inhuman quality coming from the setting of the living details of the picture between the fossilized bones and the mountains. The overall structure of the landscape also illustrates that concept of the great plain which so unfactually dominated American conceptions of the West from about this time, and which a recent geographer has brilliantly analysed in a series of articles dealing with early American conceptualizations of the country.[25] The picture itself then is an example of the way in which the art theory of generalizing from particulars coincides with a similar scientific mode and helps to conceptualize the very vision of the landscape itself.

In spite of the renewed tendency to specialized research, Seymour's picture indicates a wholeness of response governed by certain inherited concepts of nature, of art and of science, which emphasized varied relationships within an albeit somewhat aristocratic but encyclopedic world vision. In the text of James's two volumes, in spite of the numerous authorities quoted and cited (Jefferson, Humboldt, Collins, Michaux, Marquette and Joliet, Bartram, Bonpland, Benjamin Smith Barton, Nuttal, Silliman and Say) the writing still has a more catholic range of interest and reference. Accounts of soil and flora are interspersed with descriptions of camp meetings, methods of hauling boats up the Missouri by capstans, descriptions of early steam boats, and even of quotations from Daniel Boone ('I think it time to remove when I can no longer fell a tree for fuel, so that its top will lie within a few yards of the door of my cabin').[26] Unfortunately in the final stages of the expedition, Long and Say split off from the rest of the party only to be robbed of their most valuable notes and specimens by three defectors.

The main categorizations of landscape, ethnology, fauna and flora, can, in spite of the generalized interest of the narrative, still be usefully used in summarizing the main natural history interests of the account. The bluffs of the Missouri and the sandstone formations at the base of the Rocky Mountains provoke the writer into the now familiar contemplation of the immensity of geological time and catastrophe:

> It is difficult, when contemplating the present appearance and situation of these rocks, to prevent the imagination from wandering back to that remote period, when the billows of the ocean lashed the base of the Andes, depositing, during a succession of ages, that vast accumulation of rounded fragments of rocks, alternating with beds of animal remains, which now extends without interruption from the base of this range to the summits of the Alleghany mountains; and endeavouring to form

[25] See G. Malcolm Lewis, 'Early American Exploration and the Cis-Rocky Mountain Desert, 1803–1823', *Great Plains Journal*, 5 (Fall 1965) pp. 1–11; 'The Great Plains Region and its Image of Flatness', *Journal of the West*, 6 (January 1967) pp. 11–26; 'William Gilpin and the Concept of the Great Plains Region', *Annals of the Association of American Geographers*, 56 (March 1966) pp. 33–51.

[26] James, *Account*, vol. I, p. 98.

some idea of that great subsequent catastrophe by which this secondary formation has so changed its elevation, in relation to the primitive, that its margin has been broken off and thrown into an inclined or vertical position.[27]

The mountain is a visual condensation of cosmic time, with the patterns of history observable in its very constitution.

James's attitudes to the Indians and Indian legends vary in detail from those of Lewis and Clark, though, on the whole, the generalized descriptions familiar from the previous expedition are adhered to. The Indians themselves are seldom communicative, have limited abstract and metaphysical ideas, and are lazy. The Indian graves near St Louis provide an occasion for historical pieties and reflections on the passing of time:

> In everything human we are reminded what has been so often said of the pyramids of Egypt, and may with equal propriety be applied to all the words of men, 'these monuments must perish, but the grass that grows between their disappointed fragments shall be renewed from year to year.'[28]

James's attitude to Indian legends is, however, rather unusual for the time:

> Such anecdotes, however puerile and absurd they may be, if characteristic, lead us to a more accurate and complete knowledge of the manners and habits of the people, than still more copious general remarks and reflections.[29]

However, the usual observations are made on the subject of the Indians' sexual habits. Such Western moralities as 'conjugal fidelity' seemed again and again to be flouted. As if to make up in sentiment what to all observation was a somewhat unpalatable truth, James, like many others of his time, attempts to prove Indians human by inflicting on them Western cultural myths of courtly romance:

> Many circumstances tend to show that the squaw is susceptible of the most tender and permanent attachment to an individual of the opposite sex, and that on the cessation of all hope of a union with the beloved object, the consequences have sometimes been fatal.[30]

James does, however, publish certain phallic rituals which Catlin supressed some 20 years later.

---

[27] Ibid., vol. II, p. 188.
[28] Ibid., vol. I, p. 59.
[29] Ibid., vol. I, p. 257.
[30] Ibid., vol. I, p. 223.

Many hundreds of animals are described in the report, the vast herds of buffalo compelling the greatest wonder. The appendix foreshadows the more specialized reporting of the future in its tripartite division of animals, birds, reptiles; Indian language of signs; Indian speeches.

John Charles Frémont's (1813—90) three expeditions are interesting because they indicate a markedly increased public awareness of the official expedition. They begin in 1839 and end in 1845 with a court martial for Frémont over his activities in the Mexican war. Frémont's career pointedly illustrates those connections, already well-developed, between scientific interest, official exploratory policy, imperialist ethics and exploitation of natural resources. Early in his career Frémont resigned his post teaching mathematics to the Navy, and became, like so many others, a second lieutenant in the US topographical corps. In a career which uncannily follows that of Long in its early stages, Frémont's first important task was to survey a railroad route from Charleston to Cincinatti, 1836—7.[31] In the same year again under a Captain Williams, he made a reconnaissance of Cherokee territory prior to the removal of the Cherokee west of the Mississippi. A complacent paternalism accompanied topographical skills. For Frémont the two qualities 'of permanence and responsibility make the army the best and simplest as well as the safest and least expensive medium through which to control and care for these Indian wards of the nation. We have taken away from them their property and means of support and are bound to a corresponding obligation'.[32] The assumptions of absolute military power create these liberal moralizings, for Frémont recommends an efficiently costed sop to conscience without challenging his own or the nation's sense of destiny.

The first two expeditions, worked up in sentimental prose on the model of Irving's *Adventures of Captain Bonneville* (1837) by his wife Jesse, daughter of Senator Benton, was put on sale to the public at the father's expense. Benton was the mid-western mouthpiece of Manifest Destiny who dominated the senate for more than 30 years. The expedition became a literary artefact articulating the conscious aspirations of a colonizing nation already pressing for expansion in Texas, Mexico, California and Oregon. New folk heroes replaced conscious Americanizations of faithful European retainers like Cooper's Natty Bumppo. Kit Carson appeared for the first time in

---

[31] John C. Frémont, *Memoirs of my Life* (Chicago and New York 1887) p. 23.
[32] Ibid., p. 27.

the report of 1843:

> Mounted on a fine horse, without a saddle, and scouring bareheaded
> over the prairies, Kit was one of the finest pictures of a horseman I have
> even seen.[33]

Jesse's descriptions of those archetypes of Western landscape, the
white hero, Indian, buffalo, and gothic geological scenery make a
dream world which complements the daily violence. Some of the
ambiguities can be seen in the following description of the buffalo:

> A few miles brought us into the midst of the Buffalo, swarming in
> immense numbers over the plains, where they had left scarcely a blade
> of grass standing. Mr Preuss, who was sketching at a little distance in the
> rear, had at first noted them as large groves of timber. In the sight of such
> a mass of life, the traveller feels a strange emotion of grandeur. We had
> heard from a distance a dull and confused murmuring, and when we
> came in view of their dark masses, there was not one among us who did
> not feel his heart beat quicker. It was the early part of the day, when
> the herds are feeding; and everywhere they were in motion. Here and
> there a huge old bull was rolling in the grass, and clouds of dust rose in
> the air from various parts of the bands, each the scene of some obstinate
> fight. Indians and buffalo make the poetry and life of the prairie, and
> our camp was full of their exhilaration. In place of the quiet monotony
> of the march, relieved only by the cracking of the whip, and an 'avance
> donc! enfant de garce!' shouts and songs resounded from every part of
> the line, and our evening camp was always the commencement of a
> feast, which terminated only with our departure on the following
> morning.[34]

Again the description depends on the contrast of the near and far
view. Preuss, the artist, not a practical man, at first mistakes them
in an appropriately picturesque way. Burke's criteria of indefiniteness for sublime appearances is followed, and in the sense of grandeur
there is mingled a military fear. The dark masses are threatening,
sporadic fights break out, as in pre-Hollywood manner the panoramic
shot narrows down to the single solitary old bulls apparently in a
playful mood. Like a Hollywood spectacular the scene provides
visual time off from the sheer boredom of military routine—except
that the 'prospect' of a feast is instantly realizable as Frémont's men
both had their poetry and ate it. In a complementary incident
Frémont sees buffalo and the hunt through a telescope, bringing

---

[33] John Charles Frémont, *A Report on an Exploration of the Country lying between
the Missouri River and the Rocky Mountains, on the line of the Kansas and Great Platte
Rivers* (Washington, D.C. 1843) p. 13.
[34] Ibid., p. 16.

the experience near like a dream through the intensification of the visual sense:

> The apparent silence, and the dimly seen figures flitting by with such rapidity, gave it a kind of dreamy effect, and seemed more like a picture than a scene of real life.[35]

The isolating and distancing effect of the telescope simultaneously creates the sense of dream and control. The sense of wonder is distanced from practical considerations through the visual medium.

In the literary landscapes the laws of perspective, isolating foreground, middle ground and background, together with that pervasive sense of the great plain in front of a backdrop of huge mountains determine the overall structure of the picture. Fort Laramie gleams white in the uncertain light of the evening, with Indian huts clustered around like medieval cottages before a baron's castle, giving a feeling of precarious civilization obtained against the menacing beauty of nature. The Black Hills make up the background and the writer comments that with the prominent peak of Laramie mountain, strongly drawn in the clear light of the western sky, where the sun had already set, 'the whole formed at the moment a strikingly beautiful picture'.[36] For Frémont the landscape illustrates a religious symbolism of life and death. Preuss's sketch of the Wind River mountains **pl. 30** gives us all the exaggerated iconographic features of geological eternity, and Frémont commented

30 *Central Chain of the Wind River Mountains*, Preuss, del. in J. C. Fremont. A Report on an Expedition (Washington, DC, 1843). (*Courtesy of the British Library, London*.)

[35] Ibid., p. 26.
[36] Ibid., p. 35.

on the highest peaks of the Rocky Mountains:

> A stillness the most profound, and terrible solitude forced themselves
> constantly on the mind as the great features of the place.[37]

Because they are so huge, they can only be contemplated at a
distance. Since what is seen at a distance is traditionally dream-
like, the psychology of vision seemed to give confirmation to the
literary commonplaces of the symbolic role of mountains, prevalent
since Burke and Wordsworth. But for Frémont the sense of eternity
and death is juxtaposed with live nature. Of the Rockies he says,
'the gigantic disorder of enormous masses, and savage sublimity of
naked rock', is placed in 'wonderful contrast with innumerable
green spots of a rich floral beauty, shut up in their stern recesses'.[38]
It is a naturalization of a Christian vision where the eternal protects
and encloses the living.

The report itself became, for eastern readers, substitute gratification for the denial of first-hand western experience. And the public
manipulation paid off as Frémont, in traditional American double-
think, entered Washington a national hero in spite of his court
martial. Jesse Frémont revelled in the descriptions of her bewitching
husband, thrilled to his stories of barbaric feasts, of sublime mountains, of Indians and buffalo, and the envied male tasks of Carson
and his henchman Godey:

> In the afternoon a war-whoop was heard, such as Indians made when
> returning from a victorious enterprise; and soon Carson and Godey
> appeared, driving before them a band of horses, recognized by Fuentes
> as part of those they had lost. Two bloody scalps, dangling from the end
> of Godey's gun, announced that they had overtaken the Indians as well
> as the horses.[39]

It was Jesse's writing up of the first two of these expeditions that
made Carson the popular figure he was in the public imagination.
A recent writer talks of the drama, the character, and the setting,
though without realizing the historic inheritance of the vision.[40]
For it was a mindless plot of criminal exploitation, a series of
characters articulating every fantasy of violence without consequences, and a picturesque setting moralized into a presiding spectre
of death.

Frémont's own *Memoirs* give us an interesting account of the

---

[37] Ibid., p. 66.

[38] Ibid., p. 63.

[39] Quoted from K. L. Steckmesser, *The Western Hero in History and Legend* (Norman,
Oklahoma 1965) pp. 18–19.

[40] Ibid., p. 52.

possibilities for landscape painting and photography round the mid-century. In the description of the plates which accompanied this volume Jesse Benton describes how Frémont, finding himself left out of the Pacific railroad explorations, made an expedition at his own expense, and took with him photographic apparatus bought in Paris on his journey to England in 1850–1. On his way through London to take the boat to America he bought a copy of the recently published *Cosmos* by Humboldt where he was delighted to find Humboldt's advocacy of the use of photography in landscape art. Frémont bought daguerre apparatus in New York, and on his expedition was accompanied by a Mr Cavalho who performed the increasingly common dual role of painter and photographer. On their return the daguerre plates were made into photographs by Brady in order to give them a more permanent form. Jesse commented:

> This long journeying by mule through storms and snows across the Sierras, then the scorching tropical damp of the sea voyage back across the Isthmus, left them unharmed and surprisingly clear, and so far as is known, give the first of a connected series of views by daguerre of an unknown country, in pictures as truthful as they are beautiful.[41]

Throughout the winter of 1855–6, Frémont worked alongside Brady in the latter's New York studio, and Frémont turned the north drawing room of his own house into a studio where the artist Hamilton worked on the views, reproducing them in oil. Hamilton was a pupil of Turner's, 'and had great joy in the true cloud effects as well as in the stern mountains and castellated rock formations'. Not only were the views realized in oil but also in wood engravings done as Jesse sentimentally observed, 'by an artist young then, a namesake and grandson of Frank Key, the author of the *Star-Spangled Banner*.' Even then the processing was not complete. F. O. C. Darley enlarged some by means of India-ink sketches and supplied many of the figures, and the total product was then passed on to the engravers. The account thus gives us an interesting view of the eclectic processes of image-making at the time, and gives a strong caution about talking of Victorian representative accuracy and 'realism'. Humboldt, the last of the great makers of scientific cosmoses in an enlightenment tradition, always said that the details should be generalized into more artistic wholes, and his prestige gave law to the process. At the same time it is interesting that Brady supervised the practice. His own photographs were to help swing the visual consciousness away from the dramatic whole structure

---

[41] Frémont, *Memoirs*, pp. xvff. for subsequent quotations.

of linear vision, with its dual practice of generalization and category.
For the public, these pictures, in their various forms, were the mid-
nineteenth century equivalent of today's pictures of the far side
of the moon. Their sense of uniqueness and boundary-breaking
achievement guaranteeing the strange and wild beauty caught, then
as now, the public imagination. But the practices they were supposed
to redeem were not discussed. In one way they provided instant
visualization of ever-expanding American empire for armchair
imperialists.

The results of government expeditions after Frémont were published in full more and more often, as the authorities began to
realize the value of carefully controlled reports of their expansionist
activities. One of the more elaborate is Emory's *Notes of a Military
Reconnaissance*, published in 1848, which shows an army-based
surveying party actually engaged in fighting a war. The usual
scientific experts accompanied the party. Lieutenant Albert supplied
an appendix on animals and natural history. Albert gives us a good
example of the classical inheritance in action in a literal and obvious
way; a copy of Horace and a Greek New Testament accompanied
him on his travels, and there is a gentleman amateur style in his
prose. The appearance of striking mountains elaborates those
features with which we are already familiar:

> I could not but compare the legends these rocks unfold with the doubt-
> ful records of history. See with what detail they present everything to
> us, showing us specimens of birds, of plants, of animals and the like,
> telling us when and where they existed. See how they go back ages upon
> ages! behold with astonishment the mighty deeds in which they have
> been concerned, the grand convulsions they have undergone.[42]

What is new here is the sense of progress, and the psychologizing
of the visual record in an almost romantic manner. Legends become
truer than the facts of history. Here is a most literal visualization
of the history of nature. The fossils are the eternal form of nature,
with nature supplying its own museum of the historical record.

Albert is harder on the living races. The New Mexicans are natural
unconscious liars, and of the Digger Indians of California he has this
to say:

> In fact, at one place, was evidence of a former abode of Indians, (diggers)
> as they are called—probably the lowest order of the human race—living
> on lizards, bugs, seed &c., and naked as they came into the world, except

[42] W. H. Emory, *Notes of a military reconnaissance from Fort Leavenworth, in
Missouri, to San Diego, in California, including parts of the Arkansas, Del Norte, and
Gila Rivers* (Washington, DC 1848) p. 438.

the covering of grass which the women hang round their loins. How far from being arrayed in purple and fine linen, and feasting sumptuously every day, or from the enjoyment of the fruits of man's intellect, in the bright pages of modern literature![43]

The natural climax of this report is the action at San Pasqual, in which 18 officers and men were killed and 13 wounded. The party was relieved only by the redoubtable Kit Carson, penetrating the enemy lines, and bringing a relief force of 100 sailors (*tars*, Emory calls them) and 80 marines with Lieutenant Beale.

A much more lavish report of Emory's survey of the Mexican boundary was published in Washington in 1857. Its form was similar to that already being published at the same time on the Pacific railroad survey. There are four sections: the personal narrative by Emory; geological researches including meteorological records and magnetic observations by James Hall; botany by John Torrey with Dr George Engleman from St Louis dealing with *cactaceae*; and a fourth general natural history section under the control of Spencer F. Baird. The report is typical of many others. There are accounts of bureaucratic difficulties, of money voted by Congress not being paid, a multiplication of unofficial posts and difficulties with local people. The motley races of Panama were, according to Emory, 'wholly unequal to the task of receiving and entertaining in an orderly manner such an influx of strangers'.[44]

Attitudes to the Spanish Indians and other races are predictable. The failure of the Spanish empire is due to two causes: the first is that American republican soldiers are superior, and the second is that the Spanish, intermarried with the Indians, produce a race of inferior stock. According to Emory, white men should import white wives to the frontier: 'Whenever practical amalgamation of races of different colour is carried to any extent, it is from absence of the women of the cleaner [sic] colored race'.[45] As far as Emory could see:

> The white makes his alliance with his darker partner for no other purpose than to satisfy a law of nature, or to acquire property . . . Faithless to his vows, he passes from object to object with no other impulse than the gratification arising from novelty, ending at last in emasculation and disease, leaving behind no progeny at all; or if any, a very inferior and syphilitic race.[46]

[43] Ibid., p. 612.
[44] W. H. Emory, *Report on the United States and Mexican Boundary Survey, made under the direction of the Secretary of the Interior* (Washington, DC 1857) vol. I, p. 2
[45] Ibid., vol. I, p. 69.
[46] Ibid., vol. I, p. 69.

31 *Diegeños*, Arthur Schott, del., in W. H. Emory, *Report on the United States and Mexican Boundary Survey* (Washington, DC, 1857). (*Courtesy of the British Library, London.*)

Emory's hell of a miscegenation left no doubt that the white race had to preserve its integrity at all costs.

Three artists at least helped to make plates for the three volumes. Arthur Schott was principal artist and assistant to one Mr N. Michler, topographical engineer in charge of the Mexican boundary survey from the Pacific side. There were two others, A. de Vaudricourt and John E. Weyss. A special feature are the half-page steel engravings of endless topographical outline panoramas. The main patterns of the landscape and the shrubbery are sketched in unrelieved black outline on a white ground. Page after page gives the monotonous contours of the section along the 11th meridian. The visual abstraction comes half way between representational art and map-representation. Every object is seen in a space enclosed by line, there is no colour, no variation of light and shade, no shading or hachuring, no aerial perspective. It is the perfect visual equivalent of the topographical prose of Emory's landscape descriptions: a proliferation of objects in a dead space.

One painting by Schott **pl. 31** is reproduced here to give some idea of how two 'representatives of their race' were visually presented in the report. The costume was no doubt carefully copied from an original and the features generalized from portraits to give the 'typical' Diegeños 'characteristics'. The grouping is interesting, for Schott has transferred an incident in Christian iconography, 'the flight into Egypt' to the Mexican border. Also reducing them to a family group, the painter perhaps unconsciously expresses the wish that they would abandon their hectic sexual lives and become a model child, father and mother (and dog) Victorian happy family. The other print reproduced is, on the other hand, a rather striking one by Paul Roetter, a Swiss born St Louis artist, of the Giant Cactus of the Gila **pl. 32**. The expedition's botanist, C. C. Parry remarked, 'Still less can anyone who has seen the giant cactus of the Gila, in its perfection, ever forget the wild and singular features of the country in which it grows'.[47] A good Humboldtian, Parry is more interested in the pattern of plant distribution than the details of botanical analysis. In Roetter's picture these huge plants retain their terrifying gothicism in spite of the conventional groupings of the seated figures, as if the artist were fighting a rearguard action against the scientific objectification of his material. The atmosphere of science fiction captures that intersection of the European-based visualization and a new and strange landscape.

[47] Ibid., vol. I, p. 9.

32 *Giant Cactus of the Gila,* Paulus Roetter, del. in W. H. Emory, *Report on the United States and Mexican Boundary Survey* (Washington, DC, 1857). (*Courtesy of the British Library, London.*)

This lavish report, however, was superseded in lavishness by the report on the survey for the Pacific railroad which had begun two years earlier. This massive 12 volume publication marks the climax of official exploration in the first half of the century. Throughout the late forties and fifties, Americans like Asa Whitney had been arguing the need for a trans-American railroad to the Pacific coast. Senator Benton's dream of America capturing British profits from the Indian empire and China by a direct overland route to Asia had already prompted St Louis citizens to sponsor Frémont's disastrous surveying expedition in the early fifties. The route of such a railroad became a political issue; whether it should link the South with the Southwest, or the North, via Chicago or St Louis, with California, In 1855, the first volume of the government's surveying teams was submitted to Davis, the secretary for war. Unlike the Lewis and Clark journals, this report was the product of many hundreds of skilled men who collected not only the data needed to build a railroad, but gathered information on Indian tribes and natural history. Isaac Stevens was in charge of the eastern division, Captain George B. McClellan, the later Civil War general, was in charge of the western division. Each were assigned various topographical experts, scientists, landscape artists and a small military force. Expeditions were sent along the 47th and 49th parallels from St Paul, via Vancouver, to Seattle: along the 41st and 42nd parallels, via Council Bluffs, to Benicia: along the 38th and 39th parallels from West Port to San Francisco, via the Coo-che-to-pa and Madelin passes: along the 35th parallel from Fort Smith to San Pedro, and along the 32nd parallel from Fulton via San Pedro to San Francisco.

Isaac Steven's 'personal narrative' is contained in volume XII, part I of the report, and is in the conversational style of the older explorers. His own route was along the 47th and 49th parallels and the report is illustrated by George Sohon and Stanley. Steven's descriptions of landscape are only slightly more austere than those of his predecessors, but the accompanying pictures are remarkable. A special feature are the fold-out panoramas, similar to those of Barrès in the closing years of the preceding century. These are coloured and give one a sense of the size and nature of the immense stretches of land covered. Contrasting with these are the individual pictures which give a greater sense of enclosure and civilization. The description of the falls of Minnehaha with its accompanying plate **pl. 33** is almost contemporary with Longfellow's popularization of them in *Hiawatha* in 1855. 'Though the magnitude of this cascade is not such as to excite our wonder,' says Stevens, 'its picturesque beauty and pleasing melody attract the admiration of

33 *The Falls of Minnehaha,* Stanley, del. in *Reports of Explorations and Surveys,* (Washington, DC, 1855—60). (*Courtesy of the Bodleian Library, Oxford.*)

every visitor.'[48] Stanley's picture, lithographed by Sarony, Major and Knapp of New York, recalls the stylized geological formations of an older European tradition, for the lines are as clean as some architectural design by Ledoux, the French visionary architect. The neat circle of the perimeter is offset by the carefully disordered stones to the rear of the fisherman.

This desire for clean-cut architectural landscape is illustrated in another plate from Stanley which uses Indian figures to set off the grandly architectural scenery. Stanley's original sketch for this is

[48] *Reports of Explorations and Surveys, to ascertain the most Practicable and Economical Route for a Railroad from the Mississippi River to the Pacific Ocean made under the Direction of the Secretary of War, in 1853—4* (Washington, DC 1855—60), vol. XII part I, p. 39.

rather indifferent and certainly does not render outline and shape
so cleanly. But the lithograph **pl. 34** pushes the colouring nearer
black and white contrast, exaggerates shadows and gives the whole
scene a sense of Arcadian simplicity as if to reduce to essences the
primitivism much sought after by the inherited imaginations of
western observers. This landscape without vegetation emphasizes
the antiquity of geological time, thus creating a suitably literary
context for the 'primitive' Indian. For the result is a dream landscape which in the Victorian imagination could be moralized in
terms of death, time and eternity, The womb-like foreground
represents life, the way out is through the cleft, the harbour passage
through the rocks, which leads in turn to sun and mountain, twin
symbols of eternity.

George Sohon, who is clearly the better artist, made a remarkable
picture of the *Great Falls of the Missouri River* **pl. 35**, giving it an
oval frame which emphasizes a sense of circularity and boundlessness
more than the conventional frame could do. The original is strikingly
coloured, not according to the conventions of traditional representative art, but according to some wild, hallucinatory vision of his
own imagination. The washes of various shades of reds, yellows and
purple articulate a kind of overall aerial perspective, irrespective of
object or detail. In the print the contrast is of some colour against

34 *Dalles,* Stanley, del., in *Reports of Explorations and Surveys* (Washington, DC,
1855—60). (*Courtesy of the Bodleian Library, Oxford.*)

35 *Great Falls of the Missouri River,* G. Sohon, del., in *Reports of Explorations and Surveys,* vol. 12 (Washington, DC, 1855–60). (*Courtesy of the Bodleian Library, Oxford.*)

a good deal of whiteness, the dark foreground encircling precisely half the frame. The circular and enclosed landscape describes in contrast with the frame, a simultaneously contrasting sense of finiteness and limitlessness.

A strange combination of scientific interest in geology and in the grotesque patterns of nature is shown in pl. 36 from volume III of the report. The hillside is stripped bare to reveal the strata, and science and landscape art merge in a picture which defies the classifications of either. In *Cosmos* Humboldt had speculated on the functions of engravings and lithographs in books of travel and in scientific reports and asserted that:

> even in the present imperfect condition of pictorial delineations of landscape, the engravings which accompany, and too often disfigure our books of travels, have, however, contributed towards a knowledge of the physiognomy of distant regions to the taste for voyages in the tropical zones, and to a more active study of nature.[49]

The excellent reproductions in the Pacific railroad report showed that the ineptitude Humboldt complained of was certainly not represented here. For these pictures make a unique contribution, hitherto unvalued, to the development of American landscape art.

[49] Alexander von Humboldt, *Cosmos* (London 1849–58) vol. II, p. 456.

36 *A Conical Hill, 500 feet high, Standing in the valley of Lagunda, Colorado,* H. B. Molhausen, in *Reports of Explorations and Surveys,* vol. 3 (Washington, DC, 1855–60). (*Courtesy of the British Library, London.*)

Stevens's comments on ethnology are unremarkable for their originality. The Gros Ventres are sexually promiscuous, simple minded, filthy and improvident. The attitudes were fairly similar throughout the survey. The first volume relates that no difficulty was experienced with any Indian during the entire exercise, just as no one was actually harmed on the Lewis and Clark expedition. Other Indians are characterized variously. The Blackfeet are sentimentalized into the Arabs of the North, and the mountain Indians are noted, with approval, to have given up polygamy and to have started agriculture. A paternalistic nod accompanies the remark that the Assiniboines have been 'steadily improving in character since the treaty of Laramie, and now sustain an excellent reputation, they were previously considered incorrigible thieves'.[50] One of the purposes of the expedition was to take a rough census of Indian tribes just as Lewis and Clark had done.

The rest of the natural history information was specialized in separate volumes. Volume IV was largely devoted to botany under the direction of John M. Biglow. John Torrey's introduction states that the 'drawings were, with a few exceptions, executed by Sprague and Riocreux, two of the most skilful botanical artists now living. All the engraving has been done upon stone by Prestele, who excels

[50] *Reports of Explorations and Surveys etc.,* vol. I, p. 149.

in this branch of the art.' It is Paul Roetter again who draws the
cactacea. Many of the drawings were carefully copied from sketches
on the spot made by Molhausen. Most of the individual surveys
have their accompanying sections on natural history, though the
whole of volume VIII is devoted to the zoology of all the routes
under the general supervision of Baird. In volume IX a letter from
Joseph Henry, secretary of the Smithsonian Institution, to a Captain
A. A. Humphreys in charge of 'Explorations and Surveys', tells how
the vast amount of data was prepared for publishing. As the accounts
were:

> necessarily disconnected and incomplete, it was deemed advisable to
> furnish a general systematic report upon the collection as a whole; and
> this being sanctioned by the War Department, the materials were en-
> trusted to competent individuals for this purpose, the necessary drawings
> being made by a skilful artist within the walls of the Institution.

One still has a lingering sense of a commitment to a whole natural
system, before the various branches of natural history split up
entirely. But the price was a selection of particulars which was felt
to illustrate a general truth about a category rather than a rendering
of unique detail. As a whole the Pacific railroad expeditions show a
consciousness divided many ways; between generalized truth and
personal report, between the surveyor and artist, between the men
in the field and the generalizing bureaucracy in Washington, and
between the scientist and political opportunist.

More sober reflection, however, indicates that these expeditions,
divorced from any concept of democratic appeal and control started
a train of activity which was to end with a physical rape of the continent. The Pacific railroad was delayed by the Civil War but its
completion in 1869 was the main source of a new era of incredible
corruption in public life in the post-war decades. Extraordinary
amounts of money were made by the absentee landlords of the
railroad grants, as the ability to centralize the power structure
became practicable on a hitherto unheard of scale. The railroads
played an important strategic part as we have already seen in the
Civil War itself. Unfortunately many of the trends observable from
the first expeditions can be paralleled in contemporary American
life. As the quotation at the head of this chapter shows, the social
function of the topographer or astronaut has changed but little.
The men with the short hair and slide rules are the equivalent of
the army-trained topographer with a consciousness divided between
sentiment and practicality. Lieutenant Albert and his Greek Testament parallels, in a still traditionally religious country, Borman

reading from Genesis in space on Christmas day. Just as railroads were used in the Civil War, the development of modern rocketry has a primarily military function. The organization of such 'scientific' exploration then as now is under the direction of the secretary of war. Just as Lewis and Clark had Indian fighting experience, so the privileged men on the pick-up carrier are Vietnam veterans. By the end of the nineteenth century, Frank Norris viewed the railroad as an octopus strangling the lifeblood of thousands of western farmers (the Indian had already been defeated). On a vaster scale the armaments race threatens the extinction of human life altogether. The literary pieties still appear to bind a passive public who watch the television set as Easterners read the accounts of Frémont. Then as now governments quickly realized the value of an immediate publication of its offical doings, a ritualistic manipulation by word and picture of a whole populace through the creation of a plot and folk hero in a continuous American tradition. Kit Carson and Daniel Boone are the nineteenth-century counterparts of contemporary astronauts. The real figures are the nameless scientists and engineers whose unquestionable devotion, expertise, and selfless personal effacement make them tools of a machine in a tradition, stretching philosophically from the Renaissance, which divorced ends from means, intellectual endeavour from social concern, and developed a concept of reason and reality which rarely challenged the basis of its own identity.

8

The North American Indian

Most of the attitudes toward the Indian current in all forms of visual and literary artefact, from broadsheet to novel, from woodcut to history painting, at the beginning of the nineteenth century were at least 300 years old. In the middle of the sixteenth century, Amerigo Vespucci (probably describing South American Indians) complained of their lack of religion, their immoderate lust and their nakedness.[1] The Elizabethan merchant-explorer, Hakluyt the Elders remarked, 'If the people be content to live naked and to content themselves with few things of mere necessity, then traffic [i.e. trade] is not.'[2] The Elizabethan profit consciousness decided in advance that the Indian had better change his nature whether by Christianity or force. Hakluyt argued that since the savages had no 'commodities' (gold, silver, copper, iron) the best thing to do would be to acquaint them with agriculture. The interest in natural history itself rose largely from a necessity to categorize certain types of 'commodity', and from the first, one can see emerging the utilitarian categories of aborigine, soil, climate, vegetation, animals, birds, and fish. 'Ignorant' of the white man's relationship to nature which excluded all values except those of exploitation, the Indian found himself simultaneously praised for his own relationship with nature and removed from the scene. The double-mindedness many cultural historians impute to white attitudes to the Indian, between the sordid reality of the Indian condition and the myth of the noble savage, is at best only half justified.[3] The myth is supposed to be a simple cultural inheritance, the actuality a God-given fact. Such an explanation is in fact a continuance of the double-mindedness it is intended to expose, for the concept of actuality is conditioned by the myth, and the nature of the myth permits reaction to the

---

[1] Wilcomb E. Washburn, ed., *The Indian and the White Man* (New York 1964) pp. 6–8.

[2] Louis B. Wright ed., *The Elizabethan's America* (London 1965) p. 31.

[3] See Roy Harvey Pearce, *The Savages of America* (Baltimore 1965) p. 66. Pearce's book, however, is one of the most important works on the American Indian.

new or strange only in its own terms. The actuality of improvidence is determined by the Puritan doctrine of prudence, the actuality of lechery is projected by a myth of Christian chastity, filth by a vision of cleanliness, lack of agriculture (in fact Indians cultivated both tobacco and potato) by a vision of civilization based on agriculture, and ignorance by a kind of knowledge characterized by a one-dimensional vision of use and profit and an actuality of power to give it a social reality.

In 1630 John Cotton, in a sermon published in London, gave three principles by which the Indian could be deprived of his land; first on a special commission from God; second by purchase or permission; third on the grounds of vacancy. Cotton warned, nonetheless, that 'wee may not rush into any place, and never say to God, By your leave; but we must discerne how God appoints us this place'.[4] Later generations were to drop the soul-searching, assume their religious destinies, and depersonalize individual responsibility by the substitution of secularized natural law. For the Indian was no better categorized by the Linnaean method than by the pervasive Puritan view of him as an agent of the Devil. His place in a linearly constructed catalogue, was counterbalanced by baroque fantasy, as the split between 'science' and 'art' became more and more acute. A kind of balance was struck in the middle of the eighteenth century in English literature with the neo-Classical vision of the Indian as a statue of antiquity, and as one who embodied the virtues of Greek civilization, particularly those of Sparta.[5] This classical ideal died a slow death until the mid-years of the nineteenth century when the Indian of earlier captivity literature,[6] revived as archetype by the popular writers, and actual war, swung the balance the other way. First, however, we shall look at the Indian as he appears in the work of the major writers, novelists, poets and historians, then at the Indian as he appears in Indian legends both actual and rewritten, and then at the Indian as he appears in the scientific report. Lastly we shall examine the pictorial record.

In Charles Brockden Brown's *Edgar Huntley* (1799), and Thomas Campbell's *Gertrude of Wyoming* (1809) we can see two early Anglo-American syntheses of Indian characterizations which were to dominate American literature for at least half a century. In

[4] John Cotton, *God's Promise to his Plantation* (London 1630) reprinted in Washburn, *The Indian and the White Man*, pp. 102–3, 104.

[5] Benjamin Bissell, *The American Indian in English Literature of the Eighteenth Century* (New Haven, Conn. 1925) p. 5.

[6] For a good introductory account of captivity literature see Roy Harvey Pearce, 'The Significances of the Captivity Narrative' *American Literature*, 19 (1947–8) pp. 1–20.

Edgar Huntley, as William Dunlap, the first American art historian, observed, Brown linked the 'mysterious disease Somnabulism' with 'incidents of Indian hostility, and the perils of the western wilderness'.[7] Drawing on the captivity literature of the 1780s and the 1790s, and the 'gothicism' of the English novel, Brown gives us an intensely ironic exposure of the dream of reason and a sophisticated psychological analysis of the nature of power and its scientific rationales.[8] In the novel, Brown demonstrates that his hero's pursuit of knowledge has an irrational foundation which he has no techniques of coping with, and that his self-appointed investigatory mission as detective-scientist leads to an identification of victim and pursuer. The plot is complex, though less so than in Brown's other novels. The incidents often do not proceed logically and are created for psychological effect, rather than to complete a linear narrative. The novel begins with the hero, Huntley, investigating a patient-victim, Clithero, both to submit his ghost-like reality to empirical testing and because he suspects him of having killed his fiancée's brother. Huntley's role is that of policeman as man of science, and the terms of the drama expose the destructive implications of such a role. Like Poe's detective, and Hawthorne's numerous investigators later, Huntley begins by identifying himself with the 'criminal's' dream world. Huntley pursues the somnabulist suspect in a series of dream-journeys through a landscape filled with Salvator Rosa-like bogs and rocks first to a cave (natural refuge) and second to his own home (civilized refuge) where the cornered Clithero relates his story. He tells how, as the highly favoured steward of an aristocratic English woman in Ireland (one Mrs Lorimer), he had bettered himself to the extent of being engaged to her daughter. The daughter's criminal brother, returned from a transportation sentence, is killed by Clithero, who in an excess of sensibility, believed that the only way to confront him with the news of his engagement was to kill him. The interacting theme of crime and order is now stated as Clithero transports himself to America.

This moral exemplum of the dark depths of European human nature causes Huntley, the pure, upright American investigator, some mental disturbance:

> . . . my mind was full of the images unavoidably suggested by this tale,
> but they existed in a kind of chaos; and not otherwise than gradually

[7] From Dunlap's *Life of Charles Brockden Brown,* quoted in the introduction to Charles Brockden Brown, *Edgar Huntley* (London 1831) p. xiii.
[8] The best criticism of this novel is A. G. Kimball, 'Brockden Brown's Dramatic Irony', *Studies in Romanticism,* 6 (1966–7) pp. 214–25.

was I able to reduce them to distinct particulars, and subject them to a deliberate and methodical inspection.[9]

Once the processes of chaos have been reduced to order the next step is the implementation of benevolence. Huntley's prurient charity now leads him in search of the once-more vanished Clithero and a second journey to the cave. In greater darkness than before Huntley penetrates to the depths of his own soul, and after a Macbeth-like moment of indecision in which he feels that to go back is as difficult as to go on, he emerges onto a ledge from which he views a pristine American landscape:

> It was probable that human feet had never before gained this recess, that human eyes had never been fixed upon these gushing waters. The aboriginal inhabitants had no motives to lead them into caves like this, [sic] and ponder on the verge of such a precipice: their successors were still less likely to have wandered hither: since the birth of this continent, I was probably the first who had deviated thus remotely from the customary paths of men.[10]

Huntley's teacher and mentor, Sarsfield, explains his pupil's previous interest in 'explorations' in the following terms:

> . . . he was fond of penetrating into these recesses, partly from the love of picturesque scenes, partly to investigate its botanical and mineral productions, and partly to carry on more effectually that species of instruction which he had adopted with regard to me, and which chiefly consisted in moralizing narratives or synthetical reasonings.[11]

Brown dissolves the boundaries between Huntley's rational and irrational voyages of exploration, showing them in fact to be linked. For at the heart of the pristine landscape of scientific order, across the gulf from Huntley's viewpoint, as a figure in the landscape is Clithero himself. The criminal occupies the world of scientific order.

By felling a log to bridge the gulf which separates pursuer and victim, and by opening a private box of Clithero's without his knowledge, Huntley becomes more and more identified with his object of investigation. Pursuer and victim take on identical roles. Huntley, in any case, is investigating the murder of his fiancée's brother, just as Clithero is fleeing from the consequences of murdering his fiancée's brother. The dual emotion mainspring of the action is the imposition of an outside lover on the brother-sister relationship. It is family or inherited love versus the disrup-

---

[9] Charles Brockden Brown, *Edgar Huntley* (London 1831) p. 78.
[10] Ibid., p. 89.
[11] Ibid., p. 83.

tions of sexual affections. In both Clithero's and Huntley's experience it is over-reverence for the authority of family love which causes the psychic imbalance. In Clithero's case there is the additional class respect for the aristocratic family whose loyalty he fears will not extend beyond the bounds of justice.

Huntley now plunges deeper into madness. Having lost his provisions he crosses the tree bridge, which is then destroyed, only to be confronted with a fierce panther, the terrifying animal of the dream. On his return home he himself begins to sleepwalk and like Clithero, steals manuscripts from himself. At this point rational securities are further shaken by a merchant who turns up to say that Huntley's fiancée's murdered brother's fortune is his by right and not Huntley's. Faced by his own guilt and misfortune, his 'reason' comes to an end. Sleepwalking past his mentor Sarsfield (an emblem of rationality), Huntley is knocked on the head by Indians and thrown unconscious into a cave pit inside the very mountain he had previously explored.

Huntley is now literally unconscious in the very place his instructor had undertaken his education. That the Indians should appear at this point is crucial. Coming round into consciousness he sees them guarding the entrance to the cave, but not before he has drunk his own blood in order to survive, and confronted the mate of the panther in the darkness. Beginning with violence on himself he inverts the world of normal order. Reborn from the cave the picturesque landscape becomes the landscape of his tortured psyche, scientific investigation a strategy of war, and moral imperatives an unconscious acceptance of prevailing social attitudes. Huntley rescues his sister from the Indians guarding the cave by killing all four of them. Imagining her raped, he kills the last one by hand, and 'Prompted by some freak of fancy, I stuck his musket in the ground, and left it standing upright in the middle of the road'.[12] The Indian deaths are sexual killings in the cause of a world order guaranteed by a brother's proprietary control over his sister's sexual availability. Of all these fears, shared by both pursuer and victim, of sexual loss, of financial insecurity, of the gulf of terror opened up by the inadequacy of scientific observation and sense-psychology to explain the failure of will and irrational behaviour, the Indian is the literary symbol:

> The legs were naked, and scored with uncouth figures: the moccasins which lay beside them, and which were adorned in a grotesque manner, in addition to other incidents, immediately suggested the suspicion that

[12] Ibid., p. 177.

they were Indians. No spectacle was more adapted than this to excite wonder and alarm. Had some mysterious power snatched me from the earth, and cast me in a moment into the heart of the wilderness?[13]

And viewing three Indians dead by his own hand, Huntley remarked:

My anguish was mingled with astonishment: in spite of the force and uniformity with which my senses were impressed by external objects, the transition I had undergone was so wild and inexplicable. . . . [14]

But Huntley scarcely learns from his experience, and still pursuing the total explanation, he causes the document explaining the events to fall into the hands of Mrs Lorimer, thus causing her to have a miscarriage. His last attempt to 'root out' the guilt in Clithero's soul leads to the latter's suicide—a form of escape only contemplated by Huntley himself in the cave.

In spite of the book's structural weaknesses, this is perhaps the most remarkable of Brown's works, articulating as it does an image of the Indian as a dark nemesis of the white man's consciousness with his sexual, social, financial and rational fears of failure. Reason itself is shown to be a nightmare for the very dualism of dream and rationality it projects is maintained only through violence on an artificial frontier, with the Indian (uncategorizable in these terms) removed from the boundary.

Brockden Brown was later to translate Volney's *A View of the Soil and Climate of the United States of America* (1804), and disclaim against Volney as an 'enthusiast against savages'. He also reviewed Barton's *Book on the Indians* and Jonathan Edwards's 'Observations on the Language of the Muhhekaneew Indians'.[15] The first writer deliberately to draw on eyewitness accounts (Colden, Lewis and Clark, Weld, Charlevoix, Bartram and Jefferson) was an English poet, Thomas Campbell in his once popular narrative poem *Gertrude of Wyoming* (1809). Into the poem went imagery of scientifically authenticated fauna and flora, Indian myths and antiquities, and the 'character' of the Indian in relation to such things as courage, stoicism, family life and eloquence.

The poem's narrative is straightforward but realizes many of the themes and situations which were later to dominate the popular fiction and poetry of the nineteenth century. An ancient Scottish sire, Albert, and his daughter, Gertrude, the comfort of his old age, are visited by a pursued Indian who hands over to them one

[13] Ibid., p. 149.
[14] Ibid., p. 169.
[15] See Mabel Morris, 'Charles Brockden Brown and the American Indian', *American Literature*, 18 (1946–7) pp. 244–7.

Waldegrave, the son of an old friend of Albert, whose father has been killed by the Indians and whose mother has died of grief. After a brief visit to Europe, Waldegrave returns to marry Gertrude, but after a short period of happiness the War of Independence is fought, Albert is killed and Gertrude dies of grief on the hapless breast of her husband. The good Indian snatches their white child from his own avenging child. This Indian, Oneyda, with a look of 'monumental bronze', sings a song to the child before he leaves it with the father, promising its adoption into his own tribe. Two basic love situations prove of lasting endurance; the father and child (something of a cross between Lear and Cordelia, Prospero and Miranda) and the white man returning as quasi-son of the old Indian, having been cheated out of his wife through war. Gertrude's death symbolically depicts that she prefers father to husband, leaving to Waldegrave the comforting words:

> Oh! by that retrospect of happiness,
> And by the hopes of an immortal trust,
> God shall assuage thy pangs—when I am laid in dust![16]

The Oneyda chief, like Waldegrave, is now dispossessed of his land. As the last of his tribe he can no more go back to his blue western mountains than Waldegrave can return to his primitive Arcadia on the Prospero model. The implication in the eloquent final speech is that in the following day's battle, Waldegrave will dry his tears 'in glory's fires' and the old Indian chief will die. The father and daughter relation, the good ageing Indian, the white-red male friendship in the forest, the impossibility of heterosexual relationships, which are exchanged for the pleasures of memory and future spiritual bliss, set in a disappearing Indian Arcadia all form the ingredients which James Fenimore Cooper and his contemporaries were to draw on heavily.

Like Campbell, Joel Barlow also drew on captivity literature in *The Columbiad*. The death of 'Lucinda' was modelled on the death of Miss Jane McCrea and articulates that familiar iconography of white woman attacked by dark savage. Leslie Fiedler points to the heavily erotic nature of the killing, for long before Poe,[17] Barlow had made use of the most poetical subject in the world, the death of a beautiful woman:

> Two Mohawks meet the maid—historian, hold,
> She starts—with eyes upturned and fleeting breath,

---

[16] Thomas Campbell, *The Poetical Works of Thomas Campbell* (London 1887) p. 68.
[17] For Poe's use of this motif, see Edgar Allan Poe, *Works,* 7 vols (London 1900) vol. III, p. 272.

In their raised axes views her instant death.
Her hair, half lost along the shrubs she passed,
Rolls, in loose tangles, round her lovely waist;
Her kerchief torn betrays the globes of snow,
That heave responsive to her weight of woe.
With calculating pause and demon grin
They seize her hands, and through her face divine,
Drive the descending axe![18]

The passage was endlessly reprinted in Drake's *Book of the Indians* (see below p. 269) thus clearly articulating the link between a European tradition and the popular culture. A parallel in painting which captures all the essential elements can be seen in Vanderlyn's *The Death of Jane McCrea* (1803) pl. 37. Nine years later Vanderlyn was to create a puritanical scandal with his nude study of *Ariadne* in Philadelphia. *The Death of Jane McCrea*, far more sadistically provocative, received little comment.

In the foreground, two huge out-of-proportion savages emerge from the darkness one seizes her hair, the other brandishes a tomahawk. The figures tower over the woman whose exposed sensuous breasts are picked out by the picture's lighting. In contrast, difficult to see in the reproduction, the husband, a tiny figure in European dress occupies a light corner of the background in almost Italian Arcadian style. Like Brockden Brown, Vanderlyn reverses the balance of reason by the importance he assigns to the figures and to the balance of the chiaroscuro. Here order is literally a distant prospect, while the foreground illustrates a nightmare of disorder from the sexually threatening Indian.

James Fenimore Cooper's work is crucial to our understanding of the Indian as he appears in literature. Writing on Cooper's Indians has been fairly prolific but strangely off at a tangent. Everyone seems to agree that Cooper had next to no experience of Indians, but instead of then examining the images he makes of them in terms of his fiction, critics seem keen to authenticate his sources in Heckewelder, Charlevoix, Penn, Smith, Eliot, Colden, Long and Lewis and Clark.[19] Cooper, on the whole is far less sophisticated than Brockden Brown, though he is, of course, a good deal more prolific. There are good Indians and there are bad Indians who in the Leatherstocking novels are represented on the one hand by

---

[18] Quoted from S. G. Drake, *The Book of the Indians of North America* (Boston 1833) p. 35.

[19] See, for example, J. T. Frederick, 'Cooper's Eloquent Indians', *Publications of the Modern Language Association of America*, 71 (1956) pp. 1004–17: P. A. W. Wallace, 'Cooper's Indians', *New York History*, 35 (1955) pp. 423–46; A. C. Parker, 'Sources and Range of Cooper's Indian Lore', *New York History*, 35 (1955) pp. 447–56.

37 *Death of Jane McCreau,* 1803, by John Vanderlyn. (*Courtesy of Wadsworth Atheneum, Hartford, Connecticut.*)

John Mohegan, Chingachgook, Uncas, Tamenund, Hard Heart and on the other by Magua, Mahtoree, and Arrowhead. These of course balance the good and bad white characters. These dualisms are philosophically supported by the homespun wisdom of the Leather-stocking whose theories of 'gifts' (God-given character traits) are derived ultimately from Pauline doctrine: 'Now there are diversity of gifts, but the same Spirit'.[20] Cooper's secularization of the

[20] I Corinthians 12.4.

doctrine impoverishes the Christian text to the extent that it
authorizes division. And yet Cooper is able to criticize his own
divisions, though not very seriously since he puts the argument into
the mouth of woman of dubious reputation who happens to be
the nearest the Leatherstocking ever gets to a girl friend:

> 'And yet they scalp and slay young and old—women and children!'
> 'They have their gifts, Mabel, and are not to be blamed for following
> them. Natur' is natur', though the different tribes have different ways
> of showing it. For my part, I am white, and endeavour to maintain
> white feelings.'
> 'This is all unintelligible to me,' answered Mabel.[21]

Mabel is unable to accept Bumppo's contradictory rationalizations
of red-white roles, and she herself is rejected when she appears in
a dream in which Killdeer, Bumppo's rifle, fails to go off. Cooper's
image of the Indian does develop slightly, however, throughout the
novels from John Mohegan, the misanthropic victim of white progress in *The Pioneers* (1823) to Scalping Pete in *Oak Openings*
(1848) who turns from Indian to Christian nature without even
having the grace of Longfellow's Hiawatha, who, three years later,
at least had the guts not to hand himself over to the missionaries.
Perhaps Cooper's Indian is most significant in the death scenes of
which we take two examples.

The order of killing in the climactic final scenes of *The Last of the
Mohicans* (1826) gives an interesting insight into the way Cooper
solves the sexual problems of racism. First to die is Cora, whose
murderer is glimpsed by the impotent white rescuers at the exit of
Brockden Brown-like caves. Then 'Uncas', the last of the Mohicans,
whom Magua calls 'woman' dies by Magua's own hand as symbolically
ingenuous virtue is overcome by diabolical evil. Finally this dark
threatening male who has already sexually accosted the dark-white
Cora is eliminated by the Leatherstocking in the following manner.
The Leatherstocking's 'half-raised rifle played like a leaf fluttering
on the wind,' and then steadied as hard as the 'surrounding rocks'
as it 'poured out its contents' into the body of Magua who had
'drawn his knees up to his body in an effort to regain the top of the
precipice'.[22] This Indian death is a violent travesty of homosexual
red-white love. The result is death whether for the beautiful Indian
boy or the sexually threatening red male. The Leatherstocking's
rifle eliminates tension to establish moral, sexual and political

---

[21] James Fenimore Cooper, *The Pathfinder* (1840; reprinted New York 1895—6)
pp. 326—7.
[22] James Fenimore Cooper, *The Last of the Mohicans* (1826; reprinted New York
1895—6) p. 408.

order. The one is killed because he is too pure and therefore the last of his tribe, and because Cooper was too prurient, and possibly too jealous to give him to Cora, the other, because he threatens the white man politically and attempted to take the woman he had not the courage to take for himself. The Leatherstocking whom Balzac called a 'moral hermaphrodite', is left establishing control in a landscape of death.

The other death scene is the famous one in chapter seven of *The Deerslayer* (1841) when the youthful Leatherstocking kills his first Indian. The scene has in Ivor Winters' words, 'something of the tenderness and wonder of idyllic first love'.[23] Winters contents himself, however, with a lyrical elaboration of the scene and seems totally unaware of the obscenity of the romance:

> —Deerslayer took the hand of the savage, whose last breath was drawn in that attitude, gazing in admiration at the countenance of a stranger, who had shown so much readiness, skill, and firmness, in a scene that was equally trying and novel.[24]

F. O. C. Darley's engraving of the scene **pl. 38** with its clearcut lines shows the Leatherstocking, dressed in deerskins and fur hat charitably helping the huge muscular Indian to die, stoically, like a proverbial gladiator. Meanwhile the image of the Leatherstocking suggests the good American helping a buddy in trouble. In another Indian picture by Darley **pl. 39** the clear lines of the engraving, with its definition of the reality of rational benevolence, are replaced by an ink and water sketch showing the other polarity of dream image. Here the Indian chief presides over a mystic, tribal rite in which the forms are but shadows. The different media show the split conception of the Indian: dead or dying he becomes an object of rational benevolence, alive he is savage or devil who threatens white life and society. In Cooper's fictional world, there is little possibility of contact between red and white. Where dramatic variations are played between good and bad fixed points there can be no possibility of change. A good and a bad Indian ensure a continued double view of the Indian. The very notion of character and plot which Cooper took from Scott's historical romances is played out against large Manichean landscapes of war and peace. Inside this static framework, Cooper was able to encompass a set of sophisticated variations on the given elements which reached deep into the American consciousness.

[23] Yvor Winters, *In Defense of Reason* (London 1947) p. 188.
[24] James Fenimore Cooper, *The Deerslayer* (1841; reprinted New York, 1895–6) pp. 116–7.

38 *Giving Water*, 1862, by F. O. C. Darley. (*Courtesy of the Newberry Library, Chicago.*)

For the 'scientific' historian, however, of whom Francis Parkman (1823–93) is our representative example, the Indian was a product of two forces: history and nature. For the American New England (Brahmin) historian the archetype of the savage was to be found in Gibbon's *Decline and Fall of the Roman Empire* which began publication, significantly, the year of the Declaration of Independence. As we might imagine, this huge historical myth of the dissolution of the Roman state had a peculiar relevance to the neo-Classical conceptions of civilization on which the American state was founded. The savage in the historical drama is a threat to the organized boundaries of empire. The way Gibbon approaches the Sythians or Tartars, for example, gives us an archetypal response which was taken over for the American 'savage'. The 'barbarous

39 *Indian Tribal Ceremony* (?) by F. O. C. Darley. (*Courtesy of the Library of Congress, Washington, DC.*)

Sythian' had been an image of savagery since Shakespeare's time,[25] and as a 'sober historian' Gibbon uses this view to negate the current literary conceptions of him as in any way noble: 'Like the animals of prey, the savages, both of the old and new world, experience the

[25] See Edwin Muir, ed., *King Lear* (London 1966) I. i. l.116.

alternate vicissitudes of famine and plenty . . ..'[26] From the point
of view of nature and history, their nomadic and communal life
inhibits commerce, the building of cities and the development of
property. Their cold and dirty houses are fit dwellings for the
'promiscuous youth' who hunt fearlessly the boar and tiger, and
'excite the sluggish courage of the bear.'[27] These characterizations
appear consistently in Parkman's own accounts.

Early in Parkman's career his image of the Indian was derived
from the fiction of his favorite American writers, Irving and Cooper.
His own famous *Oregon Trail* (1849) took up the tradition of
Irving's *Tour on the Prairies* (1835) and like most of the New
England Brahmin historians his favorite English authors were Byron
and Scott. He was also interested in painting and on an early visit
to Europe, went to Rome and toured the colony of English and
American artists there. In London he was pleased to find Catlin's
Indian Gallery (see below p. 275) half dispersed, commenting 'he
would not suffer the fruits of his six years' labor and danger to
rot in the dampness to gratify a few ignorant cockneys. . . .'[28]
Later in Parkman's career his image of the Indian was modified
somewhat as the figure of romance moved to one caught between
the conflicting forces of history and nature. The introduction to
his book, *The Jesuits in North America in the Seventeenth Century*
(1867) reflect his mature views on the subject.

In this introduction, Parkman confines himself to the Algonquins,
the Hurons, the Huron-Iroquois family, the Iroquois and to generalized remarks on religion and superstition. Parkman quotes Morton's
infamous *Crania Americana* and J. S. Philips' *Principal Groups of
Indians in the United States,* to prove phrenologically the existence
of the Indian's 'animal propensities'.[29] When he attacks the
classical view of the Indian as noble savage he coins the phrase
'wild democracy' to characterize Indian society. He had similar
problems with Indian religion, for although he saw correctly that
previous accounts were biased owing to the monotheistic inter-
pretations foisted on them by the Jesuits, his own contempt of all
magic and legend gives us no alternative approach.

One of the most striking features of Parkman's prose are the set
descriptions of the Indian and Indian society, literary equivalents
of the historical paintings of West and his followers in the nine-

[26] Edward Gibbon, *Decline and Fall of the Roman Empire*, 6 vols (1776–88;
reprinted London 1962) vol. III, p. 6.
[27] Ibid., p. 8.
[28] Mason Wade, ed., *The Journals of Francis Parkman* (London 1946) vol. II, p. 222.
[29] Francis Parkman, *The Jesuits in North America in the Seventeenth Century* (1867;
reprinted New York 1965) p. x liii.

teenth century. The following passage has been chosen as typical and it illustrates the interior of a Huron house:

> He who entered on a winter night beheld a strange spectacle: the vista of fires lighting the smoky concave; the bronzed groups circling each, —cooking, eating, gambling, or amusing themselves with idle badinage; shrivelled squaws, hideous with threescore years of hardship; grisly old warriors, scarred with Iroquois war-clubs; young aspirants, whose honors were yet to be won; damsels gay with ochre and wampum; restless children pell-mell with restless dogs. Now a tongue of resinous flame painted each wild feature in vivid light; now the fitful gleam expired, and the group vanished from sight, as their nation has vanished from history.[30]

The passage moves from a Macbeth-like opening to a prophecy of Indian doom. Within the limits described by the chiaroscuro, the stages of Indian life are divided symbolically in roles according to age, thus presenting the whole process of life as a static moment. The arrested moment is characterized then by age or sex. Young women are frivolous, children play 'with restless dogs', and young men aspire to what old men dream of. This *tableaux vivant* symbolically expresses the totality of Indian life. According to the dramatist's whim the stage can be melodramatically lit by the 'fitful gleam' (life's fitful fever) arresting the characteristic moment like strobe lighting effects. The flame is also the spirit of the race, for when it is extinguished, the nation dies too. The group here is representative of the nation as the last sentence shows, and sight, the mode of perception of the dramatist-painter, is equated with the absolute inevitability of history itself.

Another set piece early on in *The History of the Conspiracy of Pontiac* (1851) shows the Indian, not as a victim of history but of nature:

> The Indian is a true child of the forest and the desert. The wastes and solitudes of nature are his congenial home. His haughty mind is imbued with the spirit of the wilderness, and the light of civilization falls on him with a blighting power. His unruly pride, and untamed freedom are in harmony with the lonely mountain, cataracts, and rivers among which he dwells; and primitive America, with her savage scenery and savage men, opens to the imagination a boundless world, unmatched in wild sublimity.[31]

Close to nature the savage experienced its alternating moods. In a contrasted landscape of summer and winter, Parkman uses a natural

[30] Ibid., p. xxviii.
[31] Francis Parkman, *History of the Conspiracy of Pontiac* (1851; reprinted Cambridge, Mass. 1898) vol. I, p. 1.

landscape at different points in time to exteriorize the Indian's
character. In summer the Indian, 'balanced between earth and
heaven', fishes peacefully, dreaming into fantastic shapes islands
in the river created by mirages of his imagination. According to
Parkman he fancies on the shores, 'that the evil spirits of the lake
lie basking their serpentine forms', or alternatively he 'explores the
water labyrinths where the stream sweeps among the pintufted
islands. . . .'[32] The Indian becomes a kind of latter-day Bartram
imaginatively confronting the landscape. In the winter landscape,
however, the improvident Indian discovers that imagination will
not keep a man alive, and going from disaster to disaster finally
finds himself 'among the snow drifts; till, with tooth and claw, the
famished wild-cat strives in vain to pierce the frigid marble of his
limbs'.[33] It is an American fable with Hogarthian overtones, fit
for the inmates of Gradgrind school, and the fate of Parkman's
improvident Indian father rivals any threat of the poorhouse. The
moral is that magic works only in the summer, that imagination
and reason (with connotations of art and science) are to be equated
respectively with luxury and necessity, ornament and function,
religion and reality. 'Among all savages,' states Parkman, 'the
powers of perception preponderate over those of reason and
analysis.'[34] Without Brown's irony, Parkman dramatizes himself as
the analyst in love with tales of mystery and imagination. Paralleling this double vision of imagination and reason is the very structure
of Parkman's writing with its double standard of set descriptions
which reveal character interspersed within a continuous narrative
revealing the sober facts of plot. These dualisms are further paralleled
by the double criteria of nature and history and lead to a literary
world in which Indians die dramatically and nobly and whites
painfully and messily. Those Indians who claimed nature for their
goddess perished in the labyrinths of the gothic forest, those who
operated by the light of reason survived.

   If the set scenes showed the Indian in his own historical and
social setting and paralleled the work of the history painter, Parkman's *History of the Conspiracy of Pontiac* (1851), shows how
historical biography may parallel the heroic portrait. Like Emerson's
great men, Pontiac is seen in terms of the characteristics of his
race writ large:

> He possessed commanding energy and force of mind, and in subtlety of
> craft could match the best of his wily race. But though capable of acts

[32] Ibid., vol. I, p. 39.
[33] Ibid., vol. I, p. 40.
[34] Ibid., vol. I, p. 47.

of lofty magnanimity, he was a thorough savage, with a wider range of intellect than those around him, but sharing all their passions and prejudices, their fierceness and treachery. His faults were the faults of his race; and they cannot eclipse his nobler qualities, the great powers and heroic virtues of his mind.[35]

Parkman differs from Cooper in that he reduces the pattern of good and bad Indian to a single norm of savage with good and bad characteristics. There is not a good Indian doing a good act in the whole work. Parkman claimed greater realism for himself, but even in his own terms, his realism was confined to the white point of view, while he retained a more 'poetic' style for the destiny and death of his Indian subjects.

The death of Pontiac is the final set piece, and is an occasion for melodrama. For Pontiac is the child of the forest and so dies like many another pre-pubescent child in Victorian fiction. Already Parkman had quoted Walter Scott: 'All children . . . are naturally liars; and truth and honor are developments of later education'.[36] Scott continued, 'Barbarism is to civilization what childhood is to maturity; and all savages, whatever may be their country, their color or their lineage, are prone to treachery and deceit'. Within Parkman's essentially paternalist framework, the Indian does not grow up, and his child-like polymorphous sexual behaviour is a threat to maturity and civilization. He is therefore reluctantly exterminated, with Leatherstocking-like apologies, and a magnificent epitaph granted in compensation. Near death, Pontiac reflects nobly on the progress of civilization: 'The star of his people's destiny was fading from the sky; and, to a mind like his, the black and withering future must have stood revealed in all its desolation'.[37]

In Melville and Thoreau we find a more sophisticated and complex discussion of the Indian. Melville's short review of Parkman's *The Californian and Oregon Trail* approved the historian's dismissal of the popular literary archetype of the Indian but continued:

> when in the body of the book we are informed that it is difficult for any white man, after a domestication among the Indians, to hold them much better than brutes; when we are told too, that to such a person, the slaughter of an Indian is indifferent as the slaughter of a buffalo; with all deference, we beg leave to dissent.[38]

He further stated that Parkman seems to have neglected the Christian concept of brotherhood, and the actual gratuitousness of

---

[35] Ibid., vol. I, p. 191.
[36] Ibid., vol. I, p. 238.
[37] Ibid., vol. I, p. 317.
[38] *North American Review*, 74 (January 1852) pp. 150–1.

the accident of birth:

> A misfortune is not a fault; and good luck is not meritorious. The savage
> is born a savage; and the civilized being but inherits his civilization,
> nothing more.[39]

In a well-known chapter in *The Confidence Man* (1857) called 'The
Metaphysics of Indian Hating', Melville is more concerned with the
psychology of the Indian-hater than with the Indian himself.
Parodying the moral education of a Puritan, Melville shows how the
son learns of the father the facts of Indian diabolism. The Christian
sense of conscience appears hence to be socially inherited, and not
altogether trustworthy: 'The instinct of antipathy against an Indian
grows in the backwoodsman with the sense of good and bad, right
and wrong'.[40] The whole of *The Confidence Man* debates the
trustworthiness of inherited masks, or concepts of character, which,
when adhered to in the drama of social intercourse, prove occasions
for exploitation and confidence trickery. To maintain the character
of an Indian-hater needs, therefore, a religious rigour, and it is
this cultivation of the soul that Melville draws on to outline his
parody of the type. So the confidence man concludes:

> . . . to be a consistent Indian-hater involves the renunciation of ambition,
> with its objects—the pomps and glories of the world; and since religion,
> pronouncing such things vanities, accounts it a merit to renounce them,
> therefore, so far as this goes, Indian-hating, whatever may be thought
> of it in other respects, may be regarded as not wholly without the
> efficacy of a devout sentiment.[41]

According to legend, Thoreau is supposed to have died with the
word 'Indians' on his lips. He left behind him half a million words
of undigested notes for what he projected as the definitive work on
Indians in the mid-nineteenth century. Commentators lament the
untimeliness of the death even while acknowledging that the
majority of the notes were taken from the unreliable early American
anthropologist Henry Rowe Schoolcraft. Perhaps Thoreau's work
would not have been so very different from many of the others.
The last note in the last volume is replete with Gibbonesque overtones: 'The Sythians of all the people described by Herodotus
remind me most of our Indians',[42] A recent critic has pointed out
how Thoreau re-worked the Hannah Duston story in *A Week on the*

---

[39] Ibid.
[40] Herman Melville, *The Confidence Man* (1857: reprinted New York 1964) p. 158.
[41] Ibid., p. 169.
[42] Quoted in A. Keiser, 'Thoreau's Manuscripts on the Indians,' *Journal of English
and Germanic Philology*, 27 (1928) p. 191.

Concord and Merrimac Rivers (1849) and how Thoreau retold
Alexander Henry's adventures in which a pagan brotherly com-
panionship between men in the woods is posed against the kind of
life-style dominated by the Hannah Duston figure 'with her
righteousness and sexual fears, the gloomy figure of Cotton Mather
following close behind her, ready to justify her killer-role with
appropriate scriptural quotations'.[43]

In one work of Thoreau's, however, there is a refreshing change
from mere restatements of popular mythology. In *The Maine Woods*
(1864), Thoreau, in spite of the critics,[44] relies relatively little
on notes taken from books. The three journeys described take on
mythic proportions but not of the very popular kind. The first
excursion is dominated by the mountain Ktaadn which as Thoreau
explains is an Indian word signifying 'highest land'.[45] At its most
intense moments the experience of climbing the mountain takes
on a more profound psychological meaning. At first the landscape
is described in feminine terms, a tradition in American literature
beginning with Bartram, and in the foothills he exclaims, 'It was as
if we sucked at the very teats of Nature's pine-clad bosom in these
parts.'[46] Further on, however, and nearer the summit, the earth
becomes more terrifying and takes on a masculine appearance:

> This was that Earth of which we have heard, made out of Chaos and
> Old Night. . . . It was Matter, vast, terrific—not his Mother Earth that
> we have heard of. . . .'[47]

Like Ahab penetrating to the most hostile and ancient area of
nature, Thoreau likens himself to the male figures of mythology,
Atlas, Vulcan and Prometheus. The sensation of mountain climbing
has little to do with the Indian here ('Simple races . . . do not climb
mountains'[48]) but comes rather from a psychology of secularized
self-testing. The wild mountainous scenery of America we have
already seen characterized as a record of the catastrophes of time,
and Thoreau's response is in this tradition. To confront the 'raw
materials of a planet'[49] becomes a symbolic confrontation with the
raw materials of the self. For the myth here is not buddies in the

---

[43] Leslie Fiedler, *The Return of the Vanishing American* (London 1968) p. 116.

[44] Keiser in 'Thoreau's manuscripts on the Indians' uses the *The Maine Woods* as an
example of material worked from Thoreau's notes (p. 199). His evidence, however, is
scanty and does not prove that Thoreau actually used his notes extensively in *The Maine
Woods*.

[45] Henry David Thoreau, *The Maine Woods* (1864; reprinted London 1911) p. 4.

[46] Ibid., p. 35.

[47] Ibid., p. 92.

[48] Ibid., p. 85.

[49] Ibid., p. 82.

wilderness, but a sense of man alone defying the gods, testing the forbidden areas of consciousness.

Thoreau's second excursion is dominated by the death of a moose, and the poet's revulsion from the mindless and continual killing of trees and wild life. Thoreau ranges himself against both the Indian and the hunter who are equated in their misuse of natural resources. The Indian secured for this trip does not come up to literary expectations, and Thoreau is somewhat fastidiously repelled by both his swearing and his cooking. It is on the third excursion, however, that Thoreau really seems to set out to test the myth of red-white comradeship in the forest. 'I have much to learn,' he says, 'of the Indian, nothing of the missionary'.[50] Joe Polis, the Indian, does not, however, fulfil the image. He is generally uncommunicative, more orthodoxly Christian than Thoreau himself. Thoreau's record, too, is a soberly factual one. He is keener to note difference from than conformation to archetype. Only once does he quote a literary authority and that a Jesuit on mosquitoes. It is quite obvious that Thoreau scarcely knows what to make of Joe. He is obviously good on the trail, at skinning moose, and improvising such things as candles, but he is improvident, lets his boots get wet, seems to take every opportunity for a sleep, and is quite unstoical at an attack of the 'colic'. Joe cannot understand why Thoreau should want to avoid the scattered settlements, any more than Thoreau can understand why the Indian should want to go back to New York. The gulf between them is an absolute cultural one, and Thoreau, to his distress, has few means of communication:

> As we drew near to Oldtown I asked Polis if he was not glad to get home again; but there was no relenting his wildness, and he said, 'It makes no difference to me where I am.' Such is the Indian's pretence always.[51]

The last remark is the nearest Thoreau gets to irritation, and it is an irritation born of the collapse of those literary love affairs. This is one of the more honest records. The relationship is good where red and white man exchange professional information, and where the contract, costing Thoreau two dollars a day is fulfilled. Thoreau's achievement in this relatively minor work is to forget his own reading, and to let the uniqueness of the occasion come through even where the tone is somewhat bitter. Thoreau's own mystic quest is balanced by this kind of detail of tone. Staying for an hour in Joe's house right at the end Thoreau remarks: 'Mrs P. wore a hat and had a silver brooch on her breast, but she was not introduced to us.'[52]

[50] Ibid., p. 238.
[51] Ibid., p. 390.
[52] Ibid., p. 391.

Since it was assumed that no civilization could exist unless it had some form of 'recorded history', a great deal of interest surrounded 'Indian legends', which, written down by missionaries or government officials, gave some sort of graspable artefact for the predominantly literate inquirer. In addition a fascination with Indian legends rose from a complex of interacting interests at the beginning of the nineteenth century in literature, history and religion which at this point included protopsychology and anthropology. In literary terms it was part of the same cultural movement that led Bishop Percy to collect English balladry, or Grimm to write the *Teutonic Mythology* (1835) in the name of defining nationality. In historical terms it helped to articulate notions of 'origin' and 'purity' which in fact often projected doubts about Western culture into a negative picture of those things which threatened it. In religious terms it sought either to find antecedents for Christian legend, or to prove what George Eliot parodied in *Middlemarch* that there was one indivisible key to all mythologies. An interest in Indian culture as anything other than 'primitive' was to be reserved for a later generation.

Nonetheless, men like Edwin James had felt that Indian legends gave a greater insight into Indian life than scientific investigation, and most writers on literature and art felt they were at least raw material for a genuinely American culture. Schoolcraft made the first collections of any size in *Algic Researches* (1839) and in *Oneota* (1845). In a review of these two books, the Southern critic William Gilmore Simms stated that the legends were crucial since Indians had no other cultural artefacts to prove their existence. Like Carlyle he confused existence and history:

> They build no monuments, rear no temples, leave no proofs behind them that they even had a faith, or an affection, a hero or a God. The hunter, and even the agricultural life, is necessarily thus sterile.[53]

Sterility is thus defined as an absence of totemic objects which define the eternal life of the state. In the absence also of visual proof the Indian need not have existed. Schoolcraft contradicted himself completely on the value of the legends. He dismissed the legends of origin as an 'incongruous mass of wild hyperboles and crudities'.[54] and continued, 'where so much is pure mythologic dross, or requires to be put in the crucible of allegory, there appears to be little room

---

[53] W. Gilmore Simms, *Views and Reviews in American History, Literature and Fiction* (New York 1845) p. 107.

[54] Henry Rowe Schoolcraft, *Historical and Statistical Information respecting the History, Condition, and Prospects of the Indian Tribes of the United States* (Philadelphia 1847) vol. I, p. 14.

for any fact'.[55] On the other hand, some of their 'allegories' are 'beautifully sustained. And where, as in their miscellaneous legends and traditions, there is much that is incongruous and ridiculous, there is still evidence of no little variety of intellectual invention.'[56] Schoolcraft's overall view of Indian legends is heavily injected with his evangelical pietism and he discusses them mainly as a corruption of Christian truth. The savage saw through a glass darkly unlike the American whose history, in Simms' words, had been a 'day perfect from the beginning'.[57] These attitudes had been there from the start. As early as 1632 a Jesuit had discussed Indian 'superstitions': 'how much dust there is in their eyes, and how much trouble there will be to remove it that they may see the beautiful light of truth!'[58] Another collection of Indian legends was brought out by Mrs Mary Eastman, known for her *Aunt Phillis' Cabin, or Southern Life as it is* (1852), a reply to *Uncle Tom's Cabin*. She had collected them while stationed with her soldier painter husband at Fort Snelling and she published them in 1849 under the title, *Dacotah, or Life and Legends of the Sioux around Fort Snelling*.

Parkman, in his introduction to *The Jesuits in North America* (1867) and Daniel G. Brinton in his *The Myths of the New World* (1868) made some attempt to evaluate previous collections. Of *Algic Researches* Parkman observed:

> This book is perhaps the best of Mr Schoolcraft's works, though its value is much impaired by the want of a literal rendering, and the introduction of decorations which savor more of a popular monthly magazine than of an Indian wigwam.[59]

Brinton was even more damning, and does not hesitate to label certain observations of Schoolcraft, 'literary anachronisms'.[60] Brinton's analysis is much indebted to contemporary German work on mythology. He thought, however, the major hypothesis of J. G. Muller's *Geschichte der amerikanischen Ur-religionen* (Basel 1853) too imaginary and the standard *Anthropologie der Naturvoelker* (Leipzig 1862) too irreligious.

In spite of his obvious criticism of Schoolcraft, Brinton changed few of the assumptions of the 'anthropologists' who had gone before him. He deplored the tendency to atheism of his German contemporaries, and defined mythology as the 'idea of God expressed

[55] Ibid.
[56] Ibid., vol. I, p. 316.
[57] Simms, *Views and Reviews*, p. 45.
[58] Edna Kenton, ed., *The Jesuit Relations* (New York 1954) p. 61.
[59] Parkman, *The Jesuits in North America*, p. lxxxviii.
[60] Daniel G. Brinton, *The Myths of the New World* (New York 1868) p. 20.

in symbol, figure and narrative. . . .'[61] His broadly Platonic inter-
pretations remind one of the American transcendentalists, especially
when he makes statements like 'behind all forms is one essence',
and quotes the Zend Avesta to prove it.[62] He also quotes Grimm
to state 'The idea of the Devil . . . is foreign to all primitive
religions.'[63] His prudery is also in evidence, for he roundly
condemns sexual theories of mythology such as proposed in an
early American work on the subject by E. G. Squier, *The Serpent
Symbol in America* (1851), on the grounds that it 'combines the
favorite and (may I add?) characteristic French doctrine, that the
chief topic of mythology is the adoration of the generative power.'[64]
Nonetheless he placed the whole subject on a broader base, and
anticipated Freud's work with Greek legends. Iroquois legends
point, for example, 'not to a common source in history, but in
psychology'.[65]

The change from history to psychology as the meaning defined
by legend was a significant one. Brinton, like those who followed
him, thought, however, that this pointed to a common human
nature vaguely religious in connotation and so, in political terms,
the analysis comes out as inept as the historical view. The legends
collected in these early works are unverifiable factually and as such
must be read as popular imaginative works of white civilization.
Three examples of the way in which the Indian was presented in
legend follow: the first is a supposedly authentic legend out of
Schoolcraft, the second a use of Indian raw material to make a
legend of American literature and third Longfellow's *Hiawatha* as a
literary-cultural phenomenon deriving its sources from these early
collectors.

Schoolcraft's story of *Mas-kwa-sha-kwong*[66] does indeed seem, as
Parkman suggested, to belong more to the taste of the devotee of
the popular magazine than of the scientific anthropologist. For the
story is a male fantasy of the breakdown of order within the family
group. Mash-kwa-sha-kwong's wife deserts her role as mother and
monogamously faithful mistress to her husband. In revenge
Mash-kwa-sha-kwong kills both wife and lover and flies before the
avenging relations, but not before he has given his two sons an awl,
a beaver tooth, a hone and dry coal, symbols perhaps of survival in
the male role. The sons then go south to seek the father who has

[61] Ibid., p. 43.
[62] Ibid., p. 54.
[63] Ibid., p. 59.
[64] Ibid., p. 39.
[65] Ibid., pp. 173–4.
[66] In Henry Rowe Schoolcraft, *Oneota* (New York 1845) p. 139ff.

escaped through a hollow tree into the sky. The boys are pursued by the mother's spirit but they drop the awl which turns into a thorn bush. In attempting to get through the bush the spirit mother has her head torn from her body. The head continues the chase. The revenge on the sexually aggressive woman takes the form of decapitation as the woman literally becomes 'head of the family' in a savage travesty of male leadership roles.[67] Mash-kwa-sha-kwong is killed by this avenging head only to turn into a woodpecker, and his final revenge comes when his father, the boys' grandfather, (for the males of the family stick together) dashes her brains out against a rock in the middle of a river. Fish feed on the pieces and become fat and white. These nightmare fish children are the result of denaturing the woman whose infidelity is the cause of her own destruction. Having exorcized the mother, the boys become political chieftains. Finally visited by missionaries (white messengers) they refuse to go to heaven. Upon which the white messengers shoot arrows to kill the white worms in their bodies. The white worms and white fish are the nemesis attendant on the refusal of bourgeois, Christian and male sexual authority. The white messenger gives good laws and prophesies the apocalypse:

> Then the good Indian will arise from death to enjoy a new earth, filled with the abundance of all manner of living things. . . . The bad Indian will not enjoy any portion of the new earth: they will be condemned and given to the evil spirits.[68]

In *Oneota,* Schoolcraft had explained that he collected legends so that they might be 'the medium of presenting the germs of a future mythology, which in the hands of our poets and novelists, and fictitious writers, might admit of being formed and moulded to the purposes of a purely vernacular literature'.[69] In this connection he especially recommended Charles Fenno Hoffman's *Wild Scenes in the Forest and Prairie* (1839). The strangest and longest story in this collection is *The Ghost Riders.* The narrative is based on an Indian legend in which the ghostly riders are:

> . . . as two gigantic figures, representing a man and woman locked in each other's arms, and both mounted on one horse, which is of the same unearthly make as themselves. Some pretend to have been near enough to discover their features, and these assert that the countenance of the man, though emaciated and ghastly, and writhed with the most fearful contortions, by an expression of shrinking horror, can plainly

[67] It is interesting to note that this theme of the severed head seems popular. See 'Iamo or the undying head', in Schoolcraft's *Algic researches* (1839).

[68] Schoolcraft, *Oneota.*

[69] Ibid.

be identified as the face of a white man; while the features of the woman, though collapsed and corpse-like, are evidently those of an Indian female.[70]

The way Hoffman explained the legend was to take an Indian brave Ta-in-gairo and his beautiful fair-complexioned wife, Zecana, and place them in a far western Eden where, exiled by choice from their own tribe, they live the dream existence of Western sexual romance. Once again adultery destroys married bliss and Zecana is seduced by a wily and profligate Spaniard, but unlike Mash-kwa-sha-kwong's wife she becomes insane, and on meeting her returning husband snatches a dagger from his belt and kills herself. Ta-in-gairo returns, captures the trader, burns down his fort—the fort itself is a disruption of white civilization in paradise—and binds his victim to the corpse of his wife, 'trunk for trunk, and limb for limb was he lashed to his horrible companion'. Hoffman gives a graphic description of how the putrid wounds of the dead woman feed the open scars of the trader. The reversal of the male and female roles and of life and death, in the dream, show how quickly the dream of order turns to nightmare. Cheated of the suppositions of a repressive romance ethic, the Indian hero turns avenger.

Longfellow's best known poem, *The Song of Hiawatha* (1855) is a final culmination of American attempts to redefine smatterings of information on Indian legend into a composite artefact of white American literature. It made the discoveries and the popular superstitions into a vast public myth. More than this it made an image of the Indian which summed up the presuppositions of mid-nineteenth-century culture socially, sexually and politically. Like *Uncle Tom's Cabin* it was widely translated and appealed to many types of national and social interests. Sales in England, from one publisher alone, amounted to over a million copies. Like Schoolcraft's, on which it was partly based, Longfellow's Indian mythology is strongly Christian and paternalist in tone. In the opening invocation, the Indian is the child of history: 'with feeble hands and helpless/ Groping blindly in the darkness.'[71] The Indian presiding deity, however, sends to his people 'The Master of Life' who brings peace on earth. At the peace meeting the most important of the four winds is Mudjekeewis (the west wind inevitably) who is to become the father of Hiawatha. Mudjekeewis has proved himself by killing a bear whom he taunts as an old woman. Then he seduces the

[70] Charles Fenno Hoffman, *Wild Scenes in the Forest and Prairie* (London 1838) p. 135.
[71] Henry Wadsworth Longfellow, *Poetical Works*, 6 vols (Cambridge, Mass 1904) vol. II, p. 126.

daughter of Nokomis, Wenonah, and abandons her Western style by
disappearing on the wind. Brought up by his grandmother,
Hiawatha's first act is to avenge his mother by travelling west to
kill his father. Male victory, however, is preserved when after three
days of wrestling, the father proves to be immortal, and Hiawatha
returns home with instructions to be a good ruler. In a parallel fight
with Mondamin whom he kills, and from whose grave rises corn,
Hiawatha symbolically ensures the beginning of cultivation and
agriculture to found his civilization. In this wrestling match he
takes on the characteristics of his adversary in an erotic communion,
the fruits of which are to be the creation of the state:

> At his touch he felt new courage
> Throbbing in his brain and bosom,
> Felt new life and hope and vigour
> Run through every nerve and fibre.[72]

Hiawatha himself is a pastiche of the epic hero. In his encounter
with Mishe-Nahma, the King of Fishes, Hiawatha, unlike Ahab,
successfully combats the monster. On his third encounter with
Mishe-Nahma, in a sequence that reminds one alternately of Beowulf
and Jonah, Hiawatha is swallowed up with his canoe and Walt
Disney-like squirrel. Undaunted he strikes the heart of the fish and
is reborn with seagulls acting as midwives. Another epic battle is
fought with Megissogwon, his grandmother's father, who, in a
surrealistic landscape of death, turns out to be the God of Wealth.
After war comes peace, and democratically distributing the spoils
of the last encounter among his tribe, Hiawatha is mature enough
to marry and inaugurate the 'rule by love'. The landscape changes
from the waters of death to Minnehaha or laughing water. Having
built up his tribe with his two male friends, one physically strong,
the other 'woman-like', Hiawatha is free to celebrate the marriage
feast. The woman-like Pau-Puk-Keewis entertains the company
with mystic dances, and Chibiabos sings a song of love. After the
marriage comes creation and Minnehaha wanders round the corn-
fields naked, as Longfellow somewhat prudishly transcribes
Schoolcraft's description of the ceremony in *Oneota*.

Hiawatha obligingly governs according to the notions of mid-
nineteenth century historians who believed that only a written record
could secure the actual stability of the state. The need for heroes
in Hiawatha's world is as great as in Emerson's America. Following
contemporary arguments for national monuments, Hiawatha also

[72] Ibid., vol. II, p. 162.

intends that the past will control the future:

> And he said: 'behold your grave-posts
> Have no mark, no sign, nor symbol,
> Go and paint them all with figures;
> Each one with its household symbol,
> With its own ancestral Totem;
> So that those who follow after
> May distinguish them and know them.[73]

The rest of the book is concerned with the deaths of the three more feminine types. First Chichiabos (the fair one) whose death Hiawatha laments in truly David and Jonathan fashion and then Pau-puk-Keewis (the dark one) who introduces gambling into Hiawatha's bourgeois paradise, disrupts the tribe and even makes fun of Hiawatha's authority. After various protean transformations Hiawatha eventually catches up with him on the Rocky Mountains. Finally Minnehaha herself dies after an exchange with her grandmother strangely reminiscent of Goethe's *Erlkönig*. In the penultimate section, 'The White Man's Foot,' Hiawatha moves west for the last time before the inexorable drive of Manifest Destiny.

In its sentimental and incomplete approach to an image of the Indian, the poem engaged, but could not resolve the contradictions of white paternalism. For every popular notion of white civilization was confirmed in the mirror image of Indian civilization. Here God the father remains alive, Indian legends authenticate white religion, agriculture is proved the basis of civilization, disruptors of bourgeois order are hounded to death, women are aids to creation and die beautifully, and genocide is an American destiny since even the victims admit the truth. Organized through a seasonal cycle of nature, its roots patiently exhumed from European and American folk mythology by a Harvard professor of modern languages, *Hiawatha* lent to the racist and paternalist consciousness of Europe and America a conviction of ultimate truth.

In the captivity literature, the popular stories (which increase in number after 1840), the broadsheet, the mass-selling lithograph, the primitive painting and the cartoon, the different images of the Indian reflect the anxieties of white society. We shall see how many of these images were given official stamp in a government writer-artist team such as Schoolcraft and Eastman formed. In the 'captivity literature', a phenomenon present from the beginning of American literature, all the fears arising from the insecurity of white culture in the new world were given expression whether based in fact or

---

[73] Ibid., vol. II, p. 235.

fiction. They are hardly a single genre just as the images of the
Indian they project can hardly be classified simply. The Indian
appears not only as white male's companion, or threat to the virtue
and life of women and children, but as social entrepreneur, as
trickster, as Christian convert, and as noble and ignoble savage.
Recent work has shown that the captivity literature contains as
many white types as red types.[74] But through all the categories
invented by white consciousness the image of the Indian as a threat
to social order predominates from Mrs Rowlandson, whose famous
narrative had gone through 15 editions by 1800, to Cotton Mather's
descriptions of Indians dashing the brains of children against trees
in front of their frenzied mothers. A number of earlier captivity
narratives were written by survivors, for Indians nearly always
attempted to adopt the children of victims into their tribe. Between
1780 and the early 1800s, torture scenes and sadistic fantasies
poured from the pens of an increasing number of women writers:
Mrs Rowlandson, Hannah Swarton, Mrs Duston, Elizabeth Hanson,
Mary Kinnan, Mercy Herbeson, Susannah Willar Hanson and
Jermima Howe. During these years the actual violence reported
increases, sometimes accompanied by a crude engraving such as
one in the 1794 edition of *The Affecting History of the Dreadful
Distresses of Frederick Manheim's Family*, portraying that unfor-
tunate man's daughter bound naked to the stake, surrounded by
yelling savages.[75]

After the turn of the century, however, a new form appeared in
the anthologies of collected captivity narratives. The earlier ones,
such as Archibald Loudon's *A Selection of Some of the Most
Interesting Narratives of Outrages Committed by the Indians in
their Wars with the White People*, its successors by Samuel
Metcalf, Alexander Withers, and John A. M'Clung fall short in both
accuracy and popularity of the two major collections in the
forties—Samuel Drake's *Tragedies of the Wilderness* (1841) and
J. Pritts's *Incidents of Border Life* (1839), later reprinted in *Mirror
of Olden Time Border Life* (1849).

The tone of Drake's collection is clear from his introduction,
'To observe man in his uncivilized or natural state offers an approach
to a knowledge of his natural history, without which it is hardly
obtained.'[76] Here is reprinted Mrs Rowlandson's captivity with her
comforting concluding words, 'it is good for me that I have been

---

[74] See Fiedler, *The Return of the Vanishing American.*
[75] Pearce, 'The Significances of the Captivity Narrative', p. 11.
[76] Samuel Drake, *Tragedies of the Wilderness* (Boston 1841) p. iii.

afflicted,'[77] and Sarah Gerish's captivity in which she escapes from
burning and is sold from an Indian who was a 'dull sort of fellow'
to one who was 'a much more harsh and mad sort of dragon'.[78]
Here too is John Gyles's captivity (originally 1736) in which he
seems far more worried about the Jesuits than the Indians. When
he hears that he has been sold out of captivity to the French he
weeps till he could 'scarce stand. The words *sold* and that to a
people of that persuasion which my dear mother so detested, and
in her last words manifested so great fears of my falling into'.[79]
One narrative is a little unusual. Colonel James Smith's captivity
was also reprinted in Pritts's collection. In classic manner he learns
to survive in the wilderness with his adopted brother, Tontileaugo,
but we have a sense of him actually learning to see and understand
an alien culture. He learns to find meaning in Indian dances which
he had hitherto thought 'irrational and stupid', and his heart warms
to his captors when they carefully preserve his books in spite of
his own continuously hostile attitudes. When he forgets to put out
sugar and bear's oil with the venison for a visitor, Tontileaugo
reproves him and Smith acknowledges his fault. In the aftermath
of Braddock's defeat when the Delawares adopted him into their
tribe he comments:

> At this time I did not believe their fine speech, especially that of the
> white blood being washed out of me; but since that time I have found
> that there was much sincerity in said speech; for, from that day, I never
> knew them to make any distinction between me and themselves in any
> respect whatever until I left them.[80]

The narrative, however, becomes increasingly literary with reflections on religion and inclusion of his own verses in the metre of
Watts's hymns. By the end of the book he has moved from literary
recollection to enlightenment commonplaces but even these latter
have become rarer by 1840 when his work is still on sale to the
public some hundred years after it was written:

> Let us also take a view of the advantages attending Indian polity. They
> are not oppressed or perplexed with excessive litigation; they are not
> injured by legal robbery; they have no splendid villains that make them-
> selves grand and great on other people's labour; they have neither church
> nor state erected as money making machines.[81]

[77] Ibid., p. 59.
[78] Ibid., p. 69.
[79] Ibid., p. 100.
[80] Ibid., p. 186.
[81] Ibid., p. 258.

Drake's major work, *The Book of the Indians of North America* went through 15 editions from 1834 to 1860 and was the major public source of information about the Indians throughout this period. The first edition was illustrated with prints from John Smith's narrative and these are among the earliest pictures of Indians extant. The later editions were illustrated with contemporary 'historical engravings', with artists like G. L. Brown and J. G. Chapman painting the originals in a somewhat debased post-West manner and with engravers like Schoff, Smillie, G. B. Ellis and C. A. Jewett. The nature of the pictures is evident from their titles. *Westward the Star of Empire* depicts a moonlit scene where an Indian kneels on a raised ground above a lake in the foreground with a stag bounding off to the right, while two scantily clad angels with stars on their heads lead a host of angels westward. The other titles are alike suggestive: *The Last of the Wampanoags, And will the White Man still pursue?* and *The Cherokee Mother's Last Offering.*

Drake's volume has a mosaic structure of bad verse, anecdote, captivity narrative, history and biography. The line between fantasy and the blood-besmirched record seems uncertain, for volume III carries the story down to Drake's own time. Jostling each other are reports of current atrocity in the Seminole War and quotations from Eastburn and Sand's *Yamoyden* (1820) at one time an immensely popular poem in which the Indian of King Philip's War is an embodiment of piety and virtue. One of the last accounts is a description of American soldiers taking away pieces of Tecumseh's skin as mementoes of the War of 1812. The very form of the work was like a newspaper in which the good news is the literary event in bad poetry and anecdote, and in which the bad news is current war. There is a sense of a world apart in which the contradictions cancel each other out and increase the passivity of the reading public.

Drake's work on the popular level was paralleled by the work of Henry Rowe Schoolcraft, and one of his better known illustrators Seth Eastman, in his huge disorganized master work, *Historical and Statistical Information respecting the history, condition and prospects of the Indian Tribes of the United States. . . .* which began publication in 1851. Early in life Schoolcraft enjoyed the study of languages and the natural sciences. Chief among the latter was an overriding interest in geology and mineralogy, probably deriving initially from his father's business as a prosperous glass maker. His first work was a report published in New York in 1819 which reflected these interests, *A View of the Lead Mines of Missouri.* In

1822, however, he was appointed Indian agent for the Lake Superior tribes and the following year married a quarter blood Chippewa girl who had been educated in Europe. From 1836 to 1841 he was superintendent of Indian affairs for Michigan, and in 1836 negotiated a treaty with the Chippewas by which the United States took the northern third of the lower, and the eastern half of the upper peninsula of Michigan. His most important books relating to the Indian were *Algic Researches* (1831), *Oneota* (1845), *Notes on the Iroquois* (1846) as well as the volumes of *Historical and Statistical Information . . . of the Indian Tribes of the United States* (1851—60).

Technically Schoolcraft follows the tradition of reporting on Indians begun by Jedidiah Morse in 1822. In *A Report to the Secretary of War of the United States on Indian Affairs,* Morse's quite fair liberal reforms are based on a conviction of Christian superiority in religion and on the necessity of property-based state power. He had proposed an 'Indian Improvement Society' whose patrons were Adams, Jefferson and Madison, the aim of which was to conduct a scientific examination into Indian morals, antiquities and the geology and geography of their territories. Morse advocated intermarriage to prevent Indian stock from disappearing entirely and more government-controlled trading to prevent exploitation. But like Jefferson he believed that these reforms could only be carried through with a conversion of the Indians to the individu-alistic agrarian ideal. A remark from a chief of the Six Nations did not find favour:

> As to dividing our lands into farms, and holding them as individual property, as among the white people, we think it will not now do for us. Holding our lands in common as we do now, keeps us together.[82]

Early remarks in his *Narrative Journal . . . to the sources of the Mississippi River* (1821) show Schoolcraft organizing his thought somewhat haphazardly among the categorizations of the Morse *American Geography* (1789). For the basis of his remarks on natural history he quotes Pennant, Carver, Peale, Cuvier and Humboldt, but for his description of the natural landscape he quotes, typically, Sir Walter Scott on geological formations and Alexander Pope on the Indians. In a revealing section on 'Character of the Red Man of America', in *Oneota*, Schoolcraft describes how he first became interested in Indians:

> My earliest impressions of the Indian race were drawn from the fireside rehearsals of incidents which happened during the perilous times of the

---

[82] *A Report to the Secretary of War of the United States on Indian Affairs by the Rev. Jedidiah Morse, D.D.* (New Haven, Conn. 1822), Appendix, p. 2.

American revolution; in which my father was a zealous actor, and were all inseparably connected with the fearful ideas of the Indian yell, the tomahawk, the scalping knife, and the fire brand. . . . These early ideas were sustained by printed narratives of captivity and hair-breadth escapes of men and women from their clutches, which, from time to time, fell into my hands, so that long before I was ten years old, I had a most definite and terrific idea impressed on my imagination of what was sometimes called in my native precincts, 'the bow and arrow race'.[83]

On the basis of this early impression of Indians, Schoolcraft formed the body of his ideas on Indian culture which were to change very little throughout his life. From his master work, which still contains virtually the sum of information on Indians of this period, we can outline some of these ideas through which his scientific reporting was filtered.

In his introduction Schoolcraft talks of the Indian's 'pseudo-nationality' and of his inability to understand 'industrial prosperity and happiness'.[85] In spite of the fact that the Indian male makes a good father, he is wrong in his conception of the social duties of life and doubly wrong in his conception of death and eternity. Even Indian picture writing, one of the few artefacts by which he becomes visible to white historical consciousness, is, though splendidly recorded in the coloured plates of the work, condemned by Schoolcraft: 'If letters may be called the language of Christianity, picture writing is emphatically the language of idolatry.'[85] Literacy and its association with linear organization, law and the city state controls Schoolcraft's judgement. Picture writing with its extension of sense experience into two-dimensional form, colour and multidirectional space is felt by this Puritan consciousness to be irreligious. Schoolcraft's literal belief in Christian mythology lies behind his scientific analysis, for it is some years now since the atheistical tendencies of Jeffersonian republicanism guided American enlightenment thought. 'History,' states Schoolcraft, 'as viewed in the earliest and most authentic record, namely the Pentateuch, represents man as having been created, not in the savage, but in the industrialized or civilized state.'[86] Schoolcraft's Christianity, however, is a strong-minded one. In the third volume, in a preface to the Rev. D. Lowry's article, 'Education, Christianity and the Arts', he remarks, 'The forest life is so fascinating to the Indian, that he requires, as it were, to be wrested from it with a strong hand.'[87] In fact the chapter in each

---

[83] Schoolcraft, *Oneota*, p. 129.
[84] Schoolcraft, *Historical and Statistical Information etc.*, vol. I, pp. ix–x.
[85] Ibid., vol. I, p. 342.
[86] Ibid., vol. II, p. 41.
[87] Ibid., vol. III, p. 471.

volume called 'Indian Prospects' brings out Schoolcraft's calm sense of Indian human inferiority. He talks of 'manual labour schools'[88] and of the need to create the 'intellectual and moral want'[89] which will make the Indian realize the inadequacy of his own way of life.

Seth Eastman confirms the same kind of vision pictorially. Recent critics have stressed the objectivity of his point of view and his personal detachment.[90] It seems impossible to agree with this judgement on any grounds. His sense of history and figure drawing was developed at West Point, copying engravings of the French neo-Classical school. At Fort Snelling, where his wife assiduously collected legends, he posed a half-crazed Indian for sketches which he used for his figures. The very insipidity of his genre pictures outdoes the worst in that mode, not only exploiting its inbuilt snobbery, but making the Indian look mad or foolish. His flute-playing Indian is indebted for its subject to Schoolcraft and was based on classical misconceptions of the Indian's love making role, and his illustration of *Pawnees torturing female captive* owes much to Schoolcraft's latent sadism and is, as we have seen, part of an old iconography of Indian pictorial representation. He surely never saw the reality of his most famous picture, *The Death Whoop* **pl. 40.** Eastman, who had at least one child by an Indian squaw and married a Southern belle, reflects some of the worst aspects of the senti-mental tradition.

Eastman was an army officer who had 'early conceived a passion for military life'.[91] His only recorded writing on the Indian is a journal he kept of a march from San Antonio to Laredo in August 1849 as the Americans moved in to garrison Texas after the defeat of the Mexicans. The military imperialist tone is apparent through-out. He solemnly repeats stories of Indians carrying off pregnant Mexican wives whom they then rip apart at the request of their squaws, but after having given the Comanches a good hiding he reflects that now 'no Comanche dare come into San Antonio . . ..'[92] Eastman, with his mission to save Mexican women from fates worse than death, is paralleled by his wife whose *The American Aboriginal Portfolio* (1853) he illustrated. Mrs Eastman's introduction des-cribes in pathetic detail the grief of Indian children at the death of her own daughter: 'That small white hand, that lay so powerless,

[88] Ibid., vol. IV, p. 479.
[89] Ibid.
[90] See John Francis McDermott, *Seth Eastman, Pictorial Historian of the Indian* (Norman, Oklahoma 1961) p. 103.
[91] Ibid., p. 6.
[92] Ibid., p. 73.

40 *The Death Whoop,* by Seth Eastman. (*Courtesy of the James Jerome Hill Reference Library, St Paul, Minnesota.*)

had ever been outstretched to welcome them when they came weary and hungry.'[93] As imperialist administrators go, Eastman had a reputation for fairness, but the writings and the illustrations of this husband and wife team reveal the contradictions inherent in the nature of official presuppositions which alternate practically between piety and violence.

When we turn from the writers to the painters we find that, on the whole, the painterly tradition follows the literary tradition. John White's famous watercolours are still the exception.[94] Neither spartan nor savage, the Indian White depicts, with some exceptions,

[93] Mary Eastman, *Dahcotah; or, Life and Legends of the Sioux around Fort Snelling* (New York, 1849) p. ix.
[94] See Thomas Har[r]iot, *A briefe and true report of the new found land of Virginia; . . ..* (London 1588).

is not sacrificed to white preconceptions of ideality and superiority. Le Moyne, a French artist of the same period, depicted Indians very much as Spartans engaged in sadistic tortures, though the accompanying narrative showed how the atrocities Le Moyne himself experienced were really owing to French-Spanish rivalry in South America.[95] Strikingly similar in form were the illustrations accompanying Lafitau's famous work, *Moeurs des Sauvages Américains,* of 1724. His archaeological engravings compare Indian and Roman antiquities, and his choice of Indian subject matter helps to establish the iconography of painting of Indians in America. Here are domestic scenes, ball games, funeral rituals, and Indian antiquities. Only the buffalo hunt is missing. In England, academic artists were quick to take up the new subject. Indian chiefs visiting London were painted by aristocratic command. We have already seen how the Anglo-American eighteenth-century tradition was summed up by West's legendary reaction to the *Belvedere Apollo*: 'My God, how like it is to a Mohawk Indian.' The remark conveniently synthesizes that marriage of classical ideality and sense of natural liberty to be found in the conception of the noble savage.

We have also previously noted that West introduced an Indian for the seated figure in *The Death of Wolfe.* But we find a more typically American vision of the Indian in another picture by West painted almost immediately afterwards. *Penn's Treaty with the Indians* (c. 1771) **pl. 41** was a subject close to West's Quaker heart. West's insistence on ethnographical accuracy—he painted the costumes from his own collection of Indian clothes—contrasts strangely with the generalized appearance of the figures. The picture divides along a diagonal line uniting the kneeling white man with the roll of cloth and the Indian with the outstretched arm. The chiaroscuro takes the line to the top of the picture, right, and to the bottom of the picture, left. The bale of cloth illumined like the Christ child at a nativity scene gives this dividing line its focal point, as capitalism appears under the guise of Christian iconography. Either side of the line is a different world. The landscape in which the Quakers (sober fat businessmen) stand, mirrors their achievements and their prospects. We can see the establishment of property in the finished house, and the prospect of the establishment of property in the half-built house. Nature with its blue sky and luxuriant vegetation smiles benevolently on their enterprises. To the right of this diagonal line, however, the Indian figures are

[95] Le Moyne, *Narrative of Le Moyne . . . .. Translated from the Latin of De Bry. With Heliotypes of the Engraving from the Artist's Original Drawings* (1564; reprinted Boston 1875).

41 *Penn's Treaty with the Indians* by Benjamin West. (*Courtesy of the Pennsylvania Academy of Fine Arts, Philadelphia, Joseph and Sarah Harrison Collection, 1878.*)

arranged in appropriate classical attitudes. Some of the drapery arrangements could easily have come from Poussin's own figures. Another diagonal line connects the Indian baby bent over by his Madonna-like mother with the outstretched arm of the small boy to the outstretched hand of the full grown Indian bargaining with the Quakers. The mother appears to ignore these importunate male gestures however and sits, somewhat isolated, from the male world of business and exchange.

It is in George Catlin's (1796–1872) work, however, that we find the most comprehensive guide to visual representations of the Indians. Many printed books, drawings, full scale portraits in oil, and folios of coloured engravings bear witness to a life devoted to a single purpose.[96] His literary work, with some exceptions, reflects most of the popular attitudes we have already observed in a Drake or a Schoolcraft. His first work, *Letters and Notes on the Manners, Customs, and Condition of the North American Indians* (1841), is a compendium of popular superstition, classical attitudes and literary

[96] A good popular book on Catlin is Harold McCracken, *George Catlin and the Old Frontier* (Chicago and Crawfordsville, Indiana 1959).

sentiment. Catlin's motives are to record the dying culture for posterity and, like the museum curator, Catlin's artefacts take on the function of epitaphs. In this first book we have all the attributes of the 'classic West'. With typical American eclecticism Catlin's Indians are knights of the forest, Grecian youths, and as Abyssinian chiefs and Hebrews they join in jousts, Olympic games or declaim like Demosthenes. The second half of the book deals with Indian religion, and here Catlin follows Morse and Schoolcraft in their belief that the Indians are the twelve lost tribes of Israel because of their monotheism and their predominantly 'Mosaic' mode of worship. In spite of this vast heritage of Hebraism and Hellenism, Catlin also sees them as having minds, which, like Locke's *tabula rasa,* are 'a beautiful blank, on which anything may be written'.[97]

One account of an Indian ceremony, however, which Catlin suppressed from the work of 1841 and from a more elaborate account printed as a separate work in 1867, shows Catlin ignoring public presupposition and providing more closely factual data for future anthropologists. It is of interest to us because it parallels in many ways Melville's chapter 'The Cassock' in its attempt to equate significances about the psychology of state with 'primitive' ritual. In *An Account of a Religious Ceremony . . ..*[98] Catlin describes how, in a Mandan ceremony, a man with an artificial penis ritualistically fucks eight male buffalo dancers while the surrounding women of the tribe go through a kind of communal orgasm. The dance concludes with a symbolic castration of the male dancer by one of the women of O-Ke-hee-dee who breaks off the penis, carrying it 'as she would have carried an infant', to deposit it later in 'the sacred archives of the nation'. This phallic mother claims she has power of life and death over the tribe, that 'she was father of all the buffaloes', and that it was her duty to stop the dance and begin the *Pohk-hong* or male initiation torture rites in the Medicine lodge. Catlin's fascination with the ceremony and his use of terms which show him mentally attempting to equate this ritual with equivalents in his own society show how close the order of Indian society was to mid-nineteenth-century American society. In the ritual sexual relations become communal symbols of state order. The divided roles of male and female, in Indian society as well as in white, symbolically unite the dialectic of war and peace (the dance of

    [97] George Catlin, *Letters and Notes on the Manners . . . of the North American Indians* (Boston 1841) p. 245.
    [98] George Catlin, *An Account of a Religious Ceremony, practised by the Mandan tribe of Indians at the 'Feast of the Buffaloes'. Being the suppressed chapter from Catlin's O-Kee-Pa* (London 1867) pp. i–iii.

fertility and the ceremony of physical pain to make warriors) in order to preserve the permanence of the society. Catlin felt that universal truths about human nature were embodied in this ritual, and in *O-Kee-Pa* (1867) he provided a lavishly illustrated edition for his mid-nineteenth-century audience as a kind of mirror for their own concerns. Catlin himself concluded, 'rational and conclusive deductions from the above premises—I approach with timidity.'

In order to help pay for his own interests Catlin went over to Europe with an exhibition which he set up in the Egyptian Hall in London. At first there were only pictures but with the arrival of one Arthur Rankin, accompanied by eight Ojibway Indians, the exhibition was extended to include live Indians in *tableaux vivants*. In these exhibitions the Indians were literally made into museum pieces, and to do Catlin credit he was very uneasy about the humanity of the project from the beginning. Rankin was out for mere sensationalism and squeezed every ounce of publicity he could from the marriage of one of the Indians to an English girl, with traffic blocking Trafalgar Square and the Strand on the occasion. Catlin began making arrangements with Poinsett, the secretary of war, to stop further speculators. When seven Ioway Indians brought over to London by a Mr Melody, Mr Rankin's successor, died, and after being offered a sight of one of the war-chiefs' skeletons Catlin revolted:

> . . . I went on through Piccadilly, and I know not where, meditating on the virtues of scientific and mercenary man. I thought of the heroic *Osceola*, who was captured when he was disarmed and was bearing a white flag in his hand; who died a prisoner of war, and whose head was a few months afterwards offered for sale in the city of New York! I thought also of the thousands of Indian graves I had seen on the frontier thrown open by sacrilegious hands for the skulls and trinkets they enclosed, to which the retiring relatives were lurking back to take the last glance of, and to mingle their last tears over, with the horror of seeing the bones of their fathers and children strewed over the ground by hands too averse to labour and too ruthless to cover them again.
>
> I was here forcibly struck with the fitness of Tim's remark about the hyaenas, of 'their resemblance to *Chemokimons* or pale-faces,' when I told him that they lived by digging up and devouring bodies that had been consigned to the grave.[99]

The fate of these exhibition Indians, made into objects of aristocratic curiosity (Queen Victoria asked for a visit) showed the results of the categories of natural history when literally applied to human

---

[99] George Catlin, *Catlin's Notes of Eight Years' Travel and Residence in Europe* (London 1848) p. 153.

42 *Male Indian* by George Catlin. (*Courtesy of the Newberry Library, Chicago.*)

beings. Catlin realized that the Indian was a victim equally of
capitalism and scientific analysis.

Catlin is most famous, however, for his visual representations of
Indians. His presuppositions about the kind and style of painting
he should adopt were European but fortunately his lack of formal
training saved him from the insipidity of current European norms.
If he is to be classed at all it must be with so-called primitive
painters. His 600 Indian portraits are a unique record of Indians
at the time, and however clumsy the figures are, the details of dress
and equipment are drawn and coloured with a fine precision. Perhaps even more interesting is the unique collection of pencil
drawings Catlin made from the paintings which are bound in two

43 *Female Indian* by George Catlin. (*Courtesy of the Newberry Library, Chicago.*)

volumes. These drawings, generally three quarter length figure
studies, are accompanied by manuscript notes. The drawings of the
Mandans are on the whole much more finished, though the best
drawing occurs where the costume hides Catlin's weakness in
figures. **Plate 42** is typical of Catlin's work in that it presents in
detail a composite iconography of the Indian male role. The buffalo
on the shield is emblematic of the hunter's life, and the bow
indicates male prowess in war and peace. The woman's role can be
seen in a remarkable sketch of a flat-head woman **pl. 43**. Catlin
describes her in his manuscript note as:

> (wife of the chief, on the foregoing page,) basketing salmon, at the
> Dalles, on the Columbia River. Carrying her infant in its cradle, illustrat-

ing the extraordinary mode of flattening the head, peculiar to that tribe.

The custom of flattening the head, in this tribe, is one of the most unaccountable modes to be met with amongst the Am. Indians; and like that of the Nayas tribe of wearing a block of wood in the under lip, is confined almost entirely to the females. The Author met but a very few males whose heads were flattened, and from various tests, and general enquiry, he was fully convinced that this singular process in no way impaired the intellect, or injured the health.[100]

The picture has a graceful sense of design and iconography; arm, fish and child make up the ancient triangular female symbolic shape, and the details of the cradle and the wooden board flattening the child's head are carefully articulated. Holding the fish before her like the arrow of the male, the Indian woman is seen in terms of a symbolism which indicates her domestic role and her childbearing capacity.

In his *North American Indian Portfolio*, the iconography of their life is established, particularly that of the buffalo hunt. Catlin set his Indian scenes in magnificent wide rolling landscapes coloured with beautiful yellow and light-green washes, and against magnificent sunsets. One of the most popular prints was the literary double portrait of Wi-Jun-Jon before going to Washington and after deserting his tribe **pl. 44**. The left half shows him in full Assinoboine warrior dress but with the pipe of peace in his hand. Just to the left is the White House, barely visible. The right portrait depicts him 'civilized'. His white kid glove holds a fan which he contemplates like a mirror, his top hat flaunts a feather, and the half-turned back view shows him leaning on an umbrella, with a sword between his legs. Two tell-tale gin bottles are visible in his back pocket. Catlin's accompanying narrative shows this Indian apprentice to misfortune (giving Hogarthian values an American context) corrupted by white civilization, rejected by his tribe and dying in dishonour. There is a sense of inevitable decline. For not only does the picture show Indian 'pretension' but it bitterly reflects two possible ways of life which were simply not realizable under the expanding American empire. Ridiculous in white society, denied his own, the cautionary tale Wi-Jun-Jon's fate was supposed to articulate reflects more on white society than on red.

Catlin's achievement was attained in spite of the conflicting views of art and society to which he subcribed. His sensitivity and honesty emerge from his own experience and often contradict the presuppositions he inherited. Out of his own commitment he formed a

---

[100] Catlin's two manuscript volumes are in the Ayer collection in the Newberry Library, Chicago.

44 *Wi-Jun-Jon* by George Catlin in his *North American Indian Portfolio* (London, 1844). (*Courtesy of the British Library, London.*)

transcendent and often moving iconography of the Indian way of life.

An account of the visual response to the Indian would be incomplete without a look at the work of Karl Bodmer. Although not an American, it was his American experience which caused him to produce his finest work. He is the greatest of the European painters of Indians. Born in Switzerland in 1809 and, like Delacroix, trained in Paris, in 1832 Bodmer accompanied his patron Maximilian, 'prince of Wied', up the Missouri, making sketches of Indians, landscapes and the fauna and flora of the area. What Africa was to Delacroix, America was to Bodmer, and his painting reflects a unique synthesis of a European vision and the experience of the New World.

Maximilian wrote his own account of this grand tour of natural history and it is a fine example of the best kind of scientific con-

sciousness in operation. Maximilian saw himself following in the
wake of Lewis and Clark, Bradbury and Brackenridge, Nuttall,
Long, Townsend and Wyeth. He studied under Blumenbach at
Jena, and already been to Brazil in 1815—17 after which he had
published his *Beiträge zur Naturgeschichte von Brasilien* (1825—33)
to accompany his atlas, *Abbildungen zur Naturgeschichte Brasiliens*
(1822—31). He was already familiar with the work of Thomas Say
who had been on Long's expedition, and the interpreter for his
journey was Toussaint Charbonneau who had accompanied Lewis
and Clark. He had obviously carefully read all the available information on the American West. He mentions the recent writings of
James, Schoolcraft, McKenney (see below p. 284) and Irving, and
he was familiar with European scientists, like Audubon's friendly
rival, Charles Bonaparte, and the great German botanist, Lewis
David von Schweintz. At Peale's museum in Philadelphia he commented favourably on some oil paintings of Indian villages and
scenery by Seymour. Earlier he had complained of American
attitudes to the Indian:

> As a study of the aboriginal nation of America had peculiar attractions
> for me, I searched the shops of all the booksellers and print-sellers, for
> good representations of that interesting race; but how much was I
> astonished, that I could not find, in all the towns of this country, one
> good, that is, characteristic representation of them, but only some bad
> or very indifferent copper-plates, which are in books of travel! It is
> incredible how much the original American race is hated and neglected
> by foreign usurpers.[101]

Even though Maximilian cautiously follows his old teacher, Blumenbach, in his theories of the five races, he refutes Volney and others,
maintaining that the Indian was not inferior in intellectual capacity
to the white races. But at the same time he had little of Long's feeling
for Indian legends, calling them 'silly creations of their own
imaginations'.[102] Wintering at Fort Clark, the party had leisure to
observe the Mandan tribe before their obliteration by smallpox in
1837. The descriptions reflect rather than adhere to the categorizations of the time, and the account is personalized by the diary form.
Maximilian was to endorse Catlin's account of the O-Kee-Pa
ceremony in 1867, after it had been queried by both Schoolcraft
and Mitchel whose sentimental visions could not credit the facts.

---

[101] Reuben Thwaites, ed., *Early Western Travels, 1748—1846, vols XXII—XXIV,
Maximilian, Prince of Wied's Travels in the Interior of North America* (Cleveland, Ohio
1904—7), vol. XXII., p. 70.
[102] Ibid., XXIII, p. 318.

Maximilian's journal gives an unrivalled sense of the old West, with its flora and fauna in lavish abundance, the dangers of inter-tribal Indian warfare, of the *engagés* who towed the keel boats, and above all the sheer physical beauty of the landscape.

Bodmer found it an opportunity to paint his masterpiece. He had a long subsequent career, meeting Millet in 1850, and moving over to the Barbizon school in style, finishing life as an illustrator in an age dominated by the photograph. Millet and Bodmer collaborated on several pictures including one illustration of Cooper's *Last of the Mohicans.*[103] But his best work was done as a result of this expedition and it was magnificently reproduced in the atlas accompanying Maximilian's account. If some of the pictures are drawn with the over-sophisticated eye of the academy, very often the sense of design goes far beyond what Catlin could hope to achieve. Bodmer is the first major artist to paint the Indian at war, and his picture of an incident Maximilian describes on 28 August 1833 **pl. 45** shows the Indian as an exotic and ferocious savage. One of the yelling Indians with a knife in one hand and a scalp in the other dominates the

45 *Fort Mackenzie*, from Atlas to Prince Wied-Neuwied by Karl Bodmer in *Travels in the Interior of North America* (London 1843). (*Courtesy of the Bodleian Library, Oxford.*)

[103] See B. P. Draper, 'American Indians—Barbizon Style—The Collaborative Paintings of Millet and Bodmer', *Antiques,* 44, no. 3 (Sept., 1943) pp. 108–10.

foreground, while another draws his bow with one foot on a fallen victim. To the far right an Indian with blue horns and a knife in his teeth contemplates a dead Indian and child, while above him a horse struggles desperately, reminding one of Delacroix's battle scenes, or the macabre figure relations of Géricault. The fort, however, is recognizably American as also are the bluffs which rise to the left of it. The other engravings in the volume record portraits, breathtakingly beautiful scenery, striking geological formations, and aspects of Indian life. One of the more unusual Indian pictures is the *Offering of the Mandan Indians,* **pl. 46** the foreground of which shows a circle of Indian and buffalo skulls, together with magic Indian artefacts. The details are meticulously outlined and a Baudelairian note is added by the snake moving out of the largest Buffalo skull to the right. The picture has symbolic value, too, in that it seems to furnish an ironic epitaph to the fast-disappearing Indian way of life, formulating the dark impulses behind the scientific vision which are the result of the transference of that vision to the American West.

The example of Catlin and Bodmer did not lack imitators. Thomas L. McKenney and James Hall combined together in 1836 to produce between them the most lavishly illustrated history of the Indians before Schoolcraft. Hall supplied most of the text since

46 *Offering of the Mandan Indians* by Karl Bodmer in *Travels in the Interior of North America* (London 1843). (*Courtesy of the Bodleian Library, Oxford.*)

he had already written on the West in *Legends of the West* (1832) and *Sketches of History, Life and Manners in the West* (1834—5). Beside the huge folio volume, they produced a small three volume edition in order 'to place it within reach of the thousands, who, with taste and learning equal to those of the patrons of the large edition, have no less capacity to appreciate its worth and beauties.'[104] McKenney's previous work, *Memoirs Official and Personal: with Sketches of Travels among the Northern and Southern Indians; embracing a War and descriptions of scenes along the Western Borders* (1846) had been vigorously illustrated by Darley. The joint work, *The History of the Indian Tribes of North America* has 120 portraits from the Indian Gallery at the War Department. These portraits in vivid primary colours, of shiny, thick reds, golds and blues, with the Indian in scarcely disguised European costume, prefigure the illustrations of today's *National Geographic* with its clean technicolour. The frontispiece to volume three embodies the popular image at its most sentimental pl. 47. A blazing prairie fire burns on the horizon, to the right the moon is up and night coming on. In the foreground an Indian lights the grass in order to fight fire with fire and to make a burnt area of safety for the white family group. The white man holds the two snorting horses, demonstrating *his* control of natural forces, while the woman crouches at

47 *Prairie on Fire (The Escape)*, Frontispiece to volume 3 of Thomas C. McKenney and James Hall, *History of the Indian Tribes of North America* (Philadelphia 1854). (*Courtesy of the Newberry Library, Chicago.*)

[104] See the introduction to Thomas L. McKenney and James Hall, *History of the Indian Tribes of North America* (Philadelphia 1854). This edition is used here.

his feet, clutching her child, and a rather fat parlour dog howls,
nose in air. The Indian with his knowledge of the dark forces of
fire, protects, Uncle Tom-like, master, home and dog against the
savagery of the Western landscape.

Throughout McKenney and Hall's work there is no sense of Indian
civilization having anything really valuable in human terms. 'A few
have embraced our religion, and learned our art;' states a section on
Red Jacket who is depicted as usual with Washington's medal firmly
round his neck, 'But the greater part have dwindled away under the
blasting effects of idleness, intemperance and superstition.'[105] The
authors regretfully explain the necessities of removal policy but
express a determined wish to teach the Indian the value of property.
The inevitable section on Pocahontas confirms all a recent critic
has said of the myth of the pious Indian convert.[106] The costume
she wears in the portrait upgrades her racial class to Spanish or
Italian status. 'What self-sacrificing resolution and firmness!'
exclaim the authors, 'And that in a child of twelve years old—and
that child an untaught savage of the wilderness, who had never
heard of the name of Jesus, or of that gospel which teaches us to
love our enemies, and do good to them that hate us!'[107]

One of the most revealing biographical sketches is one on an
Indian woman called Tshusick, an Ojibway woman who had the
wit to deceive 'Mrs Boyd of Washington', and all of Washington
with its moralistic high society for a considerable time. Brilliantly
manipulating white convictions of superiority she told Mrs Boyd
that her husband had died and that she wanted religion. Fèted and
laden with presents as a beautiful convert, the authors state that
'So agreeable a savage has seldom, if ever, adorned the fashionable
circles of civilized life.'[108] They continue, however, that 'The
brilliant career of Tshusick was destined to close as suddenly as that
of the conqueror of Europe at Waterloo . . .. She was a sort of
female swindler, who practised upon the *unsophisticated* nature
of her fellow men, by an *aboriginal* method of her own invention'
(my italics).[109] And the reasons for her disgrace were that 'she was
the wife of a short, squat Frenchman who officiated as a scullion in
the household of Mr Boyd, the Indian agent at Mackinaw, and who,
so far from having been spirited away from his afflicted wife, was
supporting her absence without leave with the utmost resignation.'[110]

[105] Ibid., vol. I, p. 10.
[106] See Fiedler, *The Return of the Vanishing American.*
[107] McKenney and Hall, *History of the Indian Tribes of North America,* vol. III, p. 53.
[108] Ibid., vol. I, p. 119.
[109] Ibid., vol. I, p. 126.
[110] Ibid., vol. I, p. 126.

The attitudes would not have been out of place in British India. Clearly the servants had the better of the upper house, and the evidence of stung pride and air of injured innocence is almost comic were it not for the clear evidence of the suppressed hysteria resulting from the racist snobberies of Washington society. In this work the values of the biography and portrait come together. It aimed officially to democratize the aristocratic scientific folio, but, in fact, it marked the end of that tradition which at its best attempted to embody the best of artistic skill with a genuine scientific curiosity.

Alfred Jacob Miller is a relatively recently discovered artist of the Old West.[111] Like Bodmer, Miller spent two years of his life studying painting in Paris and Rome, where he also met famous expatriots like Nathaniel Parker Willis and Horatio Greenough. In 1837 he made the grand tour of the West with a British Army officer, Captain William Stewart. The tour was sponsored by Robert Gilmor, one of the first to recognize the merit of Cole and Doughty, and who sponsored many other American artists in Europe. His style consequently swings between the presuppositions of both continents. Sometimes his Indians appear as if sketched by a Fragonard or a Boucher with Indian women lounging gracefully at the corner of a picture or swinging from tree seats, or sitting, sewing, listening to an Indian lover's blandishments. Others extend the Anglo-American iconography of Indian, buffalo and landscape established by Bodmer and Catlin, At his best, however, Miller combines Catlin's freedom from academic cliché with Bodmer's sense of design and grouping. Miller's horses' heads appear very much like Catlin's strange-looking creatures. But Miller also added new scenes of his own, archery contests, taking the hump, stampede and one, *The Yell of Triumph,* anticipating Hollywood, shows a triumphant Indian whooping on the body of a dead buffalo. In fact Miller is really better on general Western iconography, and one recent critic declares him the best painter of symbols of the American past: the cabin in the clearing, the buffalo herd, the Long Trail, the covered wagon, the Puritan and the continental soldier.[112] Nonetheless one of the very finest sketches shows what he could do with Indian subjects. The *Pawnee Indians Migrating* pl. 48 is reproduced to show the originality of the design with its deceptively casual sense of grouping. The scene of Indian women and

[111] See Bernard de Voto, *Across the Wide Missouri, Illustrated with Paintings by Alfred Jacob Miller, Charles Bodmer, and George Catlin. With an account of the discovery of the Miller collection by Mae Reed Porter.* (Boston 1947).
[112] Ibid., p. 414.

48 *Pawnee Indians Migrating* by Alfred Jacob Miller. (*Courtesy of the Walters Art Gallery, Baltimore, Maryland.*)

children packing up camp is relatively rare, the details of dog and mule pack and the mode of transportation give us a unique insight into Indian life, and the overall sense of space is skilfully suggested. In the group itself it is done by juxtaposing the light figure of the woman with the dark figure at her side with light picking out the robes of the mounted figure and the walking figure in between. The diagonal composition gives a sense of space dropping away behind the foreground group, combining in a single sketch the inheritance of genre and panorama.

Two examples of Americans under the influence of European styles show how often this phenomenon was rather less successful than the results of Bodmer's journey to America. Greenough's statue, *Rescue Group,* should be placed alongside his statue of Washington to give the full implications of the literary symbolism both enact together. If the one shows the Greek law-giving father, the other shows the violence needed to maintain the society he controls. The threat to order and family life incarnated in the Indian is controlled by the oversize figure of the white man. In

graceful fashion the Indian is overpowered while a pet dog looks
tranquilly on.

It was left to Charles Wimar (1828–62), however, to push the
representation of the Indian as the white man's nemesis to its
logical conclusion. Like many Germans he made the journey to St
Louis in the early forties and in 1849 he made a painting trip with
his teacher, one Pomarede, up the Mississippi to sketch landscape.
On this trip Pomarede advised him to paint Indians 'and to follow
it exclusively, as through it he might achieve a reputation that, in
years to come when the Indians would be a "race clean gone" would
increase to a peculiar brightness, not only in this country but on
the Continent.'[113] In 1852 he returned to Düsseldorf with its
increasingly famous school of painters. We have already seen how
Düsseldorf emphasized some of the worst tendencies of American
genre painters. For the Americans it was an eminently safe artistic
colony. A writer for the *Literary World* remarked in the year Wimar
returned there, 'It would be difficult to find anywhere, a more
respectable company of German householders and fathers of
families.'[114] The result was sentiment, as Wimar made a unique
synthesis of the literary mode of the captivity narrative, journalistic
immediacy and the theatrical implications of genre painting. In the
painting reproduced here, *The Abduction of Daniel Boone's
Daughter by the Indians*, pl. 49 the light falls on the head, shoulders
and upper white drapery of the madonna-like girl, with the lower
folds of the costume elaborately arranged in the canoe. Two savages
emerge from the tangled forest, while a third, in histrionically
fierce pose, stands in the forefront of the boat with his rifle.

Wimar made three trips altogether up the Missouri, and he lost
some of his stiffness as the academy experience receded into the
past. Like Catlin and Bodmer he painted the buffalo dance of the
Mandans, but unlike these two he achieved his effects by melodramatic chiaroscuro rather than by dynamic grouping or ethno-
graphic scrupulousness. Wimar's Indians form lurid shapes in front
of the fire while the spectators sit round as if at the theatre.
Catlin's picture of 1832 had captured the careless and informal
attitudes of the spectators scattered over the conical rooftops, and
his totems look like menacing aids to witchcraft whereas Wimar's
are stage props. Wimar could have only seen the barest remnants
of their civilization and in his picture the corpse of Mandan civilization is reanimated as a ghostly embodiment of white melodrama.

[113] City Art Museum of Saint Louis, *Charles Wimar, 1828–62, Painter of the Indian
Frontier* (St Louis 1946) p. 11.
[114] *The Literary World,* 10 (1852) p. 333.

49 *The Abduction of Daniel Boone's Daughter by the Indians*, 1853, by Charles Wimar.
(*Courtesy of The Collection, Washington University, St Louis.*)

The sensitivities of the untutored Catlin, the enlightenment
sympathies of the aristocratic Maximilian, the narrower liberalism
of Morse, the older vision of brotherhood of Colonel James Smith
could scarcely balance the image of the Indian in his multiple
clichéd roles as savage, child of nature, propertyless mendicant,
potential Christian convert, drunkard, child of the Devil, doomed
chieftain, sadist, romantic lover and museum artefact. In literature
and in the visual arts the Indian served as a composite image for the
dark doubts which lay behind the rational assumptions of civilization and nature current during these years. The Indian 'buddy' of
gothic fiction and the dark savage threatening home and family were
twin characterizations used to externalize the guilt Americans felt
in taking possession of the land. The persistent context of 'doom'
was the flimsiest objectification, in terms of history and nature,
of the socioeconomic, the political and sexual weaknesses of white
civilization.

9

Animals and Birds

After *homo sapiens* came the rest of the animal kingdom, descending in hierarchical order from primates to the lowest form of
crustacea. Again there is at least a double tradition of response which
stems back to the late sixteenth and early seventeenth centuries. In
1565, John Hawkins reported the words of a French captain who
had observed in Florida, 'a serpent with three heads and four feet,
of the bigness of a great spaniel, which for want of a harquebus he
durst not attempt to slay'.[1] The terrifying animal of the dream
remains a consistent tradition in American culture right down to the
late years of the nineteenth century. Yet ten years before Hawkins,
Thomas Browne had published his huge folio, *Pseudodoxia Epidemica*
(1546), modelled on Laurent Joubert's *Paradoxa Medica* and *De
Vulgi Erroribus* which reflected a new emphasis on visual authenticity in isolation from older cultural types of response. This visual
empirical approach with a new emphasis on dissection, comparison
and correct linear drawing originated in the early famous medical
schools of Padua and Montpellier. And yet the movement from
fantasy to reality is not really a consistent one, nor is it simply a
question of error giving way to truth. The comparative anatomists
of the mid-nineteenth century left out huge areas of possible
response to the animal kingdom, or simply divided the visual reality
from every other kind of reality. Who would not prefer Hooke's
description of a flea[2] to any equivalent in a contemporary textbook?
Even the emerging tradition of scientific drawing created its own
errors and archetypes. Gombrich has shown amusingly how Dürer's
engraving of a rhinoceros in 1515 was reproduced, complete with
non existent armour plating, right down to the end of the eighteenth-
century by artists who, like Dürer himself, claimed to be drawing
the animal from life.[3] Leonardo also misplaced important parts of

---

[1] Louis B. Wright, ed., *The Elizabethan's America* (London 1965) p. 43.
[2] Robert Hooke, *Micrographia, or some physiological descriptions of minute bodies
made by a magnifying glass . . . ..* (London 1665).
[3] E. H. Gombrich, *Art and Illusion* (London 1960) pp. 80–81.

the anatomy, and his drawings of dissected cadavers in sexual intercourse points to a return of a living reality in grotesque form to the
very heart of the morgue itself. For there is from this time a continuous split between the animal as the dead object of scientific
analysis and as the live, elusive, sometimes terrifying animal in its
own habitat. But the split is not simply a fact of nature, for the two
halves are part of a single vision. The scientists' animal was a
representative type, a *specimen*, involving all the contradictions we
have already seen operating in these concepts. In the work of
Audubon and Melville, the greatest American painter and writer
respectively of the first half of the nineteenth century, both traditions are drawn on in synthesis in their respective masterpieces. The
European separated his artistic and scientific responses. Linnaeus,
for example, wrote fulsome sentimental flower poetry, while
expunging the folk names of flowers and adducing a scientific
latinized nomenclature. Another response was to reject the scientific
movement entirely, and Wordsworth's line, 'we murder to dissect'
represented one typical revulsion from the rationalist strictures of
Enlightenment thought. Scientifically the period 1776 to 1865 is
bounded by Linnaeus and Buffon at one end and Agassiz in
America at the other. With the publication of Darwin's work,
Agassiz was rapidly becoming outmoded. Our concern is not really
with the scientists, although it must be noted that what Linnaeus
was to the botanists, the comparative anatomist Baron Cuvier was
for those with interests in other branches of natural history. Cuvier
virtually founded the subject of comparative anatomy, and his
aristocratic, visual and empirical approach to his subject determined
the development of the subject throughout the nineteenth century.
Nonetheless his empiricism and his belief in major types of animal
classification derived from his teacher's adherence to Herder's
notion of the unity of all life. Comparison in Cuvier's system
became, not so much an assessment of difference, but a process of
determining similarity among classes. For Cuvier's world was one
where the whole may be known by reasoning about its parts. The
system worked well for comparative anatomy. It was said that
Cuvier when presented with any part of a skeleton could identify
its place in the structure as a whole, and the animal and class to
which it belonged. Yet in a wider metaphysical sense he presupposed the world as a given framework of an unchanging order
made up from dead types of generalized particulars.

Given the inheritance of this mode of reasoning on the one hand,
and the fear of strange and hostile nature, on the other, it is
scarcely surprising the confrontation of two such seemingly diverse

responses should produce a number of uniquely American master-pieces. The classic American instance of the confrontation is in Edgar Allan Poe's *The Murders in the Rue Morgue,* where after consulting Cuvier's description of the orangoutang, the French detective by a series of supposedly rational deductions, in fact by a series of intuitive leaps, discovers that it is just such an animal which has committed the sexually perverse murders of the two women.[4] Poe plays off 'French' logic against the fears which threaten its clarity, as the animal becomes the representative of the forces which threaten the very structure of society itself. Here Jefferson's argument of the sexual preference (albeit in a violent form) of the lower orders for the higher, and Brockden Brown's and Bartram's dark beasts at the centre of the virgin land receive a dramatization in social and urban terms. It is almost inevitable, therefore, that the animal appears in American literature and painting as a menacing and terrifying image of a hostile and threatening nature. The grizzly bear, the buffalo, the wild horse and the sea monster in turn serve as a correlative of these fears.

Shakespeare's most famous stage direction, 'Exit pursued by a bear', in *The Winter's Tale*, serves as a dramatic instance of the savage and the primitive taking revenge on civilized tyranny. We have already seen how in Gass's account of the Lewis and Clarke expedition, the bear became a ritual victim to expiate guilt about the possession of land. In American literature from T. B. Thorpe's *The Big Bear of Arkansas* (1841) through William Faulkner's *The Bear* (1941) to Norman Mailer's parody of the phenomenon and the tradition in *Why are We in Vietnam?* (1967) the bear has been the symbol of forbidden (often with sexual connotations) territory. In the fiction of the first half of the nineteenth century, the folk hero's encounter with a bear is *de rigeur.* Maximilian said that 'almost all the hunters of the prairies related their adventures with the bears, and whole volumes might be filled with such stories'.[5] In popular literary form the first great bear killer is Davy Crockett. In the *Autobiography* (1834) he relates how, at one point, he kills 47 bears in one month and 105 in the whole year. Travellers reported how the Indian felt that to kill a bear was a more noble feat than killing a man (bears took a notoriously long time to die), and Davy Crockett as a white Indian continues the tradition. The pattern in the Crockett hunts is to pursue the bear through a wild nightmarish landscape, for which Brown's landscapes give precedent, and then kill the monster hand to hand. The land

---

[4] Poe, *Works,* vol. I, 404–41.
[5] Maximilian, *Travels in the Interior of North America,* vol. II, p. 43.

scape itself is a labyrinthine scene, a heroic stage set for the psychological drama of the self as representative man in an eternally divided and conflicting reality.[6] In this American story the ancient mythic pattern is given a Puritan iconography:

> I encouraged my dogs, and they knowed me so well, that I could have made them seize the old serpent himself, with all his horns and heads, and cloven foot and ugliness into the bargain, if he would have come to light, so that they could have seen him.[7]

Thorpe's *The Big Bear of Arkansas* is the most striking bear story of the period. Thorpe dedicated his first collection of stories, *Mysteries of the Backwoods, or Sketches of the South-West* (1846) to Hiram Powers, the American sculptor. Such a dedication implies Thorpe's association with genteel culture and points to the fact that backwoods stories were becoming popular in the increasingly urban America of the East Coast. The account opens with a steamboat trip in which the passengers vie with each other in 'tall-story' telling. The bear story is given by the narrator as an example of tenderfoot initiation rites. The futile attempts to kill the bear, early referred to as a 'she-devil', and the identification of hunter and hunted form an archetypal travesty of sexual relation. Bear and dog are 'ordained to go together as naturally as Squire Jones says a man and woman is, when he moralizes in marrying a couple'.[8] And the narrator continues:

> Well, missing that bear so often took hold of my vitals, and I wasted away . . . .. I would see that bear in everything I did: he hunted me, and that, too, like a devil, which I began to think he was . . . .. But wasn't he a beauty, I loved him like a brother.[9]

In an even more revealing sequence, the hunter pursues the bear, and 'coming to the edge of a lake, the varmit jumped in, and swam to a little island in the lake, which it reached, just a moment before the dogs'.[10] It is a totally fictionalized account very similar to Gass's actual description in his *Journal*. However Thorpe's narrator follows the bear to the island, fights it and kills it in the water where, mysteriously, it turns from a male to a female bear. What should have been a death-like embrace with a brother turns out as a rebirth with a dead woman. Thorpe recreates in comic terms that

---

[6] See Norman O. Brown's *Love's Body*, ch. II, 'Nature', for an extended discussion of the archetype.

[7] Davy Crockett, *The Autobiography of Davy Crockett* (Philadelphia 1834) p. 181.

[8] Thomas Bangs Thorpe, *The Hive of 'the Beehunter' etc.* (New York 1854) p. 78.

[9] Ibid., p. 87.

[10] Ibid., p. 89.

equation of sexual fear between the sexes or between members of one sex and the terror of the natural landscape which is so dominant a theme in American literature:

> The way matters got mixed on that island was unaccountably curious, and thinking of it made me more than ever convinced that I was hunting the Devil himself.[11]

The terms of the fraternal death pact have been betrayed. Eventually the bear dies 'when his time came', and the narrator concludes that it was a 'creation bear'. The bear's existence is established outside space and time and its transformations serve the author's fantasies of disturbing the dark heart of the forest, the erotic attraction of passivity in the face of violent assault, and of that sense of terror and impotence felt by an individual lost in an enormous landscape which are too easily compensated for by violence.

In the visual arts there are many depictions of the bear hunt. In the Crockett almanacs there are woodcuts of Crockett doing a dance with a grizzly in fine comic style. Currier and Ives captured the popular mood with a print of a bear hunt pl. 50, a man's en-

50 *The Life of a Hunter 'A Tight Fix'*, by A. F. Tait. Currier and Ives lithograph, 1861. (*Courtesy of the Harry T. Peters Collection, Museum of the City of New York.*)

[11] Ibid., p. 90.

counter in the depths of the forest armed only with a knife, based
on a painting by Arthur Fitzwilliam Tait, an Englishman who had
come out to America in 1850. Bodmer's picture **pl. 51** is one of the
finest, with the bear devouring the carcass of the buffalo. To the
left men from their boats on the river charge the bear, while its
mate slinks off to the right. The sky and lighting increase the
dramatic effect, highlighting the bones of the buffalo and forming
a triangular design with the rising ground and back of the bear. The
vultures, black against the shaft of light emphasize this structural
aspect as Bodmer draws the moral that the wilderness dissolves
boundaries between hunter and hunted.

The democratization of aristocratic delights of the chase reached
its fullest expression in the 1860s with the mass slaughter of the
buffalo. Cooper parodied the natural scientist in his comic figure
of Dr Battius in *The Prairie* (1827) confronted by a herd of charg-
ing buffalo:

> The dark forms of the herd lost their distinctness, and then the naturalist
> began to fancy he beheld a wild collection of all the creatures of the
> world, rushing upon him in a body, as if to revenge the various injuries,
> which in the course of a life of indefatigable labor on behalf of the
> natural sciences he had inflicted on their several species. The paralysis
> it occasioned in his system was like the effect of the incubus. Equally

51 *Hunt of the Grisly Bears* by Karl Bodmer. (*Courtesy of the Bodleian Library, Oxford.*)

unable to fly or to advance, he stood riveted to the spot, until the
infatuation became so complete, that the worthy naturalist was beginning, by a desperate effort of scientific resolution, even to class the
different specimens.[12]

This comic nightmare indicates precisely the connections between
the classificatory rationalization and the revenge called up when
the purely visual relation to nature fails. The loss of distinctness of
the herd is important, and the convention goes back to Burke where
obscurity is one of the characteristics of the sublime. The simile
by which Cooper describes the effect of the nightmare suggests a
kind of sexual paralysis, from which Dr Battius can only arouse
himself 'by a desperate effort of scientific resolution'. In the same
novel there is the dramatic scene where the Leatherstocking stands
face on to the herd of buffalo while they divide round his
apotheosized form.[13] In a typical manner Cooper divides his
characters to fit the divisions of the cultural inheritance. Leatherstocking's noble, god-like, instinctive and anti-intellectual relation
to nature is counterbalanced in the comic, stupid, crazy scientist
impotent in the face of the wilderness. Hence these two antago-
nistic attitudes to nature which are incomplete in themselves, hinder
the possibility of bringing 'instinctive' and 'rational' responses
together.

The mass of the buffalo herd seen at a distance is the chief
iconographic literary and pictorial response. The prairie itself
becomes a symbol of primitive undifferentiated energy where life
is transformable into any shape. In Catlin's the *Buffalo hunt
surround*, the point of view is taken from high up, men and buffalo
are reduced to tiny figures scattered among the hills. On the outside of the herd, particularized forms and shapes are distinguishable,
to the centre all is an indistinguishable blur. At long range the
buffalo was sublime, at close range, however, he was usually dying.
Washington Irving was one of the few writers who seemed to have
felt remorse after killing buffalo by his own hand. Parkman's blood-
lust was insatiable. Frederick Ruxton, in an account written for
the sporting public, is typical of the way many writers lingered over
the details of the death:

Gouts of purple blood spurt from his mouth and nostrils, and gradually
the failing limbs refuse longer to support the ponderous carcass; more
heavily rolls the body from side to side until suddenly, for a brief instant,
it becomes rigid and still; a convulsive tremor seizes it and, with a low

12 James Fenimore Cooper, *The Prairie* (1827; reprinted 1896) p. 235.
13 Ibid., p. 236.

sobbing gasp, the huge animal falls over on his side, the limbs extended stark and stiff, and the mountain of flesh without life or motion.[14]

It was Catlin again who established the iconography of the buffalo hunt: the hunt itself, the surround, the stampede, hunting in snow, the death of the single buffalo, buffalo herds crossing the river and Indians approaching the herd dressed in wolf-skins. Currier and Ives prints ensured that these basic Catlin designs reached a wider audience. Other painters took up the themes and Bodmer and Wimar have magnificent pictures of buffalo crossing the Missouri, Platte, and Yellowstone rivers respectively. As if in counterbalance, however, in the massive works of the comparative anatomists, buffalo skulls are drawn in endless lines over many pages with measurements appended. This faith in the amassing of visual facts, together with the endless literary descriptions of the same phenomenon in the works of natural history begged the question of ends and even the simplest form of scientific rationale.

The wild horse shared the same fate as the buffalo and Irving pictured him as an aristocratic victim of urban progress:

> From being a denizen of these vast pastures, ranging at will from plain to plain and mead to mead, cropping of every herb and flower, and drinking of every stream, he was suddenly reduced to perpetual and painful servitude, to pass his life under the harness and the curb, amid, perhaps, the din and dust and drudgery of cities. The transition in his lot was such as sometimes takes place in human affairs, and in the fortunes of towering individuals: one day, a prince of the prairies—the next day, a pack horse.[15]

One outstanding picture by a 'primitive' painter, called *The Neigh of an Iron Horse* (1859), **pl. 52** has as its subject the literary theme of the mechanization of transport. To the left the steam engine with its carriages can be seen blowing its steam whistle. Tapy's frightened horse in its strange anatomical shape dominates the picture. The effect depends a good deal on silhouette, for the horse itself is painted somewhat flatly, and the minimum landscape details bring out the form more distinctly. There is no mistaking the terror in the disposition of the mane and tail, and the white of the eyeball, for the picture captures that sense of frightened animal energy reminiscent of European painters like Stubbs or Géricault—albeit in an American folk manner.

Of all the monsters of the imagination, however, the sea beast

---

[14] Quoted from Bernard de Voto, *Across the Wide Missouri* (Cambridge, Mass. 1947) p. 39.

[15] J. F. McDermott, ed., *A Tour on the Prairies* (Norman, Oklahoma 1956) p. 122.

52 *The Neigh of an Iron Horse*, 1859, by A. Tapy. (*Courtesy of the Collection of Edgar William and Bernice Chrysler Garbisch.*)

seems to have the longest history, and Melville's *Moby Dick* is a mid-nineteenth-century dramatization of the heroic chase of the animal of the dream. Ahab's hunt is a psychopolitical re-enactment of an archetype of world mythology which finds expression variously in the tales of Gilgamesh, Jonah, Hercules, Vishnu, Krishna, Perseus, Beowulf and St George. By the 1840s, mainly as a result of extensive American whaling in the Pacific, the theme of the sea hunt had entered popular fiction. Besides the well-known source for *Moby Dick*, Jeremiah N. Reynolds's *Mocha Dick; or the White Whale of the Pacific* (1836), there was John S. Sleeper's *A Whale Adventure in the Pacific* (1841) and titles such as *A Chapter on Sharking* (1836), a hunt for an albino shark, *Hunting a Devil Fish* (1836) and *A Midsummer Night's Watch* (1837).[16] As early as the years immediately following the Revolution, perhaps complementing Bartram's description of his 'absolute crocodile', an outstanding picture by Copley moved toward articulating some of the central features of the beast in the American imagination. In *Watson and*

---

[16] See Thomas Philbrick, *James Fenimore Cooper and the Development of American Sea Fiction* (Cambridge, Mass. 1961).

the Shark (first version, 1778) **pl. 53** Copley turned the historical
mode to the purposes of a politically unimportant incident of
private life. Critics have pointed out that its subject is journalistic
and that it continues a tradition begun by West, which was later to

53 *Watson and the Shark* by John Singleton Copley (1738–1815). (*Courtesy of the
Detroit Institute of Arts, Dexter M. Ferry Jr Fund.*)

produce masterpieces like Géricault's *Raft of the Medusa* and
Delacroix's *Barque of Dante*.[17] Certainly the formal qualities of the
tradition of historical painting are there. The triangular groupings of
the figures, emphasized by oar and harpoon, show the conventions
of Renaissance formal construction and the background is reminiscent of Claude's diffusion of light mistily through a harbour scene.
In some ways the American's innovations seem clumsy. The naked

[17] Larkin, *Art and Life in America*, p. 65.

figure's relation to the water is awkward and the attacking shark,
threatens life and limb with open jaws. But it is precisely this
split between the serenity of classical figures, domestic Dutch
marine painting and the yellowy-green water with its struggling
naked figure and open-mouthed monster that is significant. For it
is that American sense of threat to civilized order that is important
and the threat comes, as in Bartram, from the hostile heart of nature
itself. In literature Copley's combination of interests in this picture
leads directly to *Moby Dick* and in painting to works like Winslow
Homer's *The Gulf Stream* in the second half of the nineteenth
century.

Howard Vincent has patiently uncovered many of Melville's debts
to the natural historians and explorers which helped him make up
the complex treatment of the whale in *Moby Dick*.[18] From works
like Thomas Beale's *Natural History of the Sperm Whale* (1835 and
1839), Frederick Debell Bennet's *A Whaling Voyage round the
globe from the Year 1833 to 1836* (1840), J. Ross Browne's
Etchings of a Whaling Cruise . . .. (1846), and Henry T. Cheever's
The Whale and his Captors (1849), Melville, like the 'sub-sub
librarian' in the introduction to *Moby Dick,* selected facts from
outside the academic and respectable categories of knowledge and
placed them on equal footing with the safe and secure divisions of
the academy. For in an important sense Melville's piay with
'Cetology' throughout *Moby Dick* is a parody of the claims to complete systems by the natural historians who give their pronounce-
ments the authority of religious truth. In Melville's time the equation of 'truth' as revealed in the categories of the natural historians
and religious truth inherited from the Christian tradition had a
peculiarly literal meaning as anyone knows who has visited that
gothic cathedral of science in London, the Natural History Museum.
In his chapter on 'Cetology' Melville's aim is not simply to parody
the conflicting claims of theology, but to parody the psychopolitical
phenomenon of classification. Melville takes on Linnaeus' system of
sexual division as he speculates what a common whale-man would
think of that natural historian's division of the whale from other
fish on account of *penem intrantem feminam mammis lactantem.*
Melville's point is that both the scientist and the whale-man are
one-sided in their vision in their attempts to classify the 'constituents
of a chaos'.[19] Like Buffon and unlike Buffon's successors, Melville
clearly saw that all systems are metaphysical and imaginative and

[18] H. P. Vincent, *The Trying Out of Moby Dick* (Carbondale and Edwardsville,
Illinois 1949).
[19] Melville, *Moby Dick*, p. 129.

further that claims to absolute truth are part of a sexually perverse authoritarian vision. In a series of puns Melville concludes:

> But I now leave my cetological System still standing thus unfinished, even as the great Cathedral of Cologne was left, with the crane still standing upon the top of the uncompleted tower. For small erections may be finished by their first architects; grand ones, true ones, ever leave the cope-stone to posterity.[20]

In one sense the desire not to complete the system may be seen as a Romantic gesture proving the fragment more inspired than the completed work. However, in the sense that the cathedral is a symbol of heavenly aspiration, that is, withheld gratification in time in the cause of future bliss (posterity), Melville's sexual innuendoes show that the artist-hero is similarly cheated of ultimate insights into truth by a kind of metaphysical buggery. During his lifelong struggle with his sense of the failure of the Christian tradition Melville somehow needed to keep the idea of an external authority to disprove the authoritarian nature of men who claimed complete systems of truth, but he also instinctively knew, as we have already seen, that reverence for such authority denied any kind of actual fulfilment.

If we look at what Howard Vincent calls 'Melville's iconographic essay' on whales,[21] where Melville specifically considers *visual* representations of whales, the emphasis is again on incomplete systems taken as whole visions. After soundly criticizing whale representations from Hindu sculptures of Vishnu to the plates in Cuvier's *Natural History of Whales* (1836), he comes to the heart of the matter when he states, 'Most of the scientific drawings have been taken from stranded fish'.[22] The scientific engraver takes the whale out of the landscape and then lets the skeleton or corpse represent the life. Scientific rigour becomes *rigor mortis*. Melville continues the parody by citing Jeremy Bentham's stuffed body preserved at University College, London. Here the filled-out skeleton correctly portrays the life because this was precisely how Melville felt about the utilitarian vision. The second part of the essay has Melville commending a French painter 'Ganery' (Garneray) by whom the whale is set in a foreground landscape of fury, with ships and sea at peace in the rear, in a scene which Melville calls in relation to other famous war pictures, 'sea battle pieces'.[23] This whale's jets are 'erect full and black like soot; so that from so

---

[20] Ibid., p. 129.
[21] Vincent, *The Trying out of Moby Dick*, p. 216. (*Moby Dick*, chapters 55–7.)
[22] Melville, *Moby Dick*, p. 264.
[23] Ibid., p. 267.

abounding a smoke in the chimney, you would think there must be a brave supper cooking in the great bowels below'.[24] It is almost as if this whale were a natural version of the *Pequod* itself as the interior destruction and consumption keeps the black jets of nobleness and authority high. Natural history provides the pattern for civil history. Typically in the last part of the essay Melville discards the academic painters and the natural history illustrators, for the painted board representing whales which a cripple holds before him in the London Docks. Punning on his stump, Melville describes how this mute orator comes closer to the truth than the stump-orators of the political system. Contemplating his own amputation, as the victim of the great exploiters, the old kedger illustrates not only Melville's conviction that art has its price and that all art which misses out the savage dimension is untrue, but serves as a warning as to the practical consequences of Ahab's own quest. After more exempla Melville turns finally to the whale shape as landscape itself. For the idealizing consciousness sees the same shape in everything. Melville doubtless here recalls Polonius', 'Very like a whale'—a comment on the pliable nature of the upholders of conventional morality—and also Psalm 139 in order to parody the psalmist's sense of the ubiquity of God. For Melville's concern is with the observer who projects onto the landscape externalized fears which take the form of a phantom, and again the images of the cosmos and battle are brought together:

> Nor when expandingly lifted by your subject, can you fail to trace out great whales in the starry heavens, and boats in pursuit of them; as when long filled with thoughts of war the Eastern nations saw armies locked in battle among the clouds.[25]

The heroic simile mocks the authenticity of the metaphysics of the monomaniac imagination presented as an image of externalized landscape. But even as Melville, in this essay on whaling pictures, satirized the lifeless characters of the natural historian, and the fabulous beast of pre-Renaissance mythology, he reaffirmed Blake's insight that a man sees as he is.

Besides the fabulous animals of the dream, there is another ancient tradition which the Americans took up in their relation to visual representations of animals. From Aristophanes to Aesop, from Chaucer's *Parlement of Foulys* to George Orwell's *Animal Farm* animals have been used as icons of political and social intercourse. In conscious imitation of the imperial state of Rome, the

---

[24] Ibid., p. 267.
[25] Ibid., p. 271.

Americans adopted the eagle as their national totem. But there were doubts from the first. John Heckwelder in his *Narrative* to the Wabash in 1792 quoted one Judge Symmes who recorded these comments, somewhat in the pious Indian tradition, from an Indian:

> For example there are many good, innocent birds. There is a dove which would not do harm to the smallest creature. But what is the eagle? He is the largest of all birds and the enemy of all birds. He is proud, because he is conscious of his size and strength. On a tree, as well as in flight he shows his pride and looks down disparagingly upon all the birds. His head, his eyes, his beak and his big brown talons declare his strength and hostility. Now this bird, which is terrible enough in itself you have depicted as even more dreadful and horrible. You have not only put one of the implements of war, a bundle of arrows into one of his talons, and rods in the other, but have painted him in the most fearful manner, and in a position of attack upon his prey.[26]

In the folk art of the young republic the icon of the American eagle appears again and again as one of the many objects of national consciousness, framing portraits of Washington, forming collective motifs with war-horses, flags, swords, trumpets and cannon. Even Audubon was deflected from his usual course of depicting birds in natural landscape when he deliberately named the great American sea eagle, *Falco Washingtoniensis.* In the *Ornithological Biography,* he commented on his first sight of the bird, 'Not even Herschel, when he discovered the planet which bears his name, could have experienced more rapturous feelings'. He continued, 'If America has reason to be proud of her Washington, so has she to be proud of her Great Eagle'.[27] The great appearances in nature reaffirm greatness in civil history. Anticipating the great themes of law and individual justice of the *Scarlet Letter,* Hawthorne describes the American eagle in somewhat ironic terms in the introduction to that novel. Here a wooden sculptured eagle caps the wooded portico of the Custom House with its faded imitation of Grecian grandeur as a symbolic protector of American trade and commerce. The description also contains indirect reflections on Hawthorne's own dismissal from his post as surveyor of the port of Salem owing to a change in the administration:

> Over the entrance hovers an enormous specimen of the American eagle, with outspread wings, a shield before her breast, and, if I recollect aright, a bunch of intermingled thunder-bolts and barbed arrows in each

[26] W. E. Connelley, ed., *A Narrative of the Mission of the United Brethren among the Delaware and Mohegan Indians from its commencement in the year 1740 to the close of the year 1808* (Cleveland, Ohio 1907) p. 76.
[27] See plate XI of John James Audubon, *The Birds of America* (London 1827–38) and *Ornithological Biography* (London 1831–5) vol. I, p. 58.

claw. With the customary infirmity of temper that characterizes this
unhappy fowl, she appears, by the fierceness of her beak and eye, and
the general truculency of her attitude, to threaten mischief to the in-
offensive community; and especially to warn all citizens, careful of their
safety, against intruding on the premises which she overshadows with
her wings. Nevertheless, vixenly as she looks, many people are seeking,
at this very moment, to shelter themselves under the wing of the federal
eagle; imagining, I presume, that her bosom has all the softness and
snugness of an eider-down pillow. But she has no great tenderness, even
in her best of moods, and sooner or later, oftener soon than late,—is apt
to fling off her nestlings, with a scratch of her claw, a dab of her beak, or
a rankling wound from her barbed arrows.[28]

Here Hawthorne parodies the paternalist (maternalist) deceptions of
state, as the symbolism of *pater patriae* becomes a mother with a
permanently barbed arrow of desire.

The political use of animal symbolism, however, is most noticeable in the cartoons of the post-revolutionary period, which are
dominated by it. The first of our four examples shows *Liberty in
the form of the Goddess of Youth: giving support to the Bald
Eagle* (1796) pl. 54. The images of nature and history interact. In
the background is a city wracked by tempest while the goddess of
liberty tramples the star and garter and the sceptre under foot.
Liberty succours the fledgeling eagle as its beak dips in the cup
presented to it. This semierotic imagery of the reception of spiritual
potency is paralleled in the political symbolism of the cap of
liberty atop the flagstaff from which the stars and stripes can be
seen flying. The traditional sceptre is broken only for another one
to be raised in its stead. In a travesty of the Christian iconography
of the spirit of God descending like a dove, the sun streams out
behind the outspread wings of the eagle as the warlike soul of
America is born.

A political cartoon of 1833 pl. 55 actually gives us an imagined
politician's nightmare in a parody of the hero's role as he slays the
hydra-headed monster in the service of his people. Andrew Jackson
faces the problems of his administration in the shape of the serpents'
heads. With some sophistication the cartoon is called, *Political
Quixotism, shewing the consequences of sleeping in Patent Magic
spectacles.* Besides the Cervantes-like parody of the heroic role,
the cartoonist might well have been recalling Lear's advice to
Gloucester, 'Get thee glass eyes/And, like a scurvy politician, seem/
To see the things thou dost not'.[29]

[28] Nathaniel Hawthorne, *The Writings of Nathaniel Hawthorne, The Scarlet Letter*
(1850; reprinted Boston 1900) p. 4.
[29] *King Lear*, IV. vi. l. 174.

54 *Liberty. In the form of the Goddess of Youth giving support to the Bald Eagle.* Engraving by E. Savage, 1796. (*Courtesy of the Library of Congress, Washington, DC.*)

After the copper engravings and woodcuts of the late eighteenth and early nineteenth centuries, the invention of lithography gave a boost to the popular print as we have already seen with Currier and Ives. The third cartoon reproduced here pl. 56 is by H. R. Robinson who was the biggest publisher of political lithographs between 1831 and 1849. Jackson is seen descending like a tortoise into the pool of corruption, Van Buren, elected largely through Jackson's influence is seen emerging from it, in the shape of a serpent. Above them flies William Henry Harrison, Whig compromise candidate in 1836, and president only for a month in 1840. Harrison comes off best in this lithograph as the American eagle, though in 1840 he was presented as the typical frontier hero with the famous campaign slogan 'Tippecanoe and Tyler, too' and the phrase 'Log cabin and

55 *The Diplomatic Hercules, Attacking the Political Hydra* 'From a very big picture in the Jineral's Bed-Room, drawd off from natur by Zek Downing, Historical Painter to Uncle Jack & Jineral Jackson'. General: 'Stam the horrid monster!!! Crush it!!! Nick Bittle!!! Hell & the Devil!!! Bribery and Corruption!!! Assassination!! Murder!!. . . Where are you Major?'/Major: 'Cum along to bed agin, Jineral. I tell you Bittle amt here, nor the devil nother as I no on'. (*Courtesy the New York Historical Society, New York City.*)

hard Cider'. The old natural history motif of bird and serpent is also drawn on, while the Washington monument presides over the political chicanery looking as natural as the mountain it caps. Out of time and out of nature it represents the past to which the politicians look forward.

Our fourth animal cartoon **pl. 57** crystallizes all these images in terms of a specific political event: the fight for Texas and California. A wily cigar smoking Spaniard holding back a crocodile represents Spain and John Bull, with an Abolition Society paper stuck in his pocket, represents England. The fight for Texas and California is represented as a 'Great Prize-Fight of the American Eagle against the Wolf and the Alligator', and is a defence of American imperialism over Spanish and British imperialism. England is a wolf in sheep's clothing (smashing the black man's sustenance with one foot) for her pious attitude to slavery is seen as disguised land-grabbing. Like God, Washington exhorts from the skies as the beseiged eagle

HIGH PLACES IN GOVERNMENT LIKE STEEP ROCKS ONLY ACCESSIBLE TO EAGLES AND REPTILES

56 *High Places in Government like Steep Rocks only Accessible to Eagles and Reptiles,* 1836. (*Courtesy of the New York Historical Society, New York City.*)

57 *The Slavery Question,* 1844, Great Prize Fight of the American Eagle against the Wolf and the Alligator. (*Courtesy of the New York Historical Society, New York City.*)

protects her young and the flag is upheld, surmounted by Jacobin cap (strange revolutionary emotion this), by a proud upstanding average American. In the foreground the black man sits ignored by all three parties.

But the masterpiece of this kind of animal symbolism comes in Edward Hicks's many paintings of his favourite subject, *The Peaceable Kingdom*, **pl. 58** out of a text from Isaiah.[30] It was a vision which

58 *Peaceable Kingdom* by Edward Hicks. (*Courtesy of the Collection of Edgar William and Bernice Chrysler Garbisch.*)

he himself scarcely achieved in his own lifetime fraught as it was with religious strife among his fellow Quakers. Almost then by way of compensation his most famous subject, which he painted almost a hundred times, shows us the lamb lying down with the lion and the animals led by little children. Alice Ford's work on Hicks has demonstrated how in the painter's mind there is more than a biblical symbolism here. For, in a tradition going back to the elemental divisions of Elizabethan psychology, each animal represents an

[30] Isaiah 11. 6—8.

emotion within the human psyche, often with a corresponding
element affixed. The *phlegmatic* characteristic is *water*, allied to the
bear, which connotes inertness, coldness, beastliness and unfeeling-
ness. The *choleric* characteristic is *fire* allied to the *lion* connoting
pride and arrogance. The *melancholic* characteristic is *earth* allied
to the *wolf* connoting fame, speculation, education and suicide. The
sanguine characteristic is *air* allied to the *leopard* connoting gaiety,
music, dancing, taverns and places of diversion. The male leopards
symbolize those 'beautiful monsters' who rob 'the poor negatively
innocent females of their virtue' and 'leave them in a state of
desperation, afraid to meet the tears of their parents'.[31] In a sermon
on a theme of the peaceable kingdom at the Goose Creek meeting
in February 1837 Hicks said, 'the lamb, the kid, the cow, and the
ox are emblems of good men and women, while the wolf, the
leopard, the bear and the lion are figures of the wicked'. The
animal kingdom is divided into states of war and peace and so
symbolizes an implied dualism and the very psychology of human
consciousness. This combination of Elizabethan psychology and
Christian ethic is based on a series of crucial dualisms between man
and woman, good and bad characters, good and bad characteristics
within the single symbolic human consciousness and endless war
between them in a world historically fallen from grace. 'Salvation'
is endlessly projected into the future in nonsensual, nonconflict
terms. In a sermon of 1828 Hicks said, 'The term animal body, used
to designate our Lord, is irreverent, and unbecoming a creature
dependent on him for salvation'.[32] This Christian-psychological
symbolism parallels the division of species within a kingdom and by
totemistic analogy the divisions within human kingdoms, as well.[33]
Hicks's peaceable kingdom is a vision of the impossible drawn by
reversing the normal processes of history and time, as conceived by
the Christian and the theorist of civil history. The foreground becomes
the present, the background, in the version reproduced here, is the
past achievement of the Quaker community in a shrunken version
of West's *Penn's Treaty with the Indians*. The human species make
a peaceable contract as a society, the children-led animals make
peace inside the human body. There are positive and negative
ironies here. Hicks gives us, as a good preacher, an exemplum, but
it is an exemplum of an actual achievement not a future possibility.
This is a heavenly story with an earthly meaning. Alternatively the

[31] Quoted from Alice Ford, *Edward Hicks, Painter of the Peaceable Kingdom*
(Philadelphia 1952) p. 86.
[32] Ibid., p. 59.
[33] See Brown, *Love's Body*, p. 22.

past distant prospect is based on a reality which as a Christian Hicks
could not see incarnated in present terms. Much can be gained from
the literary connotations of the iconography not all of which can
be understood by merely looking at the picture. But in a sense
Hicks transcends the cultural inheritance because he is not a formal
representational painter. The fortunately never-quite-mastered
techniques of perspective save the picture from sentimentality and
from realistic absurdity. The beautifully brightly coloured, flat,
cut-out quality of the animals arranged in mosaic patterns over the
picture space points to a conception of time and space outside the
linear progressions of history. Although the dualisms of nature and
civil society are retained there is a sense of momentary release from
perpetual tension, a child-like vision reminiscent of Blake's Beulah,
where, in the as yet undifferentiated polymorphousness of the
child, a more complete vision of release from duality can be glimpsed.
In this painterly masterpiece, one of the finest achievements of
American art in its whole history, Hicks transcends the terms of the
inheritance in a unique synthesis all the more remarkable because
it is composed of all the warring elements of his essentially Christian
vision.

The scientific and painterly traditions converged in Audubon's
masterpiece *Birds of America* published in London between 1827
and 1838. It is worth, however, taking a brief look at his lesser-
known predecessor, an emigré Scotsman by the name of Alexander
Wilson (1766–1813), who was one of the first to devote himself
seriously to writing about and painting American birds. His great
work, *American Ornithology: or, the natural history of the Birds
of the United States: . . .*, was published in Philadelphia between
1808 and 1813. For Wilson the natural landscape which the study
of natural history encompassed had, as with Jefferson, a psychological function of inducing release from social and political tension.
After a stormy political career in Scotland, Wilson sought refuge in
American ornithology:

> Books on Natural History . . . are generally welcomed by people of all
> parties. They may be compared to those benevolent and amicable
> individuals, who, amid the tumult and mutual irritation of discordant
> friends, kindly step in to reconcile them to each other.[34]

There is a dry Scots rationalism coupled with pietistic fervour in
his approach to nature, the study of which is 'worthy of rational

[34] Alexander Wilson, *American Ornithology; or, the natural history of the Birds of
the United States* (Philadelphia 1808) vol. III, p. v.

beings, and doubtless agreeable to the Deity'.[35]

The pictures themselves parallel Catesby's style in their representation of a flat two-dimensional reality. The colouring of the early editions varies, with the best ones done by a 17-year-old American artist, C. R. Leslie, who was later to settle in London as a fashionable portrait painter and to write an important biography of Constable.[36] Wilson anticipates Audubon in creating landscapes for his birds wherever space permitted and, where the birds of prey are concerned, adding a new sense of visual drama. He also anticipates Audubon in his literary sketches of bird life which are meant to be set against the visual image. These accompany, in a typically eighteenth-century dual frame of reference, exact observations on the habitat and visual appearance of the bird. Like Jefferson, Wilson is patriotically scornful of European mistakes; 'the Count [Buffon] is not the only European who has misrepresented and traduced this beautiful bird [Gold-winged Woodpecker]. One has given him brown legs, another a yellow neck; a third has declared him a Cuckoo . . ..'[37] The more literary descriptions, however, are reminiscent of Crèvecoeur or even Wordsworth and in the following example Wilson adds his own paragraph to American bird and serpent mythology:

> The eager school-boy after hazarding his neck to reach the Woodpecker's hole, at the triumphant moment when he thinks the nestlings his own, and strips his arm, launching it down the cavity, and grasping what he conceives to be the callow young, starts with horror at the sight of a hideous snake, and almost drops from his giddy pinnacle, retreating down the tree with terror and precipitation.[38]

The desire for possession, in a movement we are already familiar with, turns into a nightmarish fear of being possessed. The hunter in a classic American dream sequence becomes the hunted. The act of stealing from the sanctuary is revenged by the fall from grace.[39]

One of Wilson's plates to which Audubon was much indebted was that of the *White-headed Eagle* (vol. VI, pl. 36) from which the later painter took such details as the blood on the bird, the pose of the claw stuck into the fish with its guts spilling out. Wilson takes pains to refute Buffon's investiture of the eagle with noble and

---

[35] Ibid., vol. I, p. 3.

[36] C. R. Leslie, *Memoirs of the Life of John Constable, R.A., composed chiefly of his Letters* (London 1843).

[37] Wilson, *American Ornithology*, vol. I, p. 51.

[38] Ibid., vol. I, p. 146.

[39] It is interesting to compare this sequence with the bird nesting passage in Wordsworth's *The Prelude*, Book II, ll. 324—50.

aristocratic qualities, though his own descriptions are dramatic enough. Exact observation conflicts with the conventionalities of late eighteenth-century prose style:

> High over all these hovers one, whose action instantly arrests all his attention. By his wide curvature of wing, and sudden suspension in air, he knows him to be the Fish Hawk, settling over some denoted victim of the deep. His eye kindles at the sight, and balancing himself, with half-opened wings on the branch, he watches the result. Down, rapid as an arrow from heaven, descends the distant object of his attention, the roar of its wings reaching the ear as it disappears in the deep, making the surges foam around! At this moment, the eager looks of the Eagle are all ardour; and leveling his neck for flight, he sees the Fish Hawk once more emerge, struggling with his prey, and mounting in the air with screams of exultation.[40]

The theme is one we have already seen to be common in natural history descriptions, outlining as it does the precarious relation between hunter and hunted. In spite of commonplace images—kindling eyes and foaming surges—we have here a dramatization of experience in a triple point of view all the more powerful because of carefully noted details which take us out of cliché. The half open wings of the watching bird and the sound of the flurry of the bird's wings coming at the same time as the disappearance of the bird into the water, give us a sense of distance in the observed difference between the speed of light and sound. Yet always accompanying the commonsense search for fact we are given a sense of a wider, more insecure, even contraditory, area of truth. This underlying tension comes out very clearly in the lines Wilson composed on the suicide of Lewis (of the Lewis and Clark expedition). To Wilson, Lewis represented reason in action, a man whose scientific curiosity he admired together with his disciplined search for the facts of American natural history. As a symbol of America itself Lewis's death fascinated Wilson, and his account of it some months later is still almost the only evidence we have for judging the event. The threat to rational consciousness evinced in the more literary images of the bird contrasting with the lineality of the plates finds an echo in the valedictory lines:

> Poor Reason perished in the storm.
> And Desperation triumphed here.[41]

Although John James Audubon's (1785–1851) own literary episodes in his *Ornithological Biography* (1831–5) are mainly dull

---

[40] Wilson, *American Ornithology*, vol. IV, p. 90.
[41] Quoted from Robert Henry Welker, *Birds and Men* (Cambridge Mass. 1955) p. 218. This is the standard work on the cultural history of American ornithology.

reading, interspersed with the scientific information they give us a somewhat fanciful and arcadian image of American life some years before Currier and Ives gave similar descriptions a visual equivalent. Here are accounts of a night spent with Daniel Boone, of hairbreadth escapes from Indians, descriptions of scenery and animals, hunting scenes and anecdotes of early pioneering days. In one episode called a 'Kentucky Barbeque', he describes fourth of July celebrations in terms which make even Bartram seem unsentimental:

> Here were to be seen flagons of very beverage used in the country; 'la belle rivière' had opened her finny stores, . . . A purling stream gave its waters freely, while the grateful breezes cooled the air . . . .. On each lovely nymph attended her gay beau, who in her chance or sidelong glances ever watched an opportunity of reading his happiness.[42]

And yet the literary culture Audubon inherited is important to understanding the dramatic impact of his pictures. For like the English flower painter Robert John Thornton, Audubon was able to synthesize in his work the opposing demands of scientific representation and the areas of consciousness it repressed in its one-dimensional vision. Like many of his contemporaries he admired Milton and Shakespeare for their 'sublimity', and poets like Thomson and Byron. Approaching England in 1826 he reread Byron and Thomson again: 'When I came to his "Castle of Indolence" [Thomson] I felt the all powerful extent of his genius operating on me as a cathartic, swallowed when well aware that my body was not in fit condition (through situation) to be benefited by it'.[43] Like another of his contemporaries, Chester Harding, who a few years earlier had posed as an 'American Woodman', Audubon's self-dramatization of himself as a backwoodsman appealed to the European literary imagination and he was fêted by the elite and closed society of the English upper classes. In Liverpool he met William Roscoe, the English historian and art critic, saw Selby's *Birds of England* engraved by Lizars who was to acquatint the first ten plates of *The Birds of America* and also saw some of Bewick's fine woodcuts of animals and birds. In Edinburgh he met James Wilson, the brother of Christopher North who was to praise the first volume of *The Birds of America* in *Blackwoods Magazine*. The slightly old-fashioned Scottish critical and literary interests suited his taste, and he had appropriately gothic reactions to the thought

[42] John James Audubon, *Delineations of American Scenery and Character* (New York 1926) pp. 487–8.
[43] *The 1826 Journal of John James Audubon, transcribed with an Introduction and Notes by Alice Ford* (Norman, Oklahoma 1967) p. 22.

of meeting Sir Walter Scott: 'Ah Walter Scott, when I am presented
to thee my head will droop, my heart will swell, my limbs will
tremble, my lips quiver, my tongue congeal'.[44] Nonetheless
Audubon remained fiercely and patriotically American. He wrote
to his wife Lucy:

> Not even the metaphoric name of 'Sir John', as Sir *Wm* Jardine was
> pleased to call me at Twizel, could make me relinquish the idea of know-
> ing that in *my universe* of America, the deer runs free, and the Hunter
> as free forever.—No—America will always be my land.[45]

Audubon's masterpiece depended in the first instance on skilled
English engravers and on English patronage. Even in those times a
complete set of the bird prints would cost the aristocrat interested
in the representation of natural history approximately £1,000
sterling. But the design, conception, the energy of the execution,
the types of cultural and scientific tradition drawn on and daringly
juxtaposed, are uniquely American.

Audubon set his figures of natural history in a landscape, and
though this practice was not originated by him, on it depended
much of the strange appeal of the pictures. First we shall look
at the figures and then at the landscape and figures together.

Audubon's first concern was like Catesby's, to provide a semiotic
simplification of representational characteristics by which the bird
might be recognized in nature together with its habitat. Defending
her grandfather against the charge of flatness, Maria Audubon at the
end of the nineteenth century quoted Cuvier on the problem of
natural history representation:

> It is difficult to give a true picture of a bird with the same effect of
> perspective as a landscape, and the lack of this is no defect in a work on
> Natural History. Naturalists prefer the real color of objects to those
> accidental tints which are the result of the varied reflections of light
> necessary to complete picturesque representations, but foreign and even
> injurious to scientific truth.[46]

Thus Cuvier rationalized premises already adopted partly by default
in Catesby. The effect in painterly terms was an abandonment of
depth representation and chiaroscuro. There was a new equalization
of light throughout the figure, and representational colour seemed
to give off its own light unreflected from any source. With its
characteristics generalized from particulars the bird was essentially

---

[44] Ibid., p. 285.
[45] John James Audubon, *Letters of John James Audubon* (Boston 1930) p. 51.
[46] Maria Audubon, ed., *Audubon and his Journals* (1897; reprinted New York 1960)
vol. II, p. 522.

a *representative* of a *species*. Since the species itself was considered
a fixed category of nature in Linnaeus's view at least (though with
dissent as we have seen by Buffon) the bird itself pointed to a fixed
character type. Abandoning perspective and chiaroscuro meant
abandoning the vagaries of different shapes according to position
in the picture plane and different colour effects in relation to the
light source. The delineatory method thus confirmed the scientifico-
religious view of revealed and immutable nature. But such clarity
brought problems with it. Nondepth representation limited the
possibility of interesting profile in artistic terms. Exiled from a
context of depth space the natural figure was often represented in
the most boring of positions and the most dull of outlines. In botany
the problem was solved by the very complexity of stem and leaf,
but Audubon complained bitterly of his own first attempts which
were typical of the time in that they 'all represented *strictly orni-
thologically* which means neither more nor less than in stiff, un-
meaning profiles, such as are found in most works published to the
present day'.[47] Audubon's problem was that he wanted to give a
representational account of the live bird in its habitat without the
technological means of so doing which a contemporary camera
might have given him. He had primarily to work from the evidence
of the bird he shot, and then find some means of representing it
live. It is Audubon's desire to present the animal *live* and scientifically (hitherto almost irreconcilable wishes) that was eventually to
make his work so unique, Audubon explains this recognition in the
following manner:

> One day, while watching the habits of a pair of Pewees at Mill Grove, I
> looked so intently at their graceful attitudes that a thought struck my
> mind like a flash of light, that nothing, after all, could ever answer my
> enthusiastic desires to represent nature, except to copy her in her own
> way, alive and moving! Then I began again . . . .. I procured many indi-
> viduals of different species, and laying them on the table or on the
> ground, tried to place them in such attitudes as I had sketched. But,
> alas! they were *dead*, to all intents and purposes, and neither wing, leg,
> nor tail could I place according to my wishes. A second thought came
> to my assistance; by means of threads I raised or lowered a head, wing,
> or tail, and by fastening the threads securely, I had something like life
> before me; yet much was wanting.[48]

Finally Audubon borrowed a piece of soft board from a local miller
and the account is best given in his own words:

> When he returned he found me filing sharp points to some pieces of

[47] Ibid., vol. II pp. 523–4.
[48] Ibid., vol. II p. 524.

wire, and I proceeded to show him what I meant to do. I pierced the
body of the fishing bird, and fixed it on the board; another wire passed
above his upper mandible held the head in a pretty fair attitude, smaller
ones fixed the feet according to my notions, and even common pins
came to my assistance. The last wire proved a delightful elevator to the
bird's tail, and at last—there stood before me the *real* Kingfisher . . ..
This was what I shall call my first drawing actually from nature, for even
the eye of the Kingfisher was as if full of life whenever I pressed the lids
aside with my finger . . .. The better I understood my subjects the better
I became able to represent them in what I hoped were natural positions.
The birds once fixed with wires on squares, I studied as a lay figure before
me, its nature, previously known to me as far as habits went, and its
general form having been frequently observed. Now I could examine
more thoroughly the bill, nostrils, eyes, legs, and claws as well as the
structure of the wings and tail; the very tongue was of importance to me,
and I thought the more I understood these particulars, the better representations I made of the originals.[49]

Audubon's synthesis is truly remarkable. The American democrat
revivifies the 'still life' painting commissioned by the hunter aristocrat. Like Poe's detective Audubon reconstructs the life from the
details of the corpse with the squared background providing the
analytical framework. Memory and experience test the authenticity
of the movements of these corpse-like puppets. Critics have praised
the animation of Audubon's birds while excusing some of the more
grotesque poses, but that is to do violence to the strange appeal of
the pictures. It is precisely the tension between 'scientific rigor'
(here *rigor mortis*) and the representation of the life which give to
Audubon's paintings their grotesque quality. In painterly terms,
memory and experience provide the long-view of the bird in life,
the arranged corpse provides the details. In the picture both have
equal place in the composition so we are seeing the near and far
view, one for outline, the other for detail (tongue, claw etc.), in a
totally unrealistic synthesis.

The effects of this method can be inexhaustibly studied in the
pictures themselves. The colouring with little to no chiaroscuro effects
produces gleaming, jewel-like patterns in the globules on the neck
of the wild turkey (vol. I. pl. 1). In the plate of the Red-tailed Hawk
(vol. I, pl. 51) the violent action is controlled by the way in which
the tail and wing feathers of the hawk form a perfect circle which
the lower half of the hare's body continues. In the same plate the
blood and excreta of the hare are meticulously outlined each with
their own light values. Studies of life and still life juxtaposed complicated the philosophy of representation in such pictures as the

---

[49] Ibid., vol. II p. 526.

gap between them becomes more and more arbitrary. Precision of line, like a dissecting knife, reveals the details of the corpse. The plate of the White-headed Eagle **pl.** 59, is inspired by Wilson's own plate of the same subject. There is a death-like surrealism in the unearthly underside view of the catfish with its spikes which, as Audubon describes them, 'when the fish is in the agonies of death, stand out at right angles'.[50] The same controlling sense of design and of suspended motion can be seen in the Mocking Birds and Rattlesnake (vol. I, pl. 11) where the birds twist about the snake, illustrating the popular belief about the snake's magical powers of hypnosis.

59 *White-headed Eagle* by John James Audubon. (*Courtesy of the British Library, London.*)

Audubon has clearly drawn the birds individually and then assembled them into a decorative pattern which nonetheless gives the sense that each bird is executing a private vendetta with the central snake.

But Audubon also set the bird in a landscape. The effect of the flatly drawn bird and the three dimensional landscape-scene gives often a strangely contradictory sense of spatial values. This was especially true when Audubon painted the bird from the eye-level view of the drawing board on which it was arranged, and then superimposed the image onto a landscape having different and often contradictory perspectives. In the plate of the Barn Owls (vol. II, pl. 171) **pl.** 60, for example, the birds are painted flat, with each

[50] Ibid., vol. II p. 214.

60 *Barn Owl* by John James Audubon. (*Courtesy of the British Library, London.*)

detail of claw and feather unrealistically visible, but the back view of the river far below suddenly lets the viewer into the third dimension giving a simultaneous feeling of power and helplessness analagous to squirrel and bird, victim and conqueror, in the artist's imagination. The dark sky displays the owl's habits, the extended wing shows its anatomical structure, the victim of the owl's flight displays the type of food on which the bird exists. Yet the overall lighting gives us more than scientific information. The river retains the light of day in the third dimension while the blackness of darkness at the top of the picture uncannily merges into a dimensionless background for the owls whose sole light-source is the luminosity of their own colours. In complete contrast other pictures flatten out bird and background and give us an older sense of design and orna-

61 *Brown-headed Worm-eating Warbler* by John James Audubon. (*Courtesy of the British Library, London.*)

ment such as Catesby created. Of many such pictures that of the Brown-headed Worm Eating Warbler (vol. II, pl. 198) **pl. 61** is one of the most beautiful. The bird occupies a central position in an oval of orange coloured azalea with two butterflies. Its elegance and serenity provide an alternative to the more haunted visions of the birds of prey.

Audubon's *Birds of America,* as well as his *Viviparous Quadrupeds of North America* (1845—8) for a brief moment synthesized the artistic and scientific traditions of Europe and America. His work is unclassifiable in either's terms. After Audubon the bureaucratization of natural history research produced nothing to equal it. In the career of an early admirer of Audubon, Spencer Fullerton Baird who first saw Audubon's great folio in 1839 at the age of 16, we can see the process operating. Baird is important because his contributions to the science of natural history were scarcely surpassed in America during the century. He added more fishes and reptiles to the list of fauna than any other scientist and was in touch with every major government expedition from the 1840s onwards and supervized the natural history research.[51] He met every scientist of importance in his day, as well as Emerson and Thoreau in 1852, and many years later, he discussed with Emerson the Agassiz-Darwin debate. Yet his scientific outlook was essentially formed by a kind of Scottish faith in the reality of classification and facts. In the same year that *Moby Dick* came out also appeared his translation of the German Heck's *Iconographic Encyclopaedia,* a kind of literal embodiment of a linear cosmos with hundreds of line illustrations depicting the ten categories of knowledge: mathematics and astronomy; the natural sciences; geography and planography; history and ethnology; military sciences; the naval sciences; architecture; mythology and religious rites; the fine arts and technology. Somehow Audubon's work provided one of the moments of creative resistance to the American ethic of progress, and partly by design and partly by academic default avoided separatist conventionalities of art and science.

---

[51] See William Healy Dall, *Spencer Fullerton Baird. A Biography* (Philadelphia and London 1915).

10

Landscape

The experience of landscape defines a man's relation to his culture.
We can only understand Americans' attempts to understand their
own landscape from as many different approaches as there are
complexities in the culture they inherited. For whatever the separatist conventions of figure and landscape, self and environment,
history and nature, internal and external, earth and heaven, present
and future, representer and represented, public and private, war and
peace, material and immaterial, organic and mechanical, city and
country, which we have seen Americans coming to terms with in a
response to the inherited cultural drama of European thought, the
American impulse to inclusion and synthesis sought new ways to
reintegrate these polarities. The very experience of writing about
or painting landscape also articulates the sum total of the individual's
sense of reality. We have already seen that the layout of Colt's factory and garden tells us as much about American culture as Jefferson's country house and the University of Virginia. Kosciusko's
garden complements the fortified boundary of the defences of
state. Brockden Brown's hero dreams of virgin land from within
the labyrinths of a consciousness which has been failed by the
commonsense reality of eighteenth-century science. In this final
chapter we bring together those concerns which have hitherto been
looked at separately, by examining the highly sophisticated tradition of literary-visual, academic landscape painting in the first half
of the nineteenth century, together with some literary parallels.
Then, we shall have a brief look at similar phenomena on a more
popular level, and finally at the emergence of a new urban
landscape.

In terms reminiscent of the marriage service Sir Walter Raleigh,
on a voyage to a country to be named after a virgin queen, was
instructed 'to have, hold, occupy and enjoy . . . whatsoever we by
our letters patents may grant . . .'.[1] Already we have seen some of

[1] *Hakluyt's Voyages* with an introduction by J. Masefield, (London 1907) vol. VI,
p. 115.

the implications of the equation of the body of the earth with the human body in the politicosexual landscapes of men like Jefferson and Bartram. The concept of the earth as a body has ancient origins, but from the time America itself was discovered, and throughout the Renaissance it had an especially literal significance. The landscape artist or poet from Leonardo onwards could draw on a vast literature of 'Theories of the Earth' which articulated in purely anatomical terms the view of the universe as microcosm and macrocosm. Although the contents of Leonardo's notebooks were not public until many years after they were written, we can nonetheless find there a convenient summary of prevailing attitudes:

> So then we may say that the earth has a spirit of growth, and that its flesh is the soil; its bones are the successive strata of the rocks which form the mountains; its cartilage is the tufa stone; its blood the springs of its waters. The lake of blood that lies about the heart is the ocean. Its breathing is by the increase and decrease of the blood in its pulses, and even so in the earth is the ebb and flow of the sea. And the vital heat of the world is fire which is spread throughout the earth; and the dwelling place of its creative spirit is in the fires, which in divers parts of the earth are breathed out in baths and sulphur mines, and in volcanoes, such as Mount Etna in Sicily, and in many other places.[2]

In his essay, 'Renaissance Theory of Art and the Rise of Landscape', Gombrich points to the emergence of landscape in the late sixteenth century and shows how Leonardo described landscape as a prime area of dream consciousness which 'probes deep into the creative process itself'.[3]

> If a painter wants to see fair women to kindle his love, he has the power to create them, and if he desires to see monstrosities to arouse his fear, his amusement and laughter or even his compassion, he is their Lord and Creator. And if he wishes to bring forth sites or deserts, cool and shady places in times of heat or warm spots when it is cold, he fashions them. So if he desires valleys or wishes to discover vast tracts of land from mountain peaks and look at the sea on the distant horizon beyond them, it is in his power; and so if he wants to look up to the high mountains from low valleys, or from high mountains towards the deep valleys and coastline. In fact, whatever exists in the universe either potentially or actually or in the imagination, he has it first in his mind and then in his hands, and these (images) are of such excellence, that they present the

[2] *The Notebooks of Leonardo da Vinci* with an introduction by Edward MacCurdy, (1938; reprinted London 1954) vol. I, pp. 83–4.
[3] E. H. Gombrich, *Norm and Form, Studies in the Art of the Renaissance* (London 1966) p. 112.

same proportioned harmony to a single glance as belong to the things themselves. . . .[4]

Leonardo, celebrating an imaginative feeling of power *over* things, charts a concept of the reality of nature as a dialectic between fair and foul, heat and cold, high and low. Women and landscape partake of this double attitude which, under a double characterization of human activity as a mind then body process, originates 'first in his mind and then in his hands'. In Leonardo's *Notebooks* and elsewhere the landscapes of darkness, of deluge and of disaster complement landscapes of peace and light. Long before Burke, Leonardo charted the psychology of alternative landscapes. The twin emotions of compulsion towards the marvellous and reaction against the terrifying characterize his reaction to the body of the earth. In one description of dark caves in a threatening landscape he says that there 'awakened within me two emotions, fear and desire, fear of the dark threatening cavern, desire to see whether there might be any marvellous thing therein'.[5] The war machines he describes seem like a scientific apparatus which has the additional function of allaying his fears of the secret internal places of the earth's body: 'Also I have ways of arriving at a certain fixed spot by caverns and secret winding passages, made without any noise even though it may be necessary to pass underneath trenches or a river'.[6]

Over against the anarchy of the dark aspects of the body, Leonardo set the laws of light and perspective:

> Among the various studies of natural process, that of light gives most pleasure to those who contemplate it; and among the noteworthy characteristics of modern science, the certainty of its demonstrations is what operates most powerfully to elevate the minds of its investigators. Perspective therefore is to be preferred to all the formularities and systems of the schoolmen, for in its province the complex beam of light is made to show the stages of its development, wherein is found the play not only of the mathematical but also of the physical science, adorned as it is with the flowers of both.[7]

The properties of light and perspective satisfied both theoretical and actual visual criteria. And yet, as we have seen, the very reality of perspective opened up dream landscapes of calm and conflict. Leonardo's ambiguities, as Gombrich has shown, developed, in landscape painting, into a double tradition of epic and pastoral

---

[4] Ibid, p. 111–2.
[5] Leonardo, *Notebooks,* vol. II, p. 472.
[6] Ibid., vol. II, p. 497.
[7] Ibid., vol. II, p. 340.

landscapes which, for our purposes, reflect the dialectic of war and peace always inherent in the classical tradition. Although Leonardo fails to mention America in any of his writings, the complex of issues he raises has a kind of summarizing relevance to American culture in his characterizations of landscape, in his search for a scientific truth to replace older superstitions, and in his dialectical sense of reality. The tradition of the earth as a body, as we have seen, had scarcely died out even in the mid-years of the nineteenth century, although, beginning perhaps with Burke's treatise on the *Sublime and the Beautiful* (1757)[8] a more psychological and less literal correspondence had been found between the human and earth bodies. Burke located dualistic emotional properties in the features of landscape themselves, while Wordsworth, following in the same tradition, saw the physical world in a kind of mirror-like, mind-object correspondence.

The formal tradition of American nineteenth-century landscape painting began with the young, expatriate American painter Washington Allston, meeting Coleridge in Rome in 1805. In their famous *Preface to the Lyrical Ballads* (1798–1802)[9] Wordsworth and Coleridge agreed to split their energies in different directions with Wordsworth pursuing the realities of normal life and Coleridge concentrating on more exotic dream landscapes. We have already seen how Bartram's response to the American landscape helped to create the poetic landscape of *Kubla Khan* which, as Gombrich observed of Leonardo, 'probed deep into the creative process itself'. Because of this cultural interchange, which knows no boundary of academic category or national interest, we can fruitfully look at Coleridge's poem as a model poetic synthesis of that drama of nature and empire so variously enacted during this first independent period of American culture.[10]

The dream landscapes of the poem alternate between images of destruction and rebirth as a process analogous with the creative act itself. The poem dramatizes a momentary and threatened balance of forces before the fall of empire. The first landscape of the poem we know Coleridge partly based on the Chinoiserie landscape cult of English gardening[11] and it is a landscape of a walled garden

[8] Edmund Burke, *A Philosophical Enquiry into the Origin of our Ideas of the Sublime and the Beautiful* (1757) J. F. Boulton, ed., (London 1958).

[9] William Wordsworth, *The Prose Works of William Wordsworth*, 3 vols. A. B. Grossart, ed. (London 1876) vol. II, pp. 77–100.

[10] S. T. Coleridge, *Poetical Works* (1912; reprinted London 1967) pp. 297–8.

[11] See A. O. Lovejoy, *Essays in the History of Ideas* (1948; reprinted New York 1960) pp. 99–135.

which turns nature into art. Civilization is defined by the boundary
drawn by the all-powerful prince. But if Coleridge chooses one of
the most ancient civilizations as a model for this landscape, for the
landscape of nature which articulates a freer play of erotic forces,
he turns to Bartram's vision of the New World. Like the American's,
Coleridge's landscape resembles a human body, and yet it is of a
more androgynous nature, for the 'deep romantic chasm' produces
a male-like orgasm. The transposed images of the Carolinan sinks
articulate a view of nature as eternally and simultaneously destructive and creative. And it is this tumult which brings to Kubla Khan,
'Ancestral voices prophesying war!'. Coleridge's landscape serves as
a natural timeless icon which guarantees human civilized permanence
in which only conflict is eternal and in which time itself is never
present but only past and future. This contrasted landscape suggests
the eternal conflict between nature and civilization in which the
past controls the future in the name of boundary and war. Precarious paradoxes in which the balance of the dualisms is always
threatened can be seen in the shadow of the dome floating on the
water. Here, rock and water, traditionally opposed, become tem-
porarily one in the 'sunny pleasure dome with caves of ice'. The
sense of vision is transcended in images of music and harmony.
The Abyssinian maid sings of the mountain and opposed to her
is the 'woman wailing for her demon lover'. The one represents the
chaste paradise of symbolic spiritual elevation, the other the demonic ecstasy of physical love. The poet, in his Promethean defiance,
creates the landscape in which he consciously manipulates the alternatives which are the source of his power. In a sense he has
broken the secret of civilized reality and becomes dangerous in this
knowledge of the 'sacred' principles and his own possible exploitation of them.

In his own life Washington Allston, as an American, struggled
with similar meanings of nature and civilization. It is something of
a romantic myth that his last years were spent entirely frustrated
over his enormous *Belshazzar's Feast*.[12] Unlike John Martin in
England he was never able to finish the subject, and the theme of
the doom of empire had already been dramatically painted by Cole.
In some ways Allston was closer to the later Coleridge, than the
Coleridge of the Kubla Khan era. In a somewhat literal sense he
denied landscape a more animate form, 'There is certainly no simil-
itude in the objects that compose a landscape, and the form of an

[12] E. P. Richardson, *Washington Allston, A Study of the Romantic Artist in America*
(Chicago 1948). See especially pp. 152–5.

animal and man';[13] and in a more Wordsworthian manner he retains the archetypes of dream landscape while attempting to give them simultaneously concrete and psychological characteristics. Allston's more American and more Puritan nature edges him out of these complex philosophical and psychological problems towards blurring distinctions somewhat piously. The following passage on landscape may remind us of the tone and imagery of *Tintern Abbey* but what is lacking is Wordworth's more humanistic use of mystic experience:

> It is so with us, when we call some tall forest stately, or qualify as majestic some broad and slowly winding river, or some vast, yet un-broken waterfall, or some solitary, gigantic pine, seeming to disdain the earth, and to hold of night with their eternal communion with air; or when to the smooth and far-reaching expanse of our inland waters with their bordering and receding mountains; as they seem to march from the shores, in the pomp of their dark draperies of wood and mist, we apply the terms grand and magnificent: so onward to an endless succession of objects, imputing, as it were, our own nature, as lending our sympathies, till the headlong rush of some mighty cataract suddenly thunders upon us. But how is it then? In the twinkling of an eye, the outflowing sympathies ebb back upon the heart; the whole mind seems severed from earth, and the awful feeling to suspend the breath; — there is nothing human to which we can liken it. And here begins another kind of emotion which we call Sublime.[14]

Allston is led on not by the 'affections' but by an endless succession of *objects* which, and the word is overtasked, *impute* the nature of the observer in a crescendo of impressions which finally overwhelm him. The term 'sublime' is reserved for an end process to which the details of the physical world tend. Allston shys off sexual implications of creativity and he frequently speaks of 'refining on the physical' as part of the creative process and he states in a crucial passage, 'Next to the development of our moral nature, to have subordinated the senses to the mind is the highest triumph of our moral nature'.[15] His strange and only novel, *Monaldi* (1841) dram-atizes his dilemma. One character is destroyed because his mechan-istic philosophy is unable to cope with the fate of a ruling passion, the other, more intuitive, creates a fantastic world of the imagin-ation which also destroys him. Religion is the answer, 'For the death of a Christian — the death in hope — has no parallel in sub-

---

[13] Richard Henry Dana, ed., *Washington Allston, Lectures on Art and Poems* (New York 1850) p. 42.
[14] Ibid., p. 51.
[15] Ibid., p. 9.

limity on our earth'.[16] Allston's own landscapes vary from the
generalized ideality of the kind he painted under the influence of
the English—Italian tradition, to reddish, misty wilderness scenes
which in part anticipate the Hudson River school of painters.[17] One
late sketch, the chalk drawing, *Ship in a Squall* **pl. 62** is a dream

62 *Ship in a Squall,* before 1837, by Washington Allston. (*Courtesy of the Fogg Museum,*
Harvard University, Loan—Washington Allston Trust.)

landscape worthy of the tradition which was to include Poe and
Melville. The very medium of white chalk lines blurs traditional
landscape distinctions, and its whiteness emphasizes not objects but
a play of forces. Here is a traditional American subject of nature
drama in which the ship as representative of human society makes
a skilful stand against danger. The angle of the ship and the swirl of
the clouds capture the moment between peace and danger and the
mirror image of the ship on the horizon emphasizes the representative quality of the situation. The line of white which articulates the
tops of the waves serves only to emphasize the blackness inherent

[16] Washington Allston, *Monaldi* (Boston 1841) p. 251.
[17] Richardson, *Washington Allston,* p. 148.

in the body of the water. Like the ghostly ship of the *Ancient Mariner,* the dissolving elements point to a deeper psychological drama. And yet, unlike some of Turner's scenes, it still reveals a devotion to outline and solidity. It is the play between linear reality, the sensation of 'light through', and the undifferentiating medium of chalk which constitutes its appeal.

Allston himself painted many literary subjects from classic English writers such as Spenser and Shakespeare, and of course from the Bible. In this manner he followed an English tradition initiated by West which revived the heroes of classical and modern literature as psychological types. But the drama nearest to the centre of American consciousness was the drama of nature itself.

We have already seen in the popular entertainments of the panorama and diorama how nature itself becomes background and foreground, actor and landscape scene. In the work of James Fenimore Cooper and his contemporary, the painter Thomas Cole (1801—48), whom Cooper never met, we can find literal dramatizations of nature as plot in time and space which are peculiarly American. In 1840, Balzac, comparing Cooper and Scott in his short-lived magazine, *la Révue parisienne,* wrote:

> En resumé, l'un est l'historien de la nature, l'autre celui de l'humanité; l'un arrive au beau ideale par des images, l'autre par l'action et sans négliger aucune poésie.[18]

In a late and disillusioned work, *The Crater* (1848), Cooper wrote out his own distaste at the way American democracy had developed in a plot which dramatized nature as history and drew on sources in painters, geologists, and explorers. As is well known, Cooper, long before Henry James, contrasted the European with the American landscape. For the aspiring writer American landscape failed to provide sufficient 'associations'.[19] The American landscape, however, was at its best when 'it unites the agricultural with the savage', but as a rule it wants 'finish'. Even the Rocky Mountains, magnificent though they are, could do with associations, to make them amenable to the landscape artist. Cooper's double view of landscape as cultured or wild is crucial. The first is subject to the rules of time and change, birth, fruition and decay. Consequently it articulates a view of history in which the movement of time is toward ruin and death. The second kind of landscape, the savage

---

[18] Honoré de Balzac, *Oeuvres complètes* (Paris 1926—56) vol. XI, pp. 285—6.
[19] See James Fenimore Cooper's essay, 'American and European Scenery Compared', in *The Home Book of the Picturesque* (New York 1852). It was reprinted in *A Landscape Book* (New York 1868).

or wild variety, is nearly always mountains or rocks. Because, according to the ancient tradition which we have seen exemplified in Leonardo, these are the bones of the earth, they represent that reality not subject to change. However, the emerging science of geology had begun to cast some doubts upon the nature of the timelessness of rocks as adequate symbols of eternity. It is interesting that the main source for Cooper's landscape in *The Crater* was Lyell's *Principles of Geology* (1830–33).[20] Lyell was a 'uniformitarian' which meant that he thought all past geological change could be explained by contemporary geological events. So the process of change remains constant, uniform and predictable. In politics Lyell was a conservative, perhaps because his view of change, made analogous with the time scale of geological ages, could scarcely operate in a human life span. The conjunction of the double landscape of agriculture and of barren, savage rocks and mountains in Cooper's *The Crater* provides the symbolic context for his hero's activities. For our purposes it is also interesting that Cooper drew on the voyages of Captain Cook and of Captain Wilkes for his story.[21] *The Crater,* then, gives us a symbolic drama of those issues deep in the American consciousness. The desire to overcome nature, and the desire to recreate society according to a model of perfection reflect a fear of nature and of social anarchy.

In the story Mark Woolston, the hero, with his faithful retainer, Betts, leaves his virgin bride to cultivate virgin land in the shape of a barren crater on which he is shipwrecked. Here the two men, far from home, re-enact the American dream of men at work in the wilderness, literally fructifying the barren womb of the crater with bird dung. In this way, with due labour, Mark establishes himself as a person by creating his own agricultural property which will raise his status sufficiently to place him on an equal footing with his Philadelphia bride. The necessity of 'bettering oneself' draws on the psychic energy of pre-orgasmic foreplay. Having disciplined himself by disciplining the landscape which, uncultivated, cannot support life, he now undergoes a lesson in 'spiritual values'. Accidentally left alone on the island, and falling physically sick, he experiences a symbolic journey through the valley of the shadow of death to become spiritually a 'new man'.[22] At a time when the original conception of the American state as a divinely ordained

---

[20] See Harold H. Scudder, 'Cooper's *The Crater*', *American Literature*, IX (1947–8) pp. 109–26.

[21] See W. B. Gates, 'Cooper's *The Crater* and Two Explorers', *American Literature*, XXIII (1951–2) pp. 243–6.

[22] James Fenimore Cooper, *The Crater* (1848; reprinted New York 1895) p. 137.

model of nature was losing out to the more agressive and progressive notions of empire, Cooper, in the education of his hero, revives some of the old values. Woolston arrives at an appreciation of divine omnipotence through the arts of geometry and navigation. Able mathematically to place himself in his own universe Woolston is, by his discoveries, enabled to see into the mind of God:

> Previously to this period, he had looked into these things from curiosity and a love of science; now they impressed him with the deepest sense of the power and wisdom of the Deity, and caused him the better to understand his own position in the scale of created beings.[23]

The metaphysical discovery of himself as a figure in a landscape teaches Woolston humility and prepares him for the role of hero-saint. After this secular conversion, in a series of eruptions, an archipelago is created round the crater; a new world for a new man. Woolston now takes on the role of explorer king, an American Robinson Crusoe enacting an individualistic dream of power. The crater and the circular archipelago symbolize the female space in which the male hero is permanently erected. His own position on 'the peak', is authenticated by its mirror image in Vulcan's peak — the permanent natural erection in history of the power of the gods. As head of the body politic, Woolston lives on the highest part of his island. As the new society takes shape, the crater, the birthplace of the god, becomes a mystic centre forbidden to the natives. From now on Cooper recapitulates the decline and fall of empire, a moral fable not without significance for American imperial activities. In order, for example, to safeguard mineral wealth on one of the islands, Woolston supports with arms the weaker king against the more politically aware tyrant. Woolston proves his leadership qualities by his daring in whaling activities; and savages and pirates threatening property are blown up with modern weapons they know nothing about.

But as civilization progresses, the phallic hero, creating landscape from a single viewpoint, is threatened by the appearance of more islands and more people. Instead of the single crater and the lone hero, now there is a panorama of islands each with a different view of the whole. Literally unable to let his hero keep things in perspective, that is to maintain a view of reality from a single position, and having threatened him with the call of his own subjects for mass power and religious dissent, Cooper erupts his volcano and buries the whole archipelago with the words:

[23] Ibid., p. 144.

> Let those who would substitute the voice of the created for that of the
> Creator, who shout 'the people, the people,' instead of hymning praises
> of their God, who vainly imagine that the masses are sufficient for all
> things, remember their insignificance and tremble.[24]

Only the peak with its lone tree remains, symbol of eternity and
nature, and of the savage and agricultural landscapes. The body of
the earth is reduced to a ruined monument eternal in time, just as
Woolston is now reduced to being head of state without a body.
The price of eternity is man and nature reduced to a single function
of monumentality and power-seeking.

Cooper's life-long interest in the landscape painter, Thomas Cole,
is well known[25] and at the end of *The Crater* he compared the surviving solitary peak with the rock which remains constant throughout the changes of Cole's historic series of pictures *The Course of
Empire*:

> It might be said to resemble, in this respect, that sublime rock which
> is recognized as part of the 'everlasting hills' in Cole's series of noble
> landscapes that is called 'The March of Empire'; ever the same amid the
> changes of time, and civilization and decay.[26]

Cooper saw in Cole's work a painterly analogue of his own attempt
to unite the genres of landscape and history. In this respect he saw
it as the greatest work of art yet produced by an American, 'It is
quite a new thing to see landscape painting raised to a level with the
heroic in historical composition: but it is constantly to be traced in
the works of Thomas Cole'.[27] Not only did Cole attempt to unite
history and nature but the separate modes of literature and painting.
Lessing succinctly stated the problem Cole set himself:

> If it be true that painting employs wholly different signs or means of
> imitation from poetry, the one using forms and colors in space, the other
> articulate sounds in time — and if signs must unquestionably stand in
> convenient relation with the thing signified, then signs arranged side by
> side can represent only objects existing side by side, or whose parts so
> exist, while consecutive signs can express only objects which succeed
> each other, or whose parts succeed each other, in time.[28]

Lessing conceded that action could be represented, however, in
visual form if it confined itself to a single moment, 'the most sug-

[24] Ibid., p. 482.
[25] See James T. Callow, *Kindred Spirits* (Chapel Hill, N. Carolina 1967) pp. 61–2.
Artist and writer never met.
[26] Cooper, *The Crater*, p. 479.
[27] Louis L. Noble, *The Course of Empire* . . .. (New York 1853) p. 124.
[28] Gotthold Ephraim Lessing, *Laocoon* trans. Ellen Frothingham (New York 1957).
p. 91.

gestive what has gone before and what is to follow'.[29] Lessing's whole concept of space and time as a succession and relation of finite bodies sets the context for Cole's own mode of thinking. To overcome the problems of dramatic representation in visual form Cole simply presented a series of pictures of pregnant moments succeeding each other in time, with the same landscape presented from different points of view to give a greater illusion of its permanence. In short Cole presented in the *Course of Empire* a concept of history as a five act tragedy with time and space presented as stoic, enduring heroes.

Cooper was not quite right in asserting Cole's originality. The impulse to put drama back into painting had come from the theatre itself in the last half of the eighteenth century. Christopher Hussey points to the importance of an erstwhile scene painter de Loutherbourg who was important in creating a visual drama out of nature itself:

> As Thompson and Mrs Radcliffe had transformed pictures into poetry and novels respectively, and the gardeners had formed pictures with real trees and buildings, 'Leatherbag' contrived his panorama, which he called Eidophusikon, so as to realise pictures in all four dimensions.[30]

De Loutherbourg moved from scene painting as background to scene painting as a drama in its own right. By 1781 he produced an exclusively visual presentation of 'Various imitations of Natural Phenomena, represented by Moving Pictures'. The drama began with Aurora in London, continued with Noon in Tangiers, Sunset of a view near Naples, Moonlight on the Mediterranean and concluded with a Storm at Sea and Shipwreck. The diverse spatial aspects of the drama were united by a time pattern which, like Poussin's *Seasons,* moved from birth to death. An alternative final scene was 'the region of the fallen angels with Satan, arraying his troops on the bank of the Fiery Lake'. It showed:

> . . . in the foreground of a vista, stretching an immeasurable length between mountains ignited from their bases to their lofty summits, with many coloured flames, a chaotic mass rising in dark majesty, which gradually assumed form until it stood, the interior of a vast temple of gorgeous architecture, bright as molten brass, seemingly composed of unconsuming and unquenchable fire.[31]

The apocalyptic goal could be either a civil or natural disaster. Only

[29] Ibid., p. 92.
[30] Christopher Hussey, *The Picturesque, Studies in a Point of View* (1927; reprinted London 1967) p. 239.
[31] Ibid., p. 241.

three years after de Loutherbourg's London exhibition Charles
Willson Peale had converted the sky-lighted room at the end of the
long gallery to present a similar series of pictures.[32] Peale called his
show 'Perspective Views with Changeable Effects; or, Nature De-
lineated and in Motion'. The opening announcement emphasized
the quality of movement and change in the presentation. Whereas
de Loutherbourg's series ended in a grand climactic disaster, Peale
preferred to end quietly. His fourth picture showed Milton's scene
in Pandemonium, but his sea scene patriotically showed the fight
between the *Bon Homme Richard* and the *Serapis.* The final scene
was *Vandering's Mill* showing the local Schuylkill falls. The audience,
viewing the show from chairs in the gallery, was entertained also by
readings from Shakespeare, Milton and Sheridan and with music.
Peale's order and choice of subject show a slight Americanization
of the imported European mode. The American war scene is followed by a simple natural landscape without human figures.

  As early as the 1780s, therefore, the phenomenon of sequential
perspective landscape with an implicit literary meaning, often
borrowed, as was the fashion, from Milton and from the Bible, was
naturalized in America. Peale employed the mode to project recent
history as news, and to make a local American scene take the metaphysical weight of post-tragic emotional catharsis. We have already
noted American interest in the phenomena of panorama and diorama. Thus there was already an established American tradition
when Cole saw Burford's panorama of Pandemonium from designs
of H. C. Slous on his visit to London in 1829. As Wolfgang Born
has pointed out these designs were a source for the American's
Course of Empire.[33]

  Cole's uniqueness lies in his marriage of the popular tradition of
panorama and diorama to the conventions of history painting which
is a more aristocratic mode. The technical problems involved made
Cole's series a crucial American synthesis, for the whole unbounded
range of the panorama had to be encompassed in a picture frame.
The boundlessness of circular vision, celebrated in America in
Emerson's famous essay on *Nature* in 1836, had to be described in
a linear manner. Commenting on a later series of pictures, *The
Voyage of Life,* Cole observed:

> A picture is not like a scene in nature, where the eye can embrace the
> whole circle of the horizon, but is bounded like a view taken through a

[32] Charles Coleman Sellers, *Charles Willson Peale* (New York 1969) p. 205ff.
[33] Wolfgang Born, *American Landscape Painting* (New Haven, Conn. 1948). pp. 17–117

window. The greatest scope of vision is from the foreground to the extreme distance.[34]

Boundlessness was therefore 'represented' by the distance-measuring foreground horizon space because within the picture frame it provided the greatest sensation of distance. In this way the circle is symbolized by the line. Architecture, similarly representing geometrical principles of order, was most useful in representing depth in the picture frame, but only from a single viewpoint. Cole inveighed against the 'prevailing fashion of painting the walls and ceilings of churches in imitation of Architecture and Statuary',[35] simply because the illusion was lost if one moved about. In the *Course of Empire* different points of view could only be represented temporally and in sequence with a picture devoted to each occasion as part of a natural process of decline and fall.

Visual style and content are inseparably linked and it was this kind of linear theorizing that determined Cole's attitudes to civil and natural history in his series. Nor are these attitudes separable from the simultaneous cult of nature and ruins which Cole inherited. As early as 1807 the American natural historian, Benjamin Smith Barton, noted:

> Indeed, few are the writers of civil history who have not sullied their works, when they have had occasion to treat of, or touch upon, points of natural history. With great pleasure, however, do I mention, as an exception to this position, the vast work of Mr Gibbon on the *Decline and Fall of the Roman Empire*: a work from which even the student of natural history may collect many facts and much information; and this, too, so correctly and cautiously related, that I do not recollect a single instance in which the fidelity of Gibbon, as a *naturalist* can be called in question.[36]

Aside from factual details, the decline and fall of empire for Cole, as for Gibbon, was a natural event. According to the romantic sensibility of his biographer, Cole himself, consciously emulating Gibbon, conceived his work while seated in the twilight among the ruins of Rome. In Cole's series of pictures the past becomes the future, the end of a fore-ordained cycle. McLuhan speaks of the 'natural literary bias of all humanist ages in favour of ruins', and quoting Van Groningen on the Greeks, states; 'The idea of the past, discovered by means of the new visual chronology as an area of

---

[34] Noble, *The Course of Empire,* p. 282.
[35] MS. in Cole papers. Archives of American Art: RBC 759. 93 C67A2 Box 1.
[36] Benjamin Smith Barton, *A Discourse on some of the principal desiderata in Natural History . . ..* (Philadelphia 1807) p. 67.

peace in a distant perspective was, indeed, a novelty'.[37] It was no
novelty by Cole's time, however, and the very structure of his
Course of Empire is a visual chronology of history as natural process. The savage state is followed by the pastoral. The height of
empire with its exaggerated and architectural perspective pushes
lineality to grotesque proportions. It challenges the wrath of the
gods with its authoritative mathematical representation of the rules
of time and space. This moment of fruition is inevitably followed
by destruction, and the last act is peaceful ruin with civil and natural
history harmonized. Time (history) is conceived of as separable
units, representative moments, following each other as points in an
eternal cycle. Space (nature), on the other hand, is as immutable
as the continuous passage of time itself. This quality is emphasized
by the continually shifting point of view which depicts the same
fixed space from a different angle. The only way out of this space
is through the vanishing point where the parallel lines meet in
infinity. This irrational, autocratic view of space articulates a vision
of society as tragically doomed. As we have seen ironically, in *The
Crater*, the social consequences are total annihilation. In iconographic terms, Cole took Cooper's concerns even further. Men are
dwarfed by nature and architecture and in the last scene the artist
insisted that there must be no men at all:

> THE FIFTH must be a sunset, — the mountain river — the city a desolate
> ruin — columns standing isolated and encroaching waters — ruined temples,
> broken bridges, fountains, sarcophagi, &c. — no human figure — a
> solitary bird perhaps: a calm and silent effect. This picture must be as a
> funeral knell of departed greatness, and may be called the state of
> desolation.[38]

Only ruins survive. In notes he made in Naples in 1832, Cole reflected that the Colosseum looked 'more like a work of nature than
man'.[39] In Cole's series, architecture develops as man establishes
civilization by possessing the earth. His property, built according to
eternal principles, becomes the incarnate soul which survives him.
In this last picture pl. 63 the huge ivy-clad column in the foreground, representative of civilization, stands like an Edgar or
Fortinbras among the wreckage of history. On the horizon at the
vanishing point it is echoed by another. Here earth, air and water
meet at the exact centre of the picture. Both point to the rock of
ages, the timeless peak which has appeared in all five pictures. The

[37] Marshall McLuhan, *The Gutenberg Galaxy* (London 1962) p. 58.
[38] Noble, *The Course of Empire*, p. 176.
[39] Ibid., p. 160.

63 *Course of Empire: Desolation* by Thomas Cole. (*Courtesy of the New York Historical Society, New York City.*)

ruined architectural erection is a mirror of a more eternal natural truth. When making proposals for the Washington Monument, Cole objected to a column because it was only an 'architectural member, and not a complete whole'.[40] It is, however, just such an 'architectural member' which is the hero of this last scene. The unnatural intercourse of history and nature is an eternal cohabitation between 'the architectural member' (the human race symbolized by the single function of power-seeking) and space itself. In the series Cole progressively reduces the earth in his picture in favour of space. The last scene has more sky than in any other picture of the series. By this means Cole progressively makes time into eternity and space into infinity. Space and time so considered produced a cyclical view of history which seemed to represent reality itself. The message of inevitable decline and fall consequent upon empire is the moral of Cole's *Course of Empire*.

Even with more traditional subjects, Cole's landscapes articulate that puritannical fear of nature which turns actuality into threatening dream. In the *Expulsion from the Garden of Eden* (1827–8) Cole **pl**. 64 gives us the by now familiar death-like eroticism of the double landscape of war and peace. The picture is dominated by a massive cleft rock on the boundary separating a sunlit garden from

[40] Ibid., p. 207.

64 *Expulsion from the Garden of Eden* by Thomas Cole. (*Courtesy of the Boston Museum of Fine Art.*)

a gulf and a barren wilderness. The figures of Adam and Eve are tiny in the enormous context of space articulated by the overwhelming male–female rock guarding the pleasure garden. It is a psychological study of the myth of the Fall seen through the gothic landscape of American wilderness fears. The more one examines this side of Cole's work, the more it becomes clear that a continual meditation on death is an important aspect of his work. As a young engraver Cole made illustrations for Bunyan's *Holy War* and in many ways his dream landscapes are close to the sociopsychological landscapes of Bunyan's more famous work, *The Pilgrim's Progress*. As for other writers and painters of Cole's time, scenes from the Bible, Shakespeare, Milton and Bunyan were used as archetypes of emotional life. One of Cole's short stories provides a kind of parallel text to these kinds of paintings. It is called *The Bewilderment* and in some respects runs close to the tradition begun in Brockden Brown and so brilliantly exploited by Nathaniel Hawthorne. The narrator of the story climbs a steep and tangled path up a mountain (the Hill Difficulty) from the top of which he experiences a 'glorious prospect'[41] (like Christian's view of the Delectable Mountains). He

---

[41] Ibid., p. 71ff, for subsequent quotations.

then plunges into a cavern, 'dark as Egypt' where he experiences a symbolic valley of the shadow of death. Falling into water he struggles in the interior of the cave against a wet solid wall: 'A kind of sickness seized me, the sickness of despair'. Finally, like Bartram's fish, he is reborn through an outlet at the edge of a waterfall.[42] The whole process outlines the psychological reality of the self, individualistically conceived as a figure in a landscape. Climbing the mountain creates the character of the hero where the whole body is symbolically genitalized as a monument with glorious prospects. But the phallicization of the body makes space into a woman which threatens to swallow him up. In American terms the dream of the New World, achieved through puritanical self-polishing, is a dream of death, or what amounts to the same thing, an endless cycle of life and death which repressively governs the nature of reality.

A recent critic has remarked that the *Course of Empire* was well received by the American public, but that when it came to hanging pictures in their own homes, Americans wanted more 'American' scenes.[43] The American public instinct was undoubtedly correct, and even in Cole's work there are many indications of a dissatisfaction with landscape restricted by the linear rigidities of the single viewpoint. Cole's magnificent painting, *The Oxbow* (1836) pl. 65 for the first time has a number of vanishing points and inaugurates a tradition in formal painting which breaks down the single viewpoint in a very American manner. The elements of European archetype are still there in the contrasting landscape with its Salvator Rosa-like foreground and Claude-inspired pastoral landscape. This pastoral scene is not placed, however, at a distance, but at an apparently great depth below the foreground, emphasized by the clever placing of the artist's parasol in the foreground. Hunting the details over the picture space unable to get a single view of the whole, one at last realizes some of the qualities of boundlessness and infinite variety achieved by the early panoramas and dioramas. The organization is derived from the topography of the country but there are elements of exaggeration in treatment which are common to the whole of the Hudson River School, and which make nonsense of the critics' claims of 'realism'. There is a persistent sharpening of angles in mountains peaks, a vertical enlargement of distant mountains and an exaggerated downward direction of view.[44] Cole cer-

[42] Compare Samuel Johnson's *Rasselas* (1759) and Melville's *Typee* (1846).
[43] Barbara Novak, *American Painting of the Nineteenth Century* (London 1969) p. 69.
[44] Paul Shepherd, 'Paintings of the New England Landscape, A Scientist looks at their Geomorphology', *College Art Journal*, XVI–XVII (1956–8) pp. 30–42.

65 *The Oxbow* (The Connecticut River near Northampton), 1846, By Thomas Cole, (*Courtesy of the Metropolitan Museum of Art, New York, Gift of Mrs Russell Sage, 1908.*)

tainly emphasizes the dramatic curve of the stream which is expanded and rounded by the downward view. The two parts of the picture are also painted differently. The foreground with its reddish-brown tree stumps and minutely articulated detail of leaf and branches has a strangely luminous quality. On close inspection one can see that each leaf is painted green and enlivened by the occasional touches of pure red and pure white. This richness is offset by the flatly painted thin colours of the pastoral section. Wilderness and agriculture are again the literary subject, with the river itself a kind of dividing line. To the right, the savage thickness is reduced almost to the texture of watercolour and one recollects how Cole's friend, Durand, had admired English watercolours on his trip to Europe as giving great truth to nature. In the pastoral section every object is quite distinct, almost without chiaroscuro. In the bottom right-hand corner, a boat no more than an inch long, with its polesmen nonetheless quite distinct, crosses the ford. Above the ford sheep straggle down to the river, and higher round the bend there are several sailing boats. Below the artist's deserted seat, and over the river a line of birds flap lazily over the water in sharp contrast to those higher up to the left wheeling in fear of the storm.

Thus the picture encompasses those elements of dream landscape already extant in the American tradition while moving towards multiplication of viewpoint and vanishing point and towards equalizing light intensities in place of more conventional chiaroscuro. Stemming almost from the two halves of Cole's picture we find paintings still willing to exploit the grandiose conjunction of nature and history, and paintings loosely defined in the jargon of the art historians as belonging to the 'luminous' tradition. Both styles are uniquely American. The latter which has received much recent discussion is not particularly more realistic or 'objective' than other contemporary styles.[45] As in Mount's and Bingham's pictures light is equally distributed throughout the picture, aerial perspective is on the whole abandoned, but unlike the Impressionist revolution, a line is still retained round the objects and details of the composition, retaining them in their own space. As in Audubon one has a strange sense of contesting dimensions, a movement towards the relationship of objects rather than perspective, and a feeling for the luminosity of colour because it contains its own light value regardless of the requirements of chiaroscuro.

In the work of Cole's pupil, Frederick Church, (1826–1900) the formal landscape tradition of the first half of the century comes to a climax. Church was additionally influenced by Humboldt's instructions to make landscape painting more scientific. Humboldt had condemned the vapid extravagances of literary landscape description and the shoddy engravings in the current landscape albums. He also singled out the importance of panorama and photograph as aids to the prospective artist. Field-work became as important for the artist as for the geologist, botanist, or ornithologist. Indeed the more scientific knowledge an artist could muster, it was argued, the greater his landscapes would be.[46] Nonetheless it was only the process of organization which this scientific advice could affect. The moments of choice after the evidence has been gathered, and crucial to the artist, were ignored by Humboldt. Like Humboldt, Church became an explorer himself and yet his journeys seem dictated by other than scientific needs alone. The scientific rationale seems to provide the occasion for authenticating more dream-like impulses. Church went north to Labrador and south to Equador, between extremes of heat and cold, as if the wanderer-artist were charting the limits of human sensation and possibility. In Labrador,

---

[45] See Novak, *American Painting of the Nineteenth Century.*
[46] The chief figure here is Alexander von Humboldt. See Albert Ten Eyck Gardner, 'Scientific Sources of the Full-Length Landscape: 1850', *Metropolitan Museum of Art Bulletin,* IV (July 1945–June 1946) pp. 59–65.

for example, he consistently risked his life attempting to sketch icebergs, only to generalize the details of the work in his studio. The plates reproduced in *After Icebergs with a Painter* (1861)[47] show eerie, luminous green-white icebergs, with sharpened crags and angles, worthy of the early stanzas of *The Ancient Mariner.* In the narrative the danger is emphasized as if there is a continuous sense of trespass in the unpredictable secret areas of nature itself. As in *Moby Dick* the quest for knowledge and power carries its own dangers. Scientific authority barely counterbalances religious taboo. These natural ice rocks become images of the dream no less than Bodmer's geological engravings of the Mississippi bluffs, or Roetter's Giant Cactus of the Gila.

In *The Heart of the Andes* (1859), **pl.** 66 Cole's influence is clear. Again we have a double landscape with the line going from

66 *The Heart of the Andes* by Frederick Edwin Church. (*Courtesy of the Metropolitan Museum of Art, Bequest of Mrs David Dows, 1909.*)

bottom left to top right. Above the line is a short plain and mountains in thinly painted reds and blues and beyond these to the top left are snow-capped peaks whose whiteness finds an echo in the falls and the river. The extremes of heat and cold are present in the same picture. In contrast to strange hallucinatory lights of the mountains and sky, the right foreground is painted thickly with every streak of tulip numbered. The parakeet, for example, in the lower left hand corner might have been done by Audubon. It is

[47] Louis Legrand Noble, *After Icebergs with a painter in a summer voyage to Labrador and around Newfoundland* (New York 1861).

painted flatly with almost every tail-feather picked out. Not four
inches away one can observe black spots on the wings of two butterflies. In the bottom right hand corner are brilliant red flowers with
every vein minutely observed and a weaver bird's nest is plainly
visible. The human centre is between the mountains and the forest;
a kind of minute genre scene in mid-Victorian sentimental tradition
with Spanish Indian figures kneeling before a cross entwined with
roses scarcely bigger than pin heads. The reduction in size of the
human figures grotesquely emphasizes the overwhelming natural
landscape. Hung as the picture is at present[48] one can have little
idea of its full nineteenth-century significance. At that time, it was
exhibited in a darkened room, hung round with dried Ecuadorian
foliage and illuminated by gas jets. Since, for the audience, there
could be no dioramic effects of light through material, and no
panoramic effects of continuous space, Church found other solu-
tions. He exploited to the maximum the shifting vanishing points,
the 'photographic' details where the effect of inclusion rather than
selection keeps the spectator's eye restlessly moving over the picture space. For the viewer the total sensation derived from many
sources: the reworking of the ancient psychological characterization
of the earth as a body inherent in the literary title; the 'religious'
feeling of impotence in total space; the recognition through its
scientific claims of an exclusive and erudite reality; the pleasure of
the Cook's tour; the allegory of life represented in earth, mountain
and river; a sense of virgin wilderness; a feeling of nature as at once
eternal in general terms and transient in the particular; and above all
a feeling of participation, for in the dispersal of effects and single
viewpoint the viewer could make his own selection of the details
of his experience.

Outside the more formal tradition of landscape art, Americans
took up the audience-oriented, machine-aided representations of
landscape developed in Europe in the panorama and diorama. But
again Americans developed their own synthesis of effects. It was
aided partly, as Wolfgang Born has pointed out, by the new sensation of space created by the railway journey. Here the viewer is
stationary in front of the picture frame, but the frame itself,
rapidly moving, imparts motion to the landscape. In his own essay
on landscape, James Fenimore Cooper, contrasting the view from a
carriage moving at a leisurely pace through the old highways with
the view from a rapidly moving train along a straight line, remarked
that, in the latter, the landscape is like a 'picture placed in a false

[48] In the Metropolitan Museum of Art, New York.

light'.[49] Cooper's awareness of an utterly different sensation of
space cannot be overestimated in cultural terms. Hitherto the
feeling of landscape had been determined by a relatively static viewpoint, by movement adapted to human, or at most horse movement,
by roads adapted to the shape of the landscape, and by the human
intercourse of life established in villages also related by necessity
and convenience to the landscape. Now in the company of strangers
the landscape hurtled by at different speeds according to near or
far view, points were connected more theoretically by lines in a
more abstract space, as every place became, at least potentially,
accessible. The train was like a *camera obscura* maintaining a fixed
rectilinear frame and single viewpoint but portable along a theoretical geometric line drawn by surveyors. The scene outside was
amenable only to the sense of vision, barren of human intercourse,
of smell and touch. The same view was also infinitely repeatable
according to the base line of the railway line itself, giving a sense
of an invariable reality. The landscape so observed became a characteristic landscape according to the line, once imaginatively surveyed
according to railroad usage, which was now a corporate social viewpoint. By the same illusion which gives a traveller a sense of movement if his stationary train is passed by another moving one, the
new popular panorama, developed most successfully in America,
captured the experience of the railroad journey. Retaining the
frame of the proscenium arch and by using a painting slowly
moving by, wound on huge rollers, the entrepreneurs of this new
art form could suggest infinity expressed, not as by Cole from foreground to background, but horizontally. At the same time the
picture frame gave an older sense of reality. Even this, however,
possibly influenced by the arbitrary framing device of the camera
eye in which natural features refused to accommodate themselves
to an inclusive stage set, was challenged as objects moved endlessly
in and out of the viewpoint. By the late 1840s the technique of the
moving panorama had been perfected, and the race to see who
could have the biggest, longest and best space experience was on.

Some of the best panoramas were made in the mid-West, in St
Louis where the mechanization of viewpoint was achieved not by
the railway but by the steamboat moving along the Mississippi.
Some of the subjects of this new form are as ancient as de Loutherbourg's first panoramas.

John Barnvard, one of the most famous of the Mississippi
panoramic artists, exhibited in St Louis a 'new and terribly terrific

---

[49] James Fenimore Cooper, in *A Landscape Book* (New York 1868) p. 17.

spectacle of the INFERNAL REGIONS'.[50] Wimar's teacher, Pomerede, was praised by the St Louis *Reveille* for an Americanization of Miltonic iconography with scenes of St Louis in ruins and flames and of the prairie on fire. As with newspapers, the selection of material is according to deepest sociopsychological needs. The alternative landscapes of war and peace, charted by Leonardo as a result of the new conjunction of perspective and the study of the behaviour of light, reach a new form in the panoramas of the 1840s and were to be further developed in the Hollywood movie. The St Louis *Reveille* critic remarked that the panorama was presented in a proscenium arch *En style de la Renaissance.* Barnvard himself 'scientifically' hunted Mississippi scenery on the trail, collecting with enthusiasm his visual data like Catlin after Indians. As with Catlin there was also an elegiac quality in his summary of the effects. For perspective, like printing, seemed able to record in perpetuity a fast-fading reality. Printed to accompany the panorama was a booklet, *Barnvard's Geographical Panorama of the Mississippi River, with the Story of Mike Fink, the Last of the Boatmen, a Tale of River Life.* In the three mile roll was synthesized the total experience of the West. Here were landscapes of terror and peace, of Indian encampments, buffalo, war dances and even a grotesque geological formation called significantly, for our discussion of American landscape, *The City of the Dead.* Longfellow admired this panorama and it certainly rivalled *Hiawatha* for its pre-Hollywood fantasies. When Barnvard exhibited it in London, a reporter from the *Illustrated London News* described Barnvard relieving his 'narratives with Jonathanisms and jokes, poetry and patter, which delight his audience mightily; and a piano-forte is incidently invoked to relieve the narrative monotony'.[51] Like the early silent films it was shown in darkness, gas-lit and framed with a proscenium arch.

One description of a panorama scene captures that apocalyptic sense of disaster secularized from the Puritan inheritance of Milton and Bunyan:

> . . . as far back as the eye can reach, the prairie presents a sheet of living flames, leaving but a small unburnt space near the edge of the encampment. Here affrighted horses and buffalo are madly leaping over to certain destruction, wildly accoutred Indians standing on the edge of the chasm, with desparing [sic] countenances, are awaiting the

[50] J. F. McDermott, *The Lost Panoramas of the Mississippi* (Chicago 1958) p. 22. I am much indebted to this book for much of the subsequent discussion on panoramas.
[51] *Illustrated London News* (9 December 1848).

approaching doom, and, women with children pressed to their bosoms, are running distractedly to and fro.[52]

The vision of war in nature and society articulates the other side of the reality of the exploitation of nature and indigenous peoples. The mechanical panorama went further than its European predecessors in the sense that the movement of space could represent the passing of time. But space and time thus represented in terms of each other pointed to vision of both as uniform and continuous. The result was to push the process begun in America by Lewis and Clarke with their surveying instruments to new levels. For the experience of the West, and of the American landscape itself, became even more a dream reality, which is what the representational vision of perspective and theatre must reveal. More and more the American landscape became a vision articulated for the urban dweller, a Disneyland of the natural sciences.

The urban dweller himself was confronted with a landscape, however, which had little obvious precedent in history, although the city itself, as an externalized landscape of human intercourse reaches back into prehistory.[53] We have an excellent record of the way New York was visualized by its inhabitants from earliest times to the twentieth century in Kouvenhoven's imaginative and scholarly work, *The Columbia Historical Portrait of New York.*[54] Here we can trace the development of the way the urban landscape was visualized between the Revolution and the Civil War. It is possible to follow closely the development of the so-called urban crisis and the results of technological development structured by the insane cruelties of early industrial finance capitalism. For here is a landscape without a historic past where all changes are determined by profit making and where human functions gradually come to be dominated by the business of money. Unlike the natural landscape the city is to a large extent a humanly created fantasy area of the total activities of the society. New York's own landscape is fortunately, however, very much enlivened by natural features; the variation in height of Manhattan itself and the rivers and seas which surround it.

Some of the first views in the eighteenth century were made by British officers who had inherited that double tradition of mapmaking and perspective view, which as we have seen, belongs to

---

[52] McDermott, *The Lost Panoramas of the Mississippi*, p. 154.

[53] See Lewis Mumford, *The City in History* (1961; reprinted London 1966).

[54] John A. Kouwenhoven, *The Columbia Historical Portrait of New York: An Essay in Graphic History* (1953; reprinted New York 1972). The comments here build very much on Kouwenhoven's brilliant analysis.

military training. The simplified bird's-eye view of the one complemented the other where the city is visualized as a distant prospect
from a country seat. The rural foreground even at this early stage
was the point of view of those who held power. From the beginning
the rich moved out. Topographically this sociocultural view was
aided, as it still is, by views of the city across water. Close-up views
employed more of a rigorous theatrical perspective with the stage
being set at streetcorners so that the streets themselves could move
back at angles like the corridors in Palladio's original theatre. The
point of view is nearly always opposite the vanishing point which
makes the immediate foreground below eye-level. It is, in short,
the view from the Royal Box. Before 1800 this type of picture
showed the new civic institutions, generally without human figures,
of botanical garden, public theatre, church and state prison. The
civic abstractions of the revolutionary period, however, slowly give
way to an interest in people engaged in trade. In such pictures,
where traditional perspective is adhered to, there is a tendency to
push the buildings to the vertical sides of the picture frame, thus
widening the traditional sloping stage to accommodate more figures.
With the completion of the Erie canal in 1825, which confirmed
the primacy of New York as the nation's trading capital, the emphasis of the illustrators is placed more and more on business needs.
Older perspective scenes are reserved for depicting country homes,
or the quiet residential districts as if the older form articulated a
dream of leisure which drew on already fast-disappearing mores.
Two dimensional elevations of street scenes become more popular
with shops and warehouses stretching horizontally across the picture
frame. Here the purpose is simply to create space for advertising.
The shops narrowly crowd each other for access to the street line
and their owners' names and wares are written boldly over their
establishments, easy to read in the head-on view. Mumford has
shown how such a development is typical of the nineteenth-
century city.[55] Speculation in property prices was directly related
to the grids drawn up by the surveyors representing possible future
developments. The squared-out cities of America directly articulate
the political philosophy of financial gambling, of speculation according to the abstract reality of geometry and of action in the cause of
future needs (in fact of present profit) sanctioned by the ethic of
endless growth. In this way landscape and city-scape give way to
more descriptive terms like 'real estate' and 'vacant lot', the latter

[55] Mumford, *The City in History*, see especially chapter 14, section 4, 'The Speculative
Ground Plan'.

term summing up the whole philosophy in its multiple punning
meanings. The street becomes adapted neither to the contours of
the landscape nor to human needs but becomes a symbol of real
estate fortunes. The dizzy rise in property prices forced those who
could not afford to move out into ever smaller and more disgrace-
ful slums and emptied the urban centre of anything but commercial
value. A new form of human landscape appeared in the shape of
huge hotels symbolizing the progressive division of living from live-
lihood and of work from pleasure. The rented room, the all-male
conference and the business all-male week-end are new phenomena
where the male of the species could find some relief from the boredom of wife and family at the price of secrecy and guilt. The hotels
were not the only establishments of the new home-and-business
synthesis. The shops, the restaurants, the barber saloons and the
taverns take on lavish interior decorations only aspired to previously
in the home.

In the 1840s views of the city diverge in two complementary
directions. On the one hand the point of view gets closer to individual people and on the other there is a striking development of
panoramas which show the whole city imagined from an increasingly aerial perspective. As the city got bigger the sense of the
individual and small groups could only be retained by a close-up
view. Perhaps influenced by the development of photography,
genre-like scenes appear but are framed by a window, a drawing
room, a street corner or even no background at all. Inside an
increasingly alien environment the values of the village re-emerge.
New York remains the supreme example of multiple ways of life
whose boundaries are as sharp as the edges of the grid itself. Eisenstein's brilliant essay on 'Dickens, Griffith and the film today'
shows how Dickens' use of the 'close-up' relates to the provincialism
of the city dweller.[56] Both relate to the need to carve out a human-
sized environment inside a totality which can only be understood in
terms of map or panorama. City types begin to appear like characters
in a Dickens' novel; newsboy, banjo player and above all street
seller. But the desire to typify character according to role, an impulse at least as old as the medieval drama or even Plautus, in fact
gives way to the photographic portrait where the face is all, and to a
desire inherent in an essentially commercial world, to depict people
at leisure and not at work. In a business society the hero is a man of
leisure. Most frequently the pictures still show the people away

---

[56] Sergei Eisenstein, *Film Form: Essays in Film Theory*, ed. and trans. Jay Leyda (New
York 1949) pp. 195–255.

from their work, on parades, skating, in the drawing room, attending lectures and above all reading the newspaper. The man reading the newspaper shows the individual or a small group relating mentally to the dynamics of the whole society presented in the asyndetic, paratactic form of unrelated news over a large space, an analogue of the city itself.

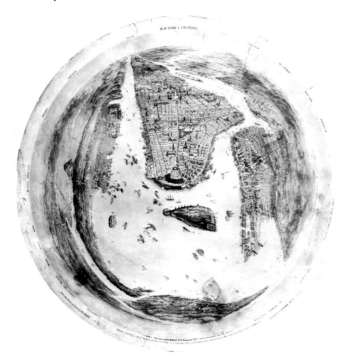

67 *New York and Environs,* lithography by John Bachman. (*Courtesy of the New York Public Library.*)

At the same time an older pictorial view of the whole society could only be achieved by the panorama. Even more important than the conventional European panorama was the attempt to fit the panorama experience into a picture frame. pl. 67 The result was a peculiarly American synthesis of map embodying three dimensional perspective. The separate visualizations of landscape as map and perspective view come together. The feeling of power and grandeur evoked by these scenes parallels that delight in searching out details which we have already seen to be one of the most striking effects of the pictures of Cole and Church. The view, however, was literally inaccessible from the ground, and the imaginative shock must have been similar to today's pictures of the earth from space. In an important sense it is a spatial point of view developed from the rural seat to the city. It is individualistic, representative and achieved with sophisticated technology at immense human cost. The fantasies of power embodied in the experience continue in the architect's aerial photographs of the conspicuously-consuming skyscrapers which house the great companies and financial aristocrats of contemporary America. Perspective scenes from ground level show the richer neighbourhoods where the wealthy buy up the modes of living of previous civilizations and its cultural artefacts.

But the hunger of literate Americans for print and news, the randomly selective view of the camera, which deeply influenced newspaper illustration, and the close-up view of hitherto unrealizable subjects like bloodstains on a slum wall, began to turn public attention towards the city's problems. There were huge slum areas where the immigrant labourers lived who were providing the manual power for the realization of the abstract grids of the property developers. For the majority of Americans, however, then as now, such problems were not a matter for very serious attention. The American dream was never an urban one — in direct contradiction to an increasing movement toward urban centres. The American's relation to his landscape was peculiar to himself. The synthesis of country and town was finally made in the *suburb*. By the Civil War, indeed by the fifties, its philosophy was entirely developed and its practice increasing.

In the best-selling works of the forties and fifties on 'villas' and 'cottages' we can best observe the new phenomenon. These works were accompanied by groundplans and perspective views of suburban houses. Two-dimensional elevations of facades were considered necessary only to the practical men who built the houses. Elevations reminded the observer rather too much of business life and the flat, head-on views of hotels and shops. These works are in effect real estate brochures as well as attempts to elevate 'taste'. Artistic effect, the twin result of cultural fantasy and practical selling, required the traditional dream visuality of perspective:

> but if the study is submitted with a view to show what sort of artistic effect may be produced, in execution, from a certain arrangement of ground plan, nothing but a perspective view will convey an accurate idea to the mind; and as the intention in this volume has been to give suggestions, rather than to supply cut-and-dried designs, the perspective mode of illustration has been adhered to as much as possible.[57]

[57] Calvert Vaux, *Villas and Cottages: A series of designs prepared for execution in the United States* (New York 1857) p. 184.

The box-like interior landscape was to be lighted by windows on not more than two sides of a room. So on the one hand the single viewpoint of the perspective view articulated the exterior effects, and inside the sense of light strove for the illumination of the proscenium arched stage.

In a book published in 1853, Andrew Downing, absorbing the increasing transatlantic influence of Ruskin, wrote down the philosophy of the American home and its many styles. 'Domestic architecture' was felt to be a uniquely American style, avoiding on the one hand the pretensions of aristocrats and on the other the exigencies of the poor. Inheriting an out-moded aesthetic vocabulary which belonged more to eighteenth-century theorists from de Piles to Mengs, Downing applies terms like beauty, symmetry, proportion, order and variety with a peculiar American twist:

> With the perception of proportion, symmetry, order and beauty awakens the desire for possession, and with them comes that refinement of manners which distinguishes a civilized from a coarse and brutal people.[58]

Gone are the abstract theories of civilization which characterized a Jefferson or a Volney. Gone is the necessity of cultivating the earth for eligibility to citizenship. What is salvaged is a sentimental image of country life viewed from the city and a concept of the basis of human society as a family, in which the father works in the city, and the women and children live in the country:

> It is the solitude and freedom of the family home in the country which constantly preserves the purity of the nation, and invigorates its intellectual powers. The battle of life, carried on in cities, gives a sharper edge to the weapon of character, but its temper is, for the most part, fixed amid those communings with nature and the family, where individuality takes its most natural and strongest development.[59]

Here in a nutshell are the half-truths of the American attitudes to land and society. Business and pleasure occupy the complementary landscapes of city and country. The half understood Romantic notion that solitude equals freedom guarantees the individualistically based 'purity' of the nation. The city is conceived as a battleground for men where, in a revealing image, the 'weapon of character' is formed. The metaphor of the tempering of the sword encompasses an ancient association of women with water and men with

---

[58] A. J. Downing, *The Architecture of Country Houses; . . .* (New York 1853) preface.
[59] Ibid.

fire. Morality is a woman's role as the most despised and hence most ignorable member of the human community. The family is visualized as a landscape of peace, an uninvolved compensatory context for the male embattled without. Here 'morality' can reign unfettered and unchallenged by either reality or social consequences:

> And much of that feverish unrest and want of balance between the desire and the fulfilment of life, is calmed and adjusted by the pursuit of tastes which result in making a little world of the family home, where truthfulness, beauty and order have the largest dominion.[60]

The point of view is strictly masculine. The home acts as refuge from external realities where women and children act as a cross between therapists and holiday camp directors. Quite apart from the literal psychic investment of energy in property, the home becomes for its owner a memory icon fixating the social and moral development of its members to the past. The contemplation of childhood is an inducement to purity:

> All to which the heart can attach itself in youth, and the memory linger fondly over in riper years, contributes largely to our stock of happiness, and to the elevation of the moral character. For this reason, the condition of the family home — in this country where every man may have a home — should be raised, till it shall symbolize the best character and pursuits, and the dearest affections and enjoyments of social life.[61]

When he turns to the details of the homes he proposes for his customers, Downing, in a traditional American manner, reviews the social and architectural history of the past before attempting to make his own synthesis. The Gothic embodies Christian love, the Roman the idea of state, and the Greek the concept of rationality. Since these are permanent realities, the American is not to ignore them necessarily, but to select from them what he thinks appropriate to his domestic life. In general terms the arguments frequently contradict themselves. Downing is rightly praised for his insistence on truth to materials, on the adaptation of building to microclimate and location, and for his directive that ornament should express structure wherever possible. Many statements are abstract enough to anticipate, without too much decontextualization, the 'organic' theories of Frank Lloyd Wright. Nonetheless many assertions reflect the ambiguities of the social situation. Beauty is different from utility because to deny that would be to deny the

---

[60] Ibid.
[61] Ibid., p. 22.

separation of business and pleasure interests conceived as part of
normal life. And yet anything which does not reflect its function is
superfluous. The way was open either to conspicuous consumption
or to a more radical expression of structure. Downing accents simplicity for the working man where indeed structure follows function,
but the 'Laborer's Cottage' looked at in conjunction with the last
design in the work, a 'Southern Villa Romanesque Style', where
Downing admits that he has no knowledge of Southern materials
for building, indicates that the former design is paternalist, even
aristocratic, in its definition of the appropriate. This final design in
the text is explained not in terms of function but in terms of the
generalized vocabulary of the eighteenth-century art critic.

Domestic architecture was the landscape of the whole private
life of man. Sometimes the European models, or what were thought
to be European models, could be easily adapted to American needs.
Steep 'gothic' roofs were good for heavy snow storms, the flat
'Italian villa' roofs, with the aid of American 'brackets' could easily
be adapted to the wooden boxlike structure of the basic American
design. The American climate forced modifications. Verandas,
piazzas, bay-windows and balconies were felt to be American necessities in view of the hot summer weather. Perhaps in these features
we can find a longing to escape the confines of the home, for they
all serve as communication with the outside world. Downing also
denuded his 'cottages' of European class association in order to
make them more suitable for the democratic American:

> The majority of such cottages in this country are occupied, not by
> tenants, dependants, or serfs, as in many parts of Europe, but by
> industrious and intelligent mechanics and working men, the bone and
> sinew of the land, who own the ground on which they stand, build them
> for their own use, and arrange them to satisfy their own peculiar wants
> and gratify their own tastes.[62]

Nonetheless Downing's division of styles into cottage, farm house,
and villa preserves the divisions in the society as strongly as any
European model. There is no talk of an architecture appropriate
to a society constantly shifting its boundaries. He speaks of the
different levels of architectural need with as much confidence as if
such divisions were natural to the society as a whole.

Downing is similarly ambiguous about materials and modes of
construction. Stone is the best material because it reflects ideals of
permanence and stability which add 'to its effects upon the reason,

---

[62] Ibid., p. 40.

though the effect upon the feelings may otherwise be equal'.[63]
Nonetheless, as Downing well knew, the material and the craftsmen
able to work suitable stone were rare in America and in any case,
using stone was pointless where wood was cheap and abundant. On
the whole, however, there is a commonsense view of materials
which should, he argued, be drawn from the character of the
country. At the same time, the vertical wooden weather boarding
(whose verticality was supposed to reflect heavenward gothic aspirations) was, in spite of philosophy, the result of mass-production
methods. Anticipating Gropius in a different medium, mass-
produced parts were turned out for American housing in the form
of steam-planed boards and grooved planks. In spite of the insistence
on 'variety' nearly every house in Downing's work is built up from
the basic concept of the box. Most materials also came from the
city. Ventilators, stoves, chimney ejectors, flue cylinders, water-
heating equipment, metal gutters, chimney tops, not to mention all
interior fittings were mass-produced by growing urban industries
and bought in the big new stores.

This applied equally to the cottage, farm house and villa. The
farm house occupied a kind of middle way. Here were to be found
the broad, honest, independent values of rural life. Anticipating
Frank Lloyd Wright, Downing argues that country places of this
kind should lie close to the earth and give a broad sense of space.
Paintwork should harmonize with the landscape. The European
visitor to New England is astonished by the assortment of grey-
browns, grey-yellows, grey-purples in which historic and modern
houses are painted. This most American sensation, however, had
European origins. Although writers state that white (the colour
nonetheless of the majority of houses) is too glaring in the New
England light, the condemnation comes from their reading of
Wordsworth, Uvedale Price and Sir Joshua Reynolds who disliked
white in a natural landscape. Reynolds advocated turning over
stones, or looking at the earth on the roots of grass to find 'correct'
colour for buildings. The painter's colours approximating the
colours of the earth decorated the farmer's property as legitimately
as his labour mixed with the earth gave him a political character.

With interior landscapes, however, Downing abandons all pretence
to American innovation. He apologizes for trespassing on feminine
preserve and simply sketches out European models. Unfettered by
the natural features of landscape or climate, interiors become a
dream of the wealthy attempting to imitate past cultural achieve-

[63] Ibid., p. 49.

ment in Italian dining rooms, gothic drawing rooms, and Elizabethan libraries. The furniture is bought to match with the proviso that chasteness and simplicity must be observed in the country while more extravagance can be indulged in in the city. Downing is appalled at New York extravagance, where, even before the Civil War, from $5,000 to $10,000 are expended in furnishing a single apartment. With these cautions, Downing recommends Hennessy in Boston for cottage furniture, and Paul for French and Elizabethan furniture. In New York, especially for library and drawing room, he recommends Roux in Broadway. The woman's world of the interior reflects her passive role of consumption. Her house reflects a dream of historical grandeur where any culture could be bought like the alternative landscapes of a Hollywood epic. A typical interior for the aspiring suburbanite would include servants' quarters and back stairs. Few Americans wanted the kitchen nearer the dining room in spite of the 'servant problem'. In addition to drawing room, dining room and bedrooms, a library and boudoir were *de rigeur*. These two latter rooms reflected male and female needs, the first much larger than the second. In later books, however, it is noticeable that the library serves purposes other than reading, as the Jeffersonian dream of the literate scientist at the centre of his universe recedes from money-making practice.

Downing's partner and successor, Calvert Vaux, pushed these trends further. By the time his *Villas and Cottages* appeared in 1857, the craze for the out-of-town-house and suburban houses was well under way. Vaux's book, however, was devoted to wealthy clients who were setting up country-style homes in the area of Newburg on the Hudson. In his obituary for Downing, who was blown up in the *Henry Clay* disaster of 1852, Vaux characterizes him as a pioneer against puritan attitudes in art. Vaux continues the campaign and speaks hopefully of the development of republican arts and social progress; and of an increase of wealthy clients as immigrants pass through the melting pot. Many of those characteristics which cultural historians like to think of as distinctly American receive short shrift here. Anything but the most generalized of religious sentiments is condemned as inhibiting art, and puritan devotion to work and self-improvement is roundly criticized. The concept that fortunes should be made and lost in successive generations, to preserve the heroic qualities of initiative and self-reliance, which Vaux states has been

> . . . reiterated over and over again, and tends to encourage the very incorrect and crude notion that a man, to be worth anything, must

begin with nothing, and make his own way by dogged perseverence at one idea for twelve or fourteen hours a day, through a series of years.[64]

Vaux dreams of the sons of the wealthy becoming 'earnest labourers' for the common good.

Unlike Downing, Vaux does not distinguish the European styles of 'Gothic' or 'Italian' as basic models for his houses. All the architectural past is at the American architect's service and he makes an interesting analogy to illustrate the point:

> Webster and Clay were orators of originality, but their words were all old. Their stock in trade is common property in the form of a dictionary, and the boundary lines, over which neither ever ventured to pass, are fairly set forth in a good grammar. Any desire on their part to invent a brand new language would have been, of course, absurd, and any wish to produce a brand new style of building is, without doubt, an equally senseless chimera.[65]

The association of boundary and grammar only allows the architect to re-arrange pre-existing elements. Vaux admits more into his architectural dictionary than Downing (Moorish architecture, for example gives good ideas for verandas, and Chinese styles for trellises and balconies) but he leaves unity of effect to 'taste'. He gives far greater priority to detail and ornament and examples fill the earlier pages. The sense of reality in architecture lies in indestructible elements which the prospective builder must generalize for himself. Vaux repeats the orthodoxies of Downing in relation to unity, symmetry and variety but somehow with less conviction. Vaux's interest lies in detail and increasingly elaborate ornament. Doors, staircases, windows, balconies, and eaves become more intricate and flamboyant in design.

The result was a grotesque eclecticism in the service of conspicuous consumption. At best, however, the energy of the elaborations and the scale on which they were performed were truly American. There was a consistent effort to break up that surface monotony of the wooden box architecture of New England. It is in just this aspect of the work that the real achievement lies. When one looks at surviving examples, it seems to be an effect achieved almost unintentionally. Downing's and Vaux's examples in their perspective drawings show stone houses with the usual variation in depth possible in such representations. However, in such designs in painted wood, surface qualities come to the fore, and so, by default, the movement toward ornamentation gives, not the effect originally

[64] Vaux, *Villas and Cottages*, p. 24.
[65] Ibid., p. 31.

desired by the architect with stone models in mind, but a marvellous sense of surface pattern. The looped 'Gothic' verandas standing in front or flush with the wall, the elaborate balconies and window porches give one not a European sensation of depth but a distinctively American pattern of relationship over a large space. It is noticeable that though Vaux inveighs against the use of 'elevations' for overall views of the houses, he does use them for the details. It is as if the plain businesslike front-on view returns to emphasize surface patterns in spite of the fact that depth interest was supposed to be socially elevated. The very quality of wood gives even recessed arches and arcades a two-dimensional rather than a depth effect.

Slowly and surely Americans modified and recreated the European sense of vision in their own terms. Even where they thought they were being most faithful to European ideals the effects were unqiue and strange. For the academic literary critic and art historian the methods may seem unusual: the conjunction of pastoral and epic modes, the mingling of popular and academic styles, syntheses of painting and literature with scientific interests, the production of new viewpoints owing to technological developments in transport, the inventions of new mediums, and machines revolving miles of painted panoramas. But the negative effects of literal readings of the European inheritance cannot be ignored either. Cooper's paternalist, scientific figure creating his own landscape anticipates the nightmarish destruction of men and landscape inherent in the individualistic ethic. The division of town and country in class and moneyed terms means the destruction of the one and the exploitation of the other. The geometry of development creates the frigid landscape of suburban neurosis and urban neglect. The panoramic view gives credence to dreams of power while neglecting human needs. Nonetheless, already in this first period the divisive vision of single viewpoint perspective was under serious attack together with its implicit hierarchies built out of a philosophy of conflict.

In spite of growing conservatism, the greatest cultural achievements of this period questioned those complex assumptions about history and nature inherent in the 'dream of reason', socially, artistically and scientifically. As one comes to a fresh sense of the achievements of this period we may ask — what happened to the sheer variety of cultural effort of early nineteenth-century America in the years following the Civil War. The answer would need a study of the post-Civil War period, but the question is inevitable given the variety, energy and sense of iconoclastic synthesis which characterize so many of the early Republic's artistic performances.

List of Plates

Bibliography

This list comprises all works quoted or cited in the text.

Agricola, Gregorius, *De Re Metallica*. . . . , translated by Herbert Clark Hoover and Lou Henry Hoover (1556; reprinted New York 1950)

Allston, Washington, *Monaldi* (Boston 1841)

Ambrose, S. E., *Duty, Honor, Country; a history of West Point* (Baltimore 1966)

The American Journal of Photography and the Allied Arts and Sciences (New York)

Anon, *A Chapter on Sharking* (1836)

Anon, *Hunting a Devil Fish* (1836)

Anon, *A Midsummer Night's Watch* (1837)

Arendt, Hannah, *On Revolution* (New York 1963)

Arnold, S. G., *The Life of George Washington* (New York 1849)

Audubon, John James, *Audubon and his Journals*, ed. Maria Audubon (1897; reprinted New York 1960)

    The Birds of America (London 1827–38)

    Delineations of American Scenery and Character (New York 1926)

    The 1826 Journal of John James Audubon, transcribed with an introduction and notes by Alice Ford (Norman, Oklahoma 1967)

    Letters of John James Audubon (Boston 1930)

    Ornithological Biography (London 1831–5)

    The Viviparous Quadrupeds of North America (London 1845–8)

Bacon, Francis, *The Advancement of Learning* (1605f; reprinted London 1915)

Bailyn, Bernard, ed., *Pamphlets of the American Revolution, 1750–1776* (Cam., Mass. 1965)

Balzac, Honoré de, *Oeuvres complètes* (Paris 1926–56)

Bancroft, Aaron, *An Essay on the Life of George Washington* (Worcester, Mass. 1807)

Barclay, Robert, *An Apology for the True Christian Divinity* (London 1678)

Barker, Vergil, *American Painting* (New York 1950)

Barlow, Joel, *The Works of Joel Barlow*, eds. W. K. Bottkorf and A. L. Ford (Gainesville, Fla. 1970)

Barnard, Henry, *Armsmear: the home, the arm and armory of Samuel Colt* (New York 1866)

Barton, Benjamin Smith, *A discourse on some of the principle desiderata in Natural History* . . . . (Philadelphia 1807)

    The Elements of Botany etc (Philadelphia 1803)

Barton, William, *Memoirs of the Life of David Rittenhouse, LLD, FRS* (Philadelphia 1813)

Bartram, William, *Travels through North and South Carolina, Georgia, East and West Florida etc* (1791; reprinted New York 1955)

Bayle, Pierre, *Historical and Critical Dictionary* . . . . (1697; reprinted London 1710)

Beale, Thomas, *Natural History of the Sperm Whale* (New York 1835 and 1839)

Beaver, Joseph, *Whitman, Poet of Science* (New York 1951)

Bennet, Frederick Debell, *A Whaling Voyage round the Globe from the Year 1833 to 1836* (London 1840)

Berry, Robert Elton, *Yankee Stargazer* (New York 1941)

Bissell, Benjamin, *The American Indian in English Literature of the Eighteenth Century*

(New Haven, Conn. 1925)

Blackwoods Magazine (Edinburgh)

Bloch, E. Maurice, *George Caleb Bingham; the evolution of an artist* (Berkeley and Los Angeles 1967)

Bolles, A. S., *Industrial History of the United States* (1881; reprinted New York 1966)

Boorstin, Daniel, *The Americans: The Colonial Experience* (1958; reprinted London 1965)

Born, Wolfgang, *American Landscape Painting* (New Haven, Conn. 1948)

Bowditch, Nathaniel, *The New American Practical Navigator* (Newberryport, Mass. 1802)

Brinton, Daniel G., *The Myths of the New World* (New York 1868)

Brown, Charles Brockden, *Edgar Huntley* (1799; reprinted London 1831)

Brown, Norman O., *Love's Body* (New York 1966)

Brown, W. H., *The History of the First Locomotives in America* (New York 1874)

Browne, J. Ross, *Etchings of a Whaling Cruise. . . .* (New York 1846)

Browne, Sir Thomas, *Pseudodoxia Epidemica* (London 1646)

Bruce, James, *Travels to Discover the Sources of the Nile, etc* 5 vols (London 1790)

Bryan, W. A., *George Washington in American Literature* (New York 1952)

Buddemeier, Heinz, *Panorama, Diorama, Entstehung und Wirkung neuer Medien im 19. Jahrhundert* (Munich 1970)

Buffon, Jean Louis Le Clerk, Comte de, *Oeuvres complètes* (Paris 1749—1804)
   Oeuvres complètes (Paris 1853—9)

Burke, Edmund, *A Philosophical Enquiry into the Origin of our Ideas of the Sublime and the Beautiful* (1757) ed. J. F. Boulton (London 1958)

Burnet, John, *An Essay on the Evolution of the Eye with Reference to Painting* (London 1837)

Caldwell, C., *Character of General Washington* (Philadelphia 1801)

Callow, James T., *Kindred Spirits* (Chapel Hill, N. Carolina 1967)

Campbell, Thomas, *The Poetical Works of Thomas Campbell* (London 1887)

Canby, H. S., *Walt Whitman, an American* (Boston 1943)

Carver, Jonathan, *Travels through the Interior Parts of Northern America in the years 1766, 1767, and 1768 etc* (London 1778)

Catesby, Mark, *The Natural History of Carolina, Florida, and the Bahaman Islands etc, 2 vols* (London 1731—1743)

Catlin, George, *An Account of a Religious Ceremony, practiced by the Mandan tribes of Indians at the 'Feast of the Buffalos'. Being the suppressed chapter from Catlin's O-Kee-Pa* (London 1867)
   Catlin's Notes of Eight Years' Travel and Residence in Europe (London 1848)
   Letters and Notes on the Manners . . . of the North American Indians (Boston 1841)
   North American Indian Portfolio (London 1844)

Chambers Cyclopaedia: or, an Universal Dictionary of Arts and Sciences (London 1786)

Channing, William, 'Review of Scott's Life of Napoleon Bonaparte', *The Christian Examiner*, IV (Boston 1827)

Chaucer, Geoffrey, *Parlement of Foulys* in *The Complete Works of Geoffrey Chaucer*, ed. Robinson, F. N. (London 1957)

Cheever, Henry T., *The Whale and his Captors . . .* (New York 1849)

Cibber, Theophilus, *The Harlot's Progress etc* (London 1733)

City Art Museum of Saint Louis, *Charles Wimar, 1828—62, Painter of the Indian Frontier* (St Louis 1946)

Coggin, J., *Arms and Equipment of the Civil War* (New York 1962)

Cohen, I. Bernard, ed., *Benjamin Franklin's Experiments* (Cam., Mass. 1941)

Cohen, I. Bernard, *Franklin and Newton, an Inquiry into Speculative Newtonian Experimental Science and Franklin's Work in Electricity as an example thereof* (Philadelphia 1956)
   Some Early Tools of American Science (Cam., Mass. 1950)

Coleridge, Samuel Taylor, *Biographia Literaria* (London 1817)
   Poetical Works (London 1967)

Connelley, W. E., ed., *A Narrative of the Mission of the United Brethren among the Delaware and Mohegan Indians from its commencement in the year 1740 to the close of the year 1808* (Cleveland, Ohio 1907)

Cook, Captain James, *The Journals of Captain James Cooke*, ed. J. C. Beaglehole (Cambridge 1955)

Cooper, James Fenimore, *Afloat and Ashore* (1844; reprinted New York 1895—6)
   The Crater (1848; reprinted New York 1895—6)
   The Deerslayer (1841; reprinted New York 1895—6)
   History of the Navy of the United States (New York 1834)
   The Last of the Mohicans (1826; reprinted New York 1895—6)
   The Pathfinder (1840; reprinted New York 1895—6)
   The Prairie (1827; reprinted New York 1895—6)
   The Red Rover (1827; reprinted New York 1895—6)

Crèvecoeur, Hector St John de, *Letters from an American Farmer* (1782; reprinted London 1912)

Crockett, David, *The Autobiography of Davy Crockett* (Philadelphia 1834)

Crombie, A. C., ed., *Scientific Change: Historical studies in the intellectual, social and technological conditions for scientific discovery . . . etc* (London 1963)

Cunliffe, Marcus, *Soldiers and Civilians; the martial spirit in America 1775—1865* (Boston 1968)

Cuvier, Baron von, with Geoffroy-Saint-Hillaire, E., *De l'histoire naturelle des cétacés* (Paris 1836)

Dall, William Healy, *Spencer Fullerton Baird. A Biography* (Philadelphia and London 1915)

Davidson, Jr., Alexander, 'How Benson J. Lossing wrote his "Field Books" of the Revolution, the War of 1812 and the Civil War', *Papers of the Bibliographical Society of America*, **32** (1938) pp. 57—64

Desaguliers, J. T., *A Course of Experimental Philosophy*, 2 vols (London 1734—44)

Dibdin, Charles, 'Jack's Gratitude' in *The Songs of Charles Dibdin etc* (London 1842)

Dickens, Charles, *American Notes, Works* (London, 1874)

Downing, A. J., *The Architecture of Country Houses* (New York 1853)

Doyle, Joseph, B., *Frederick William Steuben and the American Revolution* (Steubenville, Ohio 1913)

Drake, S. G., *The Book of the Indians of North America* (Boston 1833)
   Tragedies of the Wilderness (Boston 1841)

Draper, B. P., 'American Indians — Barbizon Style — The Collaborative Paintings of Millet and Bodmer', *Antiques*, 44, no. 3 (Sept. 1943) pp. 108—10

Dunlap, William, *The History of the Arts of Design in the United States* (Boston 1918)
   Life of Charles Brockden Brown (Philadelphia 1815)

Eastburn, J. W. and Sands, R. C., *Yamoyden; a tale of the wars of King Philip . . . .* (New York 1820)

Eastman, Mrs Mary, *The American Aboriginal Portfolio* (Philadelphia 1853)
   Aunt Phillis's Cabin, or Southern Life as it is (Philadelphia 1852)
   Dahcota; or, Life and Legends of the Sioux around Fort Snelling (New York 1849)

Edwards, Jonathan, *Images and Shadows of Divine Things*, ed. Perry Miller (New Haven 1948)
   Observations on the Language of the Muhhekaneew Indians (New Haven, Conn. 1788)
   A Treatise Concerning Religious Affections, ed. J. E. Smith (New Haven and London 1959)

Eisen, G. A., *Portraits of Washington* (New York 1932)

Eisenstein, Sergei, *Film Form: Essays in Film Theory*, ed. and trans. by Jay Leyda (New York 1949)

Emerson, Ralph Waldo, *Representative Men, Works, IV* (New York and Boston 1876)

Emory, W. H., *Notes of a military reconnaissance from Fort Leavenworth in Missouri, to San Diego, in California* (Washington, DC 1848)
   Report on the United States and Mexican Boundary Survey, made under the

　　direction of the Secretary of the Interior (Washington DC 1857)

Faulkner, William, 'The Bear' in *Go Down Moses* (New York 1942)

Ferguson, James, *Astronomy explained upon Sir Isaac Newton's Principles. . . .* (London 1773)

Fiedler, Leslie, *Love and Death in the American Novel* (New York 1960)
　　The Return of the Vanishing American (London 1968)

Fielding, Henry, *The Tragedy of Tragedies; or the Life and Death of Tom Thumb the Great* (London 1731)

Flexner, James Thomas, *That Wilder Image* (New York 1952)

Ford, Alice, *Edward Hicks, Painter of the Peaceable Kingdom* (Philadelphia 1952)

Frankenstein, Alfred, *Painter of Rural America: William Sidney Mount, 1807—1868* (Washington, DC 1968)

Franklin, Benjamin, *Poor Richard's Almanak* (Philadelphia 1733f)

Frederick, J. T., 'Cooper's Eloquent Indians', *Publications of the Modern Language Association of America, 71* (1956) pp. 1004—17

Frémont, John Charles, *Memoirs of my Life* (Chicago and New York 1887)
　　A Report on the Exploration of the Country lying between the Missouri River and the Rocky Mountains. . . . (Washington, DC 1843)

Freneau, Philip, *Poems of Philip Freneau* (Princeton, New Jersey 1907)

Frost, John, *Pictorial History of Mexico and the Mexican War* (Philadelphia 1848)

Fuller, C. E., *The Whitney Firearms* (Huntington, West Virginia 1946)

Fussell, E. S., *Frontier: American Literature and the American West* (Princeton, N.J. 1965)

Gardner, Albert Ten Eyck, 'Scientific Sources of the Full-Length Landscape: 1850', *Metropolitan Museum of Art Bulletin, IV* (July 1945—June 1946) pp. 59—65

Gardner, A. T. E. and Feld, S. P., *American Paintings* vol. I (New York 1965)

Gass, Patrick, *Journal of the Voyages and Travels of a Corps of Discovery etc.* (4th ed., Philadelphia 1812)

Gates, W. B., 'Cooper's *The Crater* and Two Explorers', *American Literature XXIII* (1951—2) pp. 243—46

Gernsheim, Helmut and Alison, *The History of Photography, from the earliest use of the camera obscura in the eleventh century up to 1914* (London 1955)
　　J. M. Daguerre, The History of the Diorama and Daguerreotype (London 1956)

Gibbon, Edward, *Decline and Fall of the Roman Empire, 6 vols* (1776—88; reprinted London 1962)

Giedion, Siegfried, *Mechanization Takes Command* (New York 1948)

Godman, John D., *American Natural History* (Philadelphia 1826)

Gombrich, E. H., *Norm and Form, Studies in the Art of the Renaissance* (London 1966)

Goodrich, S. G., *Life of George Washington* (Philadelphia 1844)

Greenough, Horatio, *Travels, Observations and Experience of a Yankee Stonecutter* (Boston 1852)

Grotius, Hugo, *The Life and Legal Writings of Hugo Grotius*, ed. Edward Dumbald (Norman, Oklahoma 1969)

Hakluyt's Voyages, with an introduction by J. Masefield (London 1907)

Hall, James, *Legends of the West* (Philadelphia 1832)
　　Sketches of History, Life and Manners in the West (Philadelphia 1834—5)

Hanson, Norwood Russell, *What I do not believe and other essays*, eds. Stephen Toulmin and Harry Woolf (Dordecht-Holland 1971)

Harris, Neil, *The Artist in American Society* (New York 1966)

Har[r]iot, Thomas, *A Brief and True Report of the New Found Land of Virginia etc* (London 1588)

Hawthorne, Nathaniel, 'The Artist of the Beautiful' in *Mosses from an Old Manse* (1842—6), *Works* (Cam., Mass. 1900)
　　'Chiefly about War-Matters. By a Peaceable Man', *Atlantic Monthly*, 10 (July—Dec. 1862)
　　The Scarlet Letter, Works (Cam., Mass. 1900)

Haydon, Benjamin Robert, *Autobiography and Memoirs* (London 1950)

Heck, Johann Georg, *Iconographic Encyclopaedia of Science, Literature and Art* (New York 1851)

Hendricks, G., 'The First Three Western Journeys of Albert Bierstadt', *Art Bulletin*, 46 (Summer, 1964) pp. 333–65

Hindle, Brooke, *The Pursuit of Science in Revolutionary America, 1735–1789* (Chapel Hill, NC 1956)

Hoffman, Charles Fenno, *Wild Scenes in the Forest and Prairie* (London 1838)

Hogarth, William, *Hogarth's Analysis of Beauty*, ed. Joseph Burke (London 1955)

Holmes, Oliver Wendell, *Soundings from the Atlantic* (Boston 1866)

The Home Book of the Picturesque (New York 1852)

Horsman, R., *The Causes of the War of 1812* (Philadelphia 1962)

Howard, Frank, *Color as a Means of Art* (London 1838)

Hugh, William, *The American Physician* (London 1672)

Humboldt, Alexander von, *Cosmos* (London 1849–50)

Humphrey's Journal (New York)

Hunt, Leigh, *The Autobiography of Leigh Hunt* (London 1850)

Hussey, Christopher, *The Picturesque, Studies in a Point of View* (1927; reprinted London 1967)

The Illustrated London News (London)

Irving, Washington, *Life of Washington, Works* (Philadelphia c. 1900)

   Tales of a Traveller (Philadelphia 1824)

   Tour on the Prairies, ed. J. F. McDermott (1835; reprinted Norman, Oklahoma 1962)

Ivins, William M., *Prints and Visual Communication* (1953; reprinted Cam., Mass. 1968)

James, Edwin, *Account of an Expedition from Pittsburgh to the Rocky Mountains* (London 1823)

Jefferson, Thomas, *Notes on the State of Virginia, 1785*, ed. Thomas Perkins Abernethy (New York 1964)

Johnson, Samuel, *[Rasselas] The Prince of Abissinia. A Tale* (London 1759)

Josselyn, John, *New England's Rarities discovered in birds, beasts, fishes, serpents and plants of that country* (London 1675)

Joubert, Laurent, *De Vulgi Erroribus* (Antwerp 1600)

   Paradoxa Medica, see Paradoxorum demonstrationum medicinalium . . . (Lugduni 1561)

Journal of Photography (London)

Jung, C. G., *Psychology of the Unconscious* (London 1922)

Keiser, A., 'Thoreua's Manuscripts on the Indians', *Journal of English and Germanic Philology*, 27 (1928)

Kernodle, George, R., *From Art to Theatre: Form and Convention in the Renaissance* (Chicago 1944)

Kimball, A. G., 'Brockden Brown's Dramatic Irony', *Studies in Romanticism*, 6 (1966–7) pp. 214–25

King, Roy and Davies, Burke, *The World of Currier and Ives* (New York 1968)

Kite, Elizabeth S., *Brigadier General Louis Lebègue Duportail. . . .* (London 1933)

Knickerbocker Magazine (New York)

Koch, Adrienne, *Jefferson and Madison; the great collaboration* (New York 1964)

Koch, Adrienne and Peden, W., *The Selected Writings of John and John Quincy Adams* (New York 1946)

Korsybzski, A., *Science and Sanity: An Introduction to Non-Aristotelian Systems and General Semantics* (Lancaster, Pennsylvania 1933)

Kouwenhoven, John A., *The Columbia Historical Portrait of New York; an Essay in Graphic History* (1953; reprinted New York 1972)

Kuhn, Thomas S., *The Copernican Revolution: Planetary Astronomy in the Development of Western Thought* (Cam., Mass. 1957)

Kurtz, K., 'The Sources and Development of Emerson's *Representative Men*', unpublished Ph.D. thesis (Yale 1947)

Lafitau, Joseph Francois, *Moeurs des sauvages Américains* (Paris 1724)

Lambeth, W. A. and Warren, H. M., *Thomas Jefferson, as an Architect and as a Designer of Landscapes* (Boston and New York 1913)

A Landscape Book (New York 1868)

Laplace, Pierre Simon, *Mécanique céleste . . . trs. Nathaniel Bowditch* (Boston 1829–39)

Larkin, Oliver W., *Art and Life in America*, rev. ed. (New York 1966)

Larson, James I., 'The Species Concept of Linnaeus', *Isis, 59* (1968)

Lawrence, D. H., *Studies in Classic American Literature* (1924; reprinted London 1964)

Lawson, John, *A New Voyage to Carolina etc* (London 1709)

Leary, Lewis, *That Rascal Freneau: A Study in Literary Failure* (New York 1964)

Leonardo da Vinci; The Notebooks of Leonardo da Vinci, with an introduction by Edward MacCurdy (1938; reprinted London 1954)

Leslie, C. R., *Memoirs of the Life of John Constable, RA, composed chiefly of his Letters* (London 1843)

Lessing, Gotthold Ephraim, *Laocoon*, trans. Ellen Frothingham (New York 1957)

Lewis, G. Malcolm, 'Early American Explorations and the Cis-Rocky Mountain Desert,' *Great Plains Journal, 5* (Fall 1965) pp. 11–26

   'William Gilpin and the Concept of the Great Plain Region', *Annals of the Association of American Geographers, 56* (March 1966) pp. 33–51

Linnaeus, Carl, *A General System of Nature*, trans. Turton, W., 7 vols (London 1806)

Lippard, George, *Washington and his Generals: or, Legends of the Revolution* (Philadelphia 1847)

The Literary World (New York)

Livermore, A. A., *The War with Mexico Reviewed* (Boston 1850)

Lewis, Meriwether and Clark, William, *Letters of the Lewis and Clark Expedition with related documents, 1783–1854* (Urbana, Illinois 1962)

   Original Journals of the Lewis and Clark Expedition, 1804–1806, ed. Reuben Gold Thwaites (1904–5; reprinted New York 1959)

Lewis, R. W. B., *The American Adam, Tragedy and Tradition in the Nineteenth Century* (Chicago and Cambridge 1955)

Longfellow, Henry Wadsworth, *Poetical Works*, 6 vols (Cam., Mass. 1904)

Lossing, Benson, *Lives of the Presidents* (New York 1848)

Loudon, Archibald, *A Selection of Some of the Most Interesting Narratives of Outrages Committed by the Indians in their Wars with the White People* (Carlisle, Pa., Press of A. Loudon 1808–11)

Lovejoy, A. O., *Essays in the History of Ideas* (1948; reprinted New York 1960)

Lowell, James Russell, *Letters of James Russell Lowell* (London 1894)

Lowes, J. Livingstone, *The Road to Xanadu* (1927; reprinted London 1951)

Lyell, Sir Charles, *Principles of Geology* (London 1830–33)

McCracken, Harold, *George Catlin and the Old Frontier* (Chicago and Crawfordsville, Indiana 1959)

McDermott, John Francis, 'George Caleb Bingham's Stump Orator', *Art Quarterly, XX,* 4 (Winter, 1957) pp. 388–99

   George Caleb Bingham, River Portraitist (Norman, Oklahoma 1959)

   Lost Panoramas of the Mississippi (Chicago 1958)

   Seth Eastman, Pictorial Historian of the Indian (Norman, Oklahoma 1961)

McKenney, T. L., *Memoirs Official and Personal; with sketches of Travels among Northern and Southern Indians; embracing a War and description of scenes along the Western borders*, 2 vols (New York 1846)

McKenney, Thomas L. and Hall, James, *History of the Indian Tribes of North America, with Biographical Sketches and Anecdotes of the Principal Chiefs. Embellished with One Hundred and Twenty Portraits from the Indian Gallery in the Department of War, at Washington*, 3 vols (Philadelphia, 1854 for 1836–44)

McLuhan, Marshall, *The Gutenberg Galaxy* (London 1962)

   Understanding Media (London 1964)

Mailer, Norman, *Why are We in Vietnam?* (New York 1967)

Martin, Benjamin, *A New and comprehensive System of Mathematical Institutions* . . .
    3 vols (London 1764)
    Philosophia Britannica . . . 4th ed. 5 vols (London 1788)
Marx, Karl and Engels, Frederick, *Marx and Frederick Engles: Selected Works*
    (London 1970)
Marx, Karl, *Capital* (Chicago 1912)
Marx, Leo, *The Machine in the Garden: Technology and the Pastoral Ideal in America*
    (New York 1964)
Matthiessen, F. O., *American Renaissance* (New York 1941)
Maximilian, Prince von Wied, *Abbildungen zur Naturgeschichte Brasiliens* (Weimar
    1822–3)
    Beiträge zur Naturgeschichte von Brasilien (Weimar 1825–33)
Maximilian, Prince von Wied *see* Reuben Thwaites, ed., *Early Western Travels,*
    1748–1846, Vols XXII–XXIV: Maximilian, Prince of Wied's Travels in the
    Interior of the North America (Cleveland, Ohio 1904–7)
Meisel, Max, *A Bibliography of American Natural History: The Pioneer Century,*
    1769–1865 (New York 1924)
Melville, Herman, *The Battle Pieces of Herman Melville*, ed. H. Cohen (New York 1963)
    The Confidence Man, (1857; reprinted New York 1964)
    Israel Potter, Works (London 1921–2)
    The Letters of Herman Melville, ed M. R. Davies and W. H. Gilman (New Haven,
    Conn. and London 1960)
    Moby Dick: or The Whale, eds. L. S. Mansfield and H. P. Vincent (New York 1962
    for 1851)
    Typee, Works (London 1921–2)
    White Jacket, Works (London, 1921–2)
Mengs, Anton Raphael, *Collected Works* (London 1796)
Miller, Perry, *The New England Mind* (New York 1938)
Montesquieu, Baron de, *The Spirit of the Laws* (New York 1949 for 1748)
The Monthly Anthology (Boston)
Morris, Mabel, 'Charles Brockden Brown and the American Indian', *American*
    Literature, 18 (1946–7) pp. 244–7
Morse, Jedidiah, *The American Geography* (New York 1789)
    A Report to the Secretary of War of the United States on Indian Affairs by the
    Rev. Jedidiah Morse (New Haven 1822)
Morse, Samuel, F. B., *Samuel F. B. Morse; his letters and journals*, ed. E. L. Morse
    (New York and Boston 1914)
Morton, S. G., *Crania Americana* (Philadelphia 1839)
Morton, Thomas, *New English Canaan* (Amsterdam 1637)
Moyne, Le, *Narrative of Le Moyne. . . . Translated from the Latin of De Bry. With*
    Heliotypes of the Engraving from the Artist's Original Drawings (1564;
    reprinted Boston 1875)
Muller, J. G., *Geschichte der amerikanischen Ur-religionen* (Basel 1853)
Mumford, Lewis, *The City in History* (London 1966)
    Herman Melville (1929; reprinted London 1963)
    Technics and Civilization (London 1946)
National Geographic Magazine (Washington, DC)
Newton, Sir Isaac, *Optics; or a treatise of the reflexions, refractions, inflections and*
    colours of light (London 1704)
    Philosophia Naturalis Principia Mathematica (London 1687)
Noble, Louis Legrand, *After Icebergs with a painter in a summer voyage to Labrador*
    and around Newfoundland (New York 1861)
    The Course of Empire etc (New York 1853)
The North American Review (Boston)
Novak, Barbara, *American Painting of the Nineteenth Century* (London 1969)
Ong, Walter, *Ramus, Method and the Decay of Dialogue* (Cam., Mass. 1958)
Orwell, George, *Animal Farm. A Fairy Story* (London 1945)

Otis, James, 'Rights of the British Colonies Asserted and Proved', in Bailyn, Bernard, ed. *Pamphlets of the American Revolution, 1750–1776* (Cam., Mass. 1965)

Paine, Thomas, *Collected Works* (New York 1954)

Palladio, Andrea, *The Architecture of Andrea Palladio. . . .* (London ?1715)

Panofsky, Erwin, *Early Netherlandish Painting* (Cam., Mass. 1953)

Parker, A. C., 'Sources and Range of Cooper's Indian Lore', *New York History 35* (1955) pp. 447–56

Parker, S., *Journal of an Exploring Tour beyond the Rocky Mountains* (1838)

Parkman, Francis, *The Californian and Oregon Trail* (New York 1849)
  France and England in North America, 9 vols (1865; reprinted New York 1965)
  History of the Conspiracy of Pontiac (1851; reprinted Cam., Mass. 1898)
  The Jesuits in North America, ed., Mason Wade (London 1946)
  The Jesuit Relations and Allied Documents , ed. Edna Kenton (New York 1954)
  Works (London, 1909)

Paul, Sherman, 'The Angle of Vision' in M. R. Konvitz and Stephen E. Wicher eds., *Emerson a Collection of Critical Essays* (Englewood Cliffs, New Jersey 1962)

Paulding, James Kirk, *Life of Washington* (New York 1835)

Peale, Charles Willson, *Introduction to a Course of Lectures. . . .* (Philadelphia 1800)
  'A Walk through the Philadelphia Museum' *Peale Papers, Archives of American Art,* Detroit

Pearce, Roy Harvey, *The Savages of America* (Baltimore 1965)
  'The Significances of the Captivity Narrative', *American Literature, 19* (1947–8) pp. 1–20

Perronet, Jean Rudolph, *Description des Projets et la construction des ponts. . . .* 2 vols (Paris 1782)

Philbrick, Thomas, *Cooper and the Development of American Sea Fiction* (Cam., Mass. 1961)

Poe, Edgar Allan, *Eureka* (1848)
  'The Murders in the Rue Morgue' (1841)
  'The Oval Portrait' (1842)
  see *Works* (London 1892)

Porta, Giovanni Battista, *Magiae Naturalis* (Neopoli 1556)

Potter, P., *Life of General George Washington* (Philadelphia 1812)

Pratt, J. W., *Expansionists of 1812* (Gloucester, Mass. 1957)

Price, Derek de Solla, *Science since Babylon* (New Haven and London 1961)

Pritts, J., *Incidents of Border Life* (Chambersburg, Pa. 1839)
  Mirror of olden time Border Life (Abingdon 1849)

Putnam's Monthly Magazine (New York)

Quimby, Robert S., *The Background of Napoleonic Warfare* (1957; reprinted New York 1968)

Rees, Alexander, *The Cyclopaedia; or Universal Dictionary of Arts, Sciences and Literature* (London 1819)

Reid, James D., *The Telegraph in America, and Morse Memorial* (New York 1886)

Renolds, Jeremiah N., *Mocha Dick; or the White Whale of the Pacific* (New York 1836)

Reports of Explorations and Surveys, to ascertain the most Practicable and Economical Route for a Railroad from the Mississippi River to the Pacific Ocean. . . . 12 vols (Washington, DC 1855–60)

Rice, Jr., Howard C., *The Rittenhouse Orrery* (Princeton, New Jersey 1954)

Richardson, E. P., *Washington Allston, a Study of the Romantic Artist in America* (Chicago 1948)

Rittenhouse, David, *An Oration . . . before the American Philosophical Society* (Philadelphia 1775)

Rohan, Jack, *Yankee Arms Maker; the incredible career of Samuel Colt* (New York and London 1935)

Rossi, Paolo, *Francis Bacon; from magic to science* (London 1968)
  Philosophy, Technology and the Arts in the Early Modern Era (1962; reprinted New York 1970)

Royal Society, *Philosophical Transactions of the Royal Society* (London 1665f)

Rufus, Karl, W., 'David Rittenhouse, as a Newtonian philosopher and defender', *Popular Astronomy*, 56 (1948) pp. 122–30

Ruiz, R. E., ed., *The Mexican War: Was it Manifest Destiny?* (New York 1963)

Sabine, Robert, *The Electric Telegraph* (London 1867)

Sala, G. A. de, *My Diary in America in the Midst of the War* (London 1865)

Say, Thomas, *American Entomology, or Description of the Insects of North America. . . .* (Philadelphia 1824)

Schneider, H. W., *A History of American Philosophy* (New York 1963)

Schoolcraft, Henry Rowe, *Algic Researches. . . .* (New York 1839)

    Historical and Statistical Information respecting the history, condition and prospects of the Indian Tribes of the United States. . . . (Philadelphia 1851–1860)

    Journal of a Tour into the Interior of Missouri and Arkansas (London 1820)

    Narrative Journal of Travels, through the North Western regions of the United States. . . . (Albany 1821)

    Notes on the Iroquois (New York 1846)

    Oneota, or Characteristics of the Red Race (New York 1845)

    A View of the Lead Mines of Missouri (New York 1819)

Scott, Sir Walter, *Life of Napoleon Bonaparte* (Paris 1827)

Scudder, Harold H., 'Cooper's *The Crater*', *American Literature*, IX (1947–8) pp. 109–126

Searle, S. L., *Washington Our Example* (Philadelphia 1865)

Selby, Prideaux John, *Birds of England*, see *Illustrations of British Ornithology* (Edinburgh 1825–33)

Sellers, Charles Coleman, *Charles Willson Peale* (New York 1969)

Shakespeare, William, *King Lear*

    A Winter's Tale

Shepherd, Paul, 'Paintings of the New England Landscape; a scientist looks at their geomorphology', *College Art Journal*, XVI–XVII (1956–8) pp. 30–42

Simms, William Gilmore, *The Letters of William Gilmore Simms*, ed. M. C. S. Oliphant *et al.* (Columbia, S. Carolina 1953)

Simms, William Gilmore, *View and Reviews in American History, Literature and Fiction* (New York 1845)

Sinclair, Angus, *Development of the Locomotive Engine* (1907; reprinted Cam., Mass. 1970)

Skelton, R. A., 'Cartography, 1750–1850' in C. Singer *et al.*, *A History of Technology* (Oxford 1957–8) vol. IV

Sleeper, John S., 'A Whale Adventure in the Pacific', in *Tales of the Ocean etc* (Boston 1841)

Smallwood, W. M. and M. S. C., *Natural History and the American Mind* (New York 1941)

Smiles, Samuel, *Lives of the Engineers* (London 1874)

Smith, Adam, *The Wealth of Nations. . . .* (1776; reprinted London 1962)

Smith, Bernard, 'European Vision and the South Pacific', *Journal of the Warburg and Courtauld Institutes*, 8 (1950) pp. 69–99

Smith, Henry Nash, *Virgin Land: The American West as Symbol and Myth* (Cam., Mass. 1950)

Smith, William, *Dictionary of Greek and Roman Biography and Mythology* (London 1846)

Squier, E. G., *The Serpent Symbol in America* (New York 1851)

Steckmesser, K. L., *The Western Hero in History and Legend* (Norman, Oklahoma 1965)

Steuben, Baron von, *A Letter on the Subject of an Established Militia, and Military Arrangements, addressed to the Inhabitants of the United States*, by *Baron de* [sic] *Steuben* (New York 1784)

    Regulations for the Order and Discipline of the Troops of the United States (Hartford, Conn. 1779)

Stowe, Harriet Beecher, *Old Town Folks* (Boston 1868)
  Uncle Tom's Cabin (Boston 1851–2)
Taft, Robert, *Photography and the American Scene* (New York 1942)
Tappan, David, *Washington's Political Legacies* (Boston 1800)
Thevet, A., *The New Found Worlde, or Antartike. . . . trans. Thomas Haket* (London 1568)
Thoreau, Henry David, *The Maine Woods* (1864; reprinted London 1911)
  Walden and Other Writings of Henry David Thoreau, ed. Brooks Atkinson (New York 1937)
  A Week on the Concord and Merrimac Rivers (1849; reprinted Cam., Mass. 1929)
Thornton, Robert John, *A New Illustration of the Sexual System of Linnaeus* (London 1797–1807)
Thorpe, Thomas Bangs, *The Hive of the Beehunter etc* (New York 1854)
  Mysteries of the Backwoods, or Sketches of the South-West (Philadelphia 1846)
Thwaites, Ruben Gold, ed., *Original Journals of the Lewis and Clark Expedition 1804–06* (1904; reprinted New York 1959)
The Times of London
Tocqueville, Alexis de, *Oeuvres complètes, Tome I, vol. 2* (Paris 1961)
Tuckerman, H. T., *The Book of the Artists: American Artist Life* (New York and London 1870)
United States Engineer School, Pamphlet on the Evolution of the Art of Fortification (Govt. Printing Office, Washington, DC 1919)
Vattel, Emmer de, *The Law of Nations* (London 1760)
Vaux, Calvert, *Villas and Cottages: A series of designs prepared for execution in the United States* (New York 1857)
Vincent, H. P., *The Trying Out of Moby Dick* (Carbondale and Edwardsville, Illinois 1949)
Vitruvius [Pollio] Marcus, *The Architecture of M. Vitruvius Pollio*; translated from the original Latin by W. Newton, 2 vols (London 1791 for 1486)
Volney, C. F., *The Ruins; or a Survey of the Revolutions of Empires* (London 1760)
  A View of the Soil and Climate of the United States of America (Philadelphia 1804)
Voto, Bernard de, *Across the Wide Missouri: Illustrated with Paintings by Alfred Jacob Miller, Charles Bodmer, and George Catlin. With an account of the discovery of the Miller collection by Mae Reed Porter* (Boston 1947)
Walker, D. P., *Spiritual and Demonic Magic from Ficino to Campanella* (London 1958)
Wallace, P. A. W., 'Cooper's Indians', *New York History*, 35 (1955) pp. 423–46
Washburn, Wilcomb E. ed., *The Indian and the White Man* (New York 1964)
Washington DC, *Proceedings of the Smithsonian Institution* (Washington DC 1847f)
Welker, Robert Henry, *Birds and Men* (Cam., Mass. 1955)
White, Gilbert, *Natural History and Antiquities of Selbourne* (London 1789)
Whitman, Walt, *Democratic Vistas* (1871) in ed. Floyd Stoval, *Prose Works* (New York 1963), vol. II
  Leaves of Grass, eds. H. W. Blodgett and S. Bradley (New York 1965)
Whittier, John Greenleaf, *Works* (London 1920)
Whorf, Benjamin Lee, *Language, Thought and Reality; selected writings of Benjamin Lee Whorf* (1956; reprinted Cam., Mass. 1970)
Williams, H. W., *The Civil War; the Artist's Record* (Washington DC 1961)
Williams, Leslie Pearce, *Michael Faraday; a biography* (London 1965)
Wilson, Alexander, *American Ornithology; or, the natural history of the Birds of the United States* (Philadelphia 1808)
Wilson, Edmund, *Patriotic Gore* (New York 1960)
Winckelmann, Johann Joachim, *History of Ancient Art* (1764; reprinted New York 1968)
Winters, Yvor, *In Defense of Reason* (London 1947)
Wise, John, 'A Vindication of the Government of New England Churches' in ed. Roy Harvey Pearce, *Colonial American Writing* (1950; reprinted New York, Chicago, San Francisco, Toronto, London 1962)

Wood, Gordon, S., *The Creation of the American Republic 1776–1787* (Chapel Hill, North Carolina 1969)

Wood, William, *New England's Prospect* (London 1634)

Wordsworth, William, *The Prelude*, in *The Poetical Works of William Wordsworth*, ed. etc by E. De Selincourt (2nd ed. Oxford 1952)

Wordsworth, William, *The Prose Works of William Wordsworth*, ed. A. B. Grossart, 3 vols (London 1876)

Wright, Louis B., ed., *The Elizabethan's America* (London 1965)

Yates, Frances A., *Theatre of the World* (London 1969)

Index